wok & stir-fry
RECIPES

wok & stir-fry
RECIPES

Discover the delights and simplicity of stir-fry cooking with 300 sensational
stove-top dishes, shown in 1000 step-by-step photographs

CONTRIBUTING EDITOR
JENNI FLEETWOOD

LORENZ BOOKS

This edition is published by Lorenz Books
an imprint of Anness Publishing Ltd
Blaby Road, Wigston
Leicestershire LE18 4SE; info@anness.com

www.lorenzbooks.com
www.annesspublishing.com

If you like the images in this book and would like to investigate
using them for publishing, promotions or advertising, please visit
our website www.practicalpictures.com for more information.

A CIP catalogue record for this book
is available from the British Library.

Publisher: Joanna Lorenz
Senior Editor: Emma Clegg
Recipes: Carla Capalbo, Kit Chan, Joanne Craig, Nicola Fowler,
Yasuko Fukuoka, Carole Handslip, Jane Hartshorn, Deh-Ta Hsiung,
Shehzad Husain, Becky Johnson, Wendy Lee, Lucy McKelvie,
Annie Nichols, Jane Stevenson, Sunil Vijayakar, Steven Wheeler
and Elizabeth Wolf-Cohen
Photography: Karl Adamson, Edward Allwright, David Armstrong,
Steve Baxter, Nicki Dowey, James Duncan, Gus Filgate,
Michelle Garrett, Amanda Heywood, Patrick McLeavey,
Michael Michaels, Thomas Odulate and Craig Robertson.
Designer: Nigel Partridge
Production Manager: Steve Lang

Previously published as part of a larger volume,
400 Wok and Stir-Fry Recipes

NOTES

Bracketed terms are intended for American readers.

For all recipes, quantities are given in both metric and imperial
measures and, where appropriate, in standard cups and spoons.
Follow one set of measures, but not a mixture, because they are
not interchangeable.

Standard spoon and cup measures are level.
1 tsp = 5ml, 1 tbsp = 15ml, 1 cup = 250ml/8fl oz.

Australian standard tablespoons are 20ml. Australian readers
should use 3 tsp in place of 1 tbsp for measuring small quantities.

American pints are 16fl oz/2 cups. American readers should use
20fl oz/2.5 cups in place of 1 pint when measuring liquids.

Electric oven temperatures in this book are for conventional ovens.
When using a fan oven, the temperature will probably need to be
reduced by about 10–20°C/20–40°F. Since ovens vary, you should
check with your manufacturer's instruction book for guidance.

The nutritional analysis given for each recipe is calculated per
portion (i.e. serving or item), unless otherwise stated. If the recipe
gives a range, such as Serves 4–6, then the nutritional analysis will
be for the smaller portion size, i.e. 6 servings. The analysis does
not include optional ingredients, such as salt added to taste.

Medium (US large) eggs are used unless otherwise stated.

Front cover shows Herb and Chilli Aubergines – for recipe, see page 332.

CONTENTS

INTRODUCTION

The wok is a wonderful invention, as suited to contemporary cooking as it is to recreating classic recipes from its country of origin. There should be one in every kitchen, as it proves its worth over and over again. In a wok you can stir-fry, deep-fry, sauté, steam and simmer. It makes short work of soups and sauces, and is as handy for poaching pears as it is for braising beef.

When it comes to design, the wok is a hugely effective cooking vessel. Heat radiates up the sides to produce a pan that cooks fast and efficiently. Its depth gives plenty of room for tossing and turning without spills, and the sloping sides ensure that the food always returns to the narrow base, where the heat is most intense.

Wok sales have rocketed in recent years. In the 1960s and 70s, a wok was something of a novelty, often bought in a burst of enthusiasm after a visit to a Chinese restaurant, then left to rust at the back of a kitchen cupboard. And rust they did, largely because people didn't know how to look after them. Part of the problem was the fact that most of the woks on sale were constructed of carbon steel. This was – and still is – an excellent material, but it needs an initial treatment to develop a non-stick, rust-resistant surface.

Fortunately, there were enough fans of this excellent pan to spread the word, and the wok gradually gained ground. It was still used mainly for Chinese food

only, however, and filled the same sort of specialist slot as the fondue pot or waffle iron. Fusion food changed all that. When chefs no longer viewed each nation's cuisine as sacrosanct, and started inventing new dishes that combined ingredients from several sources, they did us all a favour. The wok stopped being used solely for sweet and sour pork, and came to be seen as a practical pan for all sorts of dishes.

Around the same time, the pattern of everyday life was changing. People weren't just eating out more: they were

Left: The wok is a great tool for frying small pieces, or portions, of meat.

adopting more flexible eating habits. Often there wasn't enough time to cook an elaborate meal, so something that could be whizzed up in a wok was absolutely ideal. When it became apparent that this utensil was a fixture, rather than a short-lived culinary craze, manufacturers started producing woks in different materials, including non-stick ones that needed very little aftercare or special treatment. Flat-based versions were developed for use on modern electric stoves, the first electric appliances appeared, and more and more cookbooks catered for the quick and convenient style of cooking the wok promised.

Throughout all this, the wok delivered, and is still delivering. Today, it is its role in promoting healthy eating that is catching the public imagination. What the wok does extremely well is to cook a sizeable quantity of vegetables with a small amount of protein and the minimum of fat. When carbohydrate is added, in the form of noodles or rice, you have a well-balanced dish that any nutritionist would approve of. Deep-frying doesn't score a lot of brownie points in the health stakes, but if the oil is hot enough, the outer surface will be sealed immediately after the food is immersed, and the amount of oil absorbed will be limited. Steaming, however, gets a gold star. This is one of the healthiest ways to cook, since no additional fat is needed, the natural flavour of the food is preserved, and colours remain bright and true.

When you own a wok, you will find yourself discovering new uses for it, whether cooking spaghetti sauce, braising chicken portions, simmering fruit in syrup, making risotto, steaming asparagus or smoking salmon. It may not be the only pot you'll ever need, but it will be the one you use most often.

Below: Squash and pumpkin benefit from slow simmering in the wok to develop their sweet flavour.

Below: Tofu is a staple ingredient in China and Japan, and is used in many different types of wok recipes.

Right: The use of the wok has developed from its origins in Asia and the Far East, into a pan used all over the world for many different dishes.

WOKS, TOOLS AND ACCESSORIES

Left: Woks come in many different shapes and sizes and can be used to cook meals for one or for many.

using a steel wok over time, but you will gain by having an easy-care utensil that will give you very satisfactory results. It is essential to use a non-stick pan if you are cooking acidic foods such as fruits, which would discolour in a steel wok.

SIZE AND SHAPE

An average 36cm/14in wok is ideal for most kitchens, and will sit comfortably on the average burner. If you have a large family, or intend to cook whole fish on a regular basis, choose a 40cm/16in model. Whether you buy a round-based wok or a flat-based one depends on the type of stove you have, as well as your personal preference. Purists plump for round-based woks, claiming the shape gives perfect results, as the area of intense heat is very small and the upward slope uninterrupted. However, a round-based wok will wobble if placed on an electric stove. To stabilize it, you would have to use a wok stand or ring, but the round base could still reflect heat back and damage the electric

Choosing a wok isn't difficult. There are dozens of versions on the market, from conventional carbon steel and stainless steel models to modern non-stick woks that are sold solo or in gift packs with tools and even serving bowls. If you're a serious cook who likes the classical approach, begin your search at a large Asian food store, where you can examine traditional carbon steel woks in a range of shapes and sizes, hefting them in your hands to find the weight and size that suits. If you buy a good quality pan and season it properly, it will give you years of excellent service, and will actually improve with age. A cheaper wok may well have to be replaced after a year or so. Avoid very cheap woks, as they may rust despite your best efforts, or develop hot spots.

Below: A double-handled wok is ideal for using as a serving dish as well as a cooking vessel.

NON-STICK WOKS

If you prefer a non-stick wok, look for one made from reinforced titanium, which is guaranteed against scratching and can safely be washed in the dishwasher. You won't get the patina and flavour build-up that comes with

element. So, for electric stoves, or any stove with a level cooking surface, flat-based woks are best. If you have a gas stove, you can use either style of wok. You probably won't need a wok ring, but if you do, make sure that the wok sits down snugly, so that it is close to the heat source.

Both single-handled woks and twin-handled Cantonese woks are available. The single-handed wok is reckoned to be best for stir-frying, while the twin is more stable and is recommended for deep-frying, steaming and braising. Some woks offer you both features by giving you a 30cm/12in long handle matched with a short, round "helper" handle on the opposite side so that the wok can easily be moved from stove to table. Whichever type you buy, get a domed lid, so that you can use your wok for steaming or braising.

ELECTRIC WOK

The electric wok doesn't get quite as hot as a carbon steel wok over high heat, but is efficient, convenient and very good for cooking braised dishes and risotto. It can make a meal in moments, busy cooks like it because it leaves the stove free for other items, and others value its stability and the fact that the heat is thermostatically

Below: An electric wok is ideal for braising and slow cooking.

controlled. Electric woks come in various sizes but all are similar in design, with a heat element recessed in the stay-cool base. The wok that sits securely on the base will inevitably have a non-stick coating, but may need to be given a token seasoning before being used for the first time. The handbook will give instructions on how this is to be done – usually it merely means coating the wok with oil and heating it for 5 minutes, then wiping it clean and letting it cool down.

TOOLS AND ACCESSORIES

It isn't necessary to buy special tools for wok cooking, but there are a few items that will prove useful.

Cleavers and Knives

Cutting meat and vegetables for stir-frying so that the maximum surface area is exposed to the heat is quite an art, and Chinese cooks swear that the best tool for the job is a cleaver. This short-handled implement has a large, flat blade that can be used to cut everything from paper-thin vegetable slices to meat on the bone. When the blade is held flat, it can be used like a spatula, to transport the prepared food to the wok. Cleavers come in several sizes and weights. Number one is the heaviest and resembles a chopper more than a knife. Its 23cm/9in long blade is 10cm/4in wide, and is mainly used for

Above: A Chinese cleaver is finely balanced.

slicing. The medium weight number two cleaver is the most popular choice for general kitchen use. It is used for both slicing and chopping. The back of the blade is ideal for pounding meat to tenderize it, and the flat surface can be used to crush garlic or ginger. Good quality kitchen knives can be used instead of a cleaver. A 10cm/4in paring knife and a 20cm/8in cook's knife will be the most useful sizes. It is vital to keep blades sharp, either by using a steel or a stone.

Mortar and Pestle

South-east Asian cooks like to use their woks for making quick curries. These depend for their flavour on curry pastes that are freshly made using ingredients like galangal, garlic and lemon grass. A granite mortar is best for this purpose, since the rough surface amplifies the pounding action of the pestle and also helps to grip the ingredients so they do not escape from the bowl. Buy a mortar that measures at least 18cm/7in across. This is sufficient for mixtures of up to 450ml/$\frac{3}{4}$ pint/scant 2 cups.

Below: A granite mortar and pestle is useful for making traditional wet spice pastes.

Draining or Steaming Rack

Most woks, whether standard or electric, come with a rainbow-shaped metal rack that clips on to the rim. This item, sometimes called a tempura rack, is useful when deep-frying. As items cook, they can be set to drain on the rack. Surplus oil will drip back into the pan, and the drained foods can be moved to a piece of kitchen paper when the rack is full. The rack can also be used for steaming, and is particularly useful in an electric wok.

Spatulas and Scoops

It is useful to have at least two wooden spatulas for stir-frying, preferably with a rounded side that follows the contours of the wok. Another useful implement is the *charn*, a long-handled spatula shaped like a shovel, which makes it easy to scoop and toss foods that are being stir-fried. If you use a charn in a non-stick pan, take care not to scratch the surface.

Ladle

You will need a ladle for spooning soups or other liquids out of the wok. Choose one with a deep bowl. Although black nylon ladles are recommended for non-stick woks, they do scorch easily, so stainless steel ladles are a better bet. Some ladles have graduated markings inside that indicate how much liquid they contain. This is useful when you need to spoon out a specific quantity of stock. If your ladle is not marked in this

Below: You may need a wok ring on your stove top to keep the wok steady.

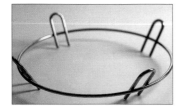

Above: Essential wok tools include a dome-shaped lid, wooden or bamboo chopsticks, a long-handled spatula and a large ladle.

way, measure the liquid it holds by filling it with water and spooning this into a measuring jug (cup). Making a note of the amount for future reference will help you when you are following a recipe that specifies a particular amount of liquid to be removed from the wok.

Chopsticks

If you wander through an Asian street market you will sometimes see food being stirred in giant woks with extra-long chopsticks. These are ideal for the dextrous, but tongs or two spatulas can be used instead.

Skimmers

These are long-handled utensils with wire or bamboo scoops at one end. These can be cup- or saucer-shaped and are used to fish food out of hot oil or stock. Saucer-shaped skimmers are also called spiders, since they resemble circular webs.

Wok Ring

This circular metal stand gives stability to a round-based wok when used on an electric or gas stove. The rings come in several sizes and designs. The most common ones look like crumpet rings or cookie cutters, and consist of solid metal that may be punched with ventilation holes. Thick wire stands are also available, and these are recommended for gas stoves. It is important to buy a ring that supports your wok securely while allowing it to be as close to the heat source as possible without putting out the flame. If your wok has a flat base you won't need a ring. If you intend using a wok ring on an electric stove, check with the manufacturer, as this practice can damage the element.

Steamers

Steaming is one of the healthiest ways of cooking, since no fat is required and the natural flavour of the food is preserved. A wok is ideal for this purpose, since its shape gives you a large surface area of water to turn into steam. There are several ways of steaming in a wok. For just a few items, you can use the semicircular rack that clips on to the side of the pan.

Left: A perforated metal scoop and a traditional wire skimmer.

Above: Racks can be clipped to the side of a wok to drain deep-fried food on.

Alternatively, you can place items to be steamed on a heatproof plate, provided you raise the plate above the surface of the water or stock by means of a trivet or upturned cup. You can also steam items by the Chinese method, using stackable bamboo baskets. An expanding metal steamer will also work well, but take care that the feet do not scratch the surface of the wok if it has a non-stick coating. Whichever means you use, you will need to trap the steam somehow, either by fitting a domed lid over the wok, or making sure the steamer itself is tightly covered.

Preparing a Steamer
Before you use a bamboo steamer for the first time, scrub it well, using a mild detergent if you like, then rinse it thoroughly, Place the wet steamer over boiling water in a wok. Steam it empty for at least 10 minutes, then leave to air dry. Store in a well-ventilated place.

Bamboo Steamers

Although stainless-steel steamers are regarded as being more hygienic, natural bamboo steamers do an excellent job, since the material allows steam to circulate freely with only minimal condensation. The steamer baskets can be bought singly or in sets and come in various sizes. Standard steamers have a diameter of 25cm/10in and are about 15cm/6in tall. This is the ideal size for a 36cm/14in wok. When the basket is in use, there should be at least 5cm/2in space between it and the side of the wok. Steamers can be stacked.

Left: A stack of steamers increases the amount of food you can cook at one time.

Seasoning a Wok
First wash the wok in warm water and detergent to remove any preservative coating. Rinse it well, shake off the excess water, then place the wok over low heat to dry. Add a little cooking oil (not olive oil) and, using kitchen paper, wipe the pan to coat it evenly. Take care not to burn yourself. Heat gently for 10–12 minutes, then wipe off the oil with clean kitchen paper. Don't be alarmed when it blackens – this is perfectly natural. Repeat the process for as long as it takes for the paper to come away clean, by which time the wok itself will have darkened. The more it is used, the better the wok's natural non-stick coating will become and the easier it will be to clean. If a wok should rust – perhaps because it has been put away wet or abandoned in a cupboard for months – it should be rubbed down with wire wool or fine sandpaper and then seasoned again. A cast iron or carbon steel wok is less likely to rust if it is oiled lightly before being stored.

Cleaning a Wok
A properly seasoned wok should never be washed with detergent. Remove any food that sticks to the surface, then wash the wok in hot water. Dry thoroughly by placing the wok over the heat for a few minutes. Leave to cool, then rub a little oil into the surface.

PREPARATION TECHNIQUES

Successful wok cooking is all about preparation, especially when you are stir-frying, which is so fast it is essential to have everything ready before you begin. That means slicing vegetables, meat or fish to the size required, having sauces handy and making sure that implements needed are within reach.

CUTTING AND SLICING VEGETABLES

Asian cooks take great care over the preparation of ingredients. There's an aesthetic reason for this – food must look as well as taste good – but careful cutting also serves a practical purpose. Cutting all the pieces to a similar size means they cook quickly and evenly.

Root Vegetables

Firm root vegetables, such as carrots, parsnips and mooli (daikon), can be diced, sliced or cut into matchsticks. Use a cook's knife or a cleaver. Trim the vegetable, then take a thin slice off each side to square it up. Slice lengthways. Pile the slices on top of each other and cut them into sticks.

Onions

Valued for their flavour, all members of the onion family are used in stir-fries and other dishes. Shallots have a mild flavour but are fiddly to prepare. Spring onions (scallions) are often used cooked, raw and as a garnish in many Asian and Eastern cooking traditions. They make a perfect stir-fry ingredient, as their flavour is retained. If shreds are called for, cut off the dark green top, then slice the portions of stem lengthways in half, then into strips.

Above: Use a mixture of peppers for maximum colour impact.

Above: Cut meat into small pieces or strips so that it cooks quickly.

Other Vegetables

Aubergines (eggplants), courgettes (zucchini), sweet (bell) peppers, green beans, mushrooms and corn are common stir-fry ingredients.

Less robust than root vegetables, courgettes shouldn't be cut too small. Ovals, sliced at an angle, work best. Aubergines are thinly sliced for tempura, cubed for slow-cooked dishes, or cut into strips for frying. If peppers

Below: Aubergine, sliced for tempura.

are called for in a dish, cut them in thin slices, as they can take longer to cook than other ingredients.

Mushrooms of all kinds are favourite ingredients. Shitake mushrooms are a particular favourite of Chinese and Thai cooks, and are often used dried for a more intense flavour.

If fresh corn is in season, and a recipe calls for it as an ingredient, use this instead of canned or frozen. To free the corn from the cob, hold the top with one hand, and slice the kernels away.

Green beans for stir-fries should be the very freshest available; if they are slightly woody, trim the sides as well as the tops and bottoms, and slice thinly. Broccoli and cauliflower should be cut into small florets for stir-fries.

PREPARING MEAT, FISH AND POULTRY

How you prepare meat and fish depends on the type and dish, but for stir-fries you should always use the best and freshest cuts. The cheaper cuts, such as stewing beef or belly pork, are ideal for slow cooked dishes that have time to tenderize. When you are using chicken or pork in a stir-fry, you need to make sure it is cooked right through, and shows no sign of pinkness.

For stir-fries cut meat and fish across the grain. This not only helps the food to cook evenly, but also prevents it from disintegrating. Prawns (shrimp) and scallops can be left whole, and need only minutes to cook. They are usually the last ingredient to be added to a stir-fry, to prevent them going rubbery.

Below: Prawns can be left in their shells or peeled.

STIR-FRYING TECHNIQUES

Most of the cooking you are likely to do in your wok will be stir-frying, so it makes sense to get to grips with the technique from the start. Have all the ingredients close at hand, including measured items such as sauces.

PREHEATING THE WOK

The most important thing to remember is that the wok must be preheated. If the wok is hot when you add the oil, it will coat the surface with a thin film, preventing food from sticking. The best way to do this is to add a trickle of oil, necklace-fashion, around the inner rim so that it runs down evenly. You don't need much – 15–30ml/1–2 tbsp will be ample. Tilt the pan, if necessary, to spread the oil evenly.

Have the heat as high as possible if you are stir-frying meat, so that it is seared the moment it touches the wok. For fish or vegetables, the heat can be slightly lower. A simple test to ensure the wok is hot enough for stir-frying is to flick a few drops of water on to the surface after oiling. If this results in a loud sizzling sound, and the water immediately boils off, add your meat. If the water sizzles but remains visible for a few seconds before vanishing, the heat is right for fish or vegetables. Use oil with a high smoking point, such as groundnut (peanut) or corn oil.

COOKING AROMATICS

Individual recipes vary, but it is usual to start a stir-fry by adding aromatics such as garlic, ginger, chillies and spring onion (scallions) to the oil, then to fry meat, if used, and finish with the

Below: Make sure the oil in the wok is hot before adding any ingredients.

vegetables. Cooking aromatics flavours the oil. If this is their only function, they are fished out before anything else is added to the wok.

STIR-FRYING MEAT

When stir-frying meat, don't overload the wok or you will bring down the temperature. Add a few pieces at a time, sear them for a few seconds, flip them over and sear the other side, then push them away from the centre, where the heat is concentrated, and add more meat to the well. When the meat has been sealed, either push the pieces on to the sloping sides of the wok, so they will stay warm without continuing to fry, or remove them to a dish.

STIR-FRYING VEGETABLES

Add the vegetables to the wok, starting with varieties that take the longest to cook, such as carrots, broccoli and

Below: When cooking aromatics, be careful not to let them burn.

Above: Sauces are added at the end of the cooking process.

sweet (bell) peppers. Vegetables that need very little cooking, such as mooli (daikon) and mushrooms should be added next, with leafy vegetables tossed in right at the end. Keep the food on the move all the time, flipping and turning it with a spatula. Although the technique is called stir-frying, use a tossing and turning action, rather than stirring.

ADDING A SAUCE

When the vegetables are lightly cooked but still crisp, mix in the meat or other ingredients and then add any suggested sauces. A cornflour (cornstarch) mixture will thicken as well as flavour the mixture. If you are using a cornflour-based sauce, make a well in the stir-fry so you can stir it on its own for a minute or so before mixing it in.

Below: The wok is ideal for frying meat because of its high and even heat.

DEEP-FRYING TECHNIQUES

Provided a few safety precautions are taken, a wok is a useful pan for shallow and deep-frying. The shape means that you need less oil than in a conventional deep-fryer, yet still have a large surface area for cooking the food.

HEATING THE OIL

Start by making sure that the wok is stable. A flat-based wok is safest for deep-frying. If you use a round-based wok, make sure it will not wobble. Use a stand if necessary. The wok must be cold when the oil is added. This is the opposite advice to that given for stir-frying, when oil is added to a hot wok. Use an oil with a low smoking point and never fill the wok more than one-third full. This is more than adequate for most foods, and there will be less risk of the cook being splashed with hot fat or, worse, of the fat catching fire.

THE RIGHT TEMPERATURE

For deep-frying, oil needs to be at just the right temperature, so that the outside of the food becomes beautifully crisp while the centre cooks through to tender perfection. The precise temperature required will depend upon the density of what is being cooked and whether it has a coating of some kind, but around 180–190°C/350–375°F is suitable for most foods. A deep-fat thermometer, which can be clipped safely to the side of the wok before the oil is heated, is the safest and surest way of checking the temperature, but you can also test it by adding a cube of bread to the hot oil. The bread should brown in 45 seconds, if it sinks or fries

Below: Make sure there is enough oil for the volume of food being fried.

Above: Coating food before frying helps retain its moisture and flavour.

Above: Wrappers create a delicious crispy coating and keep food moist.

more slowly any food cooked in the wok would be greasy; if it burns, the same fate lies in wait for the food; if it sizzles on contact and bobs up to float on the surface, the temperature is just right.

COATING

Food can be coated in batter or a simple egg-and-breadcrumb mixture before being deep-fried. This protects, adds a contrasting texture and locks in the flavour. Dip the item to be coated in to the batter and gently shake off any excess before adding it to the hot oil. Flour or cornflour (cornstarch), egg and breadcrumbs can also be used for coating. Another method of protecting delicate food is to enclose it in a dough wrapper before deep-frying. This method is used for wontons and spring rolls, and the crispy result is delicious.

DEEP-FRYING TIPS

Don't overcrowd the wok. Add a few pieces at a time, lowering them gently into the oil to avoid splashing. Lift out carefully and either drain on a rack that

Hot Tips for Safe Deep-frying
• Don't fill the wok more than one-third full.
• Make sure it is stable.
• Be extra careful when adding food to the oil or retrieving it.
• Never leave a hot wok unattended.
• If the oil does catch fire, turn off the heat if you can and cover the wok with a heavy cloth or mat to exclude the air. This will put out the fire. Never throw water on an oil fire and don't try to move the wok.

has been clipped on to the side of the wok, or drain on kitchen paper and keep hot. Wait a minute or two before cooking successive batches, so that the oil gets the chance to return to its optimum temperature.

Below: Lift deep-fried food in and out of the hot wok with a long-handled tool.

STEAMING TECHNIQUES

This is a supremely healthy method, since the food is cooked without added fat and most of the nutrients are preserved. It is also simple, fast and efficient, whether you use a steamer specifically made for the wok or improvise with a trivet and a plate.

SUITABLE FOR STEAMING

All sorts of foods can be steamed, from fish to vegetables, poultry and even pancakes, custards and breads. Tender cuts of chicken cook well in the steamer but this is not the ideal cooking method for red meat. Check your chosen recipe for any advance preparation required. If you are cooking fish, is it whole or in portions? If whole, you may be advised to slit the skin and insert flavourings, such as fresh herbs, citrus slices or even a spicy rub. Delicate foods may need to be wrapped before being steamed. Banana leaves and lettuce leaves are popular for this purpose, as wraps or to line the steamer.

SELECTING A STEAMER

A steamer is simply a device for cooking foods by means of moist heat. The food should never touch the water that generates the steam, and the moisture must be trapped. You can steam food by simply placing it on a raised plate inside your wok, but steaming is simpler in a utensil designed for the purpose. Bamboo steamers are efficient and easy to use. So are stainless-steel steamers, but they are much more expensive. It is also possible to steam foods on the rack supplied with your wok, but this will only accommodate small amounts.

Below: Whole chickens, when steamed, have a special flavour and tenderness.

Above: A bamboo steamer is best when steaming in a wok, as it fits perfectly.

ASSEMBLING THE STEAMER

Food can be placed directly in the steamer basket, but this method tends to be reserved for dim sum or breads. It is more usual for a recipe to recommend lining the steamer with baking parchment or leaves before adding the food. This stops the food sticking and prevents small pieces from slipping through the slats. If you use this technique, make sure steam can still circulate. Using leaves for lining won't pose problems as steam will find its way around them, but parchment should be pierced. Alternatively, the food can be put on a plate or bowl inside the steamer so long as the steam holes are not blocked. Custards and some fish dishes are cooked this way.

Before you use a steamer in your wok for the first time, check the fit. You may have to use a trivet or upturned cup to keep the base of the steamer above the water. If a steamer is large, the sloping sides of the wok may prevent it from descending to the water level.

Steamer baskets are stackable, so you can cook several items at once, with the most delicate foods on top. The steamer will probably have its own cover, but if it doesn't, you will need to cover the wok itself, preferably with a domed lid so that condensed water runs down the sides and drips back into the water, rather than on to the food.

GETTING UP STEAM

The liquid to generate the steam can be water or stock. Aromatic flavourings like lemon grass, ginger or seaweed can be used to scent the steam. Fill the wok to a depth of around 5cm/2in, bring the liquid to the boil, carefully insert the steamer and cover with the lid. During steaming, keep checking the water level and top up if necessary. Slope the lid away from you to avoid being scalded.

Below: Individual fish custards are steamed to retain flavour and texture.

SIMMERING <u>AND</u> SMOKING

Although the wok is most closely associated with stir-fries and steamed food, it is also great for soups and sauced dishes such as Thai curries, braised pork belly or Beef Rendang. The frying stage that is the starting point for many of these dishes is easily accomplished in a wok, and after more ingredients are added, simmering is a cinch.

RAPID REDUCTION

The shape of the wok, with a wide surface area tapering to a narrow heat base, makes for rapid reduction of sauces. Where the aim is to concentrate the liquid, this is ideal, but you need to keep an eye on what's cooking, and top up the stock or sauce if necessary. For this reason, a wok isn't the best pan for a stew or similar dish that needs to be cooked for a very long time. A heavy pan is better for that purpose, but if you do use a wok, make it a stainless steel or non-stick one. Extended slow cooking in a carbon steel wok may erode the seasoned surface.

BLANCHING AND BOILING

For stir-frying, vegetables are usually cooked in relays, as some are much denser than others. Blanching toughies such as carrots and broccoli in boiling water gives them a head start so they can be stir-fried alongside more tender

Below: The wok is ideal for boiling or blanching green leafy vegetables.

Above: Fast boiling reduces a sauce, and gives a more intense flavour.

Above: Slow, gentle simmering produces a rich creamy taste and texture.

vegetables. Bring a wok of water to the boil, add the vegetables and cook for the required length of time (usually about 2–3 minutes). Lift the vegetables out of the wok with a skimmer or spider, plunge them into cold water so that they stop cooking, then drain and pat dry.

A wok can also be used for poaching fruit and cooking rice or noodles.

Wok Smoking

You don't need elaborate equipment to smoke poultry or seafood. A carbon steel wok works well, especially if you follow the Chinese tradition and use a tea leaf mixture as the smoking medium. The only drawback is the obvious one – use an extractor fan or be prepared for your smoke alarm to go off.

1 Line a carbon steel wok (not any other type) with foil, allowing a generous overlap. Sprinkle in 30ml/2 tbsp each of raw long grain rice, sugar and tea leaves.

2 Fit a wire rack on top of the wok and place the food to be smoked in a single layer on top. Mackerel fillets, salmon and duck or chicken breast portions work well. Cover the wok with a lid or inverted pan and cook over a very high heat until you see smoke.

3 Lower the heat so that the smoke reduces to wisps that seep from under the lid, and cook until the food is done. A mackerel fillet takes around 8–10 minutes; large fresh prawns (shrimp) 5–7 minutes, duck or chicken breast portions 18–20 minutes.

COOKING RICE AND NOODLES

Many of the Chinese and Thai recipes in this book are based on rice or noodles, which may be used as an accompaniment rather than part of the main dish. If you are using your wok for the meat or vegetable accompaniment, you will probably be cooking your rice or noodles in a pan.

COOKING RICE

There are several ways of cooking rice, but the absorption method is best for jasmine rice, basmati, short grain rice and glutinous rice. The proportion of water to rice will depend on the type of rice used, but as a guide, you will need about 600ml/1 pint/2½ cups water for every 225g/8oz/generous 1 cup rice.

1 Rinse the rice thoroughly and put it in a pan. Pour in the water. Do not add salt. Bring to the boil, then reduce the heat to the lowest possible setting.

2 Cover tightly and cook for 20–25 minutes, or until the liquid is absorbed.

3 Without lifting the lid, remove the pan from the heat. Leave it to stand in a warm place for 5 minutes to rest, and complete the cooking process. If cooked rice is required for a fried rice dish, cool it quickly, then chill it before frying.

Steamed Sticky Rice

Thais like their accompanying rice to be sticky. To get the authentic texture steam it in a bamboo steamer. Make sure you buy the right rice, usually called sticky or glutinous rice.

Rinse the rice in several changes of water, then leave to soak overnight in a bowl of cold water. Line a large bamboo steamer with muslin (cheesecloth). Drain the rice and spread out evenly on the muslin. Cover the rice and steam for 25–30 minutes, until the rice is tender. (Check the water level and add more if necessary.)

Making a Risotto in the Wok

The wok is not only suitable for Asian dishes, it also makes great risotto. Have the hot stock ready in a pan.

Melt butter, oil or a mixture in a wok and fry an onion. Add risotto rice and stir to coat the grains. Add a dash of white wine, then when that is absorbed begin adding hot stock, a ladleful at a time. Stir constantly until the stock is absorbed, then add more. It will take about 20 minutes for the rice to become tender. Add a little butter and stir in. Remove the pan from the heat and cover. Leave for 2 minutes, then serve.

COOKING NOODLES

If you are cooking noodles, either to serve solo or as part of a composite dish, do not rely entirely on the recipe – check the packet, too. Par-cooked noodles only need to be soaked in hot water; others must be boiled. Ready-to-use noodles need no attention at all, and can simply be added to a stir-fry and tossed over the heat until hot.

Preparing Rice Noodles

Rice noodles have been par-cooked when you buy them, so they only need to be soaked in hot water before use.

Add the noodles to a large bowl of just-boiled water and leave for 5–10 minutes or until softened, stirring occasionally to separate.

Preparing Wheat Noodles

Wheat noodles have to be cooked in boiling water. They take very little time, however.

Bring a large pan of water to the boil, add the fresh egg noodles and cook for 2–4 minutes or until tender. Drain well. If the noodles are going to be mixed into a stir-fry and cooked further, give them just 2 minutes initially.

DIPS ᴬᴺᴰ GARNISHES

With a wok, it takes next to no time to rustle up treats like spring rolls, potato puffs and crisp-fried crab claws. Try them with these delicious dips.

Thai Red Curry Dip

This tastes good with mini spring rolls, or can be tossed with rice noodles for a simple accompaniment.

SERVES 4

200ml/7fl oz/scant 1 cup coconut cream
10–15ml/2–3 tsp Thai red curry paste
4 spring onions (scallions), plus extra, thinly sliced, to garnish
30ml/2 tbsp chopped fresh coriander (cilantro)
1 fresh red chilli, seeded and thinly sliced in rings
5 ml/1 tsp soy sauce
juice of 1 lime
sugar, to taste
25g/1oz/3 tbsp dry-roasted peanuts, finely chopped
salt and ground black pepper

Pour the coconut cream into a small bowl and stir in the curry paste. Trim the spring onions, slice them diagonally, then stir into the coconut cream with the coriander, chilli, soy sauce and lime juice. Add enough sugar to give a sweet-sour flavour and season with salt and pepper. Spoon into a serving bowl and top with the peanuts and thinly sliced spring onion.

Wasabi and Soy Dip

Try this with crab cakes or fish cakes. The combination works extremely well, especially if you add a squeeze of lime just before dipping.

SERVES 4

175ml/6fl oz/³⁄₄ cup soy sauce or shoyu
10ml/2 tsp wasabi paste
2 spring onions (scallions), diagonally sliced
1 fresh red chilli, seeded and thinly sliced in rings (optional)

Mix the soy sauce or shoyu with the wasabi paste in a bowl. Float the spring onion slices on top. The chilli slices can be added or left out, depending on how spicy you want the dip to be. Top with just one or two rings for colour.

Sweet Chilli Sauce

This sweet, spicy sauce has a wonderfully aromatic flavour and lovely translucent red colour. It can be used both for flavouring and as a dipping sauce. Any remaining sauce can be stored in the refrigerator in an airtight container for 1–2 weeks.

SERVES 4

6 large red chillies
60ml/4 tbsp white vinegar
250g/9oz caster (superfine) sugar
5ml/1tsp salt
4 garlic cloves, chopped

Place the chillies in a food processor. Add the vinegar, sugar, salt and garlic. Blend until smooth, transfer to a pan and cook over a medium heat until thickened. Leave to cool and then transfer to a bowl.

Tamarind Sauce

This sweet, tangy dipping sauce has a fruity flavour and is perfect served with spicy deep-fried snacks. The quantities here are suitable for one serving, but if there is any left over, transfer into an airtight container and store in the refrigerator for 1–2 weeks.

MAKES 1 SMALL JAR
    90ml/6 tbsp tamarind paste
    90ml/6 tbsp water
    45ml/3 tbsp caster (superfine) sugar

Place all the ingredients in a small pan and bring the mixture to the boil. Reduce the heat and cook gently for 3–4 minutes, stirring occasionally. Remove the pan from the heat and transfer to a small bowl. Leave to cool before serving.

Ginger and Hoisin Dip

Chunky and bursting with flavour, this dip is delicious with prawn (shrimp) crackers. The dip can be stored in the refrigerator for up to 1 week.

SERVES 4
    60ml/4 tbsp hoisin sauce
    120ml/4fl oz/$\frac{1}{2}$ cup passata (bottled strained tomatoes)
    4 spring onions (scallions), thinly sliced
    4cm/1$\frac{1}{2}$in piece fresh root ginger, peeled and finely chopped
    2 fresh red chillies, seeded and cut into fine strips
    2 garlic cloves, crushed
    few drops of roasted sesame oil

Mix the hoisin and passata in a bowl. Stir in the spring onions, ginger, chillies and crushed garlic. Add the sesame oil, mix well and serve.

GREAT GARNISHES

Thai cooks enjoy garnishing their dishes with beautifully cut vegetables. Here are some suggestions for easy finishing touches that look fabulous. A cucumber frill makes a lovely garnish for duck, steamed salmon, a stir-fry or salad.

Cut a cucumber in half lengthways. Scoop out the seeds from one half and place it cut side down. Using a knife held at an angle, thinly slice the cucumber, cutting almost through so the slices remain attached at the base. Fan the slices out. Turn in alternate slices to form loops, then bend into a semi-circle with the loops on the outside, so that they resemble petals.

1 Using a small pair of scissors or a slim-bladed knife, slit a fresh red chilli carefully lengthways from the tip to within 1cm/$\frac{1}{2}$in of the stem end. Repeat this at regular intervals around the chilli, keeping the stem end intact, until it resembles a tassel. Slit more chillies in the same way.

2 Rinse the chillies in cold water to wash away the seeds. Place in a bowl of iced water and chill for at least 4 hours. For very curly chilli flowers, leave the bowl in the refrigerator overnight.

Wasabi paste
This bright green paste packs a whopping punch. It is made from a Japanese herb and tastes like a cross between hot mustard and horseradish. A little goes a long way to flavour dips and sauces. Try mixing it with mayonnaise for a delicious dip to serve with steamed asparagus. The most convenient way to buy wasabi is in a tube. If you use powdered wasabi, mix it in an egg cup with the same volume of tepid water, then stand the egg cup upside down for 10 minutes to allow the flavour to develop without letting the wasabi dry out.

CRISPY
SNACKS AND
FINGER
FOOD

A wok isn't just for wonderful main courses — it is a great

accessory when it comes to the little treats that add spice to

life. Spring rolls, samosas and puff pastry parcels can be

cooked to crisp perfection in minutes, ready for dipping into

scrumptious sauces. Spiced Noodle Pancakes and Pea and

Potato Pakoras provide two more good reasons for heating the

oil and starting to sizzle. For serving with drinks, try

Roasted Coconut Cashew Nuts — piled in paper cones to

save fingers from getting sticky — or choose one of the more

substantial snacks that can double as an appetizer.

PRAWN AND SESAME TOASTS

THESE ATTRACTIVE LITTLE TOAST TRIANGLES ARE IDEAL FOR SERVING WITH PRE-DINNER DRINKS AND ARE ALWAYS A FAVOURITE HOT SNACK AT PARTIES. THEY ARE SURPRISINGLY EASY TO PREPARE AND YOU CAN COOK THEM IN YOUR WOK FOR JUST A FEW MINUTES. SERVE THEM WITH A SWEET CHILLI SAUCE.

SERVES FOUR

INGREDIENTS
    225g/8oz peeled raw prawns (shrimp)
    15ml/1 tbsp sherry
    15ml/1 tbsp soy sauce
    30ml/2 tbsp cornflour (cornstarch)
    2 egg whites
    4 slices white bread
    115g/4oz/½ cup sesame seeds
    oil, for deep-frying
    sweet chilli sauce,
        to serve

1 Process the prawns, sherry, soy sauce and cornflour in a food processor.

2 In a grease-free bowl, whisk the egg whites until stiff. Fold them into the prawn and cornflour mixture.

3 Cut each slice of bread into four triangular quarters. Spread out the sesame seeds on a large plate. Spread the prawn paste over one side of each bread triangle, then press the coated sides into the sesame seeds so that they stick and cover the prawn paste.

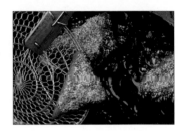

4 Heat the oil in a wok or deep-fryer, to 190°C/375°F or until a cube of bread, added to the oil, browns in about 45 seconds. Add the toasts, a few at a time, prawn side down, and deep-fry for 2–3 minutes, then turn and fry on the other side until golden.

5 Drain on kitchen paper and serve hot with sweet chilli sauce.

Energy 392Kcal/1634kJ; Protein 19.1g; Carbohydrate 21.1g, of which sugars 1.2g; Fat 25.8g, of which saturates 3.4g; Cholesterol 110mg; Calcium 270mg; Fibre 2.7g; Sodium 557mg.

CRISP-FRIED JAPANESE PANKO PRAWNS

WHEN BUTTERFLIED AND BATTERED TIGER PRAWNS ARE DEEP-FRIED IN THE WOK, THEY CURL UP BEAUTIFULLY, AND LOOK GORGEOUS ON DARK GREEN SEAWEED TOPPED WITH WHITE RICE. WASABI, SOY SAUCE, SWEET CHILLI SAUCE AND PICKLED GINGER ARE TRADITIONAL ACCOMPANIMENTS.

SERVES FOUR

INGREDIENTS

20 large raw tiger or king prawns
(jumbo shrimp), heads removed
30ml/2 tbsp cornflour (cornstarch)
3 large (US extra large) eggs,
lightly beaten
150g/5oz *panko* (Japanese-style
breadcrumbs)
sunflower oil, for frying
4 sheets of nori
400g/14oz cooked sushi rice
wasabi, soy sauce, sweet chilli sauce
and pickled ginger, to serve

1 Peel and devein the prawns, leaving the tails on. Using a small, sharp knife, cut down the back of each prawn, without cutting all the way through, and gently press the prawns out flat to butterfly them.

2 Place the cornflour, beaten eggs and *panko* in 3 separate bowls. Dip each prawn first into the cornflour, next into the egg and then into the *panko,* to coat it evenly.

3 Fill a wok one-third full of sunflower oil and heat to 180°C/350°F (or until a cube of bread, added to the oil, browns in 45 seconds).

4 Working in batches, deep-fry the prawns for 1 minute, or until lightly golden and crisp. Remove from the wok with a slotted spoon and drain the prawns on kitchen paper.

5 Carefully cut each nori sheet into a 10cm/4in square. Place each square on a serving plate and divide the sushi rice among them, then spread out the rice using the back of a spoon. Top each serving with 5 deep-fried prawns and serve with wasabi, soy sauce, sweet chilli sauce and pickled ginger.

COOK'S TIP

Panko are Japanese-style breadcrumbs, which give a fabulously crunchy result when deep-fried. They make the perfect coating for these tender, juicy prawns, which remain unbelievably succulent when cooked. If you can't find panko, use coarse, dried breadcrumbs instead.

Energy 472Kcal/1989kJ; Protein 20.2g; Carbohydrate 63g, of which sugars 1g; Fat 17.4g, of which saturates 2.8g; Cholesterol 240mg; Calcium 127mg; Fibre 0.9g; Sodium 437mg.

FIRECRACKERS

IT'S EASY TO SEE HOW THESE PASTRY-WRAPPED PRAWN SNACKS GOT THEIR NAME. NOT ONLY DO THEY WHIZ AROUND IN THE WOK LIKE ROCKETS, BUT WHEN YOU BITE INTO THEM THEIR CONTENTS EXPLODE WITH FLAVOUR. MARINATING THE PRAWNS IN CURRY PASTE MAKES ALL THE DIFFERENCE.

3 Place a wonton wrapper on the work surface at an angle so that it forms a diamond shape, then fold the top corner over so that the point is in the centre. Place a prawn, slits down, on the wrapper, with the tail projecting from the folded end, then fold the bottom corner over the other end of the prawn.

4 Fold each side of the wrapper over in turn to make a tightly folded roll. Tie a noodle in a bow around the roll and set it aside. Repeat with the remaining prawns and wrappers.

5 Heat the oil in a wok to 190°C/375°F or until a cube of bread, added to the oil, browns in 40 seconds. Fry the prawns, a few at a time, for 5–8 minutes, until golden brown and cooked through. Drain well on kitchen paper and keep hot while you cook the remaining batches.

COOK'S TIP
Soak the egg noodles to be used as ties for the rolls in a bowl of boiling water for 2–3 minutes, until soft, drain, refresh under cold running water and drain.

MAKES SIXTEEN

INGREDIENTS
16 large, raw king prawns (jumbo shrimp), heads and shells removed but tails left on
5ml/1 tsp red curry paste
15ml/1 tbsp Thai fish sauce
16 small wonton wrappers, about 8cm/3¼in square, thawed if frozen
16 fine egg noodles, soaked (see Cook's Tip)
oil, for deep-frying

1 Place the prawns on their sides and cut two slits through the underbelly of each, one about 1cm/½in from the head end and the other about 1cm/½in from the first cut, cutting across the prawn. This will prevent the prawns from curling when they are cooked.

2 Mix the curry paste with the fish sauce in a shallow dish. Add the prawns and turn them in the mixture until they are well coated. Cover and leave to marinate for 10 minutes.

Energy 71Kcal/298kJ; Protein 3.2g; Carbohydrate 7.1g, of which sugars 0.2g; Fat 3.5g, of which saturates 0.5g; Cholesterol 25mg; Calcium 20mg; Fibre 0.3g; Sodium 30mg.

DEEP-FRIED SMALL PRAWNS AND CORN

INSPIRED BY THE JAPANESE DISH CALLED TEMPURA, THIS SIMPLE SNACK FOOD IS A GOOD WAY OF USING UP SMALL QUANTITIES OF VEGETABLES, AND BECAUSE YOU CAN USE FROZEN INGREDIENTS, IT MAKES A GOOD STORECUPBOARD STANDBY. THIS IS EASY TO COOK IN A WOK.

SERVES FOUR

INGREDIENTS
200g/7oz small cooked, peeled
   prawns (shrimp)
4–5 button (white) mushrooms
4 spring onions (scallions)
75g/3oz/½ cup canned, drained or
   frozen sweetcorn, thawed
30ml/2 tbsp frozen peas, thawed
vegetable oil, for deep-frying
chives, to garnish
For the tempura batter
300ml/½ pint/1¼ cups ice-cold water
2 eggs, beaten
150g/5oz/1¼ cups plain
   (all-purpose) flour
1.5ml/¼ tsp baking powder
For the dipping sauce
400ml/14fl oz/1⅔ cups second dashi
   stock, made with instant dashi
   powder and water
100ml/3fl oz/scant ½ cup shoyu
100ml/3fl oz/scant ½ cup mirin
15ml/1 tbsp chopped chives

1 Roughly chop half the prawns. Cut the mushrooms into small cubes. Slice the white part from the spring onions and chop this roughly.

2 To make the tempura batter, mix the cold water and eggs in a medium mixing bowl.

3 Add the flour and baking powder to the eggs, and roughly fold in with a pair of chopsticks or a fork. Do not beat. The batter should be quite lumpy. Heat plenty of oil in a wok to 170°C/338°F.

4 Mix the prawns and vegetables into the batter. Pour a quarter of the batter into a small bowl, then drop gently into the oil. Using wooden spoons, carefully gather the scattered batter to form a fist-size ball. Deep-fry until golden. Drain on kitchen paper.

5 In a small pan, mix all the liquid dipping-sauce ingredients together and bring to the boil, then immediately turn off the heat. Sprinkle with chives.

6 Garnish the fritters with chives, and serve with the dipping sauce.

Energy 246Kcal/1039kJ; Protein 17.6g; Carbohydrate 37.4g, of which sugars 4.7g; Fat 4g, of which saturates 1g; Cholesterol 193mg; Calcium 117mg; Fibre 2g; Sodium 1963mg.

GRILLED EEL WRAPPED IN BACON

FRESHWATER EEL IS FIRM-FLESHED AND RICH, AND AS POPULAR IN CAMBODIA AND VIETNAM AS CATFISH AND CARP. IT IS ALSO BECOMING MORE EASILY AVAILABLE IN THE WEST. THIS RECIPE IS BEST SERVED WITH A DIPPING SAUCE, A CRUNCHY SALAD, AND JASMINE RICE.

SERVES FOUR TO SIX

INGREDIENTS

2 lemon grass stalks, trimmed
    and chopped
25g/1oz fresh root ginger, peeled
    and chopped
2 garlic cloves, chopped
2 shallots, chopped
15ml/1 tbsp palm sugar
15ml/1 tbsp vegetable or groundnut
    (peanut) oil
30ml/2 tbsp *nuoc mam* or *tuk trey*
1.2kg/2½lb fresh eel, skinned and
    cut into 2.5cm/1in pieces
12 slices streaky (fatty) bacon
freshly ground black pepper
a small bunch of fresh coriander
    (cilantro) leaves, to garnish
nuoc cham, for dipping

1 Using a mortar and pestle, pound the lemon grass, ginger, garlic and shallots with the sugar to form a paste. Add the oil and *nuoc mam* or *tuk trey*, mix well and season with black pepper. Put the eel pieces in a dish and smear them thoroughly in this paste. Cover and place in the refrigerator for 2–3 hours to marinate.

2 Wrap each piece of marinated eel in a strip of bacon, gathering up as much of the marinade as possible.

3 To cook the eel parcels, you can use a conventional grill, a well-oiled griddle pan, or a barbecue. If grilling over charcoal, you can skewer the eel parcels; otherwise, spread them over the grill (broiler) or griddle pan. Cook the eel parcels until nice and crispy, roughly 2–3 minutes on each side. Serve with fresh coriander leaves and *nuoc cham* for dipping.

COOK'S TIP
When buying fresh eel, it's worth asking the fishmonger to gut it, cut off the head, bone it, skin it and slice it for you – it makes life easier!

Energy 460Kcal/1911kJ; Protein 39.3g; Carbohydrate 0.8g, of which sugars 0.6g; Fat 33.3g, of which saturates 9g; Cholesterol 324mg; Calcium 43mg; Fibre 0.1g; Sodium 650mg.

CRISP-FRIED CRAB CLAWS

CRAB CLAWS ARE READILY AVAILABLE FROM THE FREEZER CABINET OF MANY ASIAN STORES AND SUPERMARKETS. THAW THEM THOROUGHLY AND DRY ON KITCHEN PAPER BEFORE COATING THEM. THIS DISH HAS GREAT VISUAL IMPACT, AND IS GOOD FOR A DINNER PARTY STARTER.

SERVES FOUR

INGREDIENTS
   50g/2oz/⅓ cup rice flour
   15ml/1 tbsp cornflour (cornstarch)
   2.5ml/½ tsp granulated sugar
   1 egg
   60ml/4 tbsp cold water
   1 lemon grass stalk
   2 garlic cloves, finely chopped
   15ml/1 tbsp chopped fresh
     coriander (cilantro)
   1–2 fresh red chillies, seeded and
     finely chopped
   5ml/1 tsp Thai fish sauce
   vegetable oil, for deep-frying
   12 half-shelled crab claws, thawed
     if frozen
   ground black pepper
For the chilli vinegar dip
   45ml/3 tbsp granulated sugar
   120ml/4fl oz/½ cup water
   120ml/4fl oz/½ cup red
     wine vinegar
   15ml/1 tbsp Thai fish sauce
   3 red chillies, seeded and chopped

1 First make the chilli vinegar dip. Mix the sugar and water in a pan. Heat gently, stirring until the sugar has dissolved, then bring to the boil. Lower the heat and simmer for 5–7 minutes. Stir in the rest of the ingredients, pour into a serving bowl and set aside.

2 Combine the rice flour, cornflour and sugar in a bowl. Beat the egg with the cold water, then stir the egg and water mixture into the flour mixture and beat well until it forms a light batter.

3 Cut off the lower 5cm/2in of the lemon grass stalk and chop it finely. Add the lemon grass to the batter, with the garlic, coriander, red chillies and fish sauce. Stir in pepper to taste.

4 Heat the oil in a wok or deep-fryer to 190°C/375°F or until a cube of bread browns in 40 seconds. Dip the crab claws into the batter, then fry, in batches, until golden. Serve with the dip.

Energy 222Kcal/926kJ; Protein 10.1g; Carbohydrate 16.9g, of which sugars 0g; Fat 12.8g, of which saturates 1.7g; Cholesterol 78mg; Calcium 62mg; Fibre 0.3g; Sodium 256mg.

DEEP-FRIED LAYERED SHIITAKE AND SCALLOPS

A WOK DOES DOUBLE DUTY FOR MAKING THESE MUSHROOM AND SEAFOOD TREATS. THE NAGA-IMO (A TYPE OF YAM) IS STEAMED IN A BAMBOO BASKET, AND LATER THE WOK IS USED FOR DEEP-FRYING. THE SNACKS ARE DELICATE; USE A KNIFE AND FORK IF CHOPSTICKS PROVE TRICKY.

SERVES FOUR

INGREDIENTS
    4 scallops
    8 large fresh shiitake mushrooms
    225g/8oz naga-imo, unpeeled
    20ml/4 tsp miso
    50g/2oz/1 cup fresh breadcrumbs
    cornflour (cornstarch), for dusting
    vegetable oil, for deep-frying
    2 eggs, beaten
    salt
    4 lemon wedges, to serve

1 Slice the scallops in two horizontally, then sprinkle with salt. Remove the stalks from the shiitake by cutting them off with a knife. Discard the stalks.

2 Cut shallow slits on the top of each shiitake to form a "hash" symbol or cut slits to form a white cross. Sprinkle with a little salt.

3 Heat a steamer and steam the naga-imo for 10–15 minutes, or until soft. Test with a skewer. Leave to cool.

4 Wait until the naga-imo is cool enough to handle. Skin, then mash the flesh in a bowl with a masher, getting rid of any lumps. Add the miso and mix well. Take the breadcrumbs into your hands and break them down finely. Mix half into the mashed naga-imo, reserving the rest in a shallow container.

5 Fill the underside of each shiitake cap with a scoop of mashed naga-imo. Smooth down with the flat edge of a knife and dust the mash with cornflour.

6 Add a little mash to a slice of scallop and place on top.

7 Spread another 5ml/1 tsp mashed naga-imo on to the scallop and shape to cover it completely. Make sure all the ingredients are clinging together. Repeat to make eight little mounds.

8 Heat the oil to 150°C/300°F. Place the beaten eggs in a shallow container. Dust the shiitake and scallop mounds with cornflour, then dip into the egg. Handle with care as the mash and scallop are quite soft.

9 Coat the scallop mounds well with the remaining breadcrumbs and then deep fry in the oil until golden. Drain well on kitchen paper. Serve hot on individual plates with a wedge of lemon.

VARIATION
For a vegetarian option, use 16 shiitake mushrooms. Sandwich the naga-imo mash between two shiitake to make 8 bundles. Deep-fry in the same way as the scallop version.

COOK'S TIPS
• Fresh naga-imo produces a slimy liquid when it's cut. Try not to touch this as some people may react and develop a mild rash. When it's cooked, it is perfectly safe to touch.
• If you can't find naga-imo, use yam or 115g/4oz each of potatoes and peeled Jerusalem artichokes instead. Steam the potatoes and boil the artichokes until both are tender.

Energy 247Kcal/1032kJ; Protein 14.1g; Carbohydrate 15.5g, of which sugars 4.5g; Fat 14.8g, of which saturates 2.3g; Cholesterol 113mg; Calcium 57mg; Fibre 1.9g; Sodium 213mg.

FRIED SQUID WITH SPICY SALT AND PEPPER

THIS RECIPE IS ONE OF THE SPECIALITIES OF THE CANTONESE SCHOOL OF CUISINE. SOUTHERN CHINA IS FAMOUS FOR ITS SEAFOOD, WHICH IS OFTEN FLAVOURED WITH GINGER. THE DELICIOUS SPICY SALT AND PEPPER MIX CAN BE STORED IN A JAR AND USED FOR FLAVOURING OTHER DISHES.

SERVES FOUR

INGREDIENTS
  450g/1lb fresh squid
  5ml/1 tsp ginger juice (squeezed
    from grated fresh ginger)
  15ml/1 tbsp Chinese rice wine or
    dry sherry
  about 575ml/1 pint/2½ cups
    boiling water
  vegetable oil, for deep frying
  spicy salt and pepper (see Cook's Tip)
  fresh coriander (cilantro) leaves,
    to garnish

1 Clean the squid if necessary by discarding the head and the transparent backbone as well as the ink bag; peel off and discard the thin skin, then wash the squid and dry well on kitchen paper. Open up the squid and, using a sharp knife, score the inside of the flesh in a criss-cross pattern.

COOK'S TIP
To make spicy salt and pepper, dry-fry 30ml/2 tbsp salt and 10ml/2 tsp freshly ground Szechuan or black pepper in a heavy pan until the salt darkens, then stir in 2.5ml/½ tsp Chinese five-spice powder and leave to cool.

2 Cut the squid into pieces, each about the size of a postage stamp. Marinate in a bowl with the ginger juice and rice wine or sherry for 25–30 minutes.

3 Blanch the pieces of squid in boiling water for just a few seconds – each piece will curl up and the criss-cross pattern will open out so that they resemble ears of corn. Remove and drain. Dry well.

4 Heat sufficient oil for deep-frying in a wok. Deep-fry the squid in batches for 15–20 seconds only, remove quickly and drain. Sprinkle with the spicy salt and pepper and serve garnished with fresh coriander leaves.

Energy 194kcal/812kJ; Protein 17.3g; Carbohydrate 1.4g, of which sugars 0.1g; Fat 12.9g, of which saturates 1.7g; Cholesterol 253mg; Calcium 15mg; Fibre 0g; Sodium 616mg.

DEEP FRIED PRAWN SANDWICHES

IN THE BUSY STREET MARKETS OF PHNOM PENH, THERE IS ALWAYS SOMETHING INTERESTING BEING COOKED. NEXT TO THE STALL SELLING DEEP-FRIED FURRY, BLACK SPIDERS, YOU MIGHT COME ACROSS THE LESS ALARMING SNACK OF DEEP-FRIED PRAWN SANDWICHES.

SERVES FOUR

INGREDIENTS
3–4 shallots, roughly chopped
4 garlic cloves, roughly chopped
25g/1oz fresh root ginger, peeled
   and chopped
1 lemon grass stalk, trimmed
   and chopped
1 Thai chilli, seeded and chopped
10ml/2 tsp sugar
225g/8oz fresh prawns (shrimp),
   shelled and deveined
30ml/2 tbsp *tuk trey*
1 egg, beaten
12 thin slices of day-old baguette
vegetable oil, for deep-frying
ground black pepper
chilli oil, for drizzling

1 Using a large mortar and pestle, pound the chopped shallots, garlic, ginger, lemon grass, chilli and sugar. Add the shelled prawns and pound them too to make a paste. Mix well and bind all the ingredients with the *tuk trey* and beaten egg. Season with ground black pepper.

2 Spread the mixture on each piece of bread, patting it down firmly. In a wok, heat enough oil for deep-frying. Using a slotted spoon, lower the sandwiches, prawn side down, into the oil. Cook in batches, flipping them over so they turn golden on both sides. Drain on kitchen paper and serve hot with chilli oil.

Energy 489Kcal/2065kJ; Protein 22.5g; Carbohydrate 70.6g, of which sugars 6.3g; Fat 15g, of which saturates 2g; Cholesterol 157mg; Calcium 202mg; Fibre 3.1g; Sodium 860mg.

TEMPURA SEAFOOD

THIS QUINTESSENTIALLY JAPANESE DISH ACTUALLY HAS ITS ORIGINS IN THE WEST, AS TEMPURA WAS INTRODUCED TO JAPAN BY PORTUGUESE TRADERS IN THE 17TH CENTURY.

SERVES FOUR

INGREDIENTS
8 large raw prawns (shrimp), heads
  and shells removed, tails intact
130g/4½oz squid body, cleaned
  and skinned
115g/4oz whiting fillets
4 fresh shiitake mushrooms,
  stalks removed
8 okra
⅛ nori sheet, 5 × 4cm/2 × 1½in
20g/¾oz dried harusame (a packet is
  a 150–250g/5–9oz mass)
vegetable oil and sesame oil,
  for deep-frying
plain (all-purpose) flour, for dusting
salt
For the dipping sauce
400ml/14fl oz/1⅔ cups second dashi
  stock, made with dashi powder
200ml/7fl oz/scant 1 cup shoyu
200ml/7fl oz/scant 1 cup mirin
For the condiment
450g/1lb mooli (daikon), peeled
4cm/1½in fresh root ginger, peeled
  and finely grated
For the tempura batter
ice-cold water
1 large (US extra large) egg, beaten
200g/7oz/2 cups plain (all purpose)
  flour, sifted
2–3 ice cubes

1 Remove the vein from the prawns, then make 4 × 3mm/⅛in deep cuts across the belly to stop the prawns curling up. Snip the tips of the tails and gently squeeze out any liquid. Pat dry.

2 Cut open the squid body. Lay it flat, inside down, on a chopping board, and make shallow criss-cross slits on the outside. Cut into 2.5 × 6cm/1 × 2½in rectangular strips. Cut the whiting fillets into similar-size strips.

3 Make two notched slits on the shiitake caps, in the form of a cross. Sprinkle your hands with some salt and rub over the okra, then wash the okra under running water to clean the surface.

4 Cut the nori into four long strips lengthways. Loosen the harusame noodles from the block and cut both ends with scissors to get a few strips. Make four bunches and tie them in the middle by wrapping with a nori strip. Wet the end to fix it.

5 Make the dipping sauce. In a pan, mix all the dipping sauce ingredients and bring to the boil, then immediately remove from the heat. Set aside and keep warm.

6 Prepare the condiment. Grate the daikon very finely. Drain in a sieve, then squeeze out any excess water by hand.

7 Lay clear film (plastic wrap) over an egg cup and press about 2.5ml/½ tsp grated ginger into the bottom. Add 30ml/2 tbsp grated daikon. Press and invert on to a small plate. Make three more ginger and daikon moulds in the same way.

8 Half-fill a wok with 3 parts vegetable oil to 1 part sesame oil. Bring to 175°C/347°F over a medium heat.

9 Meanwhile, make the tempura batter. Add enough ice-cold water to the egg to make 150ml/¼ pint/⅔ cup, then pour into a large bowl. Add the flour and mix roughly with chopsticks. Do not beat; leave the batter lumpy. Add some ice cubes later to keep the temperature cool.

10 Dip the okra into the batter and deep-fry until golden. Drain. Batter the underside of the shiitake, and deep-fry.

11 Increase the heat a little, then fry the harusame by holding the nori tie with chopsticks and dipping them into the oil for a few seconds. The noodles instantly turn crisp and white. Drain on kitchen paper and sprinkle with salt.

12 Hold the tail of a prawn, dust with flour, then dip into the batter. Do not put batter on the tail. Slide the prawn into the hot oil very slowly. Deep-fry one to two prawns at a time until crisp.

13 Dust the whiting strips, dip into the batter, then deep-fry until golden. Wipe the squid strips well with kitchen paper, dust with flour, then dip in batter. Deep-fry until the batter is crisp.

14 Drain excess oil from the tempura on a wire rack for a few minutes, then arrange them on individual plates. Set the condiment alongside the tempura. Reheat the dipping sauce to warm through, then pour into four small bowls.

15 Serve immediately, mixing the condiment into the dipping sauce and dunking the tempura as you eat.

Energy 401Kcal/1683kJ; Protein 27.3g; Carbohydrate 42.8g, of which sugars 4.1g; Fat 14.5g, of which saturates 2.2g; Cholesterol 231mg; Calcium 167mg; Fibre 3.2g; Sodium 1080mg.

CRISPY SALT AND PEPPER SQUID

THE CRISP, GOLDEN COATING CONTRASTS BEAUTIFULLY WITH THE SUCCULENT SQUID INSIDE. THESE
DELICIOUS MORSELS LOOK STUNNING AND ARE PERFECT SERVED WITH DRINKS, OR AS AN APPETIZER.

SERVES FOUR

INGREDIENTS
    750g/1lb 10oz fresh squid, cleaned
    juice of 4–5 lemons
    15ml/1 tbsp freshly ground
      black pepper
    15ml/1 tbsp sea salt
    10ml/2 tsp caster (superfine) sugar
    115g/4oz/1 cup cornflour
      (cornstarch)
    3 egg whites, lightly beaten
    vegetable oil, for deep-frying
    chilli sauce or sweet-and-sour sauce,
      for dipping
    skewers, to serve

1 Cut the squid into large bitesize
pieces and score a diamond pattern
on each piece, using a sharp knife
or a cleaver.

2 Trim the tentacles. Place in a large
mixing bowl and pour over the lemon
juice. Cover and marinate for 10–15
minutes. Drain well and pat dry.

3 In a separate bowl mix together the
pepper, salt, sugar and cornflour. Dip
the squid pieces in the egg whites and
then toss lightly in the seasoned flour,
shaking off any excess.

4 Fill a wok one-third full of oil and heat
to 180°C/350°F or until a cube of bread,
dropped into the oil, browns in 40
seconds. Working in batches, deep-fry
the squid for 1 minute. Drain on kitchen
paper and serve threaded on to skewers
with chilli or sweet-and-sour sauce.

COOK'S TIP
Keep egg whites in the freezer, ready to
thaw for use in dishes such as this.

Energy 346Kcal/1462kJ; Protein 31.2g; Carbohydrate 31.3g, of which sugars 2.6g; Fat 11.6g, of which saturates 1.8g; Cholesterol 422mg; Calcium 32mg; Fibre 0g; Sodium 1741mg.

FIERY TUNA SPRING ROLLS

THIS MODERN TAKE ON THE CLASSIC SPRING ROLL IS SUBSTANTIAL ENOUGH TO SERVE AS A MAIN MEAL WITH NOODLES AND STIR-FRIED GREENS. THE TUNA AND WASABI FILLING IS FANTASTIC.

SERVES FOUR

INGREDIENTS
    1 large chunk of very fresh thick
      tuna steak
    45ml/3 tbsp light soy sauce
    30ml/2 tbsp wasabi
    16 mangetout (snow peas), trimmed
    8 spring roll wrappers
    sunflower oil, for deep-frying
    soft noodles and stir-fried Asian
      greens, to serve
    soy sauce and sweet chilli sauce,
      for dipping

1 Place the tuna on a board. Using a sharp knife cut it into eight slices, each measuring about 12 x 2.5cm/4½ x 1in.

2 Place the tuna in a large, non-metallic dish in a single layer. Mix together the soy sauce and the wasabi and spoon evenly over the fish. Cover and marinate for 10–15 minutes.

3 Meanwhile, blanch the mangetout in boiling water for about 1 minute, drain and refresh under cold water. Drain and pat dry with kitchen paper.

4 Place a spring roll wrapper on a clean work surface and place a piece of tuna on top, in the centre.

COOK'S TIP
It is important to cut the tuna into neat, even slices. Chilling it briefly in the freezer, and using a very sharp knife or cleaver, makes this easier to achieve.

5 Top the tuna with 2 mangetout and fold over the sides and roll up. Brush the edges of the wrappers to seal.

6 Repeat with the remaining tuna, mangetout and wrappers.

7 Fill a large wok one-third full with oil and heat to 180°C/350°F or until a cube of bread browns in 45 seconds. Working in batches, deep-fry the rolls for 1–2 minutes, until crisp and golden.

8 Drain the rolls on kitchen paper and serve immediately with soft noodles and Asian greens. Serve the spring rolls with side dishes of soy sauce and sweet chilli sauce for dipping.

Energy 171Kcal/717kJ; Protein 14g; Carbohydrate 11.4g, of which sugars 1.7g; Fat 8g, of which saturates 1.3g; Cholesterol 14mg; Calcium 36mg; Fibre 0.8g; Sodium 825mg.

DRY-COOKED PORK STRIPS

THIS CAMBODIAN DISH IS QUICK AND LIGHT ON A HOT DAY. PORK, CHICKEN, PRAWNS (SHRIMP) AND SQUID CAN ALL BE COOKED THIS WAY. WITH THE LETTUCE AND HERBS, IT'S A VERY FLAVOURSOME SNACK, BUT YOU CAN SERVE IT WITH A DIPPING SAUCE, IF YOU LIKE.

SERVES TWO TO FOUR

INGREDIENTS
15ml/1 tbsp groundnut (peanut) oil
30ml/2 tbsp *tuk trey*
30ml/2 tbsp soy sauce
5ml/1 tsp sugar
225g/8oz pork fillet, cut into thin,
  bite-sized strips
8 lettuce leaves
chilli oil, for drizzling
fresh coriander (cilantro) leaves
a handful of fresh mint leaves

VARIATION
Try basil, flat leaf parsley, spring onions
or sliced red onion in these parcels.

1 In a wok or heavy pan, heat the oil, *tuk trey* and soy sauce with the sugar. Add the pork and stir-fry over a medium heat, until all the liquid has evaporated. Cook the pork until it turns brown, almost caramelized, but not burnt.

2 Drop spoonfuls of the cooked pork into each of the lettuce leaves, drizzle a little chilli oil over the top and add a few coriander and mint leaves. Wrap the lettuce leaves up and serve the little parcels immediately.

Energy 96Kcal/401kJ; Protein 12.2g; Carbohydrate 0.4g, of which sugars 0.4g; Fat 5g, of which saturates 1.1g; Cholesterol 35mg; Calcium 7mg; Fibre 0.1g; Sodium 300mg.

BACON-WRAPPED BEEF ON SKEWERS

In northern Vietnam, beef often features on the street menu. Grilled, stir-fried, or sitting majestically in a steaming bowl of pho, beef is used with pride. In Cambodia and southern Vietnam, snacks like this one would normally be made with pork or chicken.

SERVES FOUR

INGREDIENTS
    225g/8oz beef fillet or rump, cut
      across the grain into 12 strips
    12 thin strips of streaky (fatty) bacon
    ground black pepper
    4 bamboo skewers, soaked in water
    nuoc cham, for dipping
For the marinade
    15ml/1 tbsp groundnut (peanut) oil
    30ml/2 tbsp *nuoc mam*
    30ml/2 tbsp soy sauce
    4–6 garlic cloves, crushed
    10ml/2 tsp sugar

1 To make the marinade, mix all the marinade ingredients in a large bowl until the sugar dissolves. Season generously with black pepper. Add the beef strips, coating them in the marinade, and set aside for about an hour.

2 Preheat a griddle pan over a high heat. Roll up each strip of beef and wrap it in a slice of bacon. Thread the rolls on to the skewers, so that you have three on each one.

3 Cook the bacon-wrapped rolls for 4–5 minutes, turning once, until the bacon is golden and crispy. Serve immediately, with a bowl of *nuoc cham* for dipping.

Energy 279Kcal/1155kJ; Protein 21.7g; Carbohydrate 1.0g, of which sugars 1.0g; Fat 21.3g, of which saturates 7.1g; Cholesterol 69mg; Calcium 6mg; Fibre 0g; Sodium 750mg.

GOLDEN BEEF AND POTATO PUFFS

THESE CRISP, GOLDEN PILLOWS OF PASTRY FILLED WITH SPICED BEEF AND POTATOES ARE DELICIOUS SERVED PIPING HOT, STRAIGHT FROM THE WOK. THE LIGHT, FLAKY PASTRY PUFFS UP WONDERFULLY IN THE HOT OIL AND CONTRASTS ENTICINGLY WITH THE FRAGRANT SPICED BEEF FILLING WITHIN.

SERVES FOUR

INGREDIENTS
  15ml/1 tbsp sunflower oil
  ½ small onion, finely chopped
  3 garlic cloves, crushed
  5ml/1 tsp finely grated fresh root
  ginger
  1 fresh red chilli, seeded and finely
  chopped
  30ml/2 tbsp hot curry powder
  75g/3oz minced (ground) beef
  115g/4oz mashed potato
  60ml/4 tbsp chopped fresh
  coriander (cilantro)
  2 sheets ready-rolled, fresh
  puff pastry
  1 egg, lightly beaten
  vegetable oil, for frying
  salt and ground black pepper
  fresh coriander (cilantro), to garnish
  tomato ketchup, to serve

1 Heat the oil in a wok, then add the onion, garlic, ginger and chilli. Stir-fry over a medium heat for 2–3 minutes. Add the curry powder and beef and stir-fry over a high heat for a further 4–5 minutes, or until the beef is browned and just cooked through, then remove from the heat.

2 Transfer the beef mixture to a large bowl and add the mashed potato and chopped fresh coriander. Stir well, then season and set aside.

COOK'S TIP
For a change in texture, you can use ready-made shortcrust pastry in place of the puff pastry. The puffs will be transformed into little golden crescents that have a firmer, crisper shell but the same succulent beef filling.

3 Lay the pastry sheets on a clean, dry surface and cut out 8 rounds, using a 7.5cm/3in pastry (cookie) cutter.

4 Place a large spoonful of the beef mixture in the centre of each pastry round. Brush the edges of the pastry with the beaten egg and fold each round in half to enclose the filling. Press and crimp the edges with the tines of a fork to seal.

5 Fill a wok one-third full of oil and heat to 180°C/350°F or until a cube of bread, dropped into the oil, browns in 40 seconds.

6 Deep-fry the puffs, in batches, for 2–3 minutes until puffed up and golden brown. Drain on kitchen paper and serve garnished with fresh coriander leaves. Offer a small bowl of tomato ketchup for dipping.

VARIATION
Try equal quantities of tomato ketchup and brown sauce as an alternative dip.

Energy 408Kcal/1695kJ; Protein 9g; Carbohydrate 24.2g, of which sugars 1.8g; Fat 31.8g, of which saturates 4.2g; Cholesterol 67mg; Calcium 46mg; Fibre 0.5g; Sodium 202mg.

SPICED HONEY CHICKEN WINGS

BE PREPARED TO GET VERY STICKY WHEN YOU EAT THESE STIR-FRIED WINGS, AS THE BEST WAY TO ENJOY THEM IS BY EATING THEM WITH YOUR FINGERS. SOY SAUCE AND HONEY ADDED TO THE SPICY RESIDUE IN THE WOK CREATE A SIMPLE BUT DELICIOUS GLAZE.

SERVES FOUR

INGREDIENTS
1 red chilli, finely chopped
5ml/1 tsp chilli powder
5ml/1 tsp finely grated fresh
   root ginger or 5ml/1 tsp
   ground ginger
rind of 1 lime, finely grated
12 chicken wings
60ml/4 tbsp sunflower oil
15ml/1 tbsp fresh coriander
   (cilantro), chopped
30ml/2 tbsp soy sauce
50ml/3½ tbsp clear honey
grated lime rind and fresh
   coriander (cilantro) sprigs,
   to garnish

1 Mix the fresh chilli, chilli powder, fresh or ground ginger and grated lime rind together.

2 Rub the spice mixture into the chicken wings and leave for at least 2 hours to allow the flavours to penetrate.

3 Heat a wok and add half the oil. When the oil is hot, add half the chicken wings and stir-fry for about 10 minutes, turning regularly, until the meat is cooked through and the skins are crisp and golden. Remove and drain on kitchen paper. Add the remaining oil to the wok and cook the second batch of chicken wings in the same way. Remove and drain.

4 Add the coriander to the hot wok and stir-fry for 30 seconds, then return all the chicken wings to the wok and stir-fry for 1 minute.

5 Stir in the soy sauce and honey, and stir-fry for 1 minute. Serve the chicken wings hot with the sauce drizzled over them and garnished with lime rind and coriander sprigs.

Energy 390kcal/1624kJ; Protein 26.2g; Carbohydrate 11.5g, of which sugars 10.1g; Fat 27g, of which saturates 5.8g; Cholesterol 111mg; Calcium 16mg; Fibre 0g; Sodium 612mg.

THAI SPRING ROLLS

CRUNCHY SPRING ROLLS ARE AS POPULAR IN THAILAND AS IN CHINA. THAIS FILL THEIR VERSION WITH A DELICIOUS PORK AND VEGETABLE MIXTURE. SERVE WITH A SWEET CHILLI DIPPING SAUCE.

MAKES TWENTY-FOUR

INGREDIENTS
　　24 x 15cm/6in square spring roll
　　　wrappers, thawed if frozen
　　30ml/2 tbsp plain (all-purpose) flour
　　vegetable oil, for deep-frying
　　sweet chilli dipping sauce,
　　　to serve
For the filling
　　50g/2oz cellophane noodles
　　4–6 Chinese dried mushrooms,
　　　soaked for 30 minutes in warm
　　　water to cover
　　30ml/2 tbsp vegetable oil
　　2 garlic cloves, chopped
　　2 fresh red chillies, seeded
　　　and chopped
　　225g/8oz minced (ground) pork
　　50g/2oz peeled cooked prawns
　　　(shrimp), thawed if frozen
　　30ml/2 tbsp Thai fish sauce
　　5ml/1 tsp granulated sugar
　　1 carrot, grated
　　50g/2oz piece of canned bamboo
　　　shoot, drained and chopped
　　50g/2oz/2⁄3 cup beansprouts
　　2 spring onions (scallions),
　　　finely chopped
　　15ml/1 tbsp chopped fresh
　　　coriander (cilantro)
　　ground black pepper

2 Heat the oil in a wok, add the garlic and chillies and stir-fry for 30 seconds. Transfer to a plate. Add the pork and stir-fry until it has browned. Add the mushrooms, noodles and prawns. Stir in the fish sauce and sugar, then add pepper to taste.

3 Turn the mixture into a bowl. Stir in the carrot, bamboo shoot, beansprouts, spring onions and chopped coriander. Mix in the reserved chilli mixture.

4 Unwrap the spring roll wrappers, but cover them with a damp cloth while you are making the rolls, so that they do not dry out. Put the flour in a small bowl and stir in a little water to make a paste.

5 Place a spoonful of filling in the centre of a spring roll wrapper. Turn the bottom edge over to cover the filling, then fold in the sides. Roll up the wrapper almost to the top, then brush the top edge with the flour paste and seal. Fill the remaining wrappers.

6 Heat the oil in a wok to 190°C/375°F or until a cube of bread browns in about 40 seconds. Fry the spring rolls, in batches, until crisp and golden. Drain on kitchen paper and serve hot with sweet chilli dipping sauce.

COOK'S TIP
For an alternative dipping sauce, mix 75ml/2½ fl oz/⅓ cup plum sauce with 30ml/2 tbsp dark soy sauce and 15ml/1 tbsp fish sauce. Add a little finely chopped fresh chilli if you wish.

1 To make the filling, place the cellophane noodles in a large bowl, cover with boiling water and soak for 10 minutes. Drain the noodles and snip them into 5cm/2in lengths. Drain the soaked mushrooms. Cut off and discard the stems, then chop the caps finely.

Energy 74kcal/310kJ; Protein 3.1g; Carbohydrate 7.2g, of which sugars 0.7g; Fat 3.8g, of which saturates 0.7g; Cholesterol 10mg; Calcium 13mg; Fibre 0.4g; Sodium 12mg.

THAI AUBERGINE AND PEPPER TEMPURA WITH SWEET CHILLI DIP

THESE CRUNCHY VEGETABLES IN A BEAUTIFULLY LIGHT BATTER ARE QUICK AND EASY TO MAKE AND TASTE VERY GOOD WITH THE PIQUANT DIP. ALTHOUGH TEMPURA IS A SIGNATURE DISH OF JAPANESE CUISINE, IT HAS NOW BECOME POPULAR THROUGHOUT ASIA, WITH EACH COUNTRY ADDING ITS OWN CHARACTERISTIC TOUCH — IN THE CASE OF THAILAND, THIS CHILLI-FLAVOURED SAUCE.

SERVES FOUR

INGREDIENTS

   2 aubergines (eggplants)
   2 red (bell) peppers
   vegetable oil, for deep-frying
For the tempura batter
   250g/9oz/2¼ cups plain
     (all-purpose) flour
   2 egg yolks
   500ml/17fl oz/2¼ cups iced water
   5ml/1 tsp salt
For the dip
   150ml/¼ pint/⅔ cup water
   10ml/2 tsp granulated sugar
   1 fresh red chilli, seeded and
     finely chopped
   1 garlic clove, crushed
   juice of ½ lime
   5ml/1 tsp rice vinegar
   35ml/2½ tbsp Thai fish sauce
   ½ small carrot, finely grated

1 Using a sharp knife or a mandolin, slice the aubergines into thin batons. Halve, seed and slice the red peppers thinly.

2 Make the dip. Mix together all the ingredients in a bowl and stir until the sugar has dissolved. Cover with clear film (plastic wrap) and set aside.

VARIATIONS
Tempura batter is also good with pieces of fish or whole shellfish, such as large prawns (jumbo shrimp) or baby squid, as well as with a variety of vegetables.

3 Make the tempura batter. Set aside 30ml/2 tbsp of the flour. Put the egg yolks in a large bowl and beat in the iced water. Tip in the remaining flour with the salt and stir briefly together – the mixture should resemble thick pancake batter but be lumpy and not properly mixed. If it is too thick, add a little more iced water. Do not leave the batter to stand; use it immediately.

4 Pour the oil for deep-frying into a wok or deep-fryer and heat to 190°C/375°F or until a cube of bread, added to the oil, browns in about 40 seconds.

5 Pick up a small, haphazard handful of aubergine batons and pepper slices, dust it with the reserved flour, then dip it into the batter. Immediately drop the batter-coated vegetables into the hot oil, taking care as the oil will froth up furiously. Repeat to make two or three more fritters, but do not cook any more than this at one time, or the oil may overflow.

6 Cook the fritters for 3–4 minutes, until they are golden and crisp all over, then lift them out with a metal basket or slotted spoon. Drain thoroughly on kitchen paper and keep hot.

7 Repeat until all the vegetables have been coated in batter and cooked. Serve immediately, with the dip.

Energy 404Kcal/1699kJ; Protein 9.4g; Carbohydrate 61g, of which sugars 12.5g; Fat 15.4g, of which saturates 2.4g; Cholesterol 101mg; Calcium 124mg; Fibre 5.8g; Sodium 15mg.

PEA AND POTATO PAKORAS WITH COCONUT AND MINT CHUTNEY

THESE DELICIOUS GOLDEN BITES ARE SOLD AS STREET FOOD THROUGHOUT INDIA. THEY MAKE A WONDERFUL SNACK DRIZZLED WITH THE FRAGRANT COCONUT AND MINT CHUTNEY.

MAKES TWENTY-FIVE

INGREDIENTS
15ml/1 tbsp sunflower oil
20ml/4 tsp cumin seeds
5ml/1 tsp black mustard seeds
1 small onion, finely chopped
10ml/2 tsp grated fresh root ginger
2 fresh green chillies, seeded and
  chopped
600g/1lb 6oz potatoes, peeled, diced
  and boiled until tender
200g/7oz fresh peas
juice of 1 lemon
90ml/6 tbsp chopped fresh coriander
  (cilantro) leaves
115g/4oz/1 cup gram flour
25g/1oz/¼ cup self-raising
  (self-rising) flour
40g/1½oz/⅓ cup rice flour
large pinch of ground turmeric
10ml/2 tsp crushed coriander seeds
350ml/12fl oz/1½ cups water
vegetable oil, for deep-frying
salt and ground black pepper
For the chutney
105ml/7 tbsp coconut cream
200ml/7fl oz/scant 1 cup natural
  (plain) yogurt
50g/2oz fresh mint leaves, finely
  chopped
5ml/1 tsp golden caster
  (superfine) sugar
juice of 1 lime

1 Heat a wok and add the sunflower oil. When hot, add the cumin and mustard seeds and stir-fry for 1–2 minutes.

2 Add the onion, ginger and chillies to the wok and cook for 3–4 minutes. Add the cooked potatoes, stir a few times, then add the peas and stir-fry for 3-4 minutes. Season, then stir in the lemon juice and coriander leaves.

COOK'S TIP
Gram flour is made from ground chickpeas and is widely used in Asian cooking. It is available in most large supermarkets and Asian stores.

3 To make the batter, put the gram flour, self-raising flour and rice flour in a bowl. Season and add the turmeric and coriander seeds. Gradually whisk in the water to make a smooth, thick batter.

4 To make the chutney, place all the ingredients in a blender and process until smooth. Season, then chill.

5 Leave the mixture to cool slightly, then divide into 25 portions. Shape each portion into a ball and chill. To cook the pakoras, fill a wok one-third full of oil and heat to 180°C/350°F. Working in batches, dip the balls in the batter, then drop into the oil and deep-fry for 1–2 minutes. Drain the pakoras on kitchen paper and serve with the chutney.

Energy 126Kcal/525kJ; Protein 4.1g; Carbohydrate 8.3g, of which sugars 2.6g; Fat 8.8g, of which saturates 5.2g; Cholesterol 0mg; Calcium 35mg; Fibre 1.3g; Sodium 16mg.

POTATO, SHALLOT <u>AND</u> GARLIC SAMOSAS <u>WITH</u> GREEN PEAS

MOST SAMOSAS ARE DEEP-FRIED. THESE ARE BAKED, ALTHOUGH THEIR FILLING IS MADE IN A WOK. THEY ARE PERFECT FOR PARTIES, SINCE THE PASTRIES NEED NO LAST-MINUTE ATTENTION.

MAKES TWENTY-FIVE

INGREDIENTS

   1 large potato, about 250g/
     9oz, diced
   15ml/1 tbsp groundnut
    (peanut) oil
   2 shallots, finely chopped
   1 garlic clove, finely chopped
   60ml/4 tbsp coconut milk
   5ml/1 tsp Thai red or green
    curry paste
   75g/3oz/¾ cup peas
   juice of ½ lime
   25 samosa wrappers or 10 x 5cm/
    4 x 2in strips of filo pastry
   salt and ground black pepper
   oil, for brushing

1 Preheat the oven to 220°C/425°F/ Gas 7. Bring a small pan of water to the boil, add the diced potato, cover and cook for 10–15 minutes, until tender. Drain and set aside.

2 Meanwhile, heat the groundnut oil in a wok and cook the shallots and garlic over a medium heat, stirring occasionally, for 4–5 minutes, until softened and golden.

3 Add the drained diced potato, coconut milk, red or green curry paste, peas and lime juice to the wok. Mash together coarsely with a wooden spoon. Season to taste with salt and pepper and cook over a low heat for 2–3 minutes, then remove the pan from the heat and set aside until the mixture has cooled a little.

4 Lay a samosa wrapper or filo strip flat on the work surface. Brush with a little oil, then place a generous teaspoonful of the mixture in the middle of one end. Turn one corner diagonally over the filling to meet the long edge.

5 Continue folding over the filling, keeping the triangular shape as you work down the strip. Brush with a little more oil if necessary and place on a baking sheet. Prepare all the other samosas in the same way.

6 Bake for 15 minutes, or until the pastry is golden and crisp. Leave to cool slightly before serving.

COOK'S TIP
Many Asian food stores sell what is described as a samosa pad. This is a packet, usually frozen, containing about 50 oblong pieces of samosa pastry. Filo pastry, cut to size, can be used instead.

Energy 42Kcal/178kJ; Protein 1.2g; Carbohydrate 8.5g, of which sugars 0.6g; Fat 0.6g, of which saturates 0.1g; Cholesterol 0mg; Calcium 14mg; Fibre 0.5g; Sodium 4mg.

CORN FRITTERS

SOMETIMES IT IS THE SIMPLEST DISHES THAT TASTE THE BEST. THESE FRITTERS, PACKED WITH
CRUNCHY CORN, ARE VERY EASY TO PREPARE AND COOK QUICKLY IN A HOT WOK.

<u>MAKES TWELVE</u>

INGREDIENTS

3 corn cobs, total weight about
    250g/9oz
1 garlic clove, crushed
small bunch fresh coriander
    (cilantro), chopped
1 small fresh red or green chilli,
    seeded and finely chopped
1 spring onion (scallion),
    finely chopped
15ml/1 tbsp soy sauce
75g/3oz/⅔ cup rice flour or plain
    (all-purpose) flour
2 eggs, lightly beaten
60ml/4 tbsp water
oil, for shallow-frying
salt and ground black pepper
sweet chilli sauce, to serve

1 Using a sharp knife, slice the kernels from the cobs and place them in a large bowl. Add the garlic, chopped coriander, red or green chilli, spring onion, soy sauce, flour, beaten eggs and water and mix well. Season with salt and pepper to taste and mix again. The mixture should be firm enough to hold its shape, but not stiff.

2 Heat the oil in a wok. Add spoonfuls of the corn mixture, gently spreading each one out with the back of the spoon to make a roundish fritter. Cook for 1–2 minutes on each side.

3 Drain on kitchen paper and keep hot while frying more fritters in the same way. Serve hot with sweet chilli sauce.

Energy 77Kcal/322kJ; Protein 2.3g; Carbohydrate 7.8g, of which sugars 0.6g; Fat 4.1g, of which saturates 0.6g; Cholesterol 32mg; Calcium 24mg; Fibre 0.8g; Sodium 104mg.

GREEN CURRY PUFFS

SHRIMP PASTE AND GREEN CURRY SAUCE, USED JUDICIOUSLY, GIVE THESE PUFFS THEIR DISTINCTIVE, SPICY, SAVOURY FLAVOUR, AND THE ADDITION OF CHILLI STEPS UP THE HEAT.

MAKES TWENTY-FOUR

INGREDIENTS
24 small wonton wrappers, about
  8cm/3¼ in square, thawed if frozen
15ml/1 tbsp cornflour (cornstarch),
  mixed to a paste with 30ml/
  2 tbsp water
oil, for deep-frying
For the filling
1 small potato, about 115g/4oz,
  boiled and mashed
25g/1oz/3 tbsp cooked petits pois
  (baby peas)
25g/1oz/3 tbsp cooked corn
few sprigs fresh coriander
  (cilantro), chopped
1 small fresh red chilli, seeded and
  finely chopped
½ lemon grass stalk, finely chopped
15ml/1 tbsp soy sauce
5ml/1 tsp shrimp paste or fish sauce
5ml/1 tsp Thai green curry paste

1 Combine the filling ingredients. Lay out one wonton wrapper and place a teaspoon of the filling in the centre.

2 Brush a little of the cornflour paste along two sides of the square. Fold the other two sides over to meet them, then press together to make a triangular pastry and seal in the filling. Make more pastries in the same way.

3 Heat the oil in a wok to 190°C/375°F or until a cube of bread, added to the oil, browns in about 40 seconds. Add the pastries to the oil, a few at a time, and fry them for about 5 minutes, until golden brown.

4 Remove from the wok and drain on kitchen paper. If you intend serving the puffs hot, place them in a low oven while cooking successive batches. The puffs also taste good cold.

COOK'S TIP
Wonton wrappers dry out quickly, so keep them covered, using clear film (plastic wrap), until you are ready to use them.

Energy 69Kcal/291kJ; Protein 1.4g; Carbohydrate 9.9g, of which sugars 0.4g; Fat 3g, of which saturates 0.4g; Cholesterol 1mg; Calcium 22mg; Fibre 0.5g; Sodium 58mg.

CURRIED SWEET POTATO BALLS

THESE SWEET POTATO BALLS FROM CAMBODIA ARE DELICIOUS DIPPED IN A FIERY SAUCE, SUCH AS NUOC CHAM, FRIED BLACK CHILLI SAUCE OR HOT PEANUT DIPPING SAUCE. SIMPLE TO MAKE, THEY ARE IDEAL FOR SERVING AS A NIBBLE WITH A DRINK.

SERVES FOUR

INGREDIENTS

450g/1lb sweet potatoes or taro root,
  boiled or baked, and peeled
30ml/2 tbsp sugar
15ml/1 tbsp Indian curry powder
25g/1oz fresh root ginger, peeled
  and grated
150g/5oz/1¼ cups glutinous rice
  flour or plain (all-purpose) flour
salt
sesame seeds or poppy seeds
vegetable oil, for deep-frying
dipping sauce, to serve

1 In a bowl, mash the cooked sweet potatoes or taro root. Beat in the sugar, curry powder, and ginger. Add the rice flour (sift it if you are using plain flour) and salt, and work into a stiff dough – add more flour if necessary.

2 Pull off lumps of the dough and mould them into small balls – you should be able to make roughly 24 balls. Roll the balls on a bed of sesame seeds or poppy seeds until they are completely coated.

3 Heat enough oil for deep-frying in a wok. Fry the sweet potato balls in batches, until golden. Drain on kitchen paper. Serve the balls with wooden skewers to make it easier to dip them into a dipping sauce of your choice.

Energy 354Kcal/1495kJ; Protein 5g; Carbohydrate 61g, of which sugars 14.8g; Fat 11.8g, of which saturates 1.5g; Cholesterol 0mg; Calcium 84mg; Fibre 3.9g; Sodium 50mg.

DEEP-FRIED SWEET POTATO PATTIES

THIS DISH, BANH TOM, IS A HANOI SPECIALITY. THE STREET SELLERS IN THE CITY AND THE CAFÉS ALONG THE BANKS OF WEST LAKE ARE WELL KNOWN FOR THEIR VARIED AND DELICIOUS BANH TOM. TRADITIONALLY, THE PATTIES ARE SERVED WITH HERBS AND LETTUCE LEAVES FOR WRAPPING.

SERVES FOUR

INGREDIENTS
    50g/2oz/½ cup plain
      (all-purpose) flour
    50g/2oz/½ cup rice flour
    4ml/scant 1 tsp baking powder
    10ml/2 tsp sugar
    2.5cm/1in fresh root ginger,
      peeled and grated
    2 spring onions (scallions),
      finely sliced
    175g/6oz small fresh prawns
      (shrimp), peeled and deveined
    1 slim sweet potato, about
      225g/8oz, peeled and cut into
      fine matchsticks
    vegetable oil, for deep-frying
    salt and ground black pepper
    chopped fresh coriander (cilantro),
      to garnish
    lettuce leaves and *nuoc cham* or
      other dipping sauce, to serve

1 Sift the plain and rice flour and baking powder into a bowl. Add the sugar and about 2.5ml/½ tsp each of salt and pepper. Gradually stir in 250ml/8fl oz/1 cup water, until thoroughly combined. Add the grated ginger and sliced spring onions and leave to stand for 30 minutes. Add extra ginger if you like a strong flavour.

COOK'S TIP
Banh tom made with sweet potato are particularly popular in Hanoi, but they are also very good made with strips of winter melon or courgette (zucchini), beansprouts or bamboo shoots, or finely sliced cabbage leaves. Simply replace the sweet potato with the vegetable of your choice, add a little chilli, if you like, shape into patties and cook as before. You can make the patties any size: small for a snack or first course, or large for a main course; simply adjust the amount you spoon on to the spatula before frying. Serve the patties with a piquant or tangy dipping sauce of your own choice.

2 Add the prawns and sweet potato to the batter and fold them in, making sure they are well coated. Heat enough oil for deep-frying in a wok. Place a heaped tablespoon of the mixture on to a metal spatula. Lower it into the oil, pushing it off the spatula so that it floats in the oil. Fry for 2–3 minutes, turning it over so that it is evenly browned. Drain on kitchen paper. Continue with the rest of the batter, frying the patties in batches.

3 Arrange the patties on lettuce leaves, garnish with coriander, and serve immediately with *nuoc cham* or another dipping sauce of your choice.

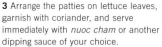

Energy 276Kcal/1159kJ; Protein 11g; Carbohydrate 35g, of which sugars 6g; Fat 11g, of which saturates 1g; Cholesterol 85mg; Calcium 83mg; Fibre 81g; Sodium 200mg.

ROASTED COCONUT CASHEW NUTS

SERVE THESE WOK-FRIED HOT AND SWEET CASHEW NUTS IN PAPER OR CELLOPHANE CONES AT PARTIES.
NOT ONLY DO THEY LOOK ENTICING AND TASTE TERRIFIC, BUT THE CONES HELP TO KEEP CLOTHES
AND HANDS CLEAN AND CAN SIMPLY BE CRUMPLED UP AND THROWN AWAY AFTERWARDS.

SERVES SIX TO EIGHT

INGREDIENTS
   15ml/1 tbsp groundnut (peanut) oil
   30ml/2 tbsp clear honey
   250g/9oz/2 cups cashew nuts
   115g/4oz/1⅓ cups desiccated (dry
   unsweetened shredded) coconut
   2 small fresh red chillies, seeded and
   finely chopped
   salt and ground black pepper

VARIATIONS
Almonds also work well, or choose
peanuts for a more economical snack.

1 Heat the oil in a wok or large frying pan and then stir in the honey. After a few seconds add the nuts and coconut and stir-fry until both are golden brown.

2 Add the chillies, with salt and pepper to taste. Toss until all the ingredients are well mixed. Serve warm or cooled in paper cones or on saucers.

Energy 301Kcal/1247kJ; Protein 7.2g; Carbohydrate 9.7g, of which sugars 5.5g; Fat 26.2g, of which saturates 11.1g; Cholesterol 0mg; Calcium 14mg; Fibre 3g; Sodium 95mg.

TUNG TONG

POPULARLY CALLED "GOLD BAGS", THESE CRISP PASTRY PURSES HAVE A CORIANDER-FLAVOURED FILLING BASED ON WATER CHESTNUTS AND CORN. THEY ARE THE PERFECT VEGETARIAN SNACK, CRISP AND CRUNCHY ON THE OUTSIDE, WITH A SUCCULENT CORN AND WATER CHESTNUT FILLING.

MAKES EIGHTEEN

INGREDIENTS
    18 spring roll wrappers, about
        8cm/3¼in square, thawed
        if frozen
    oil, for deep-frying
    plum sauce, to serve
For the filling
    4 baby corn cobs
    130g/4½oz can water chestnuts,
        drained and chopped
    1 shallot, coarsely chopped
    1 egg, separated
    30ml/2 tbsp cornflour (cornstarch)
    60ml/4 tbsp water
    small bunch fresh coriander
        (cilantro), chopped
    salt and ground black pepper

1 Make the filling. Place the baby corn, water chestnuts, shallot and egg yolk in a food processor or blender. Process to a coarse paste. Place the egg white in a cup and whisk it lightly with a fork.

2 Put the cornflour in a small pan and stir in the water until smooth. Add the corn mixture and chopped coriander and season with salt and pepper to taste. Cook over a low heat, stirring constantly, until thickened.

3 Leave the filling to cool slightly, then place 5ml/1 tsp in the centre of a spring roll wrapper. Brush the edges with the beaten egg white, then gather up the points and press them firmly together to make a pouch or bag.

4 Repeat with the remaining wrappers and filling. Heat the oil in a wok to 190°C/375°F or until a cube of bread, added to the oil, browns in about 45 seconds. Fry the bags, in batches, for about 5 minutes, until golden brown. Drain on kitchen paper and serve hot, with the plum sauce.

Energy 55Kcal/229kJ; Protein 1.2g; Carbohydrate 6.3g, of which sugars 0.4g; Fat 2.9g, of which saturates 0.4g; Cholesterol 12mg; Calcium 19mg; Fibre 0.5g; Sodium 42mg.

SPICED NOODLE PANCAKES

THE DELICATE RICE NOODLES PUFF UP IN THE HOT OIL TO GIVE A FABULOUS CRUNCHY BITE THAT MELTS IN THE MOUTH. FOR MAXIMUM ENJOYMENT, SERVE THE GOLDEN PANCAKES AS SOON AS THEY ARE COOKED AND SAVOUR THE SUBTLE BLEND OF SPICES AND WONDERFULLY CRISP TEXTURE.

SERVES FOUR

INGREDIENTS
    150g/5oz dried thin rice noodles
    1 fresh red chilli, finely diced
    10ml/2 tsp garlic salt
    5ml/1 tsp ground ginger
    ¼ small red onion, very finely diced
    5ml/1 tsp finely chopped lemon grass
    5ml/1 tsp ground cumin
    5ml/1 tsp ground coriander
    large pinch of ground turmeric
    salt
    vegetable oil, for frying
    sweet chilli sauce, for dipping

1 Roughly break up the noodles and place in a large bowl. Pour over enough boiling water to cover, and soak for 4–5 minutes. Drain and rinse under cold water. Dry on kitchen paper.

2 Transfer the noodles to a bowl and add the chilli, garlic salt, ground ginger, red onion, lemon grass, ground cumin, coriander and turmeric.

3 Toss well to mix, and season with salt, the best way to make sure the flavourings cover all the noodles is to mix them with your hands.

COOK'S TIP
For deep-frying, choose very thin rice noodles. These can be cooked dry, but here are soaked and seasoned first.

4 Heat 5–6cm/2–2½in oil in a wok. Working in batches, drop tablespoons of the noodle mixture into the oil.

5 Flatten using the back of a skimmer and cook for 1–2 minutes on each side until crisp and golden. Lift out from the wok.

6 Drain the noodle pancakes on kitchen paper and serve immediately with the chilli sauce for dipping.

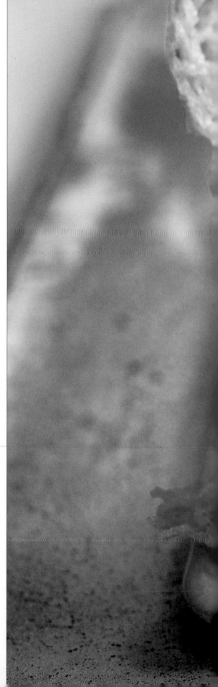

Energy 190Kcal/791kJ; Protein 2g; Carbohydrate 31.8g, of which sugars 0.9g; Fat 5.6g, of which saturates 0.7g; Cholesterol 0mg; Calcium 9mg; Fibre 0.2g; Sodium 496mg.

SOUPS

For swift soups, such as those based on ready-made stock or canned bouillon, a wok is ideal. The large surface area makes for rapid evaporation, though, so you need to keep an eye on liquid levels and top up if necessary. This is an area where an electric wok can work wonders. Any preliminary cooking can be done at a high heat, and the thermostat can then be turned down so the soup simmers well. However, there are some Asian soups that need only brief cooking, such as Spinach and Tofu Soup.

HOT-AND-SOUR FISH SOUP

THIS TANGY SOUP, CANH CHUA CA, IS FOUND THROUGHOUT SOUTH-EAST ASIA — WITH THE BALANCE OF HOT, SWEET AND SOUR FLAVOURS VARYING FROM CAMBODIA TO VIETNAM. CHILLIES PROVIDE THE HEAT, TAMARIND PRODUCES THE TARTNESS AND THE DELICIOUS SWEETNESS COMES FROM PINEAPPLE.

SERVES FOUR

INGREDIENTS

1 catfish, sea bass or red snapper,
  about 1kg/2¼ lb, filleted
30ml/2 tbsp *nuoc mam*
2 garlic cloves, finely chopped
25g/1oz dried squid, soaked in water
  for 30 minutes
15ml/1 tbsp vegetable oil
2 spring onions (scallions), sliced
2 shallots, sliced
4cm/1½ in fresh root ginger, peeled
  and chopped
2–3 lemon grass stalks, cut into
  strips and crushed
30ml/2 tbsp tamarind paste
2–3 Thai chillies, seeded and sliced
15ml/1 tbsp sugar
30–45ml/2–3 tbsp *nuoc mam*
225g/8oz fresh pineapple, peeled
  and diced
3 tomatoes, skinned, seeded and
  roughly chopped
50g/2oz canned sliced bamboo
  shoots, drained
1 small bunch fresh coriander
  (cilantro), stalks removed, leaves
  finely chopped
salt and ground black pepper
115g/4oz/½ cup beansprouts and
  1 bunch dill, fronds roughly
  chopped, to garnish
1 lime, cut into quarters, to serve

1 Cut the fish into bitesize pieces, mix with the *nuoc mam* and garlic and leave to marinate. Save the head, tail and bones for the stock. Drain and rinse the soaked dried squid.

2 Heat the oil in a wok and stir in the spring onions, shallots, ginger, lemon grass and dried squid. Add the reserved fish head, tail and bones, and sauté them gently for a minute or two. Pour in 1.2 litres/2 pints/5 cups water and bring to the boil. Reduce the heat and simmer for 30 minutes.

3 Strain the stock into another wok or a deep pan and bring to the boil. Stir in the tamarind paste, chillies, sugar and *nuoc mam* and simmer for 2–3 minutes. Add the pineapple, tomatoes and bamboo shoots and simmer for a further 2–3 minutes. Stir in the fish pieces and the chopped fresh coriander, and cook until the fish turns opaque.

4 Season to taste and ladle the soup into hot bowls. Garnish with beansprouts and dill, and serve with the lime quarters to squeeze over.

VARIATIONS

• Depending on your mood, or your palate, you can adjust the balance of hot and sour by adding more chilli or tamarind to taste. Enjoyed as a meal in itself, the soup is usually served with plain steamed rice but in Ho Chi Minh City it is served with chunks of fresh baguette, which are perfect for soaking up the spicy, fruity, tangy broth.
• Other fresh herbs, such as chopped mint and basil leaves, also complement this soup.

Energy 335Kcal/1415kJ; Protein 44g; Carbohydrate 24g, of which sugars 19g; Fat 7g, of which saturates 1g; Cholesterol 108mg; Calcium 138mg; Fibre 2.3g; Sodium 1.2g.

CRAB AND ASPARAGUS SOUP WITH NUOC CHAM

IN THIS DELICIOUS VIETNAMESE SOUP, THE RECIPE HAS CLEARLY BEEN ADAPTED FROM THE CLASSIC FRENCH ASPARAGUS VELOUTÉ TO PRODUCE A MUCH MEATIER VERSION THAT HAS MORE TEXTURE, AND THE VIETNAMESE STAMP OF NUOC CHAM AND NUOC MAM.

SERVES FOUR

INGREDIENTS
15ml/1 tbsp vegetable oil
2 shallots, finely chopped
2 garlic cloves, finely chopped
15ml/1 tbsp rice flour or
    cornflour (cornstarch)
225g/8oz/1⅓ cups cooked crabmeat,
    chopped into small pieces
450g/1lb fresh asparagus, trimmed
    and steamed
salt and ground black pepper
basil and coriander (cilantro) leaves,
    to garnish
nuoc cham, to serve

For the stock
1 meaty chicken carcass
25g/1oz dried shrimp, soaked in
    water for 30 minutes, rinsed
    and drained
2 onions, peeled and quartered
2 garlic cloves, crushed
15ml/1 tbsp *nuoc mam*
6 black peppercorns
sea salt

1 To make the stock, put the chicken carcass into a large pan. Add all the other stock ingredients, except the salt, and pour in 2 litres/3½ pints/8 cups water. Bring to the boil, boil for a few minutes, skim off any foam, then reduce the heat and simmer with the lid on for 1½–2 hours. Remove the lid and simmer for a further 30 minutes to reduce the stock. Skim off any fat, season, then strain the stock and measure out 1.5 litres/2½ pints/6¼ cups.

2 Heat the oil in a deep pan or wok. Stir in the shallots and garlic, until they begin to colour. Remove from the heat, stir in the flour, and then pour in the stock. Put the pan back over the heat and bring to the boil, stirring constantly, until smooth.

COOK'S TIP
In households close to the sea, where large crabs – some as large as 60cm/2ft in diameter – can be found in abundance, this soup may be made using a generous quantity of fresh crab. If you have a good supply of fresh crabs, you can increase the quantity of crabmeat as much as you like, to make a soup that is very rich and filling.

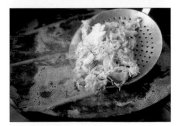

3 Add the crabmeat and asparagus, reduce the heat and leave to simmer for 15–20 minutes. Season to taste with salt and pepper, then ladle the soup into bowls, garnish with fresh basil and coriander leaves, and serve with a splash of *nuoc cham*.

Energy 142kcal/590kJ; Protein 17.1g; Carbohydrate 6.9g, of which sugars 3g; Fat 5.1g, of which saturates 0.6g; Cholesterol 72mg; Calcium 177mg; Fibre 2.1g; Sodium 584mg.

SPINACH AND TOFU SOUP

IF FRESH YOUNG SPINACH LEAVES ARE NOT AVAILABLE, WATERCRESS OR LETTUCE CAN BE USED INSTEAD. SORREL LEAVES MAY ALSO BE USED AS A SUBSTITUTE WHEN IN SEASON, BUT THEY HAVE A DISTINCTIVELY SHARP FLAVOUR SO WILL CHANGE THE CHARACTER OF THE SOUP.

SERVES FOUR

INGREDIENTS
    1 packet tofu
    115g/4oz spinach leaves
    750ml/1¼ pints/3 cups stock
    15ml/1 tbsp light soy sauce
    salt and ground black pepper

3 Add the spinach and simmer for a further minute. Skim the surface to make it clear, then adjust the seasoning and serve immediately.

1 Cut the tofu into 12 small pieces, each about 5mm/¼in thick. Wash the spinach leaves thoroughly and cut them into small pieces.

2 Put the stock into a wok and bring to a rolling boil. Add the tofu and soy sauce, bring back to the boil and simmer for about 2 minutes.

COOK'S TIP
Fresh tofu, also known as beancurd, is sold in cakes about 7.5cm/3in square in Chinese food stores. Do not confuse it with fermented tofu, which is much stronger-tasting, quite salty and usually used as a condiment.

Energy 55kcal/231kJ; Protein 7.6g; Carbohydrate 1.4g, of which sugars 1.1g; Fat 2.2g, of which saturates 0.3g; Cholesterol 25mg; Calcium 352mg; Fibre 1.3g; Sodium 300mg.

LAMB AND CUCUMBER SOUP

THIS IS A VARIATION ON THE POPULAR HOT AND SOUR SOUP, BUT IT IS EVEN SIMPLER TO PREPARE.
THE MARINADE WILL TENDERIZE THE LAMB, BUT YOU WILL STILL HAVE TO BUY A GOOD QUALITY CUT
OF MEAT SO THAT IT DOESN'T BECOME TOUGH DURING THE COOKING PROCESS.

SERVES FOUR

INGREDIENTS
225g/8oz lamb steak
15ml/1 tbsp light soy sauce
15ml/1 tbsp Chinese rice wine or
dry sherry
2.5ml/½ tsp sesame oil
7.5cm/3in piece cucumber
750ml/1¼ pints/3 cups stock
15ml/1 tbsp rice vinegar
salt and ground white pepper

1 Trim off any excess fat from the lamb and discard. Thinly slice the lamb into small pieces.

2 Put the lamb into a shallow dish and add the soy sauce, rice wine or sherry and sesame oil. Set aside to marinate for 25–30 minutes. Remove the lamb and discard the marinade.

3 Halve the cucumber lengthways and cut it into thin slices diagonally. Bring the stock to a rolling boil in a wok.

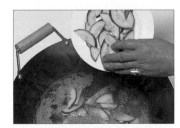

4 Add the lamb to the wok and stir to separate. Return to the boil, then add the cucumber slices, vinegar and seasoning. Bring to the boil once more, and serve at once.

COOK'S TIP
The skin on the cucumber adds an attractive bit of colour to this dish, but if the cucumber you are using has quite a tough skin, you might like to peel it.

Energy 105kcal/438kJ; Protein 11.2g; Carbohydrate 0.4g, of which sugars 0.3g; Fat 6.6g, of which saturates 3g; Cholesterol 43mg; Calcium 6mg; Fibre 0g; Sodium 316mg.

CRISPY WONTON SOUP

THE FRESHLY COOKED CRISPY WONTONS ARE SUPPOSED TO SIZZLE AND "SING" AS THE HOT FAT HITS THE SOUP, SO ADD THEM JUST BEFORE YOU TAKE THE BOWLS TO THE TABLE.

SERVES SIX

INGREDIENTS
2 cloud ear (wood ear) mushrooms,
  soaked for 30 minutes in warm
  water to cover
1.2 litres/2 pints/5 cups
  home-made chicken stock
2.5cm/1in piece fresh root ginger,
  peeled and grated
4 spring onions (scallions), chopped
2 rich-green spring green (collards)
  leaves, finely shredded
50g/2oz drained canned bamboo
  shoots, sliced
25ml/1½ tbsp dark soy sauce
2.5ml/½ tsp sesame oil
salt and ground black pepper
For the filled wontons
5ml/1 tsp sesame oil
½ small onion, finely chopped
10 drained canned water
  chestnuts, finely chopped
115g/4oz finely minced (ground) pork
24 wonton wrappers
groundnut (peanut) oil, for frying

2 Place the wonton wrappers under a slightly dampened dish towel so that they do not dry out. Next, dampen the edges of a wonton wrapper. Place about 5ml/1 tsp of the filling in the centre of the wrapper. Gather it up like a purse and twist the top or roll up as you would a baby spring roll. Fill the remaining wontons in the same way.

3 To make the soup, drain the cloud ears, discarding the soaking liquid. Trim away any rough stems, then slice thinly.

4 Bring the stock to the boil in a large pan, add the ginger and the spring onions and simmer for 3 minutes. Add the cloud ears, spring greens, bamboo shoots and soy sauce. Simmer for 10 minutes, then stir in the sesame oil. Season, cover and keep hot.

5 Heat the oil in a wok to 190°C/375°F and fry the wontons for 3–4 minutes or until they are crisp and golden. Ladle the soup into warmed bowls, share the wontons among them, and serve.

1 Make the filled wontons. Heat the sesame oil in a small pan, add the onion, water chestnuts and pork and fry, stirring occasionally, until the meat is no longer pink. Transfer to a bowl, season to taste and leave to cool.

COOK'S TIP
The wontons can be filled up to two hours ahead. Place them in a single layer on a baking sheet dusted with cornflour, to prevent them from sticking, and leave in a cool place.

Energy 132kcal/554kJ; Protein 8.4g; Carbohydrate 17g, of which sugars 3.4g; Fat 3.9g, of which saturates 0.7g; Cholesterol 12mg; Calcium 140mg; Fibre 2.7g; Sodium 332mg.

HOT AND SOUR SOUP

THIS CHINESE SOUP IS FAMED FOR ITS CLEVER BALANCE OF FLAVOURS. THE "HOT" COMES FROM PEPPER; THE "SOUR" FROM VINEGAR. SIMILAR SOUPS ARE FOUND THROUGHOUT ASIA.

SERVES SIX

INGREDIENTS

    4–6 Chinese dried mushrooms
    2–3 small pieces of cloud ear (wood
       ear) mushrooms and a few golden
       needles (lily buds) (optional)
    115g/4oz pork fillet (tenderloin), cut
       into fine strips
    45ml/3 tbsp cornflour (cornstarch)
    150ml/¼ pint/⅔ cup water
    15–30ml/1–2 tbsp sunflower oil
    1 small onion, finely chopped
    1.5 litres/2½ pints/6¼ cups good
       quality beef or chicken stock, or
       2 × 300g/11oz cans consommé made
       up to the full quantity with water
    150g/5oz fresh firm tofu, diced
    60ml/4 tbsp rice vinegar
    15ml/1 tbsp light soy sauce
    1 egg, beaten
    5ml/1 tsp sesame oil
    salt and ground white or black pepper
    2–3 spring onions (scallions),
       shredded, to garnish

1 Place the dried mushrooms in a bowl, with the pieces of cloud ear and the golden needles, if using. Add sufficient warm water to cover and leave to soak for about 30 minutes.

2 Drain the mushrooms, reserving the soaking water. Cut off and discard the mushroom stems and slice the caps finely. Trim away any tough stem from the wood ears, then chop them finely. Using kitchen string, tie the golden needles into a bundle.

3 Lightly dust the strips of pork fillet with some of the cornflour; mix the remaining cornflour to a smooth paste with the measured water.

4 Heat the oil in a wok and fry the onion until soft. Increase the heat and fry the pork until it changes colour. Add the stock or consommé, mushrooms, soaking water, and cloud ears and golden needles, if using. Bring to the boil, then simmer for 15 minutes.

5 Discard the golden needles, lower the heat and stir in the cornflour paste to thicken. Add the tofu, vinegar, soy sauce, and salt and pepper.

6 Bring the soup to just below boiling point, then drizzle in the beaten egg by letting it drop from a whisk (or to be authentic, the fingertips) so that it forms threads in the soup. Stir in the sesame oil and serve at once, garnished with spring onion shreds.

Energy 103kcal/429kJ; Protein 7.3g; Carbohydrate 7.3g, of which sugars 0.3g; Fat 5.1g, of which saturates 1g; Cholesterol 44mg; Calcium 135mg; Fibre 0g; Sodium 208mg.

TOKYO-STYLE RAMEN NOODLES IN SOUP

A WOK IS ALL YOU NEED TO MAKE THIS MULTI-LAYERED JAPANESE SOUP. THERE ARE MANY REGIONAL AND LOCAL VARIATIONS OF RAMEN, THIS IS A LEGENDARY TOKYO VERSION.

SERVES FOUR

INGREDIENTS
    250g/9oz dried ramen noodles
For the soup stock
    4 spring onions (scallions)
    7.5cm/3in fresh root ginger, quartered
    raw bones from 2 chickens, washed
    1 large onion, quartered
    4 garlic cloves, peeled
    1 large carrot, roughly chopped
    1 egg shell
    120ml/4fl oz/½ cup sake
    about 60ml/4 tbsp shoyu
    2.5ml/½ tsp salt
For the *cha-shu* (pot-roast pork)
    500g/1¼lb pork shoulder, boned
    30ml/2 tbsp vegetable oil
    2 spring onions (scallions), chopped
    2.5cm/1in fresh root ginger, peeled
        and sliced
    15ml/1 tbsp sake
    45ml/3 tbsp shoyu
    15ml/1 tbsp caster (superfine) sugar
For the toppings
    2 hard-boiled eggs
    150g/5oz pickled bamboo shoots,
        soaked for 30 minutes and drained
    ½ nori sheet, broken into pieces
    2 spring onions (scallions), chopped
    ground white pepper
    sesame oil or chilli oil

1 To make the soup stock, bruise the spring onions and ginger by hitting with the side of a large knife or a rolling pin. Pour 1.5 litres/2½ pints/6¼ cups water into a wok and bring to the boil. Add the chicken bones and boil until the colour of the meat changes. Discard the water and wash the bones under water.

2 Wash the wok, bring another 2 litres/ 3½ pints/9 cups water to the boil and add the bones and the other soup stock ingredients, except for the shoyu and salt. Reduce the heat to low, and simmer for up to 2 hours until the water has reduced by half, skimming off any scum. Strain into a bowl through a sieve lined with muslin (cheesecloth).

3 Make the *cha-shu*. Roll the meat up tightly, to 8cm/3½in in diameter, and tie it with kitchen string.

4 Wash the wok and dry over a high heat. Heat the oil to smoking point in the wok and add the chopped spring onions and ginger. Cook briefly, then add the meat. Turn often to brown the outside evenly.

5 Sprinkle with sake and add 400ml/ 14fl oz/1⅔ cups water, the shoyu and sugar. Boil, then reduce the heat to low and cover. Cook for 25–30 minutes, turning every 5 minutes. Remove from the heat.

6 Slice the pork into 12 fine slices. Use any leftover pork for another recipe.

7 Shell and halve the boiled eggs, and sprinkle some salt on to the yolks.

8 Pour 1 litre/1¾ pints/4 cups soup stock from the bowl into a large pan. Boil and add the shoyu and salt. Check the seasoning; add more shoyu if required.

9 Wash the wok again and bring 2 litres/ 3½ pints/9 cups water to the boil. Cook the ramen noodles according to the packet instructions until just soft. Stir constantly to prevent sticking. If the water bubbles up, pour in 50ml/2fl oz/ ¼ cup cold water. Drain well and divide among four bowls.

10 Pour the soup over the noodles to cover. Arrange half a boiled egg, pork slices, pickled bamboo shoots, and nori on top, and sprinkle with spring onions. Serve with pepper and sesame or chilli oil. Season to taste with a little salt, if you like.

COOK'S TIP
The cooked pork could be finely chopped and minced and used as part of the filling for spring rolls.

Energy 359kcal/1503kJ; Protein 36.1g; Carbohydrate 19.8g, of which sugars 9.8g; Fat 15.4g, of which saturates 3.4g; Cholesterol 174mg; Calcium 248mg; Fibre 1.8g; Sodium 930mg.

BEEF NOODLE SOUP

SOME WOULD SAY THAT THIS CLASSIC NOODLE SOUP, PHO, IS VIETNAM IN A BOWL. MADE WITH BEEF (PHO BO) OR CHICKEN (PHO GA), IT IS VIETNAMESE FAST FOOD, STREET FOOD, WORKING MEN'S FOOD AND FAMILY FOOD. IT IS NUTRITIOUS AND FILLING, AND MAKES AN INTENSELY SATISFYING MEAL.

SERVES SIX

INGREDIENTS
250g/9oz beef sirloin
500g/1¼lb dried noodles, soaked in
    lukewarm water for 20 minutes
1 onion, halved and finely sliced
6–8 spring onions (scallions),
    cut into long pieces
2–3 red Thai chillies, seeded and
    finely sliced
115g/4oz/½ cup beansprouts
1 large bunch each fresh coriander
    (cilantro) and mint, stalks removed,
    leaves chopped
2 limes, cut in wedges, and hoisin
    sauce, *nuoc mam* or *nuoc cham*
    to serve
For the stock
1.5kg/3lb 5oz oxtail, trimmed of fat
    and cut into thick pieces
1kg/2¼lb beef shank or brisket
2 large onions, peeled and quartered
2 carrots, peeled and cut into chunks
7.5cm/3in fresh root ginger,
    cut into chunks
6 cloves
2 cinnamon sticks
6 star anise
5ml/1 tsp black peppercorns
30ml/2 tbsp soy sauce
45–60ml/3–4 tbsp *nuoc mam*
salt

1 To make the stock, put the oxtail into a large, deep pan and cover it with water. Bring it to the boil and blanch the meat for about 10 minutes. Drain the meat, rinsing off any scum, and clean out the pan. Put the blanched oxtail back into the pan with the other stock ingredients, apart from the *nuoc mam* and salt, and cover with about 3 litres/5¼ pints/12 cups water. Bring it to the boil, reduce the heat and simmer, covered, for 2–3 hours.

2 Remove the lid and simmer for another hour, until the stock has reduced to about 2 litres/3½ pints/ 8 cups. Skim off any fat and then strain the stock into another pan.

3 Cut the beef sirloin across the grain into thin pieces, the size of the heel of your hand. Bring the stock to the boil once more, stir in the *nuoc mam*, season to taste, then reduce the heat and leave the stock simmering until ready to use.

4 Meanwhile, bring a pan filled with water to the boil, drain the rice sticks and add to the water. Cook for about 5 minutes or until tender – you may need to separate them with a pair of chopsticks if they look as though they are sticking together.

5 Drain the noodles and divide them equally among six wide soup bowls. Top each serving with the slices of beef, onion, spring onions, chillies and beansprouts.

6 Ladle the hot stock over the top of these ingredients, top with the fresh herbs and serve with the lime wedges to squeeze over. Pass around the hoisin sauce, *nuoc mam* or *nuoc cham* for those who like a little sweetening, fish flavouring or extra fire.

COOK'S TIPS
• The key to *pho* is a tasty, light stock flavoured with ginger, cinnamon, cloves and star anise, so it is worth cooking it slowly and leaving it to stand overnight to allow the flavours to develop fully.
• To enjoy this dish, use your chopsticks to lift the noodles through the layers of flavouring and slurp them up. This is the essence of Vietnam.

Energy 391Kcal/1635kJ; Protein 16g; Carbohydrate 74g, of which sugars 3g; Fat 2g, of which saturates 1g; Cholesterol 21mg; Calcium 62mg; Fibre 0.8g; Sodium 600mg.

SPICY BEEF AND AUBERGINE SOUP

A WONDERFUL KHMER DISH, THIS SOUP, SAMLAW MACHOU KROEUNG, IS SWEET, SPICY AND TANGY. THE FLAVOUR IS MAINLY DERIVED FROM THE CAMBODIAN HERBAL CONDIMENT, KROEUNG, AND THE FERMENTED FISH EXTRACT, TUK TREY.

SERVES SIX

INGREDIENTS
  4 dried New Mexico chillies
  15ml/1 tbsp vegetable oil
  75ml/5 tbsp *kroeung*
  2–3 fresh or dried red Thai chillies
  75ml/5 tbsp tamarind extract
  15–30ml/1–2 tbsp *tuk trey*
  30ml/2 tbsp palm sugar
  12 Thai aubergines (eggplants), with
    stems removed and cut into
    bitesize chunks
  1 bunch watercress or rocket
    (arugula), trimmed and chopped
  1 handful fresh curry leaves
  sea salt and ground black pepper
For the stock
  1kg/2¼lb beef shanks or brisket
  2 large onions, quartered
  2–3 carrots, cut into chunks
  90g/3½oz fresh root ginger, sliced
  2 cinnamon sticks
  4 star anise
  5ml/1 tsp black peppercorns
  30ml/2 tbsp soy sauce
  45–60ml/3–4 tbsp *tuk trey*

2 Soak the New Mexico chillies in water for 30 minutes. Split them open, remove the seeds and scrape out the pulp with a spoon.

3 Take the lid off the stock and stir in the remaining two ingredients. Simmer uncovered, for another hour, until the stock has reduced to about 2 litres/3½ pints/7¾ cups. Skim off any fat, strain the stock into a bowl and put aside. Lift the meat on to a plate, tear it into thin strips and put half of it aside for the soup.

4 Heat the oil in a wok or heavy pan. Stir in the *kroeung* along with the pulp from the New Mexico chillies and the whole Thai chillies. Stir the spicy paste as it sizzles, until it begins to darken. Add the tamarind extract, *tuk trey*, sugar and the reserved stock. Stir well and bring to the boil.

5 Reduce the heat and add the reserved beef, aubergines and watercress or rocket. Continue cooking for about 20 minutes to allow the flavours to mingle.

6 Meanwhile, dry-fry the curry leaves. Heat a small, heavy pan over a high heat, add the curry leaves and cook them until they begin to crackle. Transfer them to a plate and set aside.

7 Season the soup to taste. Stir in half the curry leaves and ladle the soup into individual bowls. Scatter the remaining curry leaves over the top and serve.

1 To make the stock, put the beef shanks into a deep pan with all the other stock ingredients, apart from the soy sauce and *tuk trey*. Cover with 3 litres/5 pints/12 cups water and bring it to the boil. Reduce the heat and simmer, covered, for 2–3 hours.

COOK'S TIP
For a greater depth of flavour, you can dry-roast the New Mexico chillies before soaking them in water.

Energy 303Kcal/1276kJ; Protein 37g; Carbohydrate 16.5g, of which sugars 14.5g; Fat 10.6g, of which saturates 4.2g; Cholesterol 90mg; Calcium 35mg; Fibre 2.4g; Sodium 300mg.

CORN AND CHICKEN SOUP

THIS POPULAR CHINESE SOUP IS DELICIOUS AND EXTREMELY EASY AND QUICK TO MAKE. IT'S A PERFECT WINTER WARMER WITH ITS MILD FLAVOURS AND CREAMY TEXTURE.

SERVES FOUR TO SIX

INGREDIENTS

1 chicken breast fillet, about 115g/
    4oz, skinned and cubed
10ml/2 tsp light soy sauce
15ml/1 tbsp Chinese rice wine or
    dry sherry
5ml/1 tsp cornflour (cornstarch)
60ml/4 tbsp cold water
5ml/ 1 tsp sesame oil
30ml/2 tbsp groundnut (peanut) oil
5ml/1 tsp grated fresh root ginger
1 litre/1¾ pints/4 cups chicken stock
425g/15oz can creamed corn
225g/8oz can corn kernels
2 eggs, beaten
salt and ground black pepper
2–3 spring onions (scallions), green
    parts only, sliced, to garnish

1 Mince (grind) the chicken breast in a food processor or blender, taking care not to over-process it. Transfer the chicken to a bowl and stir in the soy sauce, rice wine or sherry, cornflour, water, sesame oil and seasoning. Cover the bowl and leave for about 15 minutes so that the chicken absorbs the flavours of the other ingredients.

2 Heat a wok over medium heat. Add the groundnut oil and swirl it around. Add the ginger and stir-fry for a few seconds. Add the stock, creamed corn and corn kernels. Bring to just below boiling point.

3 Spoon about 90ml/6 tbsp of the hot liquid into the chicken mixture and stir to a smooth paste. Add to the wok. Slowly bring to the boil, stirring, then simmer for 2–3 minutes until cooked.

4 Pour the beaten eggs into the soup in a slow, steady stream, using a fork or chopsticks to stir the top of the soup in a figure-of-eight pattern. The egg should set in lacy threads. Serve immediately with the spring onions sprinkled over.

Energy 196kcal/831kJ; Protein 10g; Carbohydrate 29.9g, of which sugars 10.7g; Fat 4.7g, of which saturates 1g; Cholesterol 77mg; Calcium 17mg; Fibre 1.6g; Sodium 447mg.

DUCK AND LIME SOUP

THIS RICH SOUP ORIGINATES IN THE CHIU CHOW REGION OF SOUTHERN CHINA. THIS RECIPE CAN BE MADE WITH PRESERVED LIMES AND LEFTOVER DUCK MEAT FROM A ROASTED DUCK, OR BY ROASTING A DUCK, SLICING OFF THE BREAST AND THIGH MEAT FOR THE SOUP.

SERVES FOUR TO SIX

INGREDIENTS
   1 lean duck, approximately
      1.5kg/3lb 5oz
   2 preserved limes
   25g/1oz fresh root ginger,
      thinly sliced
   sea salt and ground black pepper
For the garnish
   vegetable oil, for frying
   25g/1oz fresh root ginger,
      thinly sliced into strips
   2 garlic cloves, thinly sliced
      into strips
   2 spring onions (scallions),
      finely sliced

COOK'S TIPS
• With the addition of noodles, this soup could be served as a meal in itself.
• Preserved limes have a distinct bitter flavour. Look for them in Asian markets.

1 Place the duck in a large pan with enough water to cover. Season with salt and pepper and bring the water to the boil. Reduce the heat, cover the pot, and simmer for 1½ hours.

2 Add the preserved limes and ginger. Continue to simmer for another hour, skimming off the fat from time to time, until the liquid has reduced a little and the duck is so tender that it almost falls off the bone.

3 Meanwhile heat some vegetable oil in a wok. Stir in the ginger and garlic strips and fry until gold and crispy. Drain well on kitchen paper and set aside for garnishing.

4 Remove the duck from the broth and shred the meat into individual bowls. Check the broth for seasoning, then ladle it over the duck in the bowls. Scatter the spring onions with the fried ginger and garlic over the top and serve.

Energy 124Kcal/520kJ; Protein 19.8g; Carbohydrate 0.3g, of which sugars 0.3g; Fat 6.5g, of which saturates 1.3g; Cholesterol 110mg; Calcium 19mg; Fibre 0g; Sodium 100mg.

AROMATIC BROTH WITH ROAST DUCK, PAK CHOI AND EGG NOODLES

SERVED ON ITS OWN, THIS CHINESE-INSPIRED SOUP, MI VIT TIM, *MAKES A DELICIOUS AUTUMN OR WINTER MEAL. IF YOU WANT TO ADD SOME AUTHENTIC SPICE, SERVE IT WITH A BOWL OF WHOLE FRESH OR MARINATED CHILLIES AS A FIERY SIDE DISH TO CHEW ON.*

SERVES FOUR

INGREDIENTS
    15ml/1 tbsp vegetable oil
    2 shallots, thinly sliced
    4cm/1½in fresh root ginger,
        peeled and sliced
    15ml/1 tbsp soy sauce
    5ml/1 tsp five-spice powder
    10ml/2 tsp sugar
    175g/6oz pak choi (bok choy)
    450g/1lb fresh egg noodles
    350g/12oz roast duck, thinly sliced
    sea salt
For the stock
    1 chicken or duck carcass
    2 carrots, peeled and quartered
    2 onions, peeled and quartered
    4cm/1½in fresh root ginger, peeled
        and cut into chunks
    2 lemon grass stalks, chopped
    30ml/2 tbsp *nuoc mam*
    15ml/1 tbsp soy sauce
    6 black peppercorns
For the garnish
    4 spring onions (scallions), sliced
    1–2 red Serrano chillies, seeded and
        finely sliced
    1 bunch each coriander (cilantro) and
        basil, stalks removed, leaves
        chopped

1 To make the stock, put the chicken or duck carcass into a deep pan. Add all the other stock ingredients and pour in 2.5 litres/4½ pints/10¼ cups water. Bring to the boil, and boil for a few minutes, skim off any foam, then reduce the heat and simmer gently with the lid on for 2–3 hours. Remove the lid and continue to simmer for a further 30 minutes to reduce the stock. Skim off any fat, season with salt, then strain the stock. Measure out 2 litres/3½ pints/8 cups.

2 Heat the oil in a wok or deep pan and stir in the shallots and ginger. Add the soy sauce, five-spice powder, sugar and stock and bring to the boil. Season with a little salt, reduce the heat and simmer for 10–15 minutes.

3 Meanwhile, cut the pak choi diagonally into wide strips and blanch in boiling water to soften them. Drain and refresh under cold running water to prevent them cooking any further. Bring a large pan of water to the boil, then add the fresh noodles. Cook for 5 minutes, then drain well.

4 Divide the noodles among four soup bowls, lay some of the pak choi and sliced duck over them, and then ladle over generous amounts of the simmering broth. Garnish with the spring onions, chillies and herbs, and serve immediately.

COOK'S TIP
If you can't find fresh egg noodles, you can use dried instead. Soak them in lukewarm water for 20 minutes, then cook, one portion at a time, in a sieve (strainer) lowered into the boiling water. Use a chopstick to untangle them as they soften. Ready-cooked egg noodles are also available in supermarkets.

Energy 673Kcal/2836kJ; Protein 37g; Carbohydrate 86g, of which sugars 22g; Fat 6g, of which saturates 1g; Cholesterol 81mg; Calcium 4mg; Fibre 0.7g; Sodium 700mg.

WINTER MELON SOUP <u>WITH</u> TIGER LILIES, CORIANDER <u>AND</u> MINT

THIS SOUP USES TWO TRADITIONAL SOUTH-EAST ASIAN INGREDIENTS — WINTER MELON TO ABSORB THE FLAVOURS AND TIGER LILIES TO LIFT THE BROTH WITH A FLORAL SCENT. WHEN CHOOSING TIGER LILIES, MAKE SURE THEY ARE LIGHT GOLDEN IN COLOUR.

SERVES FOUR

INGREDIENTS
350g/12oz winter melon
25g/1oz light golden tiger lilies,
   soaked in hot water
   for 20 minutes
salt and ground black pepper
1 small bunch each coriander
   (cilantro) and mint, stalks removed,
   leaves chopped, to serve
For the stock
25g/1oz dried shrimp, soaked in
   water for 15 minutes
500g/1¼lb pork ribs
1 onion, peeled and quartered
175g/6oz carrots, peeled and cut
   into chunks
15ml/1 tbsp nuoc mam
15ml/1 tbsp soy sauce
4 black peppercorns

1 To make the stock, drain and rinse the dried shrimp. Put the pork ribs in a large pan and cover with 2 litres/3½ pints/8 cups water. Bring the water to the boil, skim off any fat, and add the dried shrimp and the remaining stock ingredients. Cover and simmer for 1½ hours, then skim off any foam or fat. Continue simmering, uncovered, for a further 30 minutes. Strain and check the seasoning. You should have about 1.5 litres/2½ pints/6¼ cups.

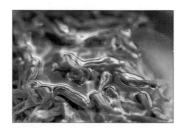

2 Halve the winter melon lengthways and remove the seeds and inner membrane. Finely slice the flesh into half-moons. Squeeze the soaked tiger lilies dry and tie them in a knot.

3 Bring the stock to the boil in a deep pan or wok. Reduce the heat and add the winter melon and tiger lilies. Simmer for 15–20 minutes, or until the winter melon is tender. Season to taste, and scatter the herbs over the top.

Energy 46Kcal/198kJ; Protein 2g; Carbohydrate 9g, of which sugars 4g; Fat 8g, of which saturates 1g; Cholesterol 44mg; Calcium 90mg; Fibre 1.4g; Sodium 400mg.

TOFU SOUP <u>WITH</u> MUSHROOMS, TOMATO, <u>AND</u> CORIANDER

THIS CLEAR BROTH WILL BALANCE A MEAL THAT MAY INCLUDE SOME HEAVIER MEAT OR POULTRY DISHES. AS THE SOUP IS RELIANT ON A WELL-FLAVOURED, AROMATIC BROTH, THE BASIC STOCK NEEDS TO BE OF THE BEST QUALITY, AND RICH IN TASTE.

SERVES FOUR

INGREDIENTS

115g/4oz/scant 2 cups dried shiitake
   mushrooms, soaked in water for
   20 minutes
15ml/1 tbsp vegetable oil
2 shallots, halved and sliced
2 Thai chillies, seeded and sliced
4cm/1½in fresh root ginger, peeled
   and grated or finely chopped
15ml/1 tbsp *nuoc mam*
350g/12oz tofu, rinsed, drained
   and cut into bitesize cubes
4 tomatoes, skinned, seeded and
   cut into thin strips
salt and ground black pepper
1 bunch coriander (cilantro),
   stalks removed, finely chopped,
   to garnish
For the stock
1 meaty chicken carcass or
   500g/1¼lb pork ribs
25g/1oz dried squid or shrimp,
   soaked in water for 15 minutes
2 onions, peeled and quartered
2 garlic cloves, crushed
7.5cm/3in fresh root ginger, chopped
15ml/1 tbsp *nuoc mam*
6 black peppercorns
2 star anise
4 cloves
1 cinnamon stick
sea salt

1 To make the stock, put the chicken carcass or pork ribs in a deep pan. Drain and rinse the dried squid or shrimp. Add to the pan with the remaining stock ingredients, except the salt, and pour in 2 litres/3½ pints/8 cups water. Bring to the boil, skim off any foam, then reduce the heat and simmer with the lid on for 1½–2 hours.

2 Remove the lid and simmer for a further 30 minutes to reduce. Skim off any fat, season, then strain and measure out 1.5 litres/2½ pints/6¼ cups.

3 Squeeze dry the soaked shiitake mushrooms, remove the stems and slice the caps into thin strips. Heat the oil in a large pan or wok and stir in the shallots, chillies and ginger. As the fragrance begins to rise, stir in the *nuoc mam*, followed by the stock.

4 Add the tofu, mushrooms and tomatoes and bring to the boil. Reduce the heat and simmer for 5–10 minutes. Season to taste and scatter the finely chopped fresh coriander over the top. Serve piping hot.

Energy 220Kcal/919kJ; Protein 12g; Carbohydrate 26g, of which sugars 4g; Fat 8g, of which saturates 1g; Cholesterol 0mg; Calcium 47.8mg; Fibre 1.1g; Sodium 500mg.

BROTH WITH STUFFED CABBAGE LEAVES

SLIGHTLY MORE COMPLEX TO MAKE, THIS SOUP COMES FROM THE ANCIENT CHINESE TRADITION OF COOKING DUMPLINGS IN A CLEAR BROTH. THIS VIETNAMESE VERSION IS OFTEN RESERVED FOR SPECIAL OCCASIONS SUCH AS THE NEW YEAR CELEBRATIONS.

SERVES FOUR

INGREDIENTS

10 Chinese leaves (Chinese cabbage) or Savoy cabbage leaves, halved, main ribs removed
4 spring onions (scallions), green tops left whole, white part finely chopped
5–6 dried cloud ear (wood ear) mushrooms, soaked in hot water for 15 minutes
115g/4oz minced (ground) pork
115g/4oz prawns (shrimp), shelled, deveined and finely chopped
1 Thai chilli, seeded and chopped
30ml/2 tbsp *nuoc mam*
15ml/1 tbsp soy sauce
4cm/1½in fresh root ginger, peeled and very finely sliced
chopped fresh coriander (cilantro), to garnish

For the stock

1 meaty chicken carcass
2 onions, peeled and quartered
4 garlic cloves, crushed
4cm/1½in fresh root ginger, chopped
30ml/2 tbsp *nuoc mam*
30ml/2 tbsp soy sauce
6 black peppercorns
a few sprigs of fresh thyme
sea salt

1 To make the chicken stock, put the chicken carcass into a deep pan. Add all the other stock ingredients except the sea salt and pour over 2 litres/3½ pints/8 cups of water. Bring to the boil, and boil for a few minutes, skim off any foam, then reduce the heat and simmer gently with the lid on for 1½–2 hours.

2 Remove the lid and simmer for a further 30 minutes to reduce the stock. Skim off any fat, season with sea salt, then strain the stock and measure out 1.5 litres/2½ pints/6¼ cups. It is important to skim off any froth or fat, so that the broth is light and fragrant.

3 Blanch the cabbage leaves in boiling water for about 2 minutes, or until tender. Remove with a slotted spoon and refresh under cold water. Add the green tops of the spring onions to the boiling water and blanch for a minute, or until tender, then drain and refresh under cold water. Carefully tear each piece into five thin strips and set aside.

4 Squeeze dry the cloud ear mushrooms, then trim and finely chop and mix with the pork, prawns, spring onion whites, chilli, *nuoc mam* and soy sauce. Lay a cabbage leaf flat on a surface and place a teaspoon of the filling about 1cm/½in from the bottom edge – the edge nearest to you.

5 Fold this bottom edge over the filling, and then fold in the sides of the leaf to seal it. Roll all the way to the top of the leaf to form a tight bundle. Wrap a piece of blanched spring onion green around the bundle and tie it so that it holds together. Repeat with the remaining leaves and filling.

6 Bring the stock to the boil in a wok or deep pan. Stir in the finely sliced ginger, then reduce the heat and drop in the cabbage bundles. Bubble very gently over a low heat for about 20 minutes to ensure that the filling is thoroughly cooked. Serve immediately, ladled into bowls with a sprinkling of fresh coriander leaves.

Energy 106Kcal/447kJ; Protein 14g; Carbohydrate 9g, of which sugars 1g; Fat 2g, of which saturates 0g; Cholesterol 77mg; Calcium 43mg; Fibre 0.3g; Sodium 1100mg.

SPICY TOMATO AND EGG DROP SOUP

POPULAR IN SOUTHERN VIETNAM AND CAMBODIA, THIS SPICY SOUP WITH EGGS IS PROBABLY ADAPTED FROM THE TRADITIONAL CHINESE EGG DROP SOUP. SERVED ON ITS OWN WITH CHUNKS OF CRUSTY BREAD, OR ACCOMPANIED BY JASMINE OR GINGER RICE, THIS IS A TASTY DISH FOR A LIGHT SUPPER.

SERVES FOUR

INGREDIENTS
    30ml/2 tbsp groundnut (peanut) or
      vegetable oil
    3 shallots, finely sliced
    2 garlic cloves, finely chopped
    2 Thai chillies, seeded and
      finely sliced
    25g/1oz galangal, shredded
    8 large, ripe tomatoes, skinned,
      seeded and finely chopped
    15ml/1 tbsp sugar
    30ml/2 tbsp *nuoc mam* or *tuk trey*
    4 lime leaves
    900ml/1½ pints/3¾ cups
      chicken stock
    15ml/1 tbsp wine vinegar
    4 eggs
    sea salt and ground black pepper
For the garnish
    chilli oil, for drizzling
    1 small bunch fresh coriander
      (cilantro), finely chopped
    1 small bunch fresh mint leaves,
      finely chopped

2 Just before serving, bring a wide pan of water to the boil. Add the vinegar and half a teaspoon of salt. Break the eggs into individual cups or small bowls.

3 Stir the water rapidly to create a swirl and drop an egg into the centre of the swirl. Follow immediately with the others, or poach two at a time, and keep the water boiling to throw the whites up over the yolks. Turn off the heat, cover the pan and leave to poach until firm enough to lift. Poached eggs are traditional, but you could use lightly fried eggs instead.

4 Using a slotted spoon, lift the eggs out of the water and slip them into the hot soup. Drizzle a little chilli oil over the eggs, sprinkle with the coriander and mint, and serve.

1 Heat the oil in a wok or heavy pan. Stir in the shallots, garlic, chillies and galangal and cook until golden and fragrant. Add the tomatoes with the sugar, *nuoc mam* and lime leaves. Stir until it resembles a sauce. Pour in the stock and bring to the boil. Reduce the heat and simmer for 30 minutes. Season.

VARIATION
The soup is very tasty without the eggs and could be served as a spicy tomato soup on its own.

Energy 181Kcal/756kJ; Protein 8g; Carbohydrate 12.3g, of which sugars 11.5g; Fat 11.7g, of which saturates 2.4g; Cholesterol 190mg; Calcium 52mg; Fibre 2.3g; Sodium 280g.

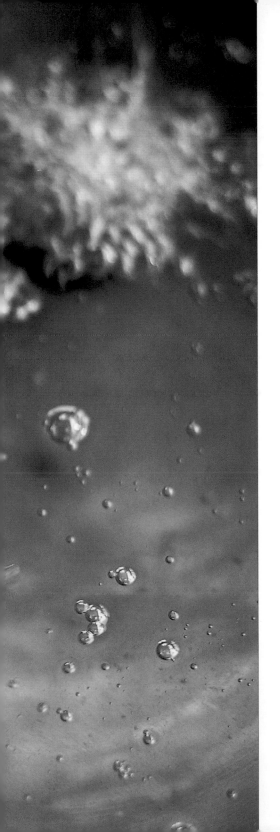

APPETIZERS

The wok is great for appetizers, whether it's a pile of crispy, tasty fish cakes, an elegant individual steamed custard, or some succulent steamed dim sum. Many of the recipes in this chapter can be half-prepared in advance, so that there is just the final step to go and you won't be spending too long away from your guests. Several of these dishes come with one of the tangy and appetizing dipping sauces that Asian food is famous for — serve individual portions and make sure you have plenty for replenishing the dishes if needed.

STEAMED OYSTERS <u>WITH</u> ZESTY TOMATO <u>AND</u> CUCUMBER SALSA

A PLATE OF LIGHTLY STEAMED FRESH OYSTERS MAKES A DELICIOUS AND IMPRESSIVE APPETIZER FOR A SPECIAL OCCASION, AND IS EASY TO PREPARE. THE FRESH, ZESTY, AROMATIC SALSA COMPLEMENTS THE DELICATE FLAVOUR AND TEXTURE OF THE OYSTERS PERFECTLY.

SERVES FOUR

INGREDIENTS
  30ml/2 tbsp sunflower oil
  1 garlic clove, crushed
  15ml/1 tbsp light soy sauce
  12–16 oysters
  sea salt, to serve
For the salsa
  1 ripe plum tomato, seeds removed
  ½ small cucumber
  ¼ small red onion
  15ml/1 tbsp very finely chopped
    coriander (cilantro)
  1 small red chilli, seeded and very
    finely chopped
  juice of 1–2 limes
  salt and ground black pepper

1 First prepare the salsa. Finely dice the tomato, cucumber and red onion. Place in a bowl with the chopped coriander and red chilli.

2 Add the lime juice to the bowl and season to taste. Set aside (at room temperature) for 15–20 minutes.

3 In a separate bowl, mix together the sunflower oil, garlic and soy sauce.

COOK'S TIP
To de-seed the tomato, cut it in half around the middle rather than over the top, and then scoop out the seeds using a teaspoon.

4 Carefully open the oysters using a special oyster knife or a strong knife with a short, blunt blade. Arrange the oysters in their half shells in a bamboo steamer and spoon over the sauce.

5 Cover the steamer and place over a wok of simmering water. Steam for 2–3 minutes. Arrange the oysters on a bed of sea salt, top each with a teaspoonful of the salsa and serve.

Energy 82Kcal/339kJ; Protein 4.5g; Carbohydrate 2.4g, of which sugars 1.3g; Fat 6.1g, of which saturates 0.8g; Cholesterol 21mg; Calcium 60mg; Fibre 0.4g; Sodium 461mg.

LEMON, CHILLI <u>AND</u> HERB STEAMED RAZOR CLAMS

RAZOR CLAMS HAVE BEAUTIFUL STRIPED GOLD AND BROWN TUBULAR SHELLS AND MAKE A WONDERFUL AND UNUSUAL APPETIZER. HERE THEY ARE LIGHTLY STEAMED AND TOSSED IN A FRAGRANT ITALIAN-STYLE DRESSING OF CHILLI, LEMON, GARLIC AND PARSLEY.

SERVES FOUR

INGREDIENTS
    12 razor clams
    90–120ml/6–8 tbsp extra virgin
      olive oil
    finely grated rind and juice of
      1 small lemon
    2 garlic cloves, very finely grated
    1 red chilli, seeded and very
      finely chopped
    60ml/4 tbsp chopped flat leaf parsley
    salt and ground black pepper
    mixed salad leaves and crusty bread,
      to serve

1 Wash the razor clams well in plenty of cold running water. Drain and arrange half the clams in a steamer, with the hinge side down.

2 Pour 5cm/2in water into a wok and bring to the boil. Carefully balance the steamer over the water and cover tightly. Steam for 3–4 minutes until the clams have opened.

3 Remove the clams from the wok and keep warm while you steam the remaining clams in the same way.

4 In a bowl, mix together the olive oil, grated lemon rind and juice, garlic, red chilli and flat leaf parsley.

5 Season the dressing well with salt and pepper. Spoon the mixture over the steamed razor clams on plates and serve immediately with a crisp mixed-leaf salad and crusty bread.

Energy 188Kcal/775kJ; Protein 6.1g; Carbohydrate 2.9g, of which sugars 0.5g; Fat 16.9g, of which saturates 2.4g; Cholesterol 20mg; Calcium 47mg; Fibre 1.1g; Sodium 364mg.

SALMON, SESAME AND GINGER FISH CAKES

THESE LIGHT FISH CAKES ARE SCENTED WITH THE EXOTIC FLAVOURS OF SESAME, LIME AND GINGER.
THEY MAKE A TEMPTING APPETIZER SERVED SIMPLY WITH A WEDGE OF LIME FOR SQUEEZING OVER, BUT
ARE ALSO PERFECT FOR A LIGHT LUNCH OR SUPPER, SERVED WITH A CRUNCHY, REFRESHING SALAD.

MAKES TWENTY-FIVE

INGREDIENTS
    500g/1¼lb salmon fillet,
        skinned and boned
    45ml/3 tbsp dried breadcrumbs
    30ml/2 tbsp mayonnaise
    30ml/2 tbsp sesame seeds
    30ml/2 tbsp light soy sauce
    finely grated rind of 2 limes
    10ml/2 tsp finely grated
        fresh root ginger
    4 spring onions (scallions),
        finely sliced
    vegetable oil, for frying
    salt and ground black pepper
    spring onions (scallions), to garnish
    lime wedges, to serve

1 Finely chop the salmon and place in a bowl. Add the breadcrumbs, mayonnaise, sesame seeds, soy sauce, lime rind, ginger and spring onions and use your fingers to mix well.

2 With wet hands, divide the mixture into 25 portions and shape each into a small round cake. Place the cakes on a baking sheet, lined with baking parchment, cover and chill for at least two hours. They can be left overnight.

3 When you are ready to cook the fish cakes, heat about 5cm/2in vegetable oil in a wok and fry the fish cakes in batches, over a medium heat, for 2–3 minutes on each side.

4 Drain the fish cakes well on kitchen paper and serve warm or at room temperature, garnished with spring onion slivers and plenty of lime wedges for squeezing over.

Energy 83Kcal/343kJ; Protein 4.6g; Carbohydrate 1.6g, of which sugars 0.2g; Fat 6.5g, of which saturates 0.9g; Cholesterol 11mg; Calcium 16mg; Fibre 0.2g; Sodium 117mg.

CRAB DIM SUM WITH CHINESE CHIVES

THESE DELECTABLE CHINESE-STYLE DUMPLINGS HAVE A WONDERFULLY STICKY TEXTURE AND MAKE A PERFECT AND ATTRACTIVE APPETIZER. YOU CAN MAKE THEM IN ADVANCE, STORING THEM IN THE REFRIGERATOR UNTIL READY TO COOK.

SERVES FOUR

INGREDIENTS
150g/5oz fresh white crab meat
115g/4oz minced (ground) pork
30ml/2 tbsp chopped Chinese chives
15ml/1 tbsp finely chopped red
  (bell) pepper
30ml/2 tbsp sweet chilli sauce
30ml/2 tbsp hoisin sauce
24 fresh dumpling wrappers
  (available from Asian stores)
Chinese chives, to garnish
chilli oil and soy sauce, to serve

1 Place the crab meat, pork and chopped chives in a bowl. Add the red pepper, sweet chilli and hoisin sauces.

VARIATION
Use chopped raw tiger prawns (jumbo shrimp) in place of the crab.

2 Working with 2–3 wrappers at a time, put a spoonful of the mixture on to each wrapper. Brush the edges of a wrapper with water and fold over to form a half-moon shape. Press and pleat the edges to seal, and flatten. Cover with a clean, damp dish towel and make the rest.

3 Arrange the dumplings on 3 lightly oiled plates and fit inside 3 tiers of a bamboo steamer.

4 Cover the steamer and place over a wok of simmering water (making sure the water does not touch the steamer). Steam for 8–10 minutes, or until the dumplings are cooked through and become slightly translucent.

5 Divide the dumplings among four plates. Garnish with Chinese chives and serve immediately with chilli oil and soy sauce for dipping.

Energy 166Kcal/700kJ; Protein 14.7g; Carbohydrate 20.5g, of which sugars 1.4g; Fat 3.3g, of which saturates 1.1g; Cholesterol 46mg; Calcium 83mg; Fibre 0.8g; Sodium 287mg.

STEAMED HERB AND CHILLI FISH CUSTARDS

THESE PRETTY LITTLE CUSTARDS MAKE AN UNUSUAL, BEAUTIFULLY PRESENTED AND RATHER EXOTIC APPETIZER FOR A DINNER PARTY, AND THEY COOK PERFECTLY IN THE WOK.

SERVES FOUR

INGREDIENTS
2 eggs
200ml/7fl oz/scant 1 cup
   coconut cream
60ml/4 tbsp chopped fresh
   coriander (cilantro)
1 fresh red chilli, seeded and sliced
15ml/1 tbsp finely chopped
   lemon grass
2 kaffir lime leaves, finely shredded
30ml/2 tbsp Thai red curry paste
1 garlic clove, crushed
5ml/1 tsp finely grated ginger
2 spring onions (scallions),
   finely sliced
300g/11oz mixed firm white fish fillets
   (cod, halibut or haddock), skinned
200g/7oz raw tiger prawns (jumbo
   shrimp), peeled and deveined
4–6 pandan leaves
salt and ground black pepper
shredded cucumber, steamed rice
   and soy sauce, to serve

2 Grease 4 ramekins and line them with the pandan leaves. Divide the fish mixture between them, then arrange in a bamboo steamer.

3 Pour 5cm/2in water into a wok and bring to the boil. Suspend the steamer over the water, cover, reduce the heat to low and steam for 25–30 minutes, or until the fish is cooked through, and the custard is set.

4 Serve the custards, still in the ramekins, straight away with some shredded cucumber, a little steamed rice and soy sauce on the side.

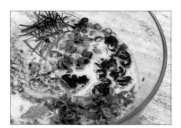

1 Beat the eggs in a bowl, then stir in the coconut cream, coriander, chilli, lemon grass, lime leaves, curry paste, garlic, ginger and spring onions. Finely chop the fish and roughly chop the prawns and add to the egg mixture. Stir well and season.

COOK'S TIP
Pandan leaves keep the custards from drying out, they are not edible and should be discarded after the cooking.

Energy 150Kcal/632kJ; Protein 26.2g; Carbohydrate 2.8g, of which sugars 2.8g; Fat 3.9g, of which saturates 1g; Cholesterol 227mg; Calcium 100mg; Fibre 0.6g; Sodium 234mg.

FISH CAKES <u>WITH</u> CUCUMBER RELISH

THESE WONDERFUL SMALL FISH CAKES ARE A VERY FAMILIAR AND POPULAR APPETIZER IN THAILAND AND INCREASINGLY THROUGHOUT SOUTH-EAST ASIA. THEY ARE USUALLY SERVED WITH THAI BEER.

MAKES ABOUT TWELVE

INGREDIENTS
8 kaffir lime leaves
300g/11oz cod fillet, cut into chunks
30ml/2 tbsp Thai red curry paste
1 egg
30ml/2 tbsp Thai fish sauce
5ml/1 tsp granulated sugar
30ml/2 tbsp cornflour (cornstarch)
15ml/1 tbsp chopped fresh
   coriander (cilantro)
50g/2oz/½ cup green beans,
   thinly sliced
vegetable oil, for deep-frying
For the cucumber relish
60ml/4 tbsp coconut or rice vinegar
50g/2oz/¼ cup granulated sugar
60ml/4 tbsp water
1 head pickled garlic
1cm/½in piece fresh root
   ginger, peeled
1 cucumber, cut into thin batons
4 shallots, thinly sliced

1 Make the cucumber relish. Mix the coconut or rice vinegar, sugar and water in a small pan. Heat gently, stirring constantly until the sugar has completely dissolved. Remove the pan from the heat and leave to cool.

2 Separate the pickled garlic into cloves. Chop the cloves finely, along with the ginger, and place in a bowl. Add the cucumber batons and shallots, pour over the vinegar mixture and mix lightly. Cover and set aside.

3 Reserve five kaffir lime leaves for the garnish and thinly slice the remainder. Put the chunks of fish, curry paste and egg in a food processor and process to a smooth paste. Transfer the mixture to a bowl and stir in the fish sauce, sugar, cornflour, sliced kaffir lime leaves, coriander and green beans. Mix well, then shape the mixture into about twelve 5mm/¼in thick cakes, each measuring about 5cm/2in in diameter.

4 Heat the oil in a wok to 190°C/375°F or until a cube of bread, added to the oil, browns in about 40 seconds. Fry the fish cakes, a few at a time, for about 4–5 minutes, until cooked and evenly brown.

5 Lift out the fish cakes and drain them on kitchen paper. Keep each batch hot while frying successive batches. Garnish with the reserved kaffir lime leaves and serve with the cucumber relish.

Energy 83Kcal/346kJ; Protein 5.5g; Carbohydrate 5.8g, of which sugars 5.6g; Fat 4.4g, of which saturates 0.6g; Cholesterol 27mg; Calcium 15mg; Fibre 0.3g; Sodium 111mg.

LETTUCE PARCELS

KNOWN AS SANG CHOY IN HONG KONG, THIS IS A POPULAR "ASSEMBLE-IT-YOURSELF" TREAT, USING CRISP LETTUCE LEAVES SPREAD WITH HOISIN SAUCE, TO WRAP THE TASTY, SUCCULENT FILING.

SERVES SIX

INGREDIENTS
2 boneless chicken breast portions,
    total weight about 350g/12oz
4 Chinese dried mushrooms, soaked
    for 30 minutes in warm water
    to cover
30ml/2 tbsp vegetable oil
2 garlic cloves, crushed
6 drained canned water chestnuts,
    thinly sliced
30ml/2 tbsp light soy sauce
5ml/1 tsp Sichuan peppercorns, dry
    fried and crushed
4 spring onions (scallions), finely
    chopped
5ml/1 tsp sesame oil
vegetable oil, for deep-frying
50g/2oz cellophane noodles
salt and ground black pepper
    (optional)
1 crisp lettuce and 60ml/4 tbsp
    hoisin sauce, to serve

1 Remove the skin from the chicken breasts, pat dry and set aside. Chop the chicken into thin strips. Drain the soaked mushrooms. Cut off and discard the mushroom stems; slice the caps finely and set aside.

2 Heat the oil in a wok. Add the garlic, then add the chicken and stir-fry until the pieces are cooked through and no longer pink. Check by lifting one of the thicker chicken strips out of the wok and cutting it in half.

3 Add the sliced mushrooms, water chestnuts, soy sauce and peppercorns. Toss for 2–3 minutes, then season, if needed. Stir in half of the spring onions, then the sesame oil. Remove from the heat and keep warm.

4 Heat the oil for deep-frying to 190°C/375°F. Cut the chicken skin into strips, deep-fry until very crisp and drain on kitchen paper. Add the noodles to the hot oil, deep-fry until crisp. Transfer to a plate lined with kitchen paper.

5 Crush the noodles and put in a serving dish. Top with the chicken skin, chicken mixture and the remaining spring onions. Arrange the lettuce leaves on a large platter.

6 Toss the chicken and noodles to mix. Invite guests to take one or two lettuce leaves, spread the inside with hoisin sauce and add a spoonful of filling, turning in the sides of the leaves and rolling them into a parcel. The parcels are traditionally eaten in the hand.

Energy 195Kcal/821kJ; Protein 28.7g; Carbohydrate 7.5g, of which sugars 0.6g; Fat 5.5g, of which saturates 0.9g; Cholesterol 82mg; Calcium 11mg; Fibre 0.1g; Sodium 428mg.

STUFFED THAI OMELETTES

OMELETTES ARE USUALLY COOKED IN A FLAT PAN, BUT A WOK WORKS EQUALLY WELL. THE HOT CHILLI IN THIS RECIPE MAKES AN INTERESTING CONTRASTING FLAVOUR TO THE DELICATE EGG.

3 To make the omelettes, put the eggs and Thai fish sauce in a bowl and beat together lightly with a fork.

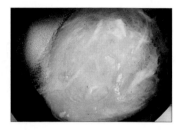

4 Heat 15ml/1 tbsp of the oil in an omelette pan or wok over a medium heat. When the oil is very hot, but not smoking, add half the beaten egg mixture and immediately tilt the pan or wok to spread the egg into a thin, even layer over the base. Cook over a medium heat until the omelette is just set and the underside is golden.

5 Spoon half the filling into the centre of the omelette. Fold into a neat square parcel by bringing the opposite sides of the omelette towards each other. Slide the parcel on to a serving dish, folded side down. Make another omelette parcel in the same way. Garnish with the coriander sprigs and chillies. Cut each omelette in half to serve.

SERVES FOUR

INGREDIENTS
  30ml/2 tbsp groundnut
    (peanut) oil
  2 garlic cloves, finely chopped
  1 small onion, finely chopped
  225g/8oz minced (ground) pork
  30ml/2 tbsp Thai fish sauce
  5ml/1 tsp granulated sugar
  2 tomatoes, peeled and chopped
  15ml/1 tbsp chopped fresh
    coriander (cilantro)
  ground black pepper
  fresh coriander (cilantro)
    sprigs and sliced fresh red
    chillies, to garnish
For the omelettes
  5 eggs
  15ml/1 tbsp Thai fish sauce
  30ml/2 tbsp groundnut
    (peanut) oil

1 Heat the oil in a wok, add the garlic and onion, and cook over a medium heat, for 3–4 minutes, until soft. Add the pork and cook until lightly browned.

2 Stir in the Thai fish sauce, sugar and tomatoes, season with pepper and simmer over a low heat until thickened. Mix in the coriander. Remove the wok from the heat, cover to keep warm and set aside while you make the omelettes.

COOK'S TIP
Making the omelette in a wok is actually easier than in a regular frying pan, since the sloping sides make it simple to flip the omelette over the filling.

Energy 305Kcal/1267kJ; Protein 19.2g; Carbohydrate 4.8g, of which sugars 4.5g; Fat 23.6g, of which saturates 5.7g; Cholesterol 275mg; Calcium 48mg; Fibre 0.7g; Sodium 130mg.

GOLDEN CORN CAKES WITH AIOLI

EAST MEETS WEST IN THESE CRISP, MOUTHWATERING CAKES THAT BRING TOGETHER CREAMY GOAT'S CHEESE AND TANGY MEDITERRANEAN PEPPERS IN THE ASIAN WOK.

SERVES FOUR

INGREDIENTS

- 300g/11oz/scant 2 cups fresh corn kernels
- 200g/7oz/scant 1 cup ricotta cheese
- 200g/7oz/scant 1 cup goat's cheese, crumbled
- 30ml/2 tbsp thyme leaves
- 50g/2oz/½ cup plain (all-purpose) flour
- 1 large (US extra large) egg, lightly beaten
- 150g/5oz natural dried breadcrumbs
- vegetable oil, for deep-frying
- salt and ground black pepper

For the aioli
- 2 red (bell) peppers, halved and seeded
- 2 garlic cloves, crushed
- 250ml/8fl oz/1 cup mayonnaise

3 Place the breadcrumbs on a plate. Roll 15ml/1 tbsp of the corn mixture into a ball, flatten slightly and coat in the breadcrumbs. Place on baking parchment and chill for 30 minutes.

4 Fill a wok one-third full of oil and heat to 180°C/350°F (or until a cube of bread, dropped into the oil, browns in 45 seconds). Working in batches, deep-fry the corn cakes for 1–2 minutes, until golden. Drain well on kitchen paper and serve with the aioli.

COOK'S TIP
If you deep-fry regularly, you will soon learn to judge when the oil has reached optimum temperature. If you need reassurance, buy a deep-fat thermometer. The safest and most reliable are those that can be clipped to the side of the wok before the oil is hot.

1 Make the aioli. Preheat the grill (broiler) to medium-high and cook the peppers, skin-side up, for 8–10 minutes, until the skins blister. Place the peppers in a plastic bag for 10 minutes and then peel away the skin. Place the flesh in a food processor with the garlic and mayonnaise and blend until fairly smooth. Transfer to a bowl and chill.

2 In a bowl, combine the corn, cheeses and thyme, then stir in the flour and egg and season well.

COOK'S TIP
If you're short on time, make the aioli with bottled peppers.

Energy 1048Kcal/4363kJ; Protein 26.1g; Carbohydrate 68.2g, of which sugars 17.3g; Fat 76.5g, of which saturates 22g; Cholesterol 162mg; Calcium 156mg; Fibre 3.9g; Sodium 1091mg.

RICE PAPER PARCELS WITH WILTED CHOI SUM

TRANSLUCENT RICE PAPER MAKES A WONDERFULLY CRISP WRAPPING FOR THE LIGHTLY SPICED VEGETABLE AND TOFU FILLING. TAKE CARE, AS THE PAPERS ARE VERY BRITTLE AND EASILY DAMAGED.

SERVES FOUR

INGREDIENTS
30ml/2 tbsp sunflower oil
90g/3½oz shiitake mushrooms, stalks
  discarded and finely chopped
30ml/2 tbsp chopped garlic
90g/3½oz water chestnuts,
  finely chopped
90g/3½oz firm tofu, finely chopped
2 spring onions (scallions),
  finely chopped
½ red (bell) pepper, seeded and
  finely chopped
50g/2oz mangetouts (snow peas),
  finely chopped
15ml/1 tbsp light soy sauce
15ml/1 tbsp sweet chilli sauce
45ml/3 tbsp chopped fresh
  coriander (cilantro)
30ml/2 tbsp chopped fresh
  mint leaves
90ml/6 tbsp plain
  (all-purpose) flour
12 medium rice paper wrappers
sunflower oil, for deep-frying
500g/1¼lb choi sum or Chinese
  greens, roughly sliced or chopped
soy sauce, to serve

1 Heat the oil in a large wok over a high heat and add the chopped mushrooms. Stir-fry for 3–4 minutes, add the garlic and fry for 1 minute.

2 Add the water chestnuts, tofu, spring onions, red pepper and mangetout to the wok, and stir-fry for 2–3 minutes.

3 Add the soy and sweet chilli sauces to the wok. Remove from the heat and stir in the chopped coriander and mint. Leave to cool completely.

4 Place the flour in a bowl and stir in 105ml/7 tbsp of cold water to make a thick, smooth paste.

5 Fill a large bowl with warm water and dip a rice paper wrapper in it for a few minutes until softened. Remove and drain on a dish towel.

6 Divide the filling into 12 portions and spoon one portion on to the softened rice wrapper. Fold in each side and roll up tightly. Seal the ends with a little of the flour paste. Repeat with the remaining wrappers and filling.

7 Fill a wok one-third full with the oil and heat to 180°C/350°F or until a cube of bread, dropped into the oil, browns in 40 seconds. Working in batches of 2–3, deep-fry the parcels for 3 minutes until crisp and lightly browned. Drain well on kitchen paper and keep warm.

8 Pour off most of the oil, reserving 30ml/2 tbsp. Place the wok over a medium heat and add the choi sum. Stir-fry for 3–4 minutes.

9 Divide the choi sum among four warmed bowls and top with the parcels. Serve immediately with soy sauce as an optional sprinkling.

Energy 252Kcal/1051kJ; Protein 10.2g; Carbohydrate 34.6g, of which sugars 6.6g; Fat 8.5g, of which saturates 1g; Cholesterol 0mg; Calcium 448mg; Fibre 6.8g; Sodium 313mg.

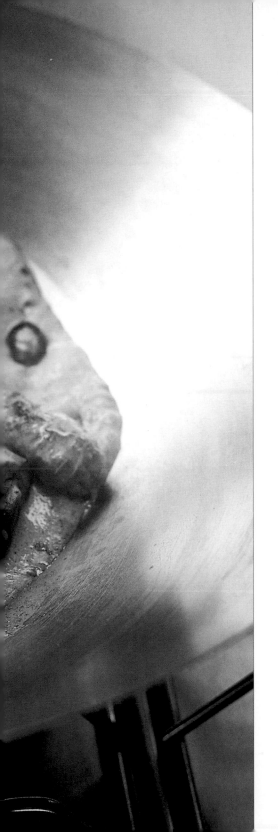

POULTRY DISHES

The wok is an excellent cooking vessel for chicken and poultry dishes, as its fast cooking ability retains the flavour and moistness of the meat. Poultry's mild taste also makes it a good protein to mix with robust oriental spices and flavours. This chapter ranges from fast and simple stir-fries such as Cashew Chicken to slow-cooked dishes like Southern Thai Chicken Curry and Adobo of Chicken and Pork. The wok doubles as a deep-fryer when Lemon and Sesame Chicken is on the menu, a dish children will love, and serves as a steamer for Vietnamese Lemon Grass Snails, or Orange and Ginger Glazed Poussins, both of which are perfect for a sophisticated supper party.

Chicken and Lemon Grass Curry

Quick-cook curries, such as this Thai speciality, work well in a wok, especially if you use an electric appliance, which allows you to adjust the heat for successful simmering.

SERVES FOUR

INGREDIENTS
45ml/3 tbsp vegetable oil
2 garlic cloves, crushed
500g/1¼lb skinless, chicken thighs,
  boned and chopped into small
  pieces
45ml/3 tbsp Thai fish sauce
120ml/4fl oz/½ cup
  chicken stock
5ml/1 tsp granulated sugar
1 lemon grass stalk, chopped into
  4 sticks and lightly crushed
5 kaffir lime leaves, rolled into
  cylinders and thinly sliced across,
  plus extra to garnish
chopped roasted peanuts
  and chopped fresh coriander
  (cilantro), to garnish
For the curry paste
1 lemon grass stalk,
  coarsely chopped
2.5cm/1in piece fresh galangal,
  peeled and coarsely chopped
2 kaffir lime leaves, chopped
3 shallots, coarsely chopped
6 coriander (cilantro) roots,
  coarsely chopped
2 garlic cloves
2 fresh green chillies, seeded and
  coarsely chopped
5ml/1 tsp shrimp paste
5ml/1 tsp ground turmeric

1 Make the curry paste. Place all the ingredients in a large mortar, or food processor, and pound with the pestle or process to a smooth paste.

2 Heat the vegetable oil in a wok or large, heavy frying pan, add the garlic and cook over a low heat, stirring frequently, until golden brown. Be careful not to let the garlic burn or it will taste bitter. Add the curry paste and stir-fry with the garlic for about 30 seconds more.

3 Add the chicken pieces to the pan and stir until thoroughly coated with the curry paste. Stir in the Thai fish sauce and chicken stock, with the sugar, and cook, stirring constantly, for 2 minutes more.

4 Add the lemon grass and lime leaves, reduce the heat and simmer for 10 minutes. If the mixture begins to dry out, add a little more stock or water.

5 Remove the lemon grass, if you like. Spoon the curry into four dishes, garnish with the lime leaves, peanuts and coriander and serve immediately.

Energy 229Kcal/959kJ; Protein 31.3g; Carbohydrate 4.3g, of which sugars 3.4g; Fat 9.7g, of which saturates 1.4g; Cholesterol 94mg; Calcium 32mg; Fibre 0.5g; Sodium 397mg.

YELLOW CHICKEN CURRY

THE PAIRING OF SLIGHTLY SWEET COCONUT MILK AND FRUIT WITH SAVOURY CHICKEN AND SPICES IS AT ONCE A COMFORTING, REFRESHING AND EXOTIC COMBINATION.

SERVES FOUR

INGREDIENTS
- 300ml/½ pint/1¼ cups chicken stock
- 30ml/2 tbsp tamarind paste mixed with a little warm water
- 15ml/1 tbsp granulated sugar
- 200ml/7fl oz/scant 1 cup coconut milk
- 1 green papaya, peeled, seeded and thinly sliced
- 250g/9oz skinless chicken breast fillets, diced
- juice of 1 lime
- lime slices, to garnish

For the curry paste
- 1 fresh red chilli, seeded and coarsely chopped
- 4 garlic cloves, coarsely chopped
- 3 shallots, coarsely chopped
- 2 lemon grass stalks, sliced
- 5cm/2in piece fresh turmeric, coarsely chopped, or 5ml/1 tsp ground turmeric
- 5ml/1 tsp shrimp paste
- 5ml/1 tsp salt

1 Make the yellow curry paste. Put the red chilli, garlic, shallots, lemon grass and turmeric in a mortar or food processor. Add the shrimp paste and salt. Pound or process to a paste, adding a little water if necessary.

COOK'S TIP
Fresh turmeric resembles root ginger in appearance and is a member of the same family. When preparing it, wear gloves to protect your hands from staining.

2 Pour the stock into a wok or medium pan and bring it to the boil. Stir in the curry paste. Bring back to the boil and add the tamarind juice, sugar and coconut milk. Add the papaya and chicken and cook over a medium to high heat for about 15 minutes, stirring frequently, until the chicken is cooked.

3 Stir in the lime juice, transfer to a warm dish and serve immediately, garnished with lime slices.

Energy 149Kcal/633kJ; Protein 17.2g; Carbohydrate 18.9g, of which sugars 17.2g; Fat 1.1g, of which saturates 0.3g; Cholesterol 50mg; Calcium 70mg; Fibre 2.8g; Sodium 153mg.

CHICKEN AND SWEET POTATO CURRY WITH COCONUT AND CARAMEL SAUCE

THIS DELICIOUS CHICKEN DISH COMBINES THE USE OF SPICY INDIAN CURRY POWDER AND SMOOTH, CREAMY COCONUT MILK. SERVE THIS CURRY WITH BAGUETTES FOR MOPPING UP THE SAUCE, OR STEAMED FRAGRANT RICE OR NOODLES.

SERVES FOUR

INGREDIENTS

45ml/3 tbsp Indian curry powder or garam masala
15ml/1 tbsp ground turmeric
500g/1¼lb skinless chicken thighs or chicken portions
25ml/1½ tbsp raw cane sugar
30ml/2 tbsp sesame oil
2 shallots, chopped
2 garlic cloves, chopped
4cm/1½in galangal, peeled and chopped
2 lemon grass stalks, chopped
10ml/2 tsp chilli paste or dried chilli flakes
2 medium sweet potatoes, peeled and cubed
45ml/3 tbsp *nuoc mam*
600ml/1 pint/2½ cups coconut milk
1 small bunch each fresh basil and coriander (cilantro), stalks removed
salt and ground black pepper

3 Heat a wok or heavy pan and add the oil. Stir-fry the shallots, garlic, galangal and lemon grass. Stir in the rest of the turmeric and curry powder with the chilli paste or flakes, followed by the chicken, and stir-fry for 2–3 minutes.

4 Add the sweet potatoes, then the *nuoc mam*, caramel sauce, coconut milk and 150ml/¼ pint/⅔ cup water, mixing thoroughly to combine the flavours. Bring to the boil, reduce the heat and cook for about 15 minutes until the chicken is cooked through. Season and stir in half the basil and coriander. Garnish with the remaining herbs and serve immediately.

VARIATION
This curry is equally good made with pork or prawns (shrimp), or a combination of the two. Galangal is available in Asian stores, but you can use fresh root ginger if you prefer.

1 In a small bowl, mix together the curry powder or garam masala and the turmeric. Put the chicken in a bowl and coat with half of the spice. Set aside.

2 To make the caramel sauce, heat the sugar in a small pan with 7.5ml/1½ tsp water, until the sugar dissolves and the syrup turns golden. Remove from the heat and set aside.

STIR-FRIED CHICKEN <u>WITH</u> CHILLIES <u>AND</u> LEMON GRASS

THIS IS GOOD HOME COOKING. THERE ARE VARIATIONS OF THIS DISH, USING PORK OR SEAFOOD, THROUGHOUT SOUTH-EAST ASIA SO, FOR A SMOOTH INTRODUCTION TO THE COOKING OF THE REGION, THIS IS A GOOD PLACE TO START. SERVE WITH A SALAD, RICE WRAPPERS AND A DIPPING SAUCE.

SERVES FOUR

INGREDIENTS
  15ml/1 tbsp sugar
  30ml/2 tbsp sesame or groundnut
    (peanut) oil
  2 garlic cloves, finely chopped
  2–3 green or red Thai chillies,
    seeded and finely chopped
  2 lemon grass stalks, finely sliced
  1 onion, finely sliced
  350g/12oz skinless chicken breast
    fillets, cut into bitesize strips
  30ml/2 tbsp soy sauce
  15ml/1 tbsp *nuoc mam*
  1 bunch fresh coriander (cilantro),
    stalks removed, leaves chopped
  salt and ground black pepper
  nuoc cham, to serve

1 To make a caramel sauce, put the sugar into a pan with 5ml/1 tsp water. Heat gently until the sugar has dissolved and turned golden. Set aside.

2 Heat a large wok or heavy pan and add the sesame or groundnut oil. Stir in the chopped garlic, chillies and lemon grass, and stir-fry until they become fragrant and golden. Add the onion and stir-fry for 1 minute, then add the chicken strips.

3 When the chicken is cooked through, add the soy sauce, *nuoc mam* and caramel sauce. Stir to mix and heat through, then season with a little salt and pepper. Toss the coriander into the chicken and serve with *nuoc cham* to drizzle over it.

Energy 202Kcal/847kJ; Protein 22g; Carbohydrate 9g, of which sugars 7g; Fat 9g, of which saturates 1g; Cholesterol 61mg; Calcium 32mg; Fibre 0.6g; Sodium 800mg.

CAMBODIAN CHICKEN <u>WITH</u> YOUNG GINGER

GINGER PLAYS A BIG ROLE IN ASIAN AND INDIAN COOKING, PARTICULARLY IN THE STIR-FRIED DISHES. WHENEVER POSSIBLE, THE JUICIER AND MORE PUNGENT YOUNG GINGER IS USED. THIS IS A SIMPLE AND DELICIOUS WAY TO COOK CHICKEN, PORK OR BEEF.

SERVES FOUR

INGREDIENTS
    30ml/2 tbsp groundnut (peanut) oil
    3 garlic cloves, finely sliced
      in strips
    50g/2oz fresh young root ginger,
      finely sliced in strips
    2 Thai chillies, seeded and finely
      sliced in strips
    4 chicken breasts or 4 boned
      chicken legs, skinned and cut
      into bitesize chunks
    30ml/2 tbsp *tuk prahoc*
    10ml/2 tsp sugar
    1 small bunch coriander (cilantro)
      stalks removed, roughly chopped
    ground black pepper
    jasmine rice and crunchy salad or
      baguette, to serve

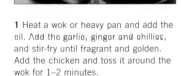

1 Heat a wok or heavy pan and add the oil. Add the garlic, ginger and chillies, and stir-fry until fragrant and golden. Add the chicken and toss it around the wok for 1–2 minutes.

COOK'S TIP
Young ginger is available in Chinese and South-east Asian markets.

2 Stir in the *tuk prahoc* and sugar, and stir fry for a further 4–5 minutes until cooked. Season with pepper and add some of the fresh coriander. Transfer the chicken to a serving dish and garnish with the remaining coriander. Serve hot with jasmine rice and a crunchy salad with fresh herbs, or with chunks of freshly baked baguette.

Energy 222Kcal/935kJ; Protein 36.4g; Carbohydrate 3g, of which sugars 2.9g; Fat 7.3g, of which saturates 1.1g; Cholesterol 105mg; Calcium 32mg; Fibre 0.6g; Sodium 100mg.

CARAMELIZED CHICKEN WINGS WITH GINGER

COOKED IN A WOK OR IN THE OVEN, THESE CARAMELIZED WINGS ARE DRIZZLED WITH CHILLI OIL AND EATEN WITH THE FINGERS, AND EVERY BIT OF TENDER MEAT IS SUCKED OFF THE BONE. OFTEN SERVED WITH RICE AND PICKLES, VARIATIONS OF THIS RECIPE CAN BE FOUND IN VIETNAM AND CAMBODIA.

SERVES TWO TO FOUR

INGREDIENTS
75ml/5 tbsp sugar
30ml/2 tbsp groundnut (peanut) oil
25g/1oz fresh root ginger, peeled and
    finely shredded or grated
12 chicken wings, split in two
chilli oil, for drizzling
mixed pickled vegetables,
    to serve

1 To make a caramel sauce, gently heat the sugar with 60ml/4 tbsp water in a small, heavy pan until it turns golden, Set aside.

2 Heat the oil in a wok or heavy pan. Add the ginger and stir-fry until fragrant. Add the chicken wings and toss them around the wok to brown.

3 Pour in the caramel sauce and make sure the chicken wings are coated in it. Reduce the heat, cover the wok or pan, and cook for about 30 minutes, until tender, and the sauce has caramelized.

4 Drizzle chilli oil over the wings and serve from the wok or pan with mixed pickled vegetables.

Energy 393Kcal/1641kJ; Protein 30.5g; Carbohydrate 14.4g, of which sugars 14.4g; Fat 24g, of which saturates 6.3g; Cholesterol 134mg; Calcium 16mg; Fibre 0g; Sodium 100mg.

STIR-FRIED CHICKEN WITH BASIL AND CHILLI

*THIS QUICK AND EASY CHICKEN DISH FROM THAILAND OWES ITS SPICY FLAVOUR TO FRESH CHILLIES
AND ITS PUNGENCY TO THAI BASIL, WHICH HAS A LOVELY AROMA WITH HINTS OF LIQUORICE.*

2 Add the pieces of chicken to the wok or pan, in batches if necessary, and stir-fry until the chicken changes colour.

3 Stir in the fish sauce, soy sauce and sugar. Continue to stir-fry the mixture for 3–4 minutes, or until the chicken is fully cooked and golden brown.

4 Stir in the fresh Thai basil leaves. Spoon the mixture on to a warm platter, or into individual dishes. Garnish with the chopped chillies and deep-fried Thai basil and serve immediately.

SERVES FOUR TO SIX

INGREDIENTS
    45ml/3 tbsp vegetable oil
    4 garlic cloves, thinly sliced
    2–4 fresh red chillies, seeded and
      finely chopped
    450g/1lb skinless chicken breast
      fillets, cut into bitesize pieces
    15ml/3 tbsp Thai fish sauce
    10ml/2 tsp dark soy sauce
    5ml/1 tsp granulated sugar
    10–12 fresh Thai basil leaves
    2 fresh red chillies, seeded and
      finely chopped, and about 20 deep-
      fried Thai basil leaves, to garnish

1 Heat the oil in a wok or large, heavy frying pan. Add the garlic and chillies and stir-fry over a medium heat for 1–2 minutes until the garlic is golden. Take care not to let the garlic burn, otherwise it will taste bitter.

COOK'S TIP
To deep-fry Thai basil leaves, first make sure that the leaves are completely dry or they will splutter when added to the oil. Heat vegetable or groundnut (peanut) oil in a wok or deep-fryer to 190°C/375°F or until a cube of bread, added to the oil, browns in about 40 seconds. Add the leaves and deep-fry them briefly until they are crisp and translucent – this will take only about 30–40 seconds, so watch them carefully. Lift out the leaves using a slotted spoon or wire basket and leave them to drain on kitchen paper before using.

Energy 138Kcal/576kJ; Protein 18.3g; Carbohydrate 1.9g, of which sugars 1.8g; Fat 6.4g, of which saturates 0.9g; Cholesterol 53mg; Calcium 6mg; Fibre 0.1g; Sodium 579mg.

SOUTHERN THAI CHICKEN CURRY

THIS IS A MILD COCONUT CURRY FLAVOURED WITH TURMERIC, CORIANDER AND CUMIN SEEDS, WHICH COMBINES THE CULINARY INFLUENCES OF MALAYSIA AND NEIGHBOURING THAILAND.

SERVES FOUR

INGREDIENTS

60ml/4 tbsp vegetable oil
1 large garlic clove, crushed
1 chicken, weighing about 1.5kg/
   3–3½lb, chopped into
   12 large pieces
400ml/14fl oz/1⅔ cups
   coconut cream
250ml/8fl oz/1 cup chicken stock
30ml/2 tbsp Thai fish sauce
30ml/2 tbsp sugar
juice of 2 limes
To garnish
2 small fresh red chillies, seeded and
   finely chopped
1 bunch spring onions (scallions),
   thinly sliced
For the curry paste
5ml/1 tsp dried chilli flakes
2.5ml/½ tsp salt
5cm/2in piece fresh turmeric or
   5ml/1 tsp ground turmeric
2.5ml/½ tsp coriander seeds
2.5ml/½ tsp cumin seeds
5ml/1 tsp shrimp paste

1 First make the curry paste. Put all the ingredients in a mortar, food processor or spice grinder and pound, process or grind to a smooth paste.

2 Heat the oil in a wok or frying pan and cook the garlic until golden. Add the chicken and cook until golden. Remove the chicken and set aside.

3 Reheat the oil and add the curry paste and then half the coconut cream. Cook for a few minutes until fragrant.

4 Return the chicken to the wok or pan, add the stock, mixing well, then add the remaining coconut cream, the fish sauce, sugar and lime juice. Stir well and bring to the boil, then lower the heat and simmer for 15 minutes.

5 Turn the curry into four warm serving bowls and sprinkle with the chopped fresh chillies and spring onions to garnish. Serve immediately.

COOK'S TIP
Shrimp paste has a very powerful flavour and should always be cooked before eating. Its strong, salty flavour mellows when cooked, but it still has a powerful kick, and should be used with care. Store, well wrapped, in the fridge.

Energy 686Kcal/2849kJ; Protein 46.8g; Carbohydrate 12.8g, of which sugars 12.8g; Fat 50g, of which saturates 12.8g; Cholesterol 246mg; Calcium 67mg; Fibre 0g; Sodium 352mg.

CASHEW CHICKEN

*ONE OF THE MOST POPULAR ITEMS ON ANY CHINESE RESTAURANT MENU, CASHEW CHICKEN IS EASY TO
RECREATE AT HOME. IT IS IMPORTANT TO HAVE THE WOK VERY HOT BEFORE ADDING THE CHICKEN OR
IT WILL STEW RATHER THAN STIR-FRY. A CARBON STEEL WOK WILL GIVE GOOD RESULTS.*

SERVES FOUR TO SIX

INGREDIENTS
  450g/1lb skinless chicken breast
  fillets
  1 red (bell) pepper
  2 garlic cloves
  4 dried red chillies
  30ml/2 tbsp vegetable oil
  30ml/2 tbsp oyster sauce
  15ml/1 tbsp soy sauce
  pinch of granulated sugar
  1 bunch spring onions (scallions), cut
  into 5cm/2in lengths
  175g/6oz/1½ cups cashews, roasted
  coriander (cilantro) leaves,
  to garnish

1 Remove and discard the skin from the chicken breasts and trim off any excess fat. With a sharp knife, cut the chicken into bitesize pieces and set aside.

2 Halve the red pepper, scrape out the seeds and membranes and discard, then cut the flesh into 2cm/¾in dice. Peel and thinly slice the garlic and chop the dried red chillies.

3 Preheat a wok and then heat the oil. The best way to do this is to drizzle a "necklace" of oil around the inner rim of the wok, so that it drops down to coat the entire inner surface. Make sure the coating is even by swirling the wok.

4 Add the garlic and dried chillies to the wok and stir-fry over a medium heat until golden. Do not let the garlic burn, otherwise it will taste bitter.

5 Add the chicken to the wok and stir-fry until it is cooked through, then add the red pepper. If the mixture is very dry, add a little water.

6 Stir in the oyster sauce, soy sauce and sugar. Add the spring onions and cashew nuts. Stir-fry for 1–2 minutes more, until heated through. Spoon into a warm dish and serve immediately, garnished with the coriander leaves.

COOK'S TIP
Cashews are also valued for the "fruit" under which each nut grows. Although they are known as cashew apples, these so-called fruits are actually bulbous portions of the stem. They may be pink, red or yellow in colour and the crisp, sweet flesh can be eaten raw or made into a refreshing drink. Cashew apples – and undried nuts – are rarely seen outside their growing regions.

Energy 314Kcal/1307kJ; Protein 24.7g; Carbohydrate 10.2g, of which sugars 6.2g; Fat 19.6g, of which saturates 3.7g; Cholesterol 53mg; Calcium 24mg; Fibre 1.7g; Sodium 268mg.

CRISPY FIVE-SPICE CHICKEN

TENDER STRIPS OF CHICKEN FILLET, WITH A DELICATELY SPICED RICE FLOUR COATING, BECOME DELICIOUSLY CRISP AND GOLDEN WHEN SHALLOW-FRIED IN A HOT WOK. THEY MAKE A GREAT MEAL SERVED ON A BED OF STIR-FRIED NOODLES WITH SWEET PEPPERS AND BROCCOLI.

SERVES FOUR

INGREDIENTS
200g/7oz thin egg noodles
30ml/2 tbsp sunflower oil
2 garlic cloves, very thinly sliced
1 fresh red chilli, seeded and sliced
½ red (bell) pepper, seeded and very
 thinly sliced
300g/11oz carrots, peeled and
 cut into thin strips
300g/11oz Chinese broccoli
 or Chinese greens, roughly sliced
45ml/3 tbsp hoisin sauce
45ml/3 tbsp soy sauce
15ml/1 tbsp caster (superfine) sugar
4 skinless chicken breast fillets,
 cut into strips
2 egg whites, lightly beaten
115g/4oz/1 cup rice flour
15ml/1 tbsp five-spice powder
salt and ground black pepper
vegetable oil, for frying

1 Cook the noodles in boiling water for 2–4 minutes, or according to the packet instructions, drain and set aside.

2 Heat a wok, add the sunflower oil, and when it is hot add the garlic, chilli, red pepper, carrots and the broccoli or greens. Stir-fry over a high heat for 2–3 minutes.

3 Add the sauces and sugar to the wok and cook for a further 2–3 minutes. Add the drained noodles, toss to combine, then remove from the heat, cover and keep warm.

4 Dip the chicken strips into the egg white. Combine the rice flour and five-spice powder in a shallow dish and season. Add the chicken strips to the flour mixture and toss to coat.

5 Heat about 2.5cm/1in oil in a clean wok. When hot, shallow-fry the chicken for 3–4 minutes until crisp and golden.

6 To serve, divide the noodle mixture between warmed plates or bowls and top each serving with the chicken.

VARIATION
The coating also works well on thin strips of fish. When frying the fish, it is best to cook just a few pieces at once, so the oil stays hot. Use a draining rack clipped to the side of the wok, and drain each batch while cooking the next.

Energy 679Kcal/2849kJ; Protein 43.9g; Carbohydrate 75.8g, of which sugars 17g; Fat 23.2g, of which saturates 3.7g; Cholesterol 104mg; Calcium 95mg; Fibre 5.5g; Sodium 667mg.

LEMON AND SESAME CHICKEN

THESE DELICATE STRIPS OF CHICKEN ARE AT THEIR BEST IF YOU
HAVE TIME TO LEAVE THEM TO MARINATE OVERNIGHT SO THAT
THEY CAN REALLY SOAK UP THE FLAVOURS. THE SUBTLE FRAGRANCE
OF LEMON PERFECTLY COMPLEMENTS THE RICH TASTE OF FRIED
CHICKEN AND THE NUTTY SESAME SEEDS.

SERVES FOUR

INGREDIENTS
  4 large chicken breast portions,
    skinned and cut into strips
  15ml/1 tbsp light soy sauce
  15ml/1 tbsp Chinese rice wine
  2 garlic cloves, crushed
  10ml/2 tsp finely grated fresh
    root ginger
  1 egg, lightly beaten
  150g/5oz cornflour (cornstarch)
  sunflower oil, for deep-frying
  toasted sesame seeds, to sprinkle
  rice or noodles, to serve
For the sauce
  15ml/1 tbsp sunflower oil
  2 spring onions (scallions),
    finely sliced
  1 garlic clove, crushed
  10ml/2 tsp cornflour (cornstarch)
  90ml/6 tbsp chicken stock
  10ml/2 tsp finely grated lemon rind
  30ml/2 tbsp lemon juice
  10ml/2 tsp sugar
  2.5ml/½ tsp sesame oil
  salt

1 Place the chicken strips in a large,
non-metallic bowl. Mix together the light
soy sauce, rice wine, garlic and ginger
and pour over the chicken. Toss
together to combine.

2 Cover the bowl of chicken with clear
film (plastic wrap) and place in the
refrigerator for 8–10 hours, or overnight
if that is more convenient.

3 When ready to cook, add the beaten
egg to the chicken and mix well, then
tip the mixture into a colander to drain
off any excess marinade and egg.

4 Place the cornflour in a large plastic
bag and add the chicken pieces. Shake
it vigorously to coat the chicken strips
thoroughly.

5 Fill a wok one-third full of sunflower
oil and heat to 180°C/350°F (or until a
cube of bread, dropped into the oil,
browns in 45 seconds).

6 Deep-fry the chicken, in batches,
for 3–4 minutes. Lift out the chicken
using a slotted spoon and drain on
kitchen paper. Reheat the oil and deep-
fry the chicken once more, in batches,
for 2–3 minutes. Remove with a slotted
spoon and drain on kitchen paper. Pour
the oil out and wipe out the wok with
kitchen paper.

7 To make the sauce, heat the wok,
then add the sunflower oil. When the oil
is hot add the spring onions and garlic
and stir-fry for 1–2 minutes. Mix
together the cornflour, stock, lemon rind
and juice, sugar, sesame oil and salt
and pour into the wok.

8 Cook over a high heat for 2–3 minutes
until thickened. Return the chicken to
the wok, toss lightly to coat with sauce,
and sprinkle over the toasted sesame
seeds. Serve with rice or noodles.

Energy 229Kcal/959kJ; Protein 31.3g; Carbohydrate 4.3g, of which sugars 3.4g; Fat 9.7g, of which saturates 1.4g;
Cholesterol 94mg; Calcium 32mg; Fibre 0.5g; Sodium 397mg.

SICHUAN CHICKEN WITH KUNG PO SAUCE

THIS RECIPE, WHICH HAILS FROM THE SICHUAN REGION OF WESTERN CHINA, HAS BECOME ONE OF THE CLASSIC RECIPES IN THE CHINESE REPERTOIRE. THE COMBINATION OF YELLOW SALTED BEANS AND HOISIN, SPIKED WITH CHILLI, MAKES FOR A VERY TASTY AND SPICY SAUCE.

SERVES THREE

INGREDIENTS
2–3 skinless chicken breast fillets,
   cut into neat pieces
1 egg white
10ml/2 tsp cornflour
2.5ml/¹/₂ tsp salt
30ml/2 tbsp yellow salted beans
15ml/1 tbsp hoisin sauce
5ml/1 tsp light brown sugar
15ml/1 tbsp rice wine or
   medium-dry sherry
15ml/1 tbsp wine vinegar
4 garlic cloves, crushed
150ml/¹/₄ pint/²/₃ cup chicken stock
45ml/3 tbsp sunflower oil
2–3 dried chillies, broken into
   small pieces
115g/4oz roasted cashew nuts
fresh coriander (cilantro), to garnish

1 Lightly whisk the egg white in a dish, whisk in the cornflour and salt, then add the chicken and stir until coated.

COOK'S TIP
Peanuts are the classic ingredient in this dish, but cashew nuts have an even better flavour and have become popular both in home cooking and in restaurants. Use roasted peanuts if you prefer.

2 In a separate bowl, mash the salted beans with a spoon. Stir in the hoisin sauce, brown sugar, rice wine or sherry, vinegar, garlic and stock.

3 Heat a wok, add the oil and then stir-fry the chicken, turning constantly, for about 2 minutes until tender. Either drain the chicken over a bowl to collect excess oil, or lift out each piece with a slotted spoon, leaving the oil in the wok.

4 Heat the reserved oil and fry the chilli pieces for 1 minute. Return the chicken to the wok and pour in the bean sauce mixture. Bring to the boil and stir in the cashew nuts. Spoon into a heated serving dish and garnish with coriander leaves.

Energy 490Kcal/2040kJ; Protein 37.7g; Carbohydrate 12.4g, of which sugars 2.6g; Fat 31.9g, of which saturates 5.6g; Cholesterol 82mg; Calcium 24mg; Fibre 1.9g; Sodium 204mg.

CHICKEN RENDANG

THIS SPICY RECIPE OF DELICIOUS, CRISPY FRIED CHICKEN, MAKES A MARVELLOUS DISH FOR A BUFFET
OR A PICNIC. SERVE IT WITH PRAWN CRACKERS OR WITH BOILED RICE AND DEEP-FRIED ANCHOVIES,
ACAR PICKLE OR A SELECTION OF SAMBALS.

SERVES FOUR

INGREDIENTS
    1 chicken, about 1.4kg/3lb
    5ml/1 tsp sugar
    75g/3oz/1 cup desiccated (dry
        unsweetened, shredded) coconut
    4 small red or white onions,
        roughly chopped
    2 garlic cloves, chopped
    2.5cm/1in piece fresh root ginger,
        peeled and sliced
    1–2 lemon grass stalks, root trimmed
    2.5cm/1in piece fresh galangal,
        peeled and sliced
    75ml/5 tbsp groundnut (peanut) oil
        or vegetable oil
    10–15ml/2–3 tsp chilli powder, or
        to taste
    400ml/14fl oz can coconut milk
    10ml/2 tsp salt
    fresh chives and deep-fried
        anchovies, to garnish

1 Joint the chicken into 8 pieces and
remove the skin, sprinkle with the
sugar and leave to stand for 1 hour.

2 Dry-fry the coconut in a wok or large
frying pan over medium to low heat,
turning all the time until it is crisp and
golden. Place the fried coconut in a
food processor and process to an oily
paste. Transfer to a bowl and reserve.

3 Add the onions, garlic and ginger to
the processor. Cut off the lower 5cm/2in
of the lemon grass, chop and add to the
processor with the galangal. Process to
a fine paste.

4 Heat the oil in a wok or large pan and
fry the onion mixture for a few minutes.
Reduce the heat, stir in the chilli powder
and cook for 2–3 minutes, stirring
constantly. Spoon in 120ml/4fl oz/½ cup
of the coconut milk and add salt to taste.

5 As soon as the mixture bubbles, add
the chicken pieces, turning them until
they are well coated with the spices.
Pour in the remaining coconut milk,
stirring constantly to prevent curdling.

6 Bruise the top of the lemon grass
stalks and add to the wok or pan. Cover
and cook gently for 40–45 minutes
until the chicken is tender.

7 Just before serving, stir in the coconut
paste. Bring to just below boiling point,
then simmer for 5 minutes. Transfer to
a serving bowl and garnish with fresh
chives and deep-fried anchovies.

Energy 501Kcal/2098kJ; Protein 55.4g; Carbohydrate 7.2g, of which sugars 7.2g; Fat 28.1g, of which saturates 12.5g; Cholesterol 158mg; Calcium 45mg; Fibre 2.6g; Sodium 1233mg.

SPICED COCONUT CHICKEN WITH CARDAMOM

YOU NEED TO PLAN AHEAD TO MAKE THIS LUXURIOUS CHICKEN CURRY. THE CHICKEN LEGS ARE MARINATED OVERNIGHT IN AN AROMATIC BLEND OF YOGURT AND SPICES BEFORE BEING GENTLY SIMMERED WITH HOT GREEN CHILLIES IN CREAMY COCONUT MILK. SERVE WITH RICE.

SERVES FOUR

INGREDIENTS

　1.6kg/3½lb large chicken drumsticks
　30ml/2 tbsp sunflower oil
　400ml/14fl oz/1⅔ cups coconut milk
　4–6 large green chillies, halved
　45ml/3 tbsp finely chopped
　　coriander (cilantro)
　salt and ground black pepper
　natural (plain) yogurt, to drizzle
For the marinade
　15ml/1 tbsp cardamom pods
　15ml/1 tbsp grated fresh root ginger
　10ml/2 tsp crushed garlic
　105ml/7 tbsp natural (plain) yogurt
　2 fresh green chillies, seeded and
　　chopped
　5ml/1 tsp ground cumin
　5ml/1 tsp ground coriander
　5ml/1 tsp ground turmeric
　finely grated rind and juice of 1 lime

1 Make the marinade. Smash the cardamom pods in a pestle so the seeds separate from the husks. Discard the husks. Put the cardamom seeds, ginger, garlic, half the yogurt, green chillies, cumin, coriander, turmeric and lime rind and juice in a blender. Process until smooth, season and pour into a large glass bowl.

2 Add the chicken to the bowl and toss to coat. Cover and marinate in the refrigerator for 6–8 hours, or overnight.

3 Heat the oil in a large, non-stick wok over a low heat. Add the chicken, reserving the marinade. Add the chicken to the wok and brown all over, then add the coconut milk, remaining yogurt, reserved marinade and green chillies and bring to the boil.

4 Reduce the heat and simmer gently, uncovered, for 30–35 minutes. Check the seasoning, adding more if needed. Stir in the coriander, ladle into warmed bowls and serve drizzled with yogurt.

Energy 691Kcal/2906kJ; Protein 107.7g; Carbohydrate 6.2g, of which sugars 6.1g; Fat 26.5g, of which saturates 6.5g; Cholesterol 540mg; Calcium 142mg; Fibre 0.6g; Sodium 805mg.

ADOBO OF CHICKEN AND PORK

FOUR INGREDIENTS ARE ESSENTIAL IN AN ADOBO, ONE OF THE BEST-LOVED RECIPES IN THE FILIPINO REPERTOIRE. THEY ARE VINEGAR, GARLIC, PEPPERCORNS AND BAY LEAVES. THE PLANTAIN CHIPS ARE THE TRADITIONAL ACCOMPANIMENT BUT SWEET POTATO CHIPS CAN BE SERVED INSTEAD.

SERVES FOUR

INGREDIENTS
1 chicken, about 1.4kg/3lb, or
    4 chicken quarters
350g/12oz pork leg steaks (with fat)
10ml/2 tsp sugar
60ml/4 tbsp sunflower oil
75ml/5 tbsp wine or cider vinegar
4 plump garlic cloves, crushed
1/2 tsp black peppercorns,
    crushed lightly
15ml/1 tbsp light soy sauce
4 bay leaves
2.5ml/1/2 tsp annatto seeds, soaked
    in 30ml/2 tbsp boiling water, or
    2.5ml/1/2 tsp ground turmeric
salt
For the plantain chips
    1–2 large plantains and/or
    1 sweet potato
    vegetable oil, for deep-frying

3 Add the vinegar, garlic, peppercorns, soy sauce and bay leaves and stir well. Strain the annatto seed liquid and stir it into the wok, stir in the turmeric. Add salt to taste.

4 Bring the stock to the boil, cover, lower the heat and simmer the chicken for 30–35 minutes. When the chicken is cooked through, remove the lid and simmer for 10 minutes more to reduce the liquid a little.

5 Meanwhile, prepare the plaintain chips. Heat the oil in a wok or deep-fryer to 195°C/390°F. Peel the plantains and slice them into rounds or chips. Deep-fry them, in batches if necessary, until cooked but not brown. Drain the chips on kitchen paper.

6 When ready to serve, reheat the oil and refry the plantains until crisp – it will take only seconds. Drain and serve with the adobo.

1 Wipe the chicken and cut into eight even-size pieces, or halve the chicken quarters, if using. Cut the pork into neat pieces. Spread out all the meat on a board, sprinkle lightly with sugar and set aside.

2 Heat the oil in a wok and fry the chicken and pork pieces, in batches if necessary, until they are golden on both sides.

COOK'S TIP
Sprinkling the chicken lightly with sugar turns the skin beautifully brown when fried, but do not have the oil too hot to begin with or they will over-brown.

Energy 676Kcal/2825kJ; Protein 60.2g; Carbohydrate 28.8g, of which sugars 8.1g; Fat 36.2g, of which saturates 6g; Cholesterol 178mg; Calcium 38mg; Fibre 1.7g; Sodium 503mg.

Chicken Pot

This nourishing main course combines meat with beans in a spicy sauce. Serve it with rice.

SERVES FOUR TO SIX

INGREDIENTS

175g/6oz dried haricot beans
3 chicken legs
15ml/1 tbsp vegetable oil
350g/12oz lean pork, diced
1 chorizo (optional)
1 small carrot, peeled and
  roughly chopped
1 onion, roughly chopped
1 clove garlic, crushed
30ml/2 tbsp tomato purée (paste)
1 bay leaf
2 chicken stock cubes
350g/12oz sweet potatoes or new
  potatoes, peeled and cubed
10ml/2 tsp chilli sauce
30ml/2 tbsp white wine vinegar
3 firm tomatoes, skinned, seeded
  and chopped
225g/8oz Chinese leaves (Chinese
  cabbage), shredded
salt and ground black pepper
3 spring onions (scallions), to garnish
boiled rice, to serve

1 Put the haricot beans in a bowl, cover with plenty of cold water and set aside to soak for 8 hours or overnight.

2 Separate the chicken drumsticks from the thighs. Chop off the narrow end of each drumstick and discard.

COOK'S TIP
This dish is intended to provide enough liquid to be served as a soup for the first course, rather like a French pot au feu. This is followed by a main course of the meat and vegetables, served with rice.

3 Heat the vegetable oil in a preheated wok, add the chicken, pork, sliced chorizo, if using, carrot and onion, then brown evenly.

4 Drain the haricot beans and add to the wok with fresh water to cover. Stir in the garlic, tomato purée and bay leaf. Bring to the boil, lower the heat and simmer for 2 hours until the beans are almost tender.

5 Crumble the chicken stock cubes into the wok, add the sweet or new potatoes and the chilli sauce, then continue to simmer for 15–20 minutes until the potatoes are cooked.

6 Add the vinegar, tomatoes and Chinese leaves to the wok, then simmer for 1–2 minutes. Season to taste with salt and pepper. Garnish with shredded spring onions and serve with rice.

Energy 309kcal/1304kJ; Protein 33.2g; Carbohydrate 30.7g, of which sugars 9.2g; Fat 6.7g, of which saturates 1.7g; Cholesterol 98mg; Calcium 79mg; Fibre 7.7g; Sodium 143mg.

BALTI BABY CHICKEN <u>IN</u> TAMARIND SAUCE

BALTI DISHES ARE USUALLY COOKED IN A KARAHI, BUT A WOK WORKS JUST AS WELL.

SERVES FOUR TO SIX

INGREDIENTS

    60ml/4 tbsp tomato ketchup
    15ml/1 tbsp tamarind paste
    60ml/4 tbsp water
    7.5ml/1½ tsp chilli powder
    7.5ml/1½ tsp salt
    15ml/1 tbsp sugar
    7.5ml/1½ tsp crushed ginger
    7.5ml/1½ tsp crushed garlic
    30ml/2 tbsp desiccated (dry
      unsweetened, shredded) coconut
    30ml/2 tbsp sesame seeds
    5ml/1 tsp poppy seeds
    5ml/1 tsp ground cumin
    7.5ml/1½ tsp ground coriander
    2 x 450g/1lb baby chickens, skinned
      and cut into 6–8 pieces
    75ml/5 tbsp corn oil
    120ml/8 tbsp curry leaves
    2.5ml/½ tsp onion seeds
    3 large dried red chillies
    2.5ml/½ tsp fenugreek seeds
    10–12 cherry tomatoes
    45ml/3 tbsp chopped fresh coriander
      (cilantro)
    2 fresh green chillies, chopped

1 Put the tomato ketchup, tamarind paste and water into a large mixing bowl and blend together with a fork.

2 Add the chilli powder, salt, sugar, ginger, garlic, coconut, sesame seeds, poppy seeds, ground cumin and ground coriander to the mixture.

3 Add the chicken pieces to the bowl and stir until they are well coated with the spice mixture. Set aside for up to 2 hours to allow the chicken to absorb the flavours of the spices.

4 Heat the oil in a preheated wok. When it is hot, add the curry leaves, onion seeds, dried red chillies and fenugreek seeds and fry for 1 minute.

5 Lower the heat to medium and add the chicken pieces, together with their sauce, 2 or 3 pieces at a time.

6 When all the chicken has been added simmer gently for 12–15 minutes or until the chicken is thoroughly cooked.

7 Add the tomatoes, fresh coriander and green chillies to the wok and serve immediately.

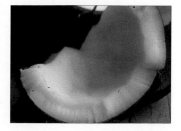

Energy 268kcal/1120kJ; Protein 26g; Carbohydrate 4.1g, of which sugars 4g; Fat 16.6g, of which saturates 4.5g; Cholesterol 70mg; Calcium 60mg; Fibre 2.2g; Sodium 152mg.

SCENTED CHICKEN WRAPS

FOR SHEER SOPHISTICATION, THESE LEAF-WRAPPED CHICKEN BITES TAKE A LOT OF BEATING. THEY ARE SURPRISINGLY EASY TO MAKE AND CAN BE DEEP-FRIED IN MINUTES IN THE WOK.

SERVES FOUR

INGREDIENTS

400g/14oz skinless chicken thighs, boned
45ml/3 tbsp soy sauce
30ml/2 tbsp finely grated garlic
15ml/1 tbsp cumin
15ml/1 tbsp ground coriander
15ml/1 tbsp golden caster (superfine) sugar
5ml/1 tsp finely grated fresh root ginger
1 fresh bird's eye chilli
30ml/2 tbsp oyster sauce
15ml/1 tbsp Thai fish sauce
1 bunch of pandan leaves, to wrap
vegetable oil, for deep-frying
sweet chilli sauce, to serve

1 Using a cleaver or sharp knife, cut the chicken into bitesize pieces and place in a large mixing bowl.

2 Place the soy sauce, garlic, cumin, coriander, sugar, ginger, chilli, oyster sauce and fish sauce in a blender and process until smooth. Pour over the chicken, cover and leave to marinate in the refrigerator for 6-8 hours.

3 When ready to cook, drain the chicken from the marinade and wrap each piece in a pandanus leaf (you will need to cut the leaves to size) and secure with a cocktail stick (toothpick).

4 Fill a wok one-third full of oil and heat to 180°C/350°F or until a cube of bread, dropped into the oil, browns in 45 seconds. Carefully add the chicken parcels, 3–4 at a time, and deep-fry for 3–4 minutes, or until cooked through. Drain on kitchen paper and serve with the chilli sauce. (Do not eat the leaves!)

COOK'S TIP

Pandan leaves are usually available from Asian supermarkets.

Energy 159Kcal/669kJ; Protein 24.5g; Carbohydrate 6.8g, of which sugars 6.6g; Fat 3.9g, of which saturates 0.6g; Cholesterol 70mg; Calcium 10mg; Fibre 0.1g; Sodium 1055mg.

HIJIKI SEAWEED AND CHICKEN

THE TASTE OF HIJIKI IS SOMEWHERE BETWEEN RICE AND VEGETABLE. IT GOES WELL WITH MEAT OR TOFU PRODUCTS, ESPECIALLY WHEN IT'S STIR-FRIED IN THE WOK FIRST WITH A LITTLE OIL.

SERVES TWO

INGREDIENTS

    90g/3½oz dried hijiki seaweed
    150g/5oz chicken breast portion
    ½ small carrot, about 5cm/2in
    15ml/1 tbsp vegetable oil
    100ml/3fl oz/scant ½ cup instant
      dashi powder plus 1.5ml/¼ tsp
      dashi-no-moto
    30ml/2 tbsp sake
    30ml/2 tbsp caster (superfine) sugar
    45ml/3 tbsp shoyu
    a pinch of cayenne pepper

1 Soak the hijiki in cold water for about 30 minutes. When ready to cook, it is easily crushed between the fingers. Pour into a sieve (strainer) and wash under running water. Drain.

2 Peel the skin from the chicken and par-boil the skin in rapidly boiling water for 1 minute, then drain. With a sharp knife, shave off all the yellow fat from the skin. Discard the clear membrane between the fat and the skin as well. Cut the skin into thin strips about 5mm/¼in wide and 2.5cm/1in long. Cut the meat into small, bitesize chunks.

3 Peel and chop the carrot into long, narrow matchsticks.

4 Heat the oil in a wok or frying pan and stir-fry the strips of chicken skin for 5 minutes, or until golden and curled up. Add the chicken meat and keep stirring until the colour changes.

5 Add the hijiki and carrot, then stir-fry for a further minute. Add the remaining ingredients. Lower the heat and toss over the heat for 5 minutes more.

6 Remove the wok from the heat and leave to stand for about 10 minutes. Serve in small individual bowls. Sprinkle with cayenne pepper.

COOK'S TIP
Chicken skin is sometimes discarded because of its high calorie content. However, in this dish the thick yellow fat is removed from the skin before cooking, thus greatly reducing the fat content. The skin curls and becomes crisp when fried, rather like pork crackling. It tastes good but can be omitted if preferred.

Energy 224Kcal/942kJ; Protein 19g; Carbohydrate 19.8g, of which sugars 19.4g; Fat 6.4g, of which saturates 1g; Cholesterol 52mg; Calcium 24mg; Fibre 0.6g; Sodium 1658mg.

SOY-BRAISED CHICKEN

WHILE THE CHICKEN IS BRAISED IN THE WOK, THE SPICY GINGER SAUCE RELEASES ITS FLAVOUR INTO
THE MEAT TO CREATE A SUCCULENT DISH. ENJOY IT HOT OR COLD.

SERVES SIX

INGREDIENTS

1 chicken, about 1.5kg/3–3½lb
15ml/1 tbsp ground Szechuan
  peppercorns
30ml/2 tbsp crushed fresh root
  ginger
45ml/3 tbsp light soy sauce
30ml/2 tbsp dark soy sauce
45ml/3 tbsp Chinese rice wine or
  dry sherry
15ml/1 tbsp soft light brown
  sugar
vegetable oil, for deep-frying
about 600ml/1 pint/2½ cups stock
  or water
10ml/2 tsp salt
25g/1oz crystal sugar
lettuce leaves, to serve

1 Rub the chicken both inside and out
with the ground Szechuan pepper and
fresh ginger. Mix together the soy
sauces, rice wine or sherry and sugar
and spoon the mixture over the chicken
in a large bowl. Leave to marinate for at
least 3 hours, turning the chicken
several times, so that the flavours
penetrate the flesh.

2 Heat the oil in a wok, remove the
chicken from the marinade and deep-
fry for 5–6 minutes, or until brown all
over. Remove and drain.

3 Pour off the excess oil, add the
marinade with the stock or water, salt
and rock sugar and bring to the boil.
Cover and braise the chicken in the
sauce for 35–40 minutes, turning once
or twice.

4 Remove the chicken from the wok
and let it cool down a little before
chopping it into approximately 30 bite-
sized pieces. Arrange in a serving dish
on a bed of lettuce leaves, then pour
some of the sauce over the chicken
and serve.

Energy 404kcal /1678kJ; protein 31.5g; carbohydrate 5.9g, of which sugars 4.9g; fat 42.5g, of which saturates 6.9g; cholesterol 165mg; calcium 18.1mg; fibre 0g; sodium 707mg.

CHICKEN WITH SPICES AND SOY SAUCE

THIS VERY SIMPLE RECIPE, CALLED AYAM KECAP, OFTEN APPEARS ON PADANG RESTAURANT MENUS.
ANY LEFTOVERS TASTE EQUALLY GOOD WHEN REHEATED THE FOLLOWING DAY.

SERVES FOUR

INGREDIENTS
  1.5kg/3–3½lb chicken, jointed and
    cut in 16 pieces
  3 onions
  about 1 litre/1¾ pints/4 cups water
  3 garlic cloves, crushed
  3–4 fresh red chillies, seeded and
    sliced, or 15ml/1 tbsp chilli powder
  45–60ml/3–4 tbsp oil
  2.5ml/½ tsp ground nutmeg
  6 whole cloves
  5ml/1 tsp tamarind pulp, soaked in
    45ml/3 tbsp warm water
  30–45ml/2–3 tbsp dark or light
    soy sauce
  salt
  fresh red chilli shreds, to garnish
  boiled rice, to serve

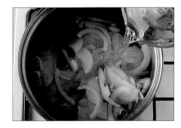

1 Place the pieces of chicken in a large pan. Slice one of the onions and add to the pan. Pour over enough cold water to just cover. Bring to the boil and then reduce the heat and simmer gently for 20 minutes.

2 Grind the remaining onions, with the garlic and chillies, to a fine paste in a food processor or with a pestle and mortar. Heat a little of the oil in a wok or large frying pan and cook the paste to bring out the flavour, but do not allow it to brown.

COOK'S TIP
Dark soy sauce is thicker and more salty than light. Adding the dark variety will give a deeper colour to the chicken.

3 When the chicken has cooked for 20 minutes, lift it out of the stock in the pan using a draining spoon and put it straight into the pan with the spiced paste. Toss everything together over a fairly high heat so that the spices permeate the chicken pieces. Reserve 300ml/½ pint/1¼ cups of the chicken stock to add to the pan later.

4 Stir in the nutmeg and cloves. Strain the tamarind and add the tamarind juice and the soy sauce to the chicken. Cook for a further 2–3 minutes, then add the reserved stock.

5 Taste and adjust the seasoning and cook, uncovered, for a further 25–35 minutes. Serve topped with shredded chilli and accompanied by boiled rice.

Energy 630kcal /2615kJ; protein 48.8g; carbohydrate 13.8g, of which sugars 10.7g; fat 42g, of which saturates 10.6g; cholesterol 247mg; calcium 51mg; fibre 2.5g; sodium 797mg.

ORANGE AND GINGER GLAZED POUSSINS

THESE MOIST, SUCCULENT POUSSINS COATED IN A SPICED CITRUS AND HONEY GLAZE MAKE A GREAT
ALTERNATIVE TO A TRADITIONAL ROAST. BE SURE TO PLAN AHEAD BECAUSE THEY NEED TO BE
MARINATED FOR AT LEAST 6 HOURS, BEFORE BEING COOKED IN THE WOK.

SERVES FOUR

INGREDIENTS

4 poussins, 300–350g/11–12oz each
juice and finely grated rind
   of 2 oranges
2 garlic cloves, crushed
15ml/1 tbsp grated fresh root ginger
90ml/6 tbsp soy sauce
75ml/5 tbsp clear honey
2–3 star anise
30ml/2 tbsp Chinese rice wine
about 20 kaffir lime leaves
a large bunch of spring onions
   (scallions), shredded
60ml/4 tbsp butter
1 large orange, segmented

1 Place the poussins in a deep, non-metallic dish. Combine the orange rind and juice, garlic, ginger, half the soy sauce, half the honey, star anise and rice wine, then pour the mixture over the poussins. Turn the poussins so they are coated all over in the marinade. Cover the dish with clear film (plastic wrap), and place in the refrigerator for at least 6 hours to marinate.

2 To cook the poussins, line a large, heatproof plate with the kaffir lime leaves and spring onions. Lift the poussins out of the marinade and place on top of the layer of leaves. Reserve the marinade in a jug (pitcher).

3 Place a trivet or steamer rack in the base of a large wok and pour in 5cm/2in water. Bring to the boil and carefully lower the plate of poussins on to the trivet or rack. Cover, reduce the heat to low and steam for 45 minutes–1 hour, or until the poussins are cooked through and tender. (Check the water level regularly and add more when necessary.)

4 Remove the poussins from the wok and keep warm while you make the glaze. Wipe out the wok and pour in the reserved marinade, butter and the remaining soy sauce and honey. Bring to the boil, reduce the heat and cook gently for 10–15 minutes, or until thick.

5 Spoon the glaze over the poussins and serve immediately, garnished with the orange segments.

COOK'S TIP
You can make easily make this for fewer people. Just use one poussin and reduce the amount of glaze accordingly. A single bird can be cooked in a steamer basket wrapped with banana leaves.

Energy 568Kcal/2378kJ; Protein 67.3g; Carbohydrate 18.7g, of which sugars 18.5g; Fat 25.3g, of which saturates 11.1g; Cholesterol 32mg; Calcium 110mg; Fibre 0.7g; Sodium 1344mg.

JUNGLE CURRY OF GUINEA FOWL

A TRADITIONAL WILD FOOD COUNTRY CURRY FROM THE NORTH-CENTRAL REGION OF THAILAND, THIS DISH CAN BE MADE USING ANY GAME, FISH OR CHICKEN. GUINEA FOWL IS NOT TYPICAL OF THAI CUISINE, BUT IS A POPULAR AND WIDELY AVAILABLE GAME BIRD IN THE WEST.

SERVES FOUR

INGREDIENTS

1 guinea fowl or similar game bird
15ml/1 tbsp vegetable oil
10ml/2 tsp Thai green curry paste
15ml/1 tbsp Thai fish sauce
2.5cm/1in piece fresh galangal,
  peeled and finely chopped
15ml/1 tbsp fresh green peppercorns
3 kaffir lime leaves, torn
15ml/1 tbsp whisky,
  preferably Mekhong
300ml/½ pint/1¼ cups
  chicken stock
50g/2oz snake beans or yard-long
  beans, cut into 2.5cm/1in lengths
  (about ½ cup)
225g/8oz/3¼ cups chestnut
  mushrooms, sliced
1 piece drained canned bamboo
  shoot, about 50g/2oz, shredded
5ml/1 tsp dried chilli flakes, to
  garnish (optional)

1 Cut up the guinea fowl, remove and discard the skin, then take all the meat off the bones. Chop the meat into bitesize pieces and set aside.

2 Heat the oil in a wok or frying pan and add the curry paste. Stir-fry over a medium heat for 30 seconds, until the paste gives off its aroma.

3 Add the fish sauce and the guinea fowl meat and stir-fry until the meat is browned all over. Add the galangal, peppercorns, lime leaves and whisky, then pour in the stock.

4 Bring to the boil. Add the vegetables, return to a simmer and cook gently for 2–3 minutes, until they are just cooked. Spoon into a dish, sprinkle with chilli flakes, if you like, and serve.

COOK'S TIPS
• Guinea fowl originated in West Africa and was regarded as a game bird. However, it has been domesticated in Europe for over 500 years. They range in size from 675g/1½lb to 2kg/4½lb, but about 1.2kg/2½lb is average. American readers could substitute two or three Cornish hens, depending on size.
• Fresh green peppercorns are simply unripe berries. They are sold on the stem and look rather like miniature Brussels sprout stalks. Look for them at Thai supermarkets. If unavailable, substitute bottled green peppercorns, but rinse well and drain them first.

Energy 321Kcal/1345kJ; Protein 42.2g; Carbohydrate 1.1g, of which sugars 0.7g; Fat 15g, of which saturates 4.4g; Cholesterol 0mg; Calcium 73mg; Fibre 1.1g; Sodium 127mg.

CHINESE DUCK CURRY

THIS RICHLY SPICED CURRY ILLUSTRATES HOW HARMONIOUSLY FIVE-SPICE POWDER MARRIES THE FLAVOURS OF DUCK, GINGER AND BUTTERNUT SQUASH. THE DUCK IS BEST MARINATED FOR AS LONG AS POSSIBLE, ALTHOUGH IT TASTES GOOD EVEN IF YOU ONLY HAVE TIME TO MARINATE IT BRIEFLY.

2 Meanwhile, bring a pan of water to the boil. Add the squash and cook for 10–15 minutes, until just tender. Drain well and set aside.

3 Pour the marinade from the duck into a wok and heat until boiling. Stir in the curry paste and cook for 2–3 minutes, until well blended and fragrant. Add the duck and cook for 3–4 minutes, stirring constantly, until browned on all sides.

4 Add the fish sauce and palm sugar and cook for 2 minutes more. Stir in the coconut milk until the mixture is smooth, then add the cooked squash, with the chillies and lime leaves.

5 Simmer gently, stirring frequently, for 5 minutes, then spoon into a dish, sprinkle with the coriander and serve with noodles.

SERVES FOUR

INGREDIENTS
    4 duck breast portions, skinned
    30ml/2 tbsp five-spice powder
    30ml/2 tbsp sesame oil
    grated rind and juice of 1 orange
    1 medium butternut squash, peeled
      and cubed
    10ml/2 tsp Thai red curry paste
    30ml/2 tbsp Thai fish sauce
    15ml/1 tbsp palm sugar or light
      muscovado (brown) sugar
    300ml/½ pint/1¼ cups coconut milk
    2 fresh red chillies, seeded
    4 kaffir lime leaves, torn
    small bunch coriander (cilantro),
      chopped, to garnish

1 Cut the duck meat into bitesize pieces and place in a bowl with the five-spice powder, sesame oil and orange rind and juice. Stir well to mix all the ingredients and coat the duck in the marinade. Cover the bowl with clear film (plastic wrap) and set aside in a cool place to marinate for at least 15 minutes.

Energy 295Kcal/1241kJ; Protein 31.4g; Carbohydrate 13.3g, of which sugars 12.3g; Fat 15.9g, of which saturates 3.1g; Cholesterol 165mg; Calcium 102mg; Fibre 2g; Sodium 427mg.

RED DUCK CURRY ᵂᴵᵀᴴ PEA AUBERGINES

THIS TASTY CURRY NEEDS TO BE SIMMERED AND THEN LEFT TO STAND TO ALLOW THE FLAVOURS TO BLEND BEAUTIFULLY. USE AN ELECTRIC WOK IF YOU HAVE ONE TO MAINTAIN THE STEADY TEMPERATURE NEEDED FOR GENTLE SIMMERING.

SERVES FOUR

INGREDIENTS
    4 duck breast portions
    400ml/14fl oz can coconut milk
    200ml/7fl oz/scant 1 cup chicken
      stock
    30ml/2 tbsp red Thai curry paste
    8 spring onions (scallions), finely
      sliced
    10ml/2 tsp grated fresh root ginger
    30ml/2 tbsp Chinese rice wine
    15ml/1 tbsp fish sauce
    15ml/1 tbsp soy sauce
    2 lemon grass stalks, halved
      lengthways
    3–4 kaffir lime leaves
    300g/11oz pea aubergines
      (eggplants)
    10ml/2 tsp sugar
    salt and ground black pepper
    10–12 fresh basil and mint leaves, to
      garnish
    steamed jasmine rice, to serve

4 Remove the wok from the heat and leave to stand, covered, for about 15 minutes. Season to taste.

5 Serve the duck curry ladled into shallow bowls, garnished with fresh mint and basil leaves. Serve with steamed jasmine rice.

COOK'S TIP
Tiny pea aubergines (eggplants) are sold in Asian stores. If you can't find them, use regular aubergines cut into chunks.

1 Using a sharp knife, cut the duck breast portions into neat bitesize pieces.

2 Place a wok over a low heat and add the coconut milk, stock, curry paste, spring onions, ginger, rice wine, fish and soy sauces, lemon grass and lime leaves. Stir well to mix, then bring to the boil over a medium heat.

3 Add the duck, aubergines and sugar to the wok and gently simmer for 25–30 minutes, stirring occasionally.

Energy 241Kcal/1017kJ; Protein 31.1g; Carbohydrate 10.2g, of which sugars 10g; Fat 10.5g, of which saturates 2.3g; Cholesterol 165mg; Calcium 65mg; Fibre 1.8g; Sodium 546mg.

SHREDDED DUCK AND NOODLE SALAD

THIS REFRESHING, PIQUANT SALAD MAKES A MOUTHWATERING FIRST COURSE OR LIGHT MEAL. THE MARINATED DUCK IS LOVELY AND MOIST, HAVING BEEN STEAMED IN THE WOK, AND TASTES SUPERB WITH THE FRESH RAW VEGETABLES, NOODLES AND ZESTY DRESSING.

SERVES FOUR

INGREDIENTS
  4 duck breast portions
  30ml/2 tbsp Chinese rice wine
  10ml/2 tsp finely grated fresh
    root ginger
  60ml/4 tbsp soy sauce
  15ml/1 tbsp sesame oil
  15ml/1 tbsp clear honey
  10ml/2 tsp Chinese five-spice powder
  toasted sesame seeds, to sprinkle
For the noodles
  150g/5oz cellophane noodles
  a small handful of fresh mint leaves
  a small handful of coriander
    (cilantro) leaves
  1 red (bell) pepper, seeded and
    finely sliced
  4 spring onions (scallions), finely
    shredded or sliced
  50g/2oz mixed salad leaves
For the dressing
  45ml/3 tbsp light soy sauce
  30ml/2 tbsp mirin
  10ml/2 tsp golden caster
    (superfine) sugar
  1 garlic clove, crushed
  10ml/2 tsp chilli oil

1 Place the duck breast portions in a non-metallic bowl. Mix together the rice wine, ginger, soy sauce, sesame oil, clear honey and five-spice powder. Toss to coat, cover and marinate in the refrigerator for 3–4 hours.

VARIATIONS
If you prefer, you can use shredded chicken in place of the duck.

2 Double over a large sheet of heavy foil. Place the foil on a heatproof plate. Place the duck breast portions on it and spoon the marinade over. Fold the foil to enclose the duck and juices and scrunch the edges to seal.

3 Place a trivet or steamer rack in a large wok and pour in water to a depth of about 5cm/2in. Bring to the boil and place the plate on to the trivet or rack. Cover tightly, reduce the heat and steam gently for 50–60 minutes. Remove the plate from the wok and leave to rest for 15 minutes.

4 Place the noodles in a large bowl and pour over boiling water to cover. Cover and soak for 5–6 minutes. Drain, refresh under cold water and drain again. Put in a bowl with the herbs, red pepper, spring onions and salad leaves.

5 Mix together all the dressing ingredients. Remove the skin from the duck breasts and roughly shred the flesh using a fork. Divide the noodle salad among four plates and top with the shredded duck. Spoon over the dressing, sprinkle with the sesame seeds and serve immediately.

Energy 398Kcal/1671kJ; Protein 32.8g; Carbohydrate 41.7g, of which sugars 10.8g; Fat 11.6g, of which saturates 2.2g; Cholesterol 165mg; Calcium 40mg; Fibre 1g; Sodium 1688mg.

DUCK AND SESAME STIR-FRY

THIS RECIPE COMES FROM NORTHERN THAILAND AND IS INTENDED FOR GAME BIRDS, AS FARMED DUCK WOULD HAVE TOO MUCH FAT. USE WILD DUCK IF YOU CAN GET IT, OR EVEN PARTRIDGE, PHEASANT OR PIGEON. IF YOU DO USE FARMED DUCK, YOU SHOULD REMOVE THE SKIN AND FAT LAYER.

SERVES FOUR

INGREDIENTS
    250g/9oz boneless wild duck meat
    15ml/1 tbsp sesame oil
    15ml/1 tbsp vegetable oil
    4 garlic cloves, finely sliced
    2.5ml/½ tsp dried chilli flakes
    15ml/1 tbsp Thai fish sauce
    15ml/1 tbsp light soy sauce
    120ml/4fl oz/½ cup water
    1 head broccoli, cut into small florets
    coriander (cilantro) and 15ml/1 tbsp
        toasted sesame seeds, to garnish

VARIATIONS
Pak choi (bok choy) or Chinese flowering
cabbage can be used instead of broccoli.

1 Cut the duck meat into bitesize pieces. Heat the wok, add the oils and, when hot, stir-fry the garlic over a medium heat until it is golden brown – do not let it burn. Add the duck to the pan and stir-fry for a further 2 minutes, until the meat begins to brown.

2 Stir in the chilli flakes, fish sauce, soy sauce and water. Add the broccoli and continue to stir-fry for about 2 minutes, until the duck is just cooked through.

3 Serve on warmed plates, garnished with coriander and sesame seeds.

Energy 192Kcal/798kJ; Protein 18.7g; Carbohydrate 2.7g, of which sugars 2.3g; Fat 12.9g, of which saturates 2.1g; Cholesterol 69mg; Calcium 104mg; Fibre 3.6g; Sodium 436mg.

VIETNAMESE LEMON GRASS SNAILS

THE LIVE SNAILS SOLD IN VIETNAMESE MARKETS ARE USUALLY DESTINED FOR THIS POPULAR DELICACY. SERVED STRAIGHT FROM THE BAMBOO STEAMER, THESE LEMON GRASS-INFUSED MORSELS ARE SERVED AS AN APPETIZER, OR AS A SPECIAL SNACK, DIPPED IN NUOC CHAM.

SERVES FOUR

INGREDIENTS

24 fresh snails in their shells
225g/8oz minced (ground) chicken,
  passed through the mincer twice
3 lemon grass stalks, trimmed
  and finely chopped or ground
  (reserve the outer leaves)
2 spring onions (scallions),
  finely chopped
25g/1oz fresh root ginger, peeled and
  finely grated
1 red Thai chilli, seeded and
  finely chopped
10ml/2 tsp sesame or groundnut
  (peanut) oil
sea salt and ground black pepper
nuoc cham or other sauce,
  for dipping

1 Pull the snails out of their shells and place them in a colander. Rinse the snails thoroughly in plenty of cold water and pat dry with kitchen paper. Rinse the shells and leave to drain.

2 Chop the snails finely and put them in a bowl. Add the minced chicken, lemon grass, spring onions, ginger, chilli and oil. Season with salt and pepper and mix all the ingredients together.

3 Select the best of the lemon grass leaves and tear each one into thin ribbons, roughly 7.5cm/3in long. Bend each ribbon in half and put it inside a snail shell, so that the ends are poking out. The idea is that each diner pulls the ends of the lemon grass ribbon to gently prize the steamed morsel out of its shell.

COOK'S TIP
The idea of eating snails may have come from the French, but the method of cooking them in Vietnam is very different. Fresh snails in their shells are available in South-east Asian markets, and in some supermarkets and delicatessens. If you ask for snails in a Vietnamese restaurant, they are likely to be cooked this way.

4 Using your fingers, stuff each shell with the snail and chicken mixture, gently pushing it between the lemon grass ends to the back of the shell so that it fills the shell completely.

5 Fill a wok or large pan a third of the way up with water and bring it to the boil. Arrange the snail shells, open side up, in a steamer that fits the wok or pan.

6 Place the lid on the steamer and steam for about 10 minutes, until the mixture is cooked. Serve hot with *nuoc cham* or another strong-flavoured dipping sauce of your choice, such as soy sauce spiked with chopped chillies.

Energy 136Kcal/573kJ; Protein 24.1g; Carbohydrate 0.2g, of which sugars 0.2g; Fat 4.3g, of which saturates 1.1g; Cholesterol 70mg; Calcium 9mg; Fibre 0.1g; Sodium 700mg.

BALTI CHICKEN WITH PANEER AND PEAS

THIS IS RATHER AN UNUSUAL COMBINATION, BUT IT REALLY WORKS WELL. SERVE WITH PLAIN BOILED RICE. PANEER IS AN INDIAN CHEESE MADE WITH WHOLE MILK, AND IS A USEFUL SOURCE OF PROTEIN IN VEGETARIAN COOKING. HERE IT ADDS EXTRA TEXTURE AND FLAVOUR TO THE DISH.

3 Heat the oil with the whole spices in a wok, then pour the sauce mixture into the oil. Lower the heat and cook gently for about 3 minutes, then pour in the water and bring to a simmer.

SERVES FOUR

INGREDIENTS
1 small chicken, about 675g/1½lb
30ml/2 tbsp tomato purée (paste)
45ml/3 tbsp natural (plain) yogurt
7.5ml/1½ tsp garam masala
5ml/1 tsp crushed garlic
5ml/1 tsp crushed ginger
pinch of ground cardamom
15ml/1 tbsp chilli powder
1.5ml/¼ tsp ground turmeric
5ml/1 tsp salt
5ml/1 tsp sugar
10ml/2 tsp oil
2.5cm/1in cinnamon stick
2 black peppercorns
300ml/½ pint/1¼ cups water
115g/4oz paneer, cubed
30ml/2 tbsp coriander (cilantro) leaves
2 green chillies, seeded and chopped
50g/2oz low fat fromage frais
75g/3oz/¾ cup frozen peas, thawed

1 Skin the chicken and cut it into 6–8 equal pieces.

2 Mix together the tomato purée, yogurt, garam masala, garlic, ginger, cardamom, chilli powder, turmeric, salt and sugar.

COOK'S TIP
As an alternative to paneer, you could use diced tofu in this dish.

4 Add the chicken pieces and stir-fry for about 2 minutes, then cover and cook over a medium heat for 10 minutes.

5 Add the paneer cubes to the pan, followed by half the coriander and half the green chillies. Mix well and cook for a further 5–7 minutes.

6 Stir in the fromage frais and peas, heat through and serve garnished with the reserved coriander and chillies.

Energy 313kcal /1302kJ; protein 27.7g; carbohydrate 7.3g, of which sugars 5.6g; fat 19.1g, of which saturates 5.8g; cholesterol 117mg; calcium 86.5mg; fibre 1.3g; sodium 686mg.

BALTI CHICKEN IN A SPICY LENTIL SAUCE

TRADITIONALLY, THIS DISH IS MADE WITH LAMB, BUT IT IS EQUALLY DELICIOUS MADE WITH CHICKEN, WHICH IS LOWER IN FAT. THE LENTILS ARE FLAVOURED WITH A TARKA, OR "FINAL FRY" OF SPICES, POURED OVER THE DISH JUST BEFORE SERVING.

SERVES FOUR

INGREDIENTS

   30ml/2 tbsp split yellow lentils
   50g/2oz/¼ cup red lentils
   15ml/1 tbsp oil
   2 medium onions, chopped
   5ml/1 tsp crushed garlic
   5ml/1 tsp crushed ginger
   2.5ml/½ tsp ground turmeric
   7.5ml/1½ tsp chilli powder
   5ml/1 tsp garam masala
   2.5ml/½ tsp ground coriander
   7.5ml/1½ tsp salt
   175g/6oz chicken breast fillets,
    skinned and cubed
   45ml/3 tbsp fresh coriander (cilantro)
    leaves
   1–2 green chillies, seeded and
    chopped
   30–45ml/2–3 tbsp lemon juice
   300ml/1/2 pint/1¼ cups water
   2 tomatoes, peeled and halved
For the *tarka*
   5ml/1 tsp oil
   2.5ml/1/2 tsp cumin seeds
   2 garlic cloves
   2 dried red chillies
   4 curry leaves

3 Add the chicken pieces and stir-fry for 5–7 minutes to seal in the juices and lightly brown the meat.

4 Add half the fresh coriander, the green chillies, lemon juice and water. Cook for 5 minutes. Add the lentils.

5 Add the tomatoes and remaining coriander. Take off the heat.

6 To make the tarka, heat the oil and add the cumin seeds, garlic cloves, dried chillies and curry leaves. When hot, pour on top of the dhal and serve.

1 Boil the yellow and red lentils together in a pan of water until soft and mushy. Set aside.

2 Heat the oil in a wok or heavy-based frying pan and fry the chopped onions until they are soft and golden brown. Stir in the garlic, ginger, turmeric, chilli powder, garam masala, ground coriander and salt.

Energy 196kcal/823kJ; Protein 20.3g; Carbohydrate 9.8g, of which sugars 2.6g; Fat 8.7g, of which saturates 1.2g; Cholesterol 47mg; Calcium 41mg; Fibre 2.5g; Sodium 51mg.

KASHMIRI CHICKEN CURRY

THIS MILD YET FLAVOURSOME DISH IS GIVEN A SPECIAL LIFT BY THE ADDITION OF SLICED APPLES.

SERVES FOUR

INGREDIENTS
   10ml/2 tsp oil
   2 medium onions, diced
   1 bay leaf
   2 cloves
   2.5cm/1in cinnamon stick
   4 black peppercorns
   1 baby chicken, about 675g/1½lb,
     skinned and cut into 8 pieces
   5ml/1 tsp garam masala
   5ml/1 tsp crushed fresh ginger
   5ml/1 tsp crushed garlic
   5ml/1 tsp salt
   5ml/1 tsp chilli powder
   15ml/1 tbsp ground almonds
   150ml/¼ pint/⅔ cup natural (plain)
     yogurt
   2 green eating apples, peeled, cored
     and roughly sliced
   15ml/1 tbsp chopped fresh coriander
     (cilantro) leaves
   15g/½oz flaked (sliced) almonds,
     toasted, and fresh coriander
     (cilantro) leaves, to garnish

1 Heat the oil in a wok or heavy-based frying pan and fry the onions with the bay leaf, cloves, cinnamon and peppercorns for about 3–5 minutes until the onions are beginning to soften without browning.

2 Add the chicken pieces and continue to stir-fry for at least another 3 minutes.

COOK'S TIP
Serve this rich and creamy chicken dish with plain rice.

3 Lower the heat and add the garam masala, ginger, garlic, salt, chilli powder and ground almonds and continue to stir for 2–3 minutes. Pour in the yogurt and stir for a couple more minutes.

4 Add the apples and chopped coriander, cover and cook for 10–15 minutes, until the chicken is cooked.

5 Garnish with flaked almonds and whole coriander leaves and serve.

Energy 384kcal /1598kJ; protein 25.4g; carbohydrate 18.4g, of which sugars 15.3g; fat 23.7g, of which saturates 5.2g; cholesterol 111mg; calcium 139mg; fibre 3.7g; sodium 616mg.

BALTI CHICKEN WITH CUMIN AND POTATOES

THE POTATOES ARE COOKED SEPARATELY IN THE OVEN BEFORE BEING ADDED TO THIS CHICKEN DISH.

SERVES FOUR

INGREDIENTS
150ml/¼ pint/⅔ cup natural (plain)
    yogurt
25g/1oz ground almonds
7.5ml/1½ tsp ground coriander
2.5ml/½ tsp chilli powder
5ml/1 tsp garam masala
15ml/1 tbsp coconut milk
5ml/1 tsp crushed garlic
5ml/1 tsp crushed fresh ginger
30ml/2 tbsp chopped fresh coriander
    (cilantro) leaves
1 red chilli, seeded and chopped
225g/8oz skinless chicken breasts,
    boned and cubed
15ml/1 tbsp oil
2 medium onions, sliced
3 green cardamom pods
2.5cm/1in cinnamon stick
2 cloves
For the potatoes
15ml/1 tbsp oil
8 baby potatoes, thickly sliced
1.5ml/1/4 tsp cumin seeds
15ml/1 tbsp finely chopped
    fresh coriander (cilantro)

1 In a bowl, mix together the yogurt, ground almonds, ground coriander, chilli powder, garam masala, coconut milk, garlic, ginger, half the fresh coriander and half the red chilli.

2 Place the chicken pieces in the mixture, mix well and leave to marinate for about 2 hours.

VARIATION
Fresh mint may be added to the potatoes if you like them with a minty flavour.

3 Heat the oil in a wok or heavy frying pan. Add the sliced potatoes, cumin seeds and fresh coriander and quickly stir-fry for 2–3 minutes.

4 Transfer to an ovenproof dish and cook in the oven at 180°C/ 350°F/Gas 4 for 30 minutes, until cooked.

5 Heat the oil in the wok with the onions, cardamoms, cinnamon and cloves for about 2 minutes. Add the chicken mixture and stir-fry for 5 minutes. Lower the heat and cook for 8 minutes. Serve with the potatoes, garnished with coriander and chilli.

Energy 169kcal/711kJ; Protein 16.8g; Carbohydrate 16.2g, of which sugars 5.9g; Fat 4.6g, of which saturates 0.6g; Cholesterol 39mg; Calcium 128mg; Fibre 4.4g; Sodium 75mg.

BALTI CHICKEN WITH LENTILS

THIS IS RATHER AN UNUSUAL COMBINATION OF FLAVOURS, BUT IT IS CERTAINLY WORTH TRYING. THE MANGO POWDER GIVES A DELICIOUS TANGY FLAVOUR TO THIS SPICY DISH.

SERVES FOUR TO SIX

INGREDIENTS
   75g/3oz split yellow lentils
   60ml/4 tbsp corn oil
   2 medium leeks, chopped
   6 large dried red chillies
   4 curry leaves
   5ml/1 tsp mustard seeds
   10ml/2 tsp mango powder
   2 medium tomatoes, roughly
     chopped
   2.5ml/½ tsp chilli powder
   5ml/1 tsp ground coriander
   450g/1lb boneless chicken, skinned
     and cubed
   salt
   15ml/1 tbsp chopped fresh coriander
     (cilantro), to garnish

1 Put the lentils in a sieve (strainer) and wash under cold running water.

2 Put the lentils in a pan and add water just to cover. Bring to the boil and cook for 10 minutes or until they are soft but not mushy. Drain thoroughly, transfer to a bowl and set aside.

3 Heat the oil in a wok and add the leeks, dried red chillies, curry leaves and mustard seeds. Stir-fry gently for 2–3 minutes.

4 Add the mango powder, tomatoes, chilli powder, ground coriander, chicken and salt and stir-fry for 7–10 minutes.

5 Mix in the cooked lentils and fry for a further 2 minutes or until the chicken is cooked through. Garnish with fresh coriander and serve immediately.

COOK'S TIP
Split yellow lentils, known as *chana dhal*, are available from Asian stores. However, if you cannot get them, split yellow peas are a good substitute.

Energy 199kcal/835kJ; Protein 24.9g; Carbohydrate 8.1g, of which sugars 2.2g; Fat 7.6g, of which saturates 1.1g; Cholesterol 62mg; Calcium 36mg; Fibre 2.1g; Sodium 63mg.

AROMATIC CHICKEN FROM MADURA

*THIS DISH IS BEST COOKED AHEAD SO THAT THE FLAVOURS HAVE TIME TO PERMEATE THE CHICKEN
FLESH, MAKING IT EVEN MORE DELICIOUS. A COOL CUCUMBER SALAD IS A GOOD ACCOMPANIMENT.*

SERVES FOUR

INGREDIENTS

1.5kg/3½lb chicken, cut in
    quarters, or 4 chicken quarters
5ml/1 tsp sugar
30ml/2 tbsp coriander seeds
10ml/2 tsp cumin seeds
6 whole cloves
2.5ml/½ tsp ground nutmeg
2.5ml/½ tsp ground turmeric
1 small onion
2.5cm/1in fresh root ginger, peeled
    and sliced
300ml/½ pint/1¼ cups chicken stock
    or water
salt and freshly ground black pepper
boiled rice and deep-fried onion
    rings, to serve

1 Cut each chicken quarter in half and
place in a flameproof casserole or wok,
sprinkle with sugar and salt and toss
together. Use any remaining bones to
make chicken stock for use later in the
recipe if you like.

2 Dry-fry the coriander, cumin and
whole cloves until the spices give off a
good aroma. Add the nutmeg and
turmeric and heat briefly. Grind in a
food processor or a pestle and mortar.

3 If using a processor, process the
onion and ginger until finely chopped.
Otherwise, finely chop the onion and
ginger and pound to a paste with a
pestle and mortar. Add the spices and
stock or water and mix well.

COOK'S TIP
Add a large piece of bruised ginger and
a small onion when making the chicken
stock to ensure a good flavour.

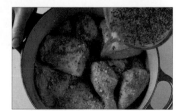

4 Pour the spice mixture over the
chicken joints in the casserole or wok.
Cover with a lid and cook over a gentle
heat until the chicken pieces are really
tender and the sauce is reduced, about
45–50 minutes.

5 Serve portions of the chicken, with
the sauce, on a bed boiled rice,
scattered with crisp deep-fried
onion rings.

Energy 604kcal/2514kJ; Protein 55.7g; Carbohydrate 4.1g, of which sugars 2.2g; Fat 40.6g, of which saturates 10.8g; Cholesterol 330mg; Calcium 66mg; Fibre 1.7g; Sodium 269mg.

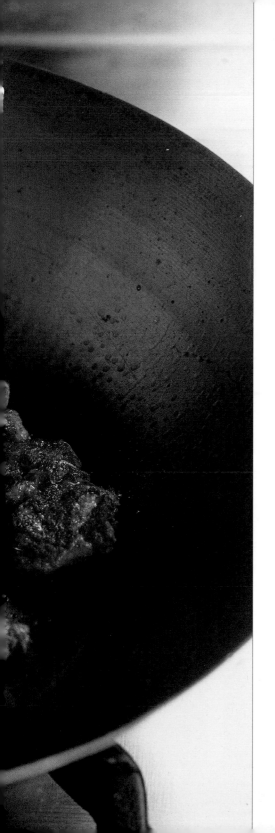

MEAT DISHES

Rich meat curries and gently simmered dishes lend themselves perfectly to wok cooking, with great depths of flavour coming from ingredients such as chillies, garlic, shallots, ginger or galangal. Fresh lemon grass and coriander are often included, and smooth, sweet coconut milk is often the liquid that marries these robust tastes together and tames their stridency. From this chapter try Beef Rendang for a typically intense dish, or you could opt for the less spicy — but still flavoursome — Chinese Braised Pork Belly with Greens.

GREEN BEEF CURRY WITH THAI AUBERGINES

THIS IS A VERY QUICK CURRY SO BE SURE TO USE GOOD QUALITY MEAT. SIRLOIN IS RECOMMENDED, BUT TENDER RUMP STEAK COULD BE USED INSTEAD. IF YOU BUY THE CURRY PASTE, THERE'S VERY LITTLE ADDITIONAL PREPARATION, BUT YOU COULD MAKE IT FROM SCRATCH IF YOU PREFER.

SERVES FOUR TO SIX

INGREDIENTS

   450g/1lb sirloin steak
   15ml/1 tbsp vegetable oil
   45ml/3 tbsp Thai green curry paste
   600ml/1 pint/2½ cups coconut milk
   4 kaffir lime leaves, torn
   15–30ml/1–2 tbsp Thai fish sauce
   5ml/1 tsp palm sugar or light
     muscovado (brown) sugar
   150g/5oz small Thai aubergines
     (eggplant), halved
   small handful of fresh Thai basil
   2 fresh green chillies, to garnish

1 Trim off any excess fat from the beef. Using a sharp knife, cut it into long, thin strips. This is easiest to do if it is well chilled. Set it aside.

2 Heat the oil in a wok. Add the curry paste and cook for 1–2 minutes, until you can smell the fragrances.

3 Stir in half the coconut milk, a little at a time. Cook, stirring frequently, for about 5–6 minutes, until an oily sheen appears on the surface of the liquid.

4 Add the beef to the pan with the kaffir lime leaves, Thai fish sauce, sugar and aubergine halves. Cook for 2–3 minutes, then stir in the remaining coconut milk.

5 Bring back to a simmer and cook until the meat and aubergines are tender. Stir in the Thai basil just before serving. Finely shred the green chillies and use to garnish the curry.

GREEN CURRY PASTE
To make the curry paste from scratch, put 15 fresh green chillies, 2 chopped lemon grass stalks, 3 sliced shallots, 2 garlic cloves, 15ml/1 tbsp chopped galangal, 4 chopped kaffir lime leaves, 2.5ml/½ tsp grated kaffir lime rind, 5ml/1 tsp chopped coriander root, 6 black peppercorns, 5ml/1 tsp each roasted coriander and cumin seeds, 15ml/1 tbsp granulated sugar, 5ml/1 tsp salt and 5ml/1 tsp shrimp paste into a food processor and process until smooth. Gradually add 30ml/2 tbsp vegetable oil, processing after each addition.

Energy 146Kcal/615kJ; Protein 18.2g; Carbohydrate 6.2g, of which sugars 6.1g; Fat 5.6g, of which saturates 1.9g; Cholesterol 38mg; Calcium 36mg; Fibre 0.5g; Sodium 163mg.

DRY BEEF CURRY WITH PEANUT AND LIME

ALTHOUGH THIS IS CALLED A DRY CURRY, THE DESCRIPTION SIMPLY MEANS THE MEAT ISN'T SWIMMING IN LIQUID. THE METHOD OF COOKING IN THE WOK ENSURES THAT THE BEEF ABSORBS THE COCONUT MILK AND PEANUT BUTTER MIXTURE AND STAYS SUCCULENT.

SERVES FOUR TO SIX

INGREDIENTS
    400g/14oz can coconut milk
    900g/2lb stewing steak,
        finely chopped
    300ml/½ pint/1¼ cups beef stock
    30ml/2 tbsp crunchy peanut butter
    juice of 2 limes
    lime slices, shredded coriander
        (cilantro) and fresh red chilli slices,
        to garnish
For the red curry paste
    30ml/2 tbsp coriander seeds
    5ml/1 tsp cumin seeds
    seeds from 6 green cardamom pods
    2.5ml/½ tsp grated or ground nutmeg
    1.5ml/¼ tsp ground cloves
    2.5ml/½ tsp ground cinnamon
    20ml/4 tsp paprika
    pared rind of 1 mandarin orange,
        finely chopped
    4–5 small fresh red chillies, seeded
        and finely chopped
    25ml/1½ tsp granulated sugar
    2.5ml/½ tsp salt
    1 piece lemon grass, about 10cm/4in
        long, shredded
    3 garlic cloves, crushed
    2cm/¾in piece fresh galangal,
        peeled and finely chopped
    4 red shallots, finely chopped
    1 piece shrimp paste,
        2cm/¾in square
    50g/2oz coriander (cilantro) root or
        stem, chopped
    juice of ½ lime
    30ml/2 tbsp vegetable oil

1 Strain the coconut milk into a bowl, retaining the thicker coconut milk in the strainer or sieve.

2 Pour the thin coconut milk from the bowl into a large, heavy pan, then scrape in half the residue from the sieve. Reserve the remaining thick coconut milk. Add the chopped steak. Pour in the beef stock and bring to the boil. Reduce the heat, cover the pan and simmer gently for 50 minutes.

3 Make the curry paste. Dry-fry all the seeds for 1–2 minutes. Tip into a bowl and add the nutmeg, cloves, cinnamon, paprika and orange rind. Pound the chillies with the sugar and salt. Add the spice mixture, lemon grass, garlic, galangal, shallots and shrimp paste and pound to a paste. Work in the coriander, lime juice and oil.

4 Strain the beef, reserving the cooking liquid, and place a cupful of liquid in a wok. Stir in 30–45ml/2–3 tbsp of the curry paste, according to taste. Boil rapidly until all the liquid has evaporated. Stir in the reserved thick coconut milk, the peanut butter and the beef. Simmer, uncovered, for 15–20 minutes, adding a little more cooking liquid if the mixture starts to stick to the pan, but keep the curry dry.

5 Just before serving, stir in the lime juice. Serve in warmed bowls, garnished with the lime slices, shredded coriander and sliced red chillies.

VARIATION
The curry is equally delicious made with lean leg or shoulder of lamb.

Energy 296Kcal/1238kJ; Protein 35.2g; Carbohydrate 4.9g, of which sugars 4.5g; Fat 15.2g, of which saturates 4.8g; Cholesterol 103mg; Calcium 66mg; Fibre 0.7g; Sodium 262mg.

BEEF STEW <u>WITH</u> STAR ANISE <u>AND</u> BASIL

THE VIETNAMESE PRIZE THIS DISH FOR BREAKFAST, AND ON CHILLY MORNINGS PEOPLE QUEUE UP FOR A BOWL OF THIT BO KHO ON THEIR WAY TO WORK. TRADITIONALLY, IT HAS AN ORANGE HUE FROM THE OIL IN WHICH ANNATTO SEEDS HAVE BEEN FRIED, BUT HERE THE COLOUR COMES FROM TURMERIC.

SERVES FOUR TO SIX

INGREDIENTS

500g/1¼lb lean beef, cut into
  bitesize cubes
15ml/1 tbsp ground turmeric
30ml/2 tbsp sesame or
  vegetable oil
3 shallots, chopped
3 garlic cloves, chopped
2 red chillies, seeded and chopped
2 lemon grass stalks, cut into several
  pieces and bruised
15ml/1 tbsp curry powder
4 star anise, roasted and ground to
  a powder
700ml/scant 1¼ pints hot beef or
  chicken stock, or boiling water
45ml/3 tbsp *nuoc mam*
30ml/2 tbsp soy sauce
15ml/1 tbsp raw cane sugar
1 bunch fresh basil, stalks removed
salt and ground black pepper
1 onion, halved and finely sliced, and
  chopped fresh coriander (cilantro)
  leaves, to garnish
steamed fragrant or sticky rice, or
  chunks of baguette, to serve

2 Add the curry powder, all but 10ml/ 2 tsp of the roasted star anise, and the beef. Brown the beef, then pour in the stock or water, *nuoc mam*, soy sauce and sugar. Stir and bring to the boil. Reduce the heat and cook gently for about 40 minutes, or until the meat is tender and the liquid has reduced.

3 Season to taste with salt and pepper, stir in the reserved roasted star anise, and add the basil. Transfer the stew to a serving dish and garnish with the sliced onion and coriander leaves.

4 Serve with steamed fragrant or sticky rice, or chunks of baguette.

1 Toss the beef in the ground turmeric and set aside. Heat a wok or heavy pan and add the oil. Stir in the shallots, garlic, chillies and lemon grass, and cook until they become fragrant.

COOK'S TIP
If you prefer to use annatto seeds instead of turmeric, they can be found in some Asian supermarkets. Fry 15ml/1 tbsp seeds in a little oil.

Energy 314Kcal/1312kJ; Protein 33g; Carbohydrate 17g, of which sugars 11g; Fat 14g, of which saturates 4g; Cholesterol 64mg; Calcium 64mg; Fibre 1.7g; Sodium 150mg.

MINCED MEAT WITH CHARRED AUBERGINE

VARIATIONS OF THIS DISH CROP UP IN DIFFERENT PARTS OF SOUTH-EAST ASIA. TO ATTAIN THE UNIQUE, SMOKY FLAVOUR, THE AUBERGINES ARE CHARRED OVER A FLAME, OR CHARCOAL GRILL, THEN SKINNED, CHOPPED TO A PULP AND ADDED TO THE DISH.

SERVES FOUR

INGREDIENTS

   2 aubergines (eggplants)
   15ml/1 tbsp vegetable or groundnut
     (peanut) oil
   2 shallots, finely chopped
   4 garlic cloves, peeled and
     finely chopped
   1 red Thai chilli, finely chopped
   350g/12oz minced (ground) beef
   30ml/2 tbsp *tuk trey* or *nuoc mam*
   sea salt and ground black pepper
   crusty bread or rice and salad,
     to serve

VARIATION

This dish can also be made with beef or pork   either way it is delicious served with chunks of fresh, crusty bread.

1 Place the aubergines directly over an open flame. Turn them over from time to time, until the skin is charred all over. Put the aubergines into a plastic bag to sweat for a few minutes.

2 Hold each aubergine by its stalk under running cold water, while you peel off the skin. Squeeze out the excess water and chop them roughly on a board.

3 Heat the oil in a large, heavy pan. Stir in the shallots, garlic and chilli and fry until golden. Add the minced beef and stir-fry for about 5 minutes.

4 Stir in the *tuk trey* or *nuoc mam* and the aubergine and cook gently for about 20 minutes, until the meat is tender. Season with salt and pepper and serve with crusty bread or rice and a salad.

Energy 245Kcal/1019kJ; Protein 19g; Carbohydrate 4g, of which sugars 3.4g; Fat 17g, of which saturates 6g; Cholesterol 53mg; Calcium 23mg; Fibre 2.2g; Sodium 607mg.

SEARED GARLIC BEEF DIPPED IN LIME JUICE

THIS DISH CAN BE MADE WITH BEEF OR QUAIL. FLAVOURED WITH LOTS OF GARLIC, THE MARINADED CHUNKS OF BEEF ARE WRAPPED IN LETTUCE LEAVES AND DIPPED IN A PIQUANT LIME SAUCE. THE BEEF CAN BE SEARED IN A WOK, OR CHARGRILLED.

SERVES FOUR

INGREDIENTS
  350g/12oz beef fillet or sirloin, cut
    into bitesize chunks
  15ml/1 tbsp sugar
  juice of 3 limes
  2 garlic cloves, crushed
  7.5ml/1½ tsp ground black pepper
  30ml/2 tbsp unsalted roasted
    peanuts, finely chopped
  12 lettuce leaves
For the marinade
  15ml/1 tbsp groundnut (peanut) oil
  45ml/3 tbsp mushroom soy sauce
  10ml/2 tsp soy sauce
  15ml/1 tbsp sugar
  2 garlic cloves, crushed
  7.5ml/1½ tsp ground black pepper

1 To make the marinade, beat together the oil, the two soy sauces and the sugar in a bowl, until the sugar has dissolved. Add the garlic and pepper and mix well. Add the beef and coat in the marinade. Leave for 1–2 hours.

2 In a small bowl, stir the sugar into the lime juice, until it has dissolved. Add the garlic and black pepper and beat well. Stir in the peanuts and put aside.

3 Heat a wok or heavy pan and sear the meat on all sides. Serve immediately with lettuce leaves for wrapping and the lime sauce for dipping.

Energy 237Kcal/986kJ; Protein 22g; Carbohydrate 5.2g, of which sugars 4.7g; Fat 14g, of which saturates 4g; Cholesterol 51mg; Calcium 12mg; Fibre 0.5g; Sodium 324mg.

STIR-FRIED BEEF IN OYSTER SAUCE

THIS IS ANOTHER SIMPLE BUT DELICIOUS RECIPE. IT IS OFTEN MADE WITH JUST ONE TYPE OF MUSHROOM, SUCH AS OYSTER, BUT USING A MIXTURE MAKES THE DISH MORE INTERESTING. OYSTER SAUCE ADDS A SAVOURY DEPTH TO THE DISH AND IS AN ESSENTIAL INGREDIENT.

3 Heat half the oil in a wok or large, heavy frying pan. Add the garlic and ginger and cook for 1–2 minutes, until fragrant. Drain the steak, add it to the wok or pan and stir well to separate the strips. Cook, stirring frequently, for a further 1–2 minutes, until the steak is browned all over and tender. Remove from the wok or pan and set aside.

4 Heat the remaining oil in the wok or pan. Add the shiitake, oyster and straw mushrooms. Stir-fry over a medium heat until golden brown.

5 Return the steak to the wok and mix it with the mushrooms. Spoon in the oyster sauce and sugar, mix well, then add ground black pepper to taste. Toss over the heat until all the ingredients are thoroughly combined.

6 Stir in the spring onions. Tip the mixture on to a serving platter, garnish with the strips of red chilli and serve.

SERVES FOUR TO SIX

INGREDIENTS
  450g/1lb rump (round) or sirloin
    steak
  30ml/2 tbsp soy sauce
  15ml/1 tbsp cornflour (cornstarch)
  45ml/3 tbsp groundnut (peanut) oil
    or vegetable oil
  15ml/1 tbsp chopped garlic
  15ml/1 tbsp chopped fresh
    root ginger
  225g/8oz/3¼ cups mixed mushrooms
    such as shiitake, oyster and straw
  30ml/2 tbsp oyster sauce
  5ml/1 tsp granulated sugar
  4 spring onions (scallions), cut into
    short lengths
  ground black pepper
  2 fresh red chillies, seeded and cut
    into strips, to garnish

1 Place the steak in the freezer for 30–40 minutes, until firm, then, using a sharp knife, slice it on the diagonal into long thin strips.

2 Mix together the soy sauce and cornflour in a large bowl. Add the steak, turning to coat well, cover with clear film (plastic wrap) and leave to marinate at room temperature for 1–2 hours.

Energy 160Kcal/670kJ; Protein 17.6g; Carbohydrate 2.9g, of which sugars 2.7g; Fat 8.8g, of which saturates 2g; Cholesterol 44mg; Calcium 10mg; Fibre 0.6g; Sodium 485mg.

THIS IS CRISPY NOODLES WITH BEEF

THIS IS A GREAT WOK-BASED MEAL — WHEN THE VERMICELLI IS ADDED TO THE HOT OIL IT EXPANDS TO AT LEAST FOUR TIMES ITS ORIGINAL SIZE. THE STRANDS ALSO BECOME CRISP AND CRUNCHY, ADDING A GREAT CONTRAST TO THE BEEF AND VEGETABLE STIR-FRY.

SERVES FOUR

INGREDIENTS

450g/1lb rump (round) steak
teriyaki sauce, for brushing
175g/6oz rice vermicelli
groundnut (peanut) oil, for deep-
  frying and stir-frying
8 spring onions (scallions),
  diagonally sliced
2 garlic cloves, crushed
4–5 carrots, cut into julienne strips
1–2 fresh red chillies, seeded and
  finely sliced
2 small courgettes (zucchini),
  diagonally sliced
5ml/1 tsp grated fresh root ginger
60ml/4 tbsp rice vinegar
90ml/6 tbsp light soy sauce
about 475ml/16fl oz/2 cups
  beef stock

1 Beat the steak to about 2.5cm/1in thick. Place in a shallow dish, brush generously with the teriyaki sauce and set aside for 2–4 hours to marinate.

2 Separate the rice vermicelli into manageable loops. Pour oil into a large wok to a depth of about 5cm/2in, and heat until a strand of vermicelli cooks as soon as it is lowered into the oil.

3 Carefully add a loop of vermicelli to the oil. Almost immediately, turn to cook on the other side, then remove and drain on kitchen paper. Repeat with the remaining loops. Transfer the cooked noodles to a deep serving bowl and keep them warm.

4 Strain the oil from the wok into a heatproof bowl and set it aside. Return 15ml/1 tbsp oil to a clean wok. When it sizzles, fry the steak for about 30 seconds on each side, until browned. Transfer to a board and cut into thick slices. The meat should be well browned on the outside but still pink inside. Set aside.

5 Add a little extra oil to the wok, add the spring onions, garlic and carrots and stir-fry over a medium heat for 5–6 minutes, until the carrots are slightly soft and have a glazed appearance. Add the chillies, courgettes and ginger and stir-fry for 1–2 minutes.

6 Stir in the rice vinegar, soy sauce and stock. Cook for 4 minutes, or until the sauce has thickened slightly. Return the slices of steak to the wok and cook for a further 1–2 minutes.

7 Spoon the steak, vegetables and sauce over the noodles and toss lightly and carefully to mix. Serve immediately.

COOK'S TIP
As soon as you add the meat mixture to the noodles, they will begin to soften in the sauce. If you wish to keep a few crispy noodles, leave some on the surface so that they do not come into contact with the hot liquid.

Energy 410Kcal/1712kJ; Protein 30.7g; Carbohydrate 41.4g, of which sugars 6.6g; Fat 13.5g, of which saturates 3g; Cholesterol 66mg; Calcium 49mg; Fibre 1.9g; Sodium 1687mg.

BEEF RENDANG

IN INDONESIA, WHERE THIS SPICY DISH ORIGINATED, IT IS USUALLY SERVED WITH THE MEAT QUITE DRY; IF YOU PREFER MORE SAUCE, SIMPLY ADD MORE WATER WHEN STIRRING IN THE POTATOES. THE DEEP-FRIED ONIONS, TRADITIONALLY SERVED WITH THE BEEF, ADD A DELICIOUS, CRISPY CONTRAST.

SERVES SIX–EIGHT

INGREDIENTS
  2 onions or 5–6 shallots, chopped
  4 garlic cloves, chopped
  2.5cm/1in piece fresh galangal,
    peeled and sliced, or 15ml/1 tbsp
    galangal paste
  2.5cm/1in piece fresh root ginger,
    peeled and sliced
  4–6 fresh red chillies, seeded
    and roughly chopped
  lower part only of 1 lemon grass
    stem, sliced
  2.5cm/1in piece fresh turmeric,
    peeled and sliced, or 5ml/1 tsp
    ground turmeric
  1kg/2¼lb prime beef in one piece
  5ml/1 tsp coriander seeds,
    dry-fried
  5ml/1 tsp cumin seeds, dry-fried
  2 kaffir lime leaves, torn into
    pieces
  2 x 400ml/14fl oz cans coconut
    milk
  300ml/½ pint/1¼ cups water
  30ml/2 tbsp dark soy sauce
  5ml/1 tsp tamarind pulp, soaked in
    60ml/4 tbsp warm water
  8–10 small new potatoes, well
    scrubbed and eyed
  salt and ground black pepper
  deep-fried onions (see below),
    sliced fresh red chillies and spring
    onions (scallions), to garnish

1 Put the onions or shallots in a food processor. Add the garlic, galangal, ginger, chillies, sliced lemon grass and fresh or ground turmeric. Process to a fine paste or grind in a mortar, using a pestle.

2 Cut the meat into cubes using a large sharp knife, then place the cubes in a bowl.

3 Grind the dry-fried coriander and cumin seeds, then add to the meat with the onion, chilli paste and kaffir lime leaves; stir well. Cover and leave in a cool place to marinate while you prepare the other ingredients.

COOK'S TIP
This dish is even better if you can cook it a day or two in advance of serving, which allows the flavours to mellow beautifully. Add the potatoes on reheating and simmer until tender.

4 Pour the coconut milk and water into a wok, then stir in the spiced meat and the soy sauce. Strain the tamarind water and add to the wok. Stir over medium heat until the liquid boils, then simmer gently, half-covered, for 1½ hours.

5 Add the potatoes and simmer for 20–25 minutes, or until the meat and the potatoes are tender. Add water if you prefer. Season and serve, garnished with the deep-fried onions, chillies and spring onions.

DEEP-FRIED ONIONS

KNOWN AS BAWANG GORENG, THESE ARE A TRADITIONAL GARNISH AND ACCOMPANY MANY INDONESIAN DISHES. ORIENTAL STORES SELL THEM READY-PREPARED, BUT IT IS EASY TO MAKE THEM. THE SMALL RED ONIONS SOLD IN ASIAN STORES ARE EXCELLENT BECAUSE THEY CONTAIN LESS WATER.

MAKES 450G/1LB

INGREDIENTS
  450g/1lb onions
  vegetable oil, for deep-frying

1 Thinly slice the onions with a sharp knife or in a food processor. Spread the slices out in a single layer on several sheets of kitchen paper and leave them to dry, in an airy place, for no less than 30 minutes and up to 2 hours.

2 Heat the oil in a wok to 190°C/375°F. Fry the onions in batches, until crisp and golden, turning all the time. Drain well on kitchen paper, cool and store in an airtight container, unless you are using them immediately.

Energy 289Kcal/1210kJ; Protein 30.2g; Carbohydrate 15.4g, of which sugars 8.6g; Fat 12.2g, of which saturates 5g; Cholesterol 73mg; Calcium 63mg; Fibre 1.4g; Sodium 465mg.
Energy 854Kcal/3521kJ; Protein 5.4g; Carbohydrate 35.5g, of which sugars 25.2g; Fat 77.8g, of which saturates 9g; Cholesterol 0mg; Calcium 113mg; Fibre 6.3g; Sodium 14mg.

BEEF AND BUTTERNUT SQUASH WITH CHILLI

STIR-FRIED BEEF AND SWEET, ORANGE-FLESHED SQUASH FLAVOURED WITH WARM SPICES, OYSTER SAUCE AND FRESH HERBS MAKES A ROBUST MAIN COURSE WHEN SERVED WITH RICE OR EGG NOODLES. THE ADDITION OF CHILLI AND FRESH ROOT GINGER GIVES THE DISH A WONDERFUL VIGOROUS BITE.

SERVES FOUR

INGREDIENTS

30ml/2 tbsp sunflower oil
2 onions, cut into thick slices
500g/1¼lb butternut squash,
   peeled, seeded and cut into thin
   strips
675g/1½lb fillet steak
   (beef tenderloin)
60ml/4 tbsp soy sauce
90g/3½oz/½ cup golden caster
   (superfine) sugar
1 fresh bird's eye chilli, seeded
   and chopped
15ml/1 tbsp finely shredded fresh
   root ginger
30ml/2 tbsp Thai fish sauce
5ml/1 tsp ground star anise
5ml/1 tsp five-spice powder
15ml/1 tbsp oyster sauce
4 spring onions (scallions), shredded
a small handful of sweet basil leaves
a small handful of mint leaves

1 Heat a wok over a medium-high heat and add the oil, trickling it down just below the rim so that it coats the surface. When hot, stir in the onions and squash. Stir-fry for 2–3 minutes, then reduce the heat, cover and cook gently for 5–6 minutes, or until the vegetables are just tender.

2 Place the beef between 2 sheets of clear film (plastic wrap) and beat, with a mallet or rolling pin, until thin. Using a sharp knife, cut into thin strips.

3 In a separate wok, mix the soy sauce, sugar, chilli, ginger, fish sauce, star anise, five-spice powder and oyster sauce. Stir-fry for 3–4 minutes.

4 Add the beef to the soy sauce mixture in the wok and cook over a high heat for 3–4 minutes. Remove from the heat. Add the onion and squash slices to the beef and toss well with the spring onions and herbs. Serve immediately.

Energy 500Kcal/2093kJ; Protein 41.3g; Carbohydrate 36.9g, of which sugars 33.8g; Fat 21.7g, of which saturates 7.2g; Cholesterol 98mg; Calcium 91mg; Fibre 2.9g; Sodium 1243mg.

SPICY SHREDDED BEEF

THE ESSENCE OF THIS RECIPE IS THAT THE BEEF IS CUT INTO VERY FINE STRIPS BEFORE BEING STIR-FRIED. THIS IS EASIER TO ACHIEVE IF THE PIECE OF BEEF IS PLACED IN THE FREEZER FOR 30 MINUTES UNTIL IT IS VERY FIRM BEFORE BEING SLICED WITH A SHARP KNIFE.

SERVES TWO

INGREDIENTS

225g/8oz rump (round) steak
15ml/1 tbsp each light and dark
   soy sauce
15ml/1 tbsp rice wine or
   medium-dry sherry
5ml/1 tsp dark brown soft sugar or
   golden granulated sugar
90ml/6 tbsp vegetable oil
1 large onion, thinly sliced
2.5cm/1in piece fresh root ginger,
   peeled and grated
1–2 carrots, cut into matchsticks
2–3 fresh or dried chillies, halved,
   seeded (optional) and chopped
salt and ground black pepper
fresh chives, to garnish

3 Heat a wok and add half the oil. When it is hot, stir-fry the onion and ginger for 3–4 minutes, then transfer to a plate. Add the carrot, stir-fry for 3–4 minutes until slightly softened, then transfer to a plate and keep warm.

4 Heat the remaining oil in the wok, then quickly add the beef, with the marinade, followed by the chillies.

5 Cook over high heat for 2 minutes, stirring all the time. Return the fried onion and ginger to the wok and stir-fry for 1 minute more.

6 Season with salt and pepper to taste, cover and cook for 30 seconds. Spoon the meat into two warmed bowls and add the strips of carrots. Garnish with fresh chives and serve.

1 With a sharp knife, slice the well-chilled beef very thinly, then cut each slice into fine strips or shreds.

2 Mix together the light and dark soy sauces with the rice wine or sherry and sugar in a bowl. Add the strips of beef and stir well to ensure they are evenly coated with the marinade.

COOK'S TIP
Remove and discard the seeds from the chillies before you chop them – unless, of course, you like really fiery food. In which case, you could add some or all of the seeds with the chopped chillies.

Energy 532Kcal/2207kJ; Protein 27.3g; Carbohydrate 19.3g, of which sugars 15.4g; Fat 38.1g, of which saturates 5.8g; Cholesterol 66mg; Calcium 59mg; Fibre 3.3g; Sodium 1154mg.

STIR-FRIED PORK WITH PEANUTS AND BASIL

PORK OR CHICKEN STIR-FRIED WITH NUTS AND HERBS, WITH A SPLASH OF CITRUS FLAVOUR OR FISH SAUCE, IS EVERYDAY HOME COOKING IN VIETNAM. THE COMBINATION OF LIME, BASIL AND MINT IN THIS RECIPE MAKES IT PARTICULARLY REFRESHING AND TASTY.

SERVES FOUR

INGREDIENTS
- 45ml/3 tbsp groundnut (peanut) oil
- 450g/1lb pork tenderloin, cut into fine strips
- 4 spring onions (scallions), chopped
- 4 garlic cloves, finely chopped
- 4cm/1½in fresh root ginger, peeled and finely chopped
- 2 green or red Thai chillies, seeded and finely chopped
- 100g/3½oz/generous ½ cup shelled, unsalted peanuts
- grated rind and juice of 2 limes
- 30ml/2 tbsp *nuoc mam*
- 30ml/2 tbsp grated fresh coconut
- 25g/1oz/½ cup chopped fresh mint leaves
- 25g/1oz/½ cup chopped fresh basil leaves
- 25g/1oz/½ cup chopped fresh coriander (cilantro) leaves
- steamed or sticky rice or rice wrappers, salad and a dipping sauce, to serve

1 Heat a large wok or heavy pan and pour in 30ml/2 tbsp of the oil. Add the pork tenderloin and sear over a high heat until browned. Transfer the meat and juices to a plate and set aside.

2 Wipe the wok or pan clean and return to the heat. Pour in the remaining oil and add the spring onions, garlic, ginger and chillies. Stir-fry until the aromas rise, then add the peanuts and stir-fry for 1–2 minutes.

3 Return the meat and its juices to the wok or pan, then stir in the lime rind and juice, and the *nuoc mam*. Add the fresh coconut and herbs, and serve with steamed or sticky rice or with rice wrappers, salad and a dipping sauce.

Energy 401Kcal/1668kJ; Protein 32g; Carbohydrate 7g, of which sugars 3g; Fat 27g, of which saturates 5g; Cholesterol 71mg; Calcium 42mg; Fibre 1.8g; Sodium 400mg.

VIETNAMESE STIR-FRIED PORK RIBS

ADAPTED FROM THE CLASSIC CHINESE SWEET-AND-SOUR SPARE RIBS, THE VIETNAMESE VERSION INCLUDES BASIL LEAVES AND THE FISH SAUCE, NUOC MAM. THIS IS FINGER FOOD, REQUIRING FINGER BOWLS, AND IS PERFECT SERVED WITH STICKY RICE AND A SALAD.

SERVES FOUR TO SIX

INGREDIENTS
  45ml/3 tbsp hoisin sauce
  45ml/3 tbsp *nuoc mam*
  10ml/2 tsp Chinese five-spice powder
  45ml/3 tbsp vegetable or sesame oil
  900g/2lb pork ribs
  3 garlic cloves, crushed
  4cm/1½in fresh root ginger, peeled and grated
  1 bunch fresh basil, stalks removed, leaves shredded

1 In a bowl, mix together the hoisin sauce, *nuoc mam* and five-spice powder with 15ml/1 tbsp of the oil.

2 Bring a large wok or pan of water to the boil, then add the pork ribs, bring back to the boil and blanch for 10 minutes. Lift the pork ribs out with a slotted spoon and drain thoroughly, then set aside.

3 Heat the remaining oil in a clean wok. Add the crushed garlic and grated ginger and cook, stirring, until fragrant, then add the blanched pork ribs.

4 Stir-fry for about 5 minutes, or until the ribs are well browned, then add the hoisin sauce mixture, turning the ribs so that each one is thoroughly coated. Continue stir-frying for 10–15 minutes, or until there is almost no liquid in the wok and the ribs are caramelized and slightly blackened. Add the shredded basil leaves and stir. Serve the ribs straight from the pan, offering dinner guests finger bowls and plenty of napkins to wipe sticky fingers.

Energy 470Kcal/1965kJ; Protein 44g; Carbohydrate 6g, of which sugars 3g; Fat 31g, of which saturates 12g; Cholesterol 149mg; Calcium 98mg; Fibre 0.1g; Sodium 800mg.

GRILLED PORK MEATBALLS WITH SWEET-
AND-SOUR PEANUT SAUCE

COOKED AT HOME, OR IN STREET STALLS, THESE VIETNAMESE MEATBALLS ARE USUALLY SERVED WITH NOODLES AND A DIPPING SAUCE. IN VIETNAM A PEANUT DIPPING SAUCE IS TRADITIONAL. THEY ARE ALSO GOOD SERVED WITH CHOPPED CORIANDER AND LIME WEDGES.

SERVES FOUR

INGREDIENTS
10ml/2 tsp groundnut (peanut) or
   sesame oil
4 shallots, chopped
2 garlic cloves, finely chopped
450g/1lb/2 cups minced
   (ground) pork
30ml/2 tbsp *nuoc mam*
10ml/2 tsp Chinese five-spice powder
10ml/2 tsp sugar
115g/4oz/2 cups breadcrumbs or
   30ml/2 tbsp potato starch
1 bunch fresh coriander (cilantro),
   stalks removed
salt and ground black pepper
For the sauce
10ml/2 tsp groundnut (peanut) oil
1 garlic clove, finely chopped
1 red Thai chilli, seeded and
   finely chopped
30ml/2 tbsp roasted peanuts,
   finely chopped
15ml/1 tbsp *nuoc mam*
30ml/2 tbsp rice wine vinegar
30ml/2 tbsp hoisin sauce
60ml/4 tbsp coconut milk
100ml/3½fl oz/scant ½ cup water
5ml/1 tsp sugar

VARIATION
A speciality of central Vietnam, these meatballs, *nem nuong*, are best threaded on to skewers and grilled on a barbecue, but they can also be cooked under a grill (broiler), or fried in a wok or steamed.

COOK'S TIP
Breadcrumbs make the paste easier to work with and don't interfere with the meaty texture of the cooked ball. However, many Vietnamese prefer potato starch because it gives the meatball a smooth, springy texture, although this does make the paste very sticky to handle. Work with wet hands to make it easier.

1 To make the sauce, heat the oil in a small wok or heavy pan, and stir in the garlic and chilli. When they begin to colour, add the peanuts. Stir-fry for a few minutes, or until the natural oil from the peanuts begins to weep. Add the remaining ingredients, except the sugar, and boil the mixture for a minute. Adjust the sweetness and seasoning to your taste by adding sugar and salt, and set aside.

2 To make the meatballs, heat the oil in a wok or small pan and add the shallots and garlic. Stir-fry until golden, then remove from the heat and leave to cool. Put the minced pork into a bowl, add the stir-fried shallots and garlic, and add the *nuoc mam*, five-spice powder and sugar. Season with a little salt and plenty of pepper. Using your hand, knead the mixture until well combined. Cover the bowl and chill in the refrigerator for 2–3 hours to allow the flavours to mingle. You can make this mixture a day ahead and leave it to marinate in the refrigerator overnight.

3 Soak eight wooden skewers in water for 30 minutes. Meanwhile, knead the mixture again, then add the breadcrumbs or potato starch. Knead well to bind. Divide the mixture into 20 pieces and roll into balls. Thread the balls on to the skewers. Cook either over the barbecue or under the grill (broiler), turning the skewers from time to time, until well browned.

4 Reheat the sauce, stirring constantly, and pour into a serving bowl. Arrange the meatballs on a serving dish with coriander leaves to wrap around them, or chop the coriander and use as a garnish. Serve with the sauce.

Energy 291Kcal/1216kJ; Protein 28g; Carbohydrate 15g, of which sugars 8g; Fat 14g, of which saturates 3g; Cholesterol 71mg; Calcium 69mg; Fibre 1.3g; Sodium 700mg.

PORK CHOPS <u>WITH</u> FIELD MUSHROOMS

EVEN THOUGH THE PORK CHOPS AND MUSHROOMS ARE COOKED ON THE BARBECUE OR GRIDDLE, THE WOK IS USED FOR MAKING THE QUICK, EASY SAUCE THAT IS SPOONED OVER THEM. SERVE THE PORK AND MUSHROOMS OVER NOODLES OR WITH THAI JASMINE RICE.

SERVES FOUR

INGREDIENTS

  4 pork chops
  4 large field (portabello) mushrooms
  45ml/3 tbsp vegetable oil
  4 fresh red chillies, seeded and
    thinly sliced
  45ml/3 tbsp Thai fish sauce
  90ml/6 tbsp fresh lime juice
  4 shallots, chopped
  5ml/1 tsp roasted ground rice
  30ml/2 tbsp spring onions
    (scallions), chopped, plus shredded
    spring onions to garnish
  coriander (cilantro) leaves, to garnish
For the marinade
  2 garlic cloves, chopped
  15ml/1 tbsp granulated sugar
  15ml/1 tbsp Thai fish sauce
  30ml/2 tbsp soy sauce
  15ml/1 tbsp sesame oil
  15ml/1 tbsp whisky or dry sherry
  2 lemon grass stalks, finely chopped
  2 spring onions (scallions), chopped

1 Make the marinade. Combine the garlic, sugar, sauces, oil and whisky or sherry in a large, shallow dish. Stir in the lemon grass and spring onions.

2 Add the pork chops, turning to coat them in the marinade. Cover and leave to marinate for 1–2 hours.

3 Lift the chops out of the marinade and place them on a barbecue grid over hot coals or on a grill (broiler) rack. Add the mushrooms and brush them with 15ml/1 tbsp of the oil. Cook the pork chops for 5–7 minutes on each side and the mushrooms for about 2 minutes. Brush both with the marinade while cooking

4 Heat the remaining oil in a wok or small frying pan, then remove the pan from the heat and stir in the chillies, fish sauce, lime juice, shallots, ground rice and chopped spring onions. Put the pork chops and mushrooms on a large serving plate and spoon over the sauce. Garnish with the coriander leaves and shredded spring onion.

Energy 293Kcal/1229kJ; Protein 44.4g; Carbohydrate 2.9g, of which sugars 1.4g; Fat 11.1g, of which saturates 3.3g; Cholesterol 126mg; Calcium 24mg; Fibre 0.9g; Sodium 411mg.

CURRIED PORK WITH PICKLED GARLIC

THIS VERY RICH CURRY IS BEST ACCOMPANIED BY LOTS OF PLAIN RICE AND PERHAPS A LIGHT VEGETABLE DISH. IT COULD SERVE FOUR WITH A VEGETABLE CURRY. ASIAN STORES SELL PICKLED GARLIC. IT IS WELL WORTH INVESTING IN A JAR, AS THE TASTE IS SWEET AND DELICIOUS.

SERVES TWO

INGREDIENTS

- 130g/4½oz lean pork steaks
- 30ml/2 tbsp vegetable oil
- 1 garlic clove, crushed
- 15ml/1 tbsp Thai red curry paste
- 130ml/4½fl oz/generous ½ cup coconut cream
- 2.5cm/1in piece fresh root ginger, finely chopped
- 30ml/2 tbsp vegetable or chicken stock
- 30ml/2 tbsp Thai fish sauce
- 5ml/1 tsp granulated sugar
- 2.5ml/½ tsp ground turmeric
- 10ml/2 tsp lemon juice
- 4 pickled garlic cloves, finely chopped
- strips of lemon and lime rind, to garnish

1 Place the pork steaks in the freezer for 30–40 minutes, until firm, then, using a sharp knife, cut the meat into fine slivers, trimming off any excess fat.

2 Heat the oil in a wok or large, heavy frying pan and cook the garlic over a low to medium heat until golden brown. Do not let it burn. Add the curry paste and stir it in well.

3 Add the coconut cream and stir until the liquid begins to reduce and thicken. Stir in the pork. Cook for 2 minutes more, until the pork is cooked through.

4 Add the ginger, stock, fish sauce, sugar and turmeric, stirring constantly, then add the lemon juice and pickled garlic and heat through. Serve in bowls, garnished with strips of rind.

Energy 227Kcal/947kJ; Protein 16.3g; Carbohydrate 9.8g, of which sugars 6.1g; Fat 14g, of which saturates 2.4g; Cholesterol 41mg; Calcium 30mg; Fibre 1g; Sodium 474mg.

SWEET AND SOUR PORK, THAI-STYLE

IT WAS THE CHINESE WHO ORIGINALLY CREATED SWEET AND SOUR COOKING, BUT THE THAIS ALSO DO IT VERY WELL. THIS VERSION HAS A FRESHER AND CLEANER FLAVOUR THAN THE ORIGINAL. IT MAKES A SUBSTANTIAL MEAL WHEN SERVED WITH RICE.

SERVES FOUR

INGREDIENTS

350g/12oz lean pork
30ml/2 tbsp vegetable oil
4 garlic cloves, thinly sliced
1 small red onion, sliced
30ml/2 tbsp Thai fish sauce
15ml/1 tbsp granulated sugar
1 red (bell) pepper, seeded and diced
½ cucumber, seeded and sliced
2 plum tomatoes, cut into wedges
115g/4oz piece of fresh pineapple,
   cut into small chunks
2 spring onions (scallions), cut into
   short lengths
ground black pepper
coriander (cilantro) leaves and spring
   onions (scallions), shredded to
   garnish

1 Place the pork in the freezer for 30–40 minutes, until firm. Using a sharp knife, cut it into thin strips.

2 Heat the oil in a wok or large frying pan. Add the garlic. Cook over a medium heat until golden, then add the pork and stir-fry for 4–5 minutes. Add the onion slices and toss to mix.

3 Add the fish sauce, sugar and ground black pepper to taste. Toss the mixture over the heat for 3–4 minutes more.

4 Stir in the red pepper, cucumber, tomatoes, pineapple and spring onions. Stir-fry for 3–4 minutes more, then spoon into a bowl. Garnish with the coriander and spring onions and serve.

Energy 211Kcal/881kJ; Protein 20.3g; Carbohydrate 11.8g, of which sugars 10.7g; Fat 9.5g, of which saturates 2g; Cholesterol 55mg; Calcium 31mg; Fibre 2g; Sodium 70mg.

SWEET AND SOUR PORK

This classic Chinese-style dish, with its stunning colours, piquant sweet and sour sauce and gloriously sticky texture makes a tasty supper dish. Serve with fried rice and steamed Asian greens to create an authentic Chinese meal.

SERVES FOUR

INGREDIENTS
1 carrot
1 red (bell) pepper
4 spring onions (scallions)
45ml/3 tbsp light soy sauce
15ml/1 tbsp Chinese rice wine
15ml/1 tbsp sesame oil
5ml/1 tsp freshly ground
  black pepper
500g/1¼lb pork loin, cut into
  1cm/½in cubes
65g/2½oz/9 tbsp cornflour
  (cornstarch)
65g/2½oz/9 tbsp plain
  (all-purpose) flour
5ml/1 tsp bicarbonate of soda
  (baking soda)
sunflower oil, for deep-frying
10ml/2 tsp finely grated garlic
5ml/1 tsp finely grated fresh
  root ginger
60ml/4 tbsp tomato ketchup
30ml/2 tbsp caster (superfine) sugar
15ml/1 tbsp rice vinegar
15ml/1 tbsp cornflour (cornstarch)
  blended with 120ml/4fl oz/
  ½ cup water
egg fried rice or noodles, to serve
salt

2 In a large mixing bowl, combine 15ml/1 tbsp of the soy sauce with the rice wine, sesame oil and pepper. Add the pork and toss to mix. Cover and chill for 3–4 hours.

4 Fill a wok one-third full with the sunflower oil and heat to 180°C/350°F or until a cube of bread browns in 45 seconds. Separate the pork cubes and deep-fry them, in batches, for 1–2 minutes, or until golden. Remove and drain on kitchen paper.

5 Mix together the garlic, ginger, tomato ketchup, sugar, the remaining soy sauce, rice vinegar and cornflour mixture. Place a small pan over a medium heat. Add the mixture and heat for 2–3 minutes, until thickened. Add the carrot, red pepper and spring onions, stir and remove from the heat.

1 Using a sharp knife or cleaver, chop the carrots in half, then in slices, and then into thin shreds. Cut the pepper into sections and shred into similar sized pieces. Cut the spring onions in half, then cut each half into shreds.

3 Combine the cornflour, plain flour and bicarbonate of soda in a bowl. Add a pinch of salt and mix in 150ml/¼ pint/⅔ cup cold water to make a thick batter. Add the pork to the batter and mix well with your hands to coat evenly.

6 Reheat the deep-frying oil in the wok to 180°C/350°F and then re-fry the pork pieces in batches for 1–2 minutes, until golden and crisp. Drain and add to the sauce and toss to mix well. Serve with egg fried rice or noodles.

Energy 445Kcal/1873kJ; Protein 29.8g; Carbohydrate 52.2g, of which sugars 17.4g; Fat 13.9g, of which saturates 2.9g; Cholesterol 79mg; Calcium 55mg; Fibre 2g; Sodium 1154mg.

STIR-FRIED PORK <u>WITH</u> DRIED SHRIMP

YOU MIGHT EXPECT THE DRIED SHRIMPS TO GIVE THIS DISH A FISHY FLAVOUR, BUT INSTEAD THEY SIMPLY IMPART A DELICIOUS SAVOURY TASTE, WHICH GOES VERY WELL WITH THE PORK AND WILTED GREENS. THIS IS GOOD JUST AS IT IS, BUT COULD BE SERVED WITH NOODLES OR JASMINE RICE.

SERVES FOUR

INGREDIENTS

  250g/9oz pork fillet
    (tenderloin), sliced
  30ml/2 tbsp vegetable oil
  2 garlic cloves, finely chopped
  45ml/3 tbsp dried shrimps
  10ml/2 tsp dried shrimp paste
  30ml/2 tbsp soy sauce
  juice of 1 lime
  15ml/1 tbsp palm sugar or light
    muscovado (brown) sugar
  1 small fresh red or green chilli,
    seeded and finely chopped
  4 pak choi (bok choy) or 450g/1lb
    spring greens (collards), shredded

1 Place the pork in the freezer for about 30 minutes, until firm. Using a sharp knife, cut it into thin slices.

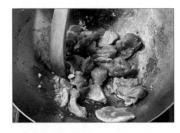

2 Heat the oil in a wok or frying pan and cook the garlic until golden brown. Add the pork and stir-fry for about 4 minutes, until just cooked through.

3 Add the dried shrimp, then stir in the shrimp paste, with the soy sauce, lime juice and sugar. Add the chilli and pak choi or spring greens and toss over the heat until the vegetables are just wilted.

4 Transfer the stir-fry to warm individual bowls and serve immediately.

Energy 200Kcal/833kJ; Protein 23.1g; Carbohydrate 6.3g, of which sugars 6.2g; Fat 9.2g, of which saturates 1.7g; Cholesterol 96mg; Calcium 334mg; Fibre 2.4g; Sodium 1223mg.

LEMON GRASS PORK

CHILLIES AND LEMON GRASS FLAVOUR THIS SIMPLE STIR-FRY, WHILE CHOPPED, UNSALTED PEANUTS ADD AN INTERESTING CONTRAST IN TEXTURE. LOOK OUT FOR JARS OF CHOPPED LEMON GRASS, WHICH ARE HANDY WHEN THE FRESH VEGETABLE ISN'T AVAILABLE, AND WILL KEEP IN THE REFRIGERATOR.

SERVES FOUR

INGREDIENTS

    675g/1½lb boneless
      pork loin
    2 lemon grass stalks,
      finely chopped
    4 spring onions (scallions),
      thinly sliced
    5ml/1 tsp salt
    12 black peppercorns,
      coarsely crushed
    30ml/2 tbsp groundnut
      (peanut) oil
    2 garlic cloves, chopped
    2 fresh red chillies, seeded
      and chopped
    5ml/1 tsp soft light brown sugar
    30ml/2 tbsp Thai fish sauce
    25g/1oz/¼ cup roasted unsalted
      peanuts, chopped
    ground black pepper
    coarsely torn coriander (cilantro)
      leaves, to garnish
    cooked rice noodles, to serve

1 Trim any excess fat from the pork. Cut the meat across into 5mm/¼in thick slices, then cut each slice into 5mm/¼in strips. Put the pork into a bowl with the lemon grass, spring onions, salt and crushed peppercorns; mix well. Cover with clear film (plastic wrap) and leave to marinate in a cool place for 30 minutes.

2 Preheat a wok, add the oil and swirl it around. Add the pork mixture and stir-fry over a medium heat for about 3 minutes, until browned all over.

3 Add the garlic and red chillies and stir-fry for a further 5–8 minutes over a medium heat, until the pork is cooked through and tender.

4 Add the sugar, fish sauce and chopped peanuts and toss to mix, then season to taste with black pepper. Serve immediately on a bed of rice noodles, garnished with the coarsely torn coriander leaves.

COOK'S TIP
The most intense heat in chillies is in the membrane surrounding the seeds, so make sure you remove it all.

Energy 297Kcal/1240kJ; Protein 37.9g; Carbohydrate 2.1g, of which sugars 1.7g; Fat 15.2g, of which saturates 3.6g; Cholesterol 106mg; Calcium 20mg; Fibre 0.5g; Sodium 119mg.

PAN-FRIED PORK <u>WITH</u> GINGER SAUCE

REPUTEDLY CREATED BY A CANTEEN DINNER LADY AT A TOKYO UNIVERSITY DURING THE 1970S, THIS DISH, KNOWN AS BUTA-NIKU SHOGA YAKI, IS PARTICULARLY POPULAR WITH YOUNGSTERS.

SERVES FOUR

INGREDIENTS
  450g/1lb pork chops, boned
    and trimmed
  15ml/1 tbsp vegetable oil
  1 small onion, thinly sliced
    lengthwise
  50g/2oz/1 cup beansprouts
  50g/2oz mangetouts (snow peas),
    trimmed
  salt
For the marinade
  15ml/1 tbsp shoyu
  15ml/1 tbsp sake
  15ml/1 tbsp mirin
  4cm/1½in piece fresh root ginger,
    very finely grated,
    plus juice

1 Wrap the pork chops in clear film (plastic wrap) and freeze for 2 hours. Cut into 3mm/⅛in slices, then into 4cm/1½in wide strips.

2 To make the marinade, mix all the ingredients in a plastic container. Add the pork and marinate for 15 minutes.

3 Heat the vegetable oil in a wok on a medium-high heat. Add the onion and stir-fry for 3 minutes.

4 Take half of the pork slices out of the marinade and add to the wok. Transfer the meat to a plate when its colour changes; this will take only about 2–3 minutes. Reserve the marinade.

5 Repeat the process with the rest of the meat. Transfer all the cooked pork and onions to the plate.

6 Pour the reserved marinade into the wok and simmer until it has reduced by one-third. Add the beansprouts and mangetouts, then the pork and increase the heat to medium-high for 2 minutes.

7 Heap the beansprouts on individual serving plates and lean the meat, onions and mangetouts against them. Serve immediately.

DEEP-FRIED PORK FILLET

THIS INVIGORATING JAPANESE DISH IS SO GOOD THAT SOME RESTAURANTS SERVE NOTHING ELSE. THE PORK IS ALWAYS GARNISHED WITH A HEAP OF VERY FINELY SHREDDED WHITE CABBAGE.

SERVES FOUR

INGREDIENTS
  1 white cabbage
  4 pork loin chops or cutlets, boned
  plain (all-purpose) flour, to dust
  vegetable oil, for deep-frying
  2 eggs, beaten
  50g/2oz/1 cup dried
    white breadcrumbs
  salt and ready-ground mixed pepper
  prepared English (hot) mustard,
    to garnish
  Japanese pickles, to serve
For the sauce
  60ml/4 tbsp Worcestershire sauce
  30ml/2 tbsp good-quality
    tomato ketchup
  5ml/1 tsp shoyu

1 Quarter the cabbage and remove the central core. Slice the wedges very finely with a vegetable slicer or a sharp knife.

2 Make a few deep cuts horizontally across the fat of the meat. This prevents the meat curling up while cooking. Rub a little salt and pepper into the meat and dust with the flour, then shake off any excess.

3 Heat the oil to 180°C/350°F, or until a cube of bread browns in 45 seconds.

4 Dip the meat in the beaten eggs, then coat with breadcrumbs. Deep-fry two pieces at a time for 8–10 minutes, or until golden brown. Drain on a wire rack or on kitchen paper. Repeat until all the pieces of pork are deep-fried.

5 Heap the cabbage on four individual serving plates. Cut the pork crossways into 2cm/¾in thick strips and arrange them to your liking on the cabbage.

6 To make the *ton-katsu* sauce, mix the Worcestershire sauce, ketchup and shoyu in a jug (pitcher) or gravy boat. Serve the pork and cabbage immediately, with the sauce, mustard and Japanese pickles. Pickles can also be served in separate dishes, if you like.

Energy 179Kcal/747kJ; Protein 25.3g; Carbohydrate 2.8g, of which sugars 2.1g; Fat 7.4g, of which saturates 1.9g; Cholesterol 71mg; Calcium 21mg; Fibre 0.7g; Sodium 614mg.
Energy 311Kcal/1304kJ; Protein 31.1g; Carbohydrate 21.7g, of which sugars 12g; Fat 11.6g, of which saturates 2.9g; Cholesterol 166mg; Calcium 141mg; Fibre 3.5g; Sodium 522mg.

CHINESE BRAISED PORK BELLY ᵂᴵᵀᴴ GREENS

PORK BELLY BECOMES MELTINGLY TENDER IN THIS SLOW-BRAISED DISH FLAVOURED WITH ORANGE, CINNAMON, STAR ANISE AND GINGER. THE FLAVOURS MELD AND MELLOW DURING COOKING TO PRODUCE A RICH, COMPLEX, ROUNDED TASTE. SERVE SIMPLY WITH RICE AND STEAMED GREENS.

SERVES FOUR

INGREDIENTS

800g/1¾lb pork belly, trimmed
400ml/14fl oz/1⅔ cups beef stock
75ml/5 tbsp soy sauce
finely grated rind and juice
  of 1 large orange
15ml/1 tbsp finely shredded fresh
  root ginger
2 garlic cloves, sliced
15ml/1 tbsp hot chilli powder
15ml/1 tbsp muscovado (molasses)
  sugar
3 cinnamon sticks
3 cloves
10 black peppercorns
2–3 star anise
steamed greens and rice, to serve

COOK'S TIP

Any type of Asian greens will go with this dish. Try pak choi (bok choy), choi sum or Chinese broccoli.

1 Cut the pork belly into 12 equal pieces. Place the pork in a wok and pour over water to cover. Bring the water to the boil. Cover, reduce the heat and cook gently for 30 minutes.

2 Drain the pork and return to the wok with the stock, soy sauce, orange rind and juice, ginger, garlic, chilli powder, muscovado sugar, cinnamon sticks, cloves, peppercorns and star anise.

3 Pour over water to just cover the pork belly pieces and cook on a high heat until the mixture comes to a boil.

4 Cover the wok tightly with a lid, then reduce the heat to low and cook gently for 1½ hours, stirring occasionally to prevent the pork from sticking.

5 Uncover the wok and simmer for 30 minutes, stirring occasionally until the meat is very tender. Serve with steamed greens and rice.

Energy 543Kcal/2260kJ; Protein 38.9g; Carbohydrate 6.6g, of which sugars 6.4g; Fat 40.4g, of which saturates 14.6g; Cholesterol 142mg; Calcium 19mg; Fibre 0g; Sodium 1475mg.

AROMATIC PORK WITH BASIL

THE COMBINATION OF MOIST, JUICY PORK AND MUSHROOMS, CRISP GREEN MANGETOUTS AND FRAGRANT BASIL IN THIS GINGER- AND GARLIC-INFUSED STIR-FRY IS ABSOLUTELY DELICIOUS. SERVED WITH SIMPLE STEAMED JASMINE RICE, IT MAKES A PERFECT QUICK SUPPER DURING THE WEEK.

SERVES FOUR

INGREDIENTS

40g/1½oz cornflour (cornstarch)
500g/1¼lb pork fillet (tenderloin),
   thinly sliced
15ml/1 tbsp sunflower oil
10ml/2 tsp sesame oil
15ml/1 tbsp very finely shredded
   fresh root ginger
3 garlic cloves, thinly sliced
200g/7oz mangetouts (snow peas),
   halved lengthwise
300g/11oz/generous 4 cups mixed
   mushrooms, such as shiitake,
   button (white) or oyster, sliced
   if large
120ml/4fl oz/½ cup Chinese
   cooking wine
45ml/3 tbsp soy sauce
a small handful of sweet basil leaves
salt and ground black pepper
steamed jasmine rice, to serve

1 Place the cornflour in a strong plastic bag. Season well and add the sliced pork. Shake the bag to coat the pork in flour and then remove the pork and shake off any excess flour. Set aside.

2 Preheat the wok over a high heat and add the oils. When very hot, stir in the ginger and garlic and cook for 30 seconds. Add the pork and cook over a high heat for about 5 minutes, stirring often, until sealed.

3 Add the mangetouts and mushrooms to the wok and stir-fry for 2–3 minutes. Add the Chinese cooking wine and soy sauce, stir-fry for 2–3 minutes and remove from the heat.

4 Just before serving, stir the sweet basil leaves into the pork. Serve with steamed jasmine rice.

Energy 298Kcal/1248kJ; Protein 30.4g; Carbohydrate 14.6g, of which sugars 4.8g; Fat 9.8g, of which saturates 2.4g; Cholesterol 79mg; Calcium 41mg; Fibre 2g; Sodium 903mg.

CELLOPHANE NOODLES <u>WITH</u> PORK

SIMPLE, SPEEDY AND SATISFYING, THIS IS THE SORT OF DISH THE WOK WAS MADE FOR. IT LOOKS SPECTACULAR, WITH THE CLEAR, GLASS-LIKE NOODLES CURLING OVER THE COLOURFUL VEGETABLE MIXTURE. A POPULAR THAI DISH, IT IS NOW SERVED ALL OVER THE WORLD.

SERVES TWO

INGREDIENTS

200g/7oz cellophane noodles
30ml/2 tbsp vegetable oil
15ml/1 tbsp magic paste
200g/7oz minced (ground) pork
1 fresh green or red chilli, seeded
   and finely chopped
300g/11oz/3½ cups beansprouts
bunch spring onions (scallions),
   finely chopped
30ml/2 tbsp soy sauce
30ml/2 tbsp Thai fish sauce
30ml/2 tbsp sweet chilli sauce
15ml/1 tbsp palm sugar or light
   muscovado (brown) sugar
30ml/2 tbsp rice vinegar
30ml/2 tbsp roasted peanuts,
   chopped and small bunch fresh
   coriander (cilantro), chopped,
   to garnish

1 Place the noodles in a large bowl, cover with boiling water and soak for 10 minutes. Drain the noodles and set aside until ready to use.

2 Heat the oil in a wok or large, heavy frying pan. Add the magic paste and stir-fry for 2–3 seconds, then add the pork. Stir-fry the meat, breaking it up with a wooden spatula, for 2–3 minutes, until browned all over.

3 Add the chopped chilli to the meat and stir-fry for 3–4 seconds, then add the beansprouts and chopped spring onions, stir-frying for a few seconds after each addition.

4 Snip the noodles into 5cm/2in lengths and add to the wok, with the soy sauce, Thai fish sauce, sweet chilli sauce, sugar and rice vinegar.

5 Toss the ingredients together over the heat until well combined and the noodles have warmed through. Pile on to a platter or into a large bowl. Sprinkle over the peanuts and coriander and serve immediately.

COOK'S TIP

Magic Paste, or *Prig gang nam ya,* is a blend of garlic, coriander root and white pepper. It is available in Asian stores.

Energy 755Kcal/3153kJ; Protein 39.8g; Carbohydrate 96.8g, of which sugars 14.6g; Fat 23.3g, of which saturates 4.2g; Cholesterol 63mg; Calcium 94mg; Fibre 4g; Sodium 1158mg.

FIVE-FLAVOUR NOODLES

THE JAPANESE NAME FOR THIS DISH TRANSLATES AS "FIVE DIFFERENT INGREDIENTS"; HOWEVER, THERE'S NOTHING TO STOP YOU ADDING AS MANY DIFFERENT INGREDIENTS AS YOU LIKE TO MAKE AN EXCITING AND TASTY NOODLE STIR-FRY. THE SEASONING MIX IMPARTS A GREAT FLAVOUR.

SERVES FOUR

INGREDIENTS

300g/11oz dried Chinese thin egg
 noodles or 500g/1¼lb fresh yaki-
 soba noodles
200g/7oz lean boneless pork,
 thinly sliced
22ml/4 tsp sunflower oil
10g/¼oz grated fresh root ginger
1 garlic clove, crushed
200g/7oz green cabbage,
 roughly chopped
115g/4oz/2 cups beansprouts
1 green (bell) pepper, seeded and cut
 into fine strips
1 red (bell) pepper, seeded and cut
 into fine strips
salt and ground black pepper
20ml/4 tsp ao-nori seaweed, to
 garnish (optional)
For the seasoning mix
 60ml/4 tbsp Worcestershire sauce
 15ml/1 tbsp Japanese soy sauce
 15ml/1 tbsp oyster sauce
 15ml/1 tbsp sugar
 2.5ml/½ tsp salt
 ground white pepper

3 Heat 7.5ml/1½ tsp of the oil in a wok. Stir-fry the pork until just cooked, then remove it from the pan.

4 Wipe the wok with kitchen paper, and heat the remaining oil in it. Add the ginger, garlic and cabbage and stir-fry for 1 minute.

5 Add the beansprouts, stir until softened, then add the peppers and stir-fry for 1 minute more.

6 Return the pork to the pan and add the noodles. Stir in all the ingredients for the seasoning mix and stir-fry for 2–3 minutes. Serve immediately, sprinkled with ao-nori seaweed (if using).

1 Cook the noodles according to the instructions on the packet. Drain well and set aside.

2 Cut the pork into 3–4cm/1¼–1½in strips and season with salt and pepper.

VARIATION
Try this with strips of tender chicken breast instead of pork.

Energy 471Kcal/1988kJ; Protein 22.8g; Carbohydrate 71g, of which sugars 17.4g; Fat 12.6g, of which saturates 3g; Cholesterol 54mg; Calcium 95mg; Fibre 5.2g; Sodium 652mg.

CINNAMON MEAT LOAF

SIMILAR TO THE VIETNAMESE STEAMED PÂTÉS, THIS TYPE OF MEAT LOAF IS USUALLY SERVED AS A SNACK OR LIGHT LUNCH, WITH A CRUSTY BAGUETTE. ACCOMPANIED WITH EITHER TART PICKLES OR A CRUNCHY SALAD WITH A ZINGY DRESSING, AND SPLASHED WITH PIQUANT SAUCE, IT IS LIGHT AND TASTY.

SERVES FOUR TO SIX

INGREDIENTS

  30ml/2 tbsp *nuoc mam*
  25ml/1½ tbsp ground cinnamon
  10ml/2 tsp sugar
  5ml/1 tsp ground black pepper
  15ml/1 tbsp potato starch
  450g/1lb lean minced (ground) pork
  25g/1oz pork fat, very finely chopped
  2–3 shallots, very finely chopped
  oil, for greasing
  chilli oil or *nuoc cham*, for drizzling
  red chilli strips, to garnish
  bread or noodles, to serve

1 In a large bowl, mix together the *nuoc mam*, ground cinnamon, sugar and ground black pepper. Beat in the potato starch.

2 Add the minced pork, the chopped pork fat, and the shallots to the bowl and mix thoroughly. Cover and put in the refrigerator for 3–4 hours. Preheat the oven to 180°C/350°F/Gas 4.

3 Lightly oil a baking tin (pan) and spread the pork mixture in it – it should feel springy from the potato starch.

4 Cover with foil and bake in the oven for 35–40 minutes. If you want the top to turn brown and crunchy, remove the foil for the last 10 minutes.

5 Turn the meat loaf out on to a board and slice it into strips. Drizzle the strips with chilli oil or *nuoc cham*, and serve them hot with bread or noodles.

Energy 111Kcal/465kJ; Protein 16g; Carbohydrate 4.8g, of which sugars 2.3g; Fat 3g, of which saturates 1g; Cholesterol 47mg; Calcium 9mg; Fibre 0.2g; Sodium 54mg.

SPICED LAMB WITH SPINACH

THE SPINACH IS ADDED AT THE END OF COOKING TO MELT INTO AND ENRICH THE SPICY SAUCE.
SERVE WITH SPICED BASMATI RICE OR WARM NAAN BREAD TO SCOOP UP THE DELICIOUS JUICES.

SERVES THREE TO FOUR

INGREDIENTS
45ml/3 tbsp vegetable oil
500g/1¼lb lean boneless lamb
1 onion, chopped
3 garlic cloves, finely chopped
1cm/½in fresh root ginger,
   finely chopped
6 black peppercorns
4 whole cloves
1 bay leaf
3 green cardamom pods, crushed
5ml/1 tsp ground cumin
5ml/1 tsp ground coriander
generous pinch of cayenne pepper
150ml/¼ pint/⅔ cup water
2 tomatoes
5ml/1 tsp salt
400g/14oz fresh spinach
5ml/1 tsp garam masala
crisp-fried onions and fresh coriander
   (cilantro) sprigs, to garnish

1 Cut the lamb into 2.5cm/1in cubes. Wash, trim and finely chop the spinach. Peel and chop the tomatoes. Pre-heat a wok or large frying pan.

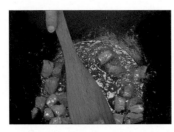

2 Add 30ml/2 tbsp of the oil and swirl it around. When hot, stir-fry the pieces of lamb in batches until they are evenly browned. Remove the lamb and set aside. Heat the remaining oil in the pan, add the onion, garlic and ginger and stir-fry for 2–3 minutes.

3 Add the peppercorns, cloves, bay leaf, cardamom pods, cumin, ground coriander and cayenne pepper. Stir-fry for 30–45 seconds.

4 Return the lamb and add the water, tomatoes and salt and bring to the boil. Simmer, covered, over a very low heat for about 1 hour, stirring occasionally until the meat is cooked and tender.

5 Increase the heat, then gradually add the spinach to the lamb, stirring to mix. Keep stirring and cooking until the spinach wilts completely and most, but not all, of the liquid has evaporated and you are left with a thick green sauce.

6 Stir in the garam masala and season to taste. Garnish with crisp-fried onions and sprigs of fresh coriander.

COOK'S TIP
If fresh spinach is not available you can use frozen, or replace it with another finely chopped dark green leaf, such as spring greens or curly kale.

Energy 359kcal/1494kJ; Protein 28.7g; Carbohydrate 7.1g, of which sugars 4.7g; Fat 24.1g, of which saturates 7.7g; Cholesterol 95mg; Calcium 237mg; Fibre 4.8g; Sodium 780mg.

GLAZED LAMB

LEMON AND HONEY MAKE A CLASSICAL STIR-FRY COMBINATION IN SWEET DISHES, AND THIS LAMB
RECIPE SHOWS HOW WELL THEY WORK TOGETHER IN SAVOURY DISHES, TOO.

SERVES FOUR

INGREDIENTS
450g/1lb boneless lean lamb
15ml/1 tbsp grapeseed oil
175g/6oz mangetouts (snow peas),
   topped and tailed
3 spring onions (scallions), sliced
30ml/2 tbsp clear honey
juice of ½ lemon
30ml/2 tbsp chopped fresh
   coriander (cilantro)
15ml/1 tbsp sesame seeds
salt and ground black pepper

1 Using a cleaver, cut the lamb across
the grain into thin strips.

COOK'S TIP
This recipe would work just as well made
with pork or chicken instead of lamb.
You could substitute chopped fresh basil
for the coriander if using chicken.

2 Heat the wok, then add the oil. When
the oil is hot, stir-fry the lamb until
browned all over. Remove from the wok
and keep warm.

3 Add the mangetouts and spring
onions to the hot wok and stir-fry for
30 seconds.

4 Return the lamb to the wok and add
the honey, lemon juice, chopped
coriander and sesame seeds and
season well. Stir thoroughly to mix.
Bring to the boil, then allow to bubble
vigorously for 1 minute until the lamb is
completely coated in the honey mixture.
Serve immediately.

Energy 223kcal/932kJ; Protein 19g; Carbohydrate 7.8g, of which sugars 7.4g; Fat 13.1g, of which saturates 4.9g; Cholesterol 67mg; Calcium 34mg; Fibre 1.2g; Sodium 78mg.

STIR-FRIED BEEF <u>WITH</u> SESAME <u>AND</u> CHILLI SAUCE

VARIATIONS OF THIS CLASSIC DISH CAN BE FOUND IN MANY ASIAN COUNTRIES. SIMILAR TO STIR-FRIED BEEF WITH SATÉ, THE SPICY PEANUT SAUCE, THIS IS A CAMBODIAN VARIATION, WHICH HAS A DELICIOUSLY RICH, SPICY AND NUTTY FLAVOUR. SERVE THE BEEF WITH PLAIN BOILED RICE.

SERVES FOUR

INGREDIENTS
   450g/1lb beef sirloin or fillet,
      cut into thin strips
   15ml/1 tbsp groundnut (peanut)
      or sesame oil
   2 garlic cloves, finely chopped
   2 red Thai chillies, seeded and
      finely chopped
   7.5ml/1½ tsp sugar
   30ml/2 tbsp sesame paste
   30–45ml/2–3 tbsp beef stock
      or water
   sea salt and ground black pepper
   red chilli strips, to garnish
   1 lemon, cut into quarters, to serve
For the marinade
   15ml/1 tbsp groundnut (peanut) oil
   30ml/2 tbsp *tuk trey*
   30ml/2 tbsp soy sauce

4 Stir in the sesame paste and enough stock or water to thin it down. Cook for 1–2 minutes, making sure the beef is coated with the sauce.

5 Season with salt and pepper, garnish with chilli strips and and serve with lemon wedges, and boiled rice.

VARIATION
Chicken breast fillet or pork fillet can be used instead of beef.

1 In a bowl, mix together the ingredients for the marinade. Toss in the beef, making sure it is well coated. Leave to marinate for 30 minutes.

2 Heat the groundnut or sesame oil in a wok or heavy pan. Stir in the garlic and chillies and cook until golden and fragrant.

3 Stir the sugar into the wok, then add the beef, tossing it around in the wok to sear it.

Energy 269Kcal/1119kJ; Protein 26.2g; Carbohydrate 2/0g, of which sugars 2.0g; Fat 18g, of which saturates 5g; Cholesterol 65mg; Calcium 31mg; Fibre 0.3g; Sodium 73mg.

WARM LAMB AND NOODLE SALAD WITH MINT

THIS THAI-INSPIRED SALAD COMBINES THIN SLICES OF WOK-FRIED LAMB WITH LIGHTLY COOKED FRESH VEGETABLES AND RICE NOODLES, ALL TOSSED TOGETHER WITH A DELICIOUSLY FRAGRANT, AROMATIC, ASIAN-STYLE DRESSING, THEN HEAPED ARTISTICALLY ON INDIVIDUAL PLATES.

SERVES FOUR

INGREDIENTS
  30ml/2 tbsp red Thai curry paste
  60ml/4 tbsp sunflower oil
  750g/1lb 11oz lamb neck fillets,
    thinly sliced
  250g/9oz sugar snap peas
  500g/1¼lb fresh rice noodles
  1 red (bell) pepper, seeded and
    very thinly sliced
  1 cucumber, cut into very thin
    slices with a vegetable peeler
  6–7 spring onions (scallions),
    sliced diagonally
  a large handful of fresh mint leaves
For the dressing
  15ml/1 tbsp sunflower oil
  juice of 2 limes
  1 garlic clove, crushed
  15ml/1 tbsp sugar
  15ml/1 tbsp Thai fish sauce
  30ml/2 tbsp soy sauce

1 In a shallow dish, mix together the red curry paste and half the oil. Add the lamb slices and toss to coat. Cover and leave to marinate in the refrigerator for up to 24 hours.

2 Blanch the sugar snap peas in a wok of lightly salted boiling water for 1–2 minutes. Drain, refresh under cold water, drain again thoroughly and transfer to a large bowl.

3 Put the noodles in a separate bowl and pour over boiling water to cover. Leave to soak for 5–10 minutes, until tender, then drain well and separate into strands with your fingers.

4 Add the noodles to the bowl containing the sugar snap peas, then add the sliced red pepper, cucumber and spring onions. Toss lightly to mix.

5 Heat a wok over a high heat and add the remaining sunflower oil. Stir-fry the lamb, in two batches, for 3–4 minutes, or until cooked through, then add to the bowl of salad ingredients.

6 Place all the dressing ingredients in a screw-top jar, screw on the lid and shake well to combine. Pour the dressing over the warm salad, sprinkle over the fresh mint leaves and toss well to combine. Serve immediately.

Energy 820Kcal/3418kJ; Protein 46g; Carbohydrate 76.4g, of which sugars 9.4g; Fat 36g, of which saturates 11.7g; Cholesterol 143mg; Calcium 55mg; Fibre 4.1g; Sodium 709mg.

COCONUT SPICED LAMB ᴼᴺ POPPADUMS

CRISP, MELT-IN-THE-MOUTH MINI POPPADUMS MAKE A GREAT BASE FOR THESE DIVINE LITTLE BITES.
TOP THEM WITH A DRIZZLE OF YOGURT AND A SPOONFUL OF MANGO CHUTNEY, THEN SERVE IMMEDIATELY.
TO MAKE AN EQUALLY TASTY VARIATION, USE CHICKEN OR PORK IN PLACE OF THE LAMB.

MAKES TWENTY-FIVE

INGREDIENTS
30ml/2 tbsp sunflower oil
4 shallots, finely chopped
30ml/2 tbsp medium curry paste
300g/11oz minced (ground) lamb
90ml/6 tbsp tomato purée (paste)
5ml/1 tsp caster (superfine) sugar
200ml/7fl oz/scant 1 cup
    coconut cream
juice of 1 lime
60ml/4 tbsp chopped fresh
    mint leaves
vegetable oil, for deep-frying
salt and ground black pepper
25 mini poppadums
natural (plain) yogurt and
    mango chutney, to drizzle
1 red chilli cut into slivers and mint
    leaves, to garnish

1 Heat the oil in a wok over a medium heat and stir-fry the shallots for 4–5 minutes, then add the curry paste. Stir-fry for 1 minute and then add the lamb. Stir-fry over a high heat for a further 4–5 minutes, then stir in the tomato purée, sugar and coconut cream.

2 Simmer the lamb for 25–30 minutes, until the liquid has been absorbed. Season and stir in the lime juice and mint. Turn off the heat and keep warm.

3 Fill a separate wok one-third full of oil and heat to 180°C/350°F or until a cube of bread browns in 40 seconds. Deep-fry the poppadums for 30–40 seconds. Drain on kitchen paper.

4 Place the poppadums on a serving platter. Put a spoonful of spiced lamb on each one, then top with a little yogurt and mango chutney. Serve immediately, garnished with slivers of red chilli and mint leaves.

Energy 63Kcal/260kJ; Protein 2.7g; Carbohydrate 2.7g, of which sugars 1.3g; Fat 4.7g, of which saturates 1.4g; Cholesterol 9mg; Calcium 7mg; Fibre 0.3g; Sodium 45mg.

BALTI KEEMA <u>WITH</u> CURRY LEAVES <u>AND</u> CHILLIES

MINCED LAMB IS COOKED IN ITS OWN JUICES WITH A FEW SPICES AND HERBS, BUT NO OTHER LIQUID.

SERVES FOUR

INGREDIENTS

   350g/12oz lean minced
     (ground) lamb
   5ml/1 tsp crushed garlic
   5ml/1 tsp crushed fresh root ginger
   5ml/1 tsp chilli powder
   1.5ml/¼ tsp ground turmeric
   5ml/1 tsp salt
   10ml/2 tsp oil
   2 medium onions, chopped
   10 curry leaves
   6 green chillies
   2 tomatoes, peeled and quartered
   15ml/1 tbsp chopped fresh coriander
     (cilantro)

1 Put the minced lamb into a bowl and blend it thoroughly with the crushed garlic and fresh ginger. Add the chilli powder, ground turmeric and salt and mix again.

2 Heat the oil and fry the onions together with the curry leaves and 3 of the whole green chillies.

3 Add the lamb to the onions and stir-fry for 7–10 minutes.

4 Add the quartered tomatoes, coriander and the remaining chillies and stir-fry for 2 minutes.

Energy 229kcal /957kJ; protein 19.0g; carbohydrate 11.2g, of which sugars 7.2g; fat 12.5g, of which saturates 5.6g; cholesterol 67.5mg; calcium 50.8mg; fibre 2g; sodium 560mg.

STIR FRIED LAMB <u>WITH</u> BABY ONIONS <u>AND</u> PEPPERS

THE BABY ONIONS ARE USED WHOLE IN THIS RECIPE. SERVE THE DISH WITH RICE OR LENTILS.

SERVES FOUR

INGREDIENTS
    225g/8oz boned lean lamb, cut
      into strips
    5ml/1 tsp ground cumin
    5ml/1 tsp ground coriander
    15ml/1 tbsp tomato purée (paste)
    5ml/1 tsp chilli powder
    5ml/1 tsp salt
    15ml/1 tbsp lemon juice
    15ml/1 tbsp oil
    8 baby onions
    2.5ml/½ tsp onion seeds
    4 curry leaves
    300ml/½ pint/1¼ cups water
    1 small red (bell) pepper, sliced
    1 small green (bell) pepper, sliced
    15ml/1 tbsp chopped fresh coriander
      (cilantro)
    15ml/1 tbsp chopped fresh mint

1 Mix the lamb with the cumin, ground coriander, tomato purée, chilli powder, salt and lemon juice and set aside.

2 Heat the oil in a wok and stir-fry the whole baby onions for about 3 minutes. Using a slotted spoon, remove the onions and set aside to drain.

3 Reheat the oil and briskly stir-fry the onion seeds and curry leaves for 2–3 minutes. Add the lamb and spice mixture and stir-fry for about 5 minutes, then pour in the water, lower the heat and cook gently for about 10 minutes, until the lamb is cooked through.

4 Add the sliced red and green peppers and half the fresh coriander and mint. Stir-fry for a further 2 minutes. Finally, add the reserved baby onions and allow to heat through. Sprinkle over the remaining chopped fresh coriander and mint and serve.

Energy 171kcal /717kJ; protein 12.8g; carbohydrate 8.5g, of which sugars 6.6g; fat 9.9g, of which saturates 3.5g; cholesterol 42mg; calcium 24mg; fibre 1.7g; sodium 554mg.

SPICY LAMB AND POTATO STEW

THIS SIMPLE STEW OF MEAT AND POTATOES IS TRANSFORMED INTO A TASTY DISH WITH THE ADDITION
OF A SUBTLE BLEND OF INDIAN SPICES.

SERVES SIX

INGREDIENTS

   675g/1½lb lean lamb fillet
   15ml/1 tbsp oil
   1 onion, finely chopped
   2 bay leaves
   1 green chilli, seeded and
     finely chopped
   2 garlic cloves, finely chopped
   10ml/2 tsp ground coriander
   5ml/1 tsp ground cumin
   2.5ml/½ tsp ground turmeric
   2.5ml/½ tsp chilli powder
   2.5ml/½ tsp salt
   225g/8oz tomatoes, peeled and
     finely chopped
   600ml/1 pint/2½ cups chicken stock
   2 large potatoes, cut into
    2.5cm/1in chunks
   chopped fresh coriander (cilantro), to
    garnish

1 Using a sharp knife, remove any visible fat from the lamb and cut the meat into 2.5cm/1in cubes.

2 Heat the oil and fry the onion, bay leaves, chilli and garlic for 5 minutes.

3 Add the meat and cook for about 6–8 minutes until lightly browned.

4 Add the ground coriander, ground cumin, ground turmeric, chilli powder and salt and cook for 3–4 minutes, stirring all the time to prevent the spices sticking to the bottom of the pan.

5 Add the tomatoes and stock and simmer for 5 minutes until the sauce thickens. Bring to the boil, cover and simmer for 1 hour.

6 Add the potatoes and cook for a further 30–40 minutes or until the meat is tender. Garnish with chopped fresh coriander and serve.

COOK'S TIP
This stew is absolutely delicious served with warm, freshly made chappatis.

Energy 426kcal /1787kJ; protein 36g; carbohydrate 21.2g, of which sugars 4g; fat 22.6g, of which saturates 9.4g; cholesterol 128mg; calcium 35mg; fibre 1.9g; sodium 163mg.

BALTI BHOONA LAMB

BHOONA DESCRIBES A TRADITIONAL WAY OF STIR-FRYING, USING SEMI-CIRCULAR MOVEMENTS TO SCRAPE THE BOTTOM OF THE WOK EACH TIME IN THE CENTRE. SERVE THIS DISH WITH CHAPPATIS.

SERVES SIX

INGREDIENTS
225–275g/8–10oz boned lean
    lamb, cubed
3 medium onions, finely diced
15ml/1 tbsp oil
15ml/1 tbsp tomato purée (paste)
5ml/1 tsp crushed garlic
7 ml/1 tsp crushed fresh root ginger
5ml/1 tsp salt
1.5ml/¼ tsp ground turmeric
600ml/1 pint/2½ cups water
15ml/1 tbsp lemon juice
15ml/1 tbsp crushed fresh root
    ginger
15ml/1 tbsp chopped fresh
    coriander (cilantro)
15ml/1 tbsp chopped fresh mint
1 red chilli, chopped

1 Heat the oil in a wok and fry the onions until soft. Mix the tomato purée, with the garlic and ginger, salt and turmeric. Add the mixture to the onions and stir-fry for a few seconds.

2 Add the lamb and stir-fry for about 2–3 minutes. Stir in the water, lower the heat, cover, and cook for 20 minutes.

3 When the water has almost evaporated, stir constantly over a medium heat for 5–7 minutes, making sure that the sauce does not catch on the bottom of the wok.

4 When the sauce is thick and the meat tender, lower the heat and pour in the lemon juice, followed by the shredded fresh ginger, coriander, mint and red chilli, then serve.

Energy 126kcal /526kJ; protein 8.9g; carbohydrate 8.8g, of which sugars 5.9g; fat 6.4g, of which saturates 2.2g; cholesterol 28.5mg; calcium 31mg; fibre 1.5g; sodium 42mg.

SHELLFISH AND FISH

Some of the finest recipes for the wok feature shellfish and fish, and no wonder, for stir-frying, deep-frying and steaming are perfect methods for cooking these ingredients. Whether your taste is for a hearty fish soup, or for something with a crisp and crunchy coating, such as Deep-fried Skate Wings with Wasabi, or the sumptuous Langoustines with Lemon Grass Risotto, the wok will prove to be the perfect utensil. If your wok will accommodate a large steamer, you can even steam fish whole, wrapped in banana leaves to seal in the superb flavours. You can also use a stack of bamboo steamers, and steam vegetables at the same time.

CURRIED SEAFOOD WITH COCONUT MILK

THIS QUICK CURRY IS BASED ON A THAI CLASSIC. THE LOVELY GREEN COLOUR COMES FROM THE FINELY CHOPPED CHILLI AND FRESH HERBS ADDED DURING THE LAST FEW MOMENTS OF COOKING.

SERVES FOUR

INGREDIENTS

225g/8oz small ready-prepared squid
225g/8oz raw tiger prawns
  (jumbo shrimp)
400ml/14fl oz/1⅔ cups coconut milk
2 kaffir lime leaves, finely shredded
30ml/2 tbsp Thai fish sauce
450g/1lb firm white fish fillets,
  skinned, boned and cut into chunks
2 fresh green chillies, seeded and
  finely chopped
30ml/2 tbsp torn fresh basil or
  coriander (cilantro) leaves
squeeze of fresh lime juice
cooked Thai jasmine rice,
  to serve

For the curry paste

6 spring onions (scallions),
  coarsely chopped
4 fresh coriander (cilantro) stems,
  coarsely chopped, plus 45ml/3 tbsp
  chopped fresh coriander (cilantro)
4 kaffir lime leaves, shredded
8 fresh green chillies, seeded and
  coarsely chopped
1 lemon grass stalk,
  coarsely chopped
2.5cm/1in piece fresh root ginger,
  peeled and coarsely chopped
45ml/3 tbsp chopped fresh basil
15ml/1 tbsp vegetable oil

1 Make the curry paste. Put all the ingredients, except the oil, in a food processor and process to a paste. Alternatively, pound together in a mortar with a pestle. Stir in the oil.

2 Rinse the squid and pat dry with kitchen paper. Cut the bodies into rings and halve the tentacles, if necessary.

3 Heat a wok until hot, add the prawns and stir-fry, without any oil, for about 4 minutes, until they turn pink.

4 Remove the prawns from the wok and leave to cool slightly, then peel off the shells, saving a few shells on for the garnish. Make a slit along the back of each one and remove the black vein.

5 Pour the coconut milk into the wok, then bring to the boil over a medium heat, stirring constantly. Add 30ml/ 2 tbsp of curry paste, the shredded lime leaves and fish sauce and stir well to mix. Reduce the heat to low and simmer gently for about 10 minutes.

6 Add the squid, prawns and chunks of fish and cook for about 2 minutes, until the seafood is tender. Take care not to overcook the squid as it will become tough very quickly.

7 Just before serving, stir in the chillies and basil or coriander. Taste and adjust the flavour with a squeeze of lime juice. Garnish with prawns in their shells, and serve with Thai jasmine rice.

VARIATIONS
• You can use any firm-fleshed white fish for this curry, such as monkfish, cod, haddock or John Dory.
• If you prefer, you could substitute shelled scallops for the squid. Slice them in half horizontally and add them with the prawns (shrimp). As with the squid, be careful not to overcook them.

Energy 238Kcal/1005kJ; Protein 40.6g; Carbohydrate 7g, of which sugars 6.2g; Fat 5.5g, of which saturates 0.9g; Cholesterol 288mg; Calcium 145mg; Fibre 1.4g; Sodium 622mg.

STIR-FRIED PRAWNS <u>WITH</u> TAMARIND

THIS DISH PERFECTLY ILLUSTRATES HOW VERSATILE THE WOK IS: IT IS USED FIRST FOR DEEP-FRYING, THEN DRY-FRYING THE CHILLIES, AND THEN STIR-FRYING FOR THIS DELICIOUS DISH. LEAVE A FEW PRAWNS IN THEIR SHELLS FOR VISUAL EFFECT.

SERVES FOUR TO SIX

INGREDIENTS

15ml/1 tbsp chopped garlic
30ml/2 tbsp sliced shallots
vegetable oil for deep-frying
6 dried red chillies
30ml/2 tbsp vegetable oil
30ml/2 tbsp chopped onion
30ml/2 tbsp palm sugar or light
  muscovado (brown) sugar
30ml/2 tbsp chicken stock or water
15ml/1 tbsp Thai fish sauce
90ml/6 tbsp tamarind juice, made
  by mixing tamarind paste with
  warm water
450g/1lb prawns (shrimp), peeled
2 spring onions (scallions), chopped,
  to garnish

1 Deep-fry the chopped garlic and sliced shallots, drain on kitchen paper and set aside. Drain the oil from the wok and wipe clean.

2 Add the dried chillies and dry-fry by pressing them against the surface of the wok with a spatula, turning them occasionally. Do not let them burn. Set them aside to cool slightly.

3 Add the oil to the wok and reheat. Add the chopped onion and cook over a medium heat, stirring occasionally, for 2–3 minutes, until softened and golden brown. Add the sugar, stock or water, fish sauce, dry-fried red chillies and the tamarind juice, stirring until the sugar has dissolved.

4 Bring the mixture to the boil, then lower the heat slightly.

5 Add the prawns, and deep-fried garlic and shallots. Toss over the heat for 3–4 minutes, until the prawns are pink and cooked through. Garnish with the spring onions and serve.

Energy 117Kcal/493kJ; Protein 13.6g; Carbohydrate 6.8g, of which sugars 6.4g; Fat 4.2g, of which saturates 0.5g; Cholesterol 146mg; Calcium 69mg; Fibre 0.3g; Sodium 144mg.

FRAGRANT TIGER PRAWNS WITH DILL

THIS ELEGANT DISH HAS A FRESH, LIGHT FLAVOUR AND IS EQUALLY GOOD SERVED AS A SIMPLE SUPPER OR FOR A DINNER PARTY. THE DELICATE TEXTURE OF FRESH PRAWNS GOES REALLY WELL WITH MILD CUCUMBER AND FRAGRANT DILL, AND ALL YOU NEED IS SOME RICE OR NOODLES TO SERVE.

SERVES FOUR TO SIX

INGREDIENTS

500g/1¼lb raw tiger prawns
(jumbo shrimp), heads and shells
removed but tails left on
500g/1¼lb cucumber
30ml/2 tbsp butter
15ml/1 tbsp olive oil
15ml/1 tbsp finely chopped garlic
45ml/3 tbsp chopped fresh dill
juice of 1 lemon
salt and ground black pepper
steamed rice or noodles, to serve

1 Using a small, sharp knife, carefully make a shallow slit along the back of each prawn and use the point of the knife to remove the black vein. Set the prawns aside.

2 Peel the cucumber and slice in half lengthways. Using a small teaspoon, gently scoop out all the seeds and discard. Cut the cucumber into 4 x 1cm/1½ x ½in sticks.

3 Heat a wok over a high heat, then add the butter and oil. When the butter has melted, add the cucumber and garlic and fry over a high heat for 2–3 minutes, stirring continuously.

4 Add the prepared prawns to the wok and continue to stir-fry over a high heat for 3–4 minutes, or until the prawns turn pink and are just cooked through, then remove from the heat.

5 Add the fresh dill and lemon juice to the wok and toss to combine. Season with salt and ground black pepper and serve immediately accompanied by steamed rice or noodles.

Energy 192Kcal/798kJ; Protein 23.2g; Carbohydrate 2.5g, of which sugars 1.9g; Fat 9.8g, of which saturates 4.4g; Cholesterol 260mg; Calcium 123mg; Fibre 0.9g; Sodium 287mg.

SATAY PRAWNS

AN ENTICING AND TASTY DISH BASED ON THE SPICY PEANUT SAUCE THAT IS TRADITIONALLY SERVED WITH SKEWERED MEAT OR FISH IN SOUTH-EAST ASIA. SERVE WITH GREENS AND JASMINE RICE.

SERVES FOUR TO SIX

INGREDIENTS

450g/1lb large raw prawns (shrimp), shelled, tails left on, and deveined
½ bunch coriander (cilantro), to garnish
4 red chillies, finely sliced, to garnish
spring onions (scallions), cut diagonally, to garnish

For the peanut sauce
45ml/3 tbsp vegetable oil
15ml/1 tbsp chopped garlic
1 small onion, chopped
3–4 red chillies, chopped
3 kaffir lime leaves, torn
1 stalk lemon grass, bruised and chopped
5ml/1 tsp medium curry paste
250ml/8fl oz/1 cup coconut milk
1.5cm/½in cinnamon stick
75g/3oz crunchy peanut butter
45ml/3 tbsp tamarind juice
30ml/2 tbsp Thai fish sauce
30ml/2 tbsp palm sugar
juice of ½ lemon

1 To make the sauce, heat half the oil in a wok or large frying pan and add the garlic and onion. Cook until it softens, about 3–4 minutes.

2 Add the chillies, kaffir lime leaves, lemon grass and curry paste. Cook for a further 2–3 minutes.

COOK'S TIP
Curry pastes have a better and more authentic flavour than curry powders. Once opened, they should be kept in the refrigerator and used within 2 months.

3 Stir in the coconut milk, cinnamon stick, peanut butter, tamarind juice, fish sauce, palm sugar and lemon juice.

4 Reduce the heat and simmer gently for 15–20 minutes until the sauce thickens, stirring occasionally to ensure the sauce doesn't stick to the bottom of the pan.

5 Heat the rest of the oil in a wok or large frying pan. Add the prawns and stir-fry for about 3–4 minutes or until the prawns turn pink and are slightly firm to the touch.

6 Mix the prawns with the sauce. Serve garnished with coriander leaves, red chillies and spring onions.

Energy 219kcal/913kJ; Protein 16.6g; Carbohydrate 10.1g, of which sugars 9g; Fat 12.7g, of which saturates 2.4g; Cholesterol 146mg; Calcium 98mg; Fibre 1.2g; Sodium 414mg.

SPICED PRAWNS WITH COCONUT

THIS SPICY DISH IS BASED ON THE TRADITIONAL INDONESIAN DISH SAMBAL GORENG UDANG.
SAMBALS ARE PUNGENT, VERY HOT DISHES POPULAR THROUGHOUT SOUTH-EAST ASIA.

SERVES SIX

INGREDIENTS

2–3 red chillies, seeded and chopped
3 shallots, chopped
1 lemon grass stalk, chopped
2 garlic cloves, chopped
thin sliver of dried shrimp paste
2.5ml/½ tsp ground galangal
5ml/1 tsp ground turmeric
5ml/1 tsp ground coriander
15ml/1 tbsp groundnut (peanut) oil
250ml/8fl oz/1 cup water
2 fresh kaffir lime leaves
5ml/1 tsp light brown soft sugar
2 tomatoes, skinned, seeded
   and chopped
250ml/8fl oz/1 cup coconut milk
675g/1½lb large raw prawns (shrimp),
   peeled and deveined
squeeze of lemon juice
salt
shredded spring onions (scallions)
   and flaked coconut, to garnish

1 In a mortar, pound together the chillies, shallots, lemon grass, garlic, shrimp paste, galangal, turmeric and coriander with a pestle until the mixture forms a paste.

COOK'S TIP
Dried shrimp paste is available from Asian food stores, as is ground galangal, which is similar to ground ginger and comes from the same family. It is sold in blocks, and you simply cut off however much you need. The remaining paste can be stored in the refrigerator, wrapped in several layers of foil.

2 Heat a wok, add the oil and swirl it around. Add the spice paste and stir-fry for 2 minutes. Pour in the water and add the kaffir lime leaves, sugar and tomatoes. Simmer for 8–10 minutes until most of the liquid has evaporated.

3 Add the coconut milk and prawns and cook gently, stirring, for 4 minutes until the prawns are pink. Season with lemon juice and salt to taste.

4 Transfer the mixture to a warmed serving dish, garnish with the spring onions and flaked coconut and serve.

Energy 141kcal/590kJ; Protein 15.7g; Carbohydrate 9.9g, of which sugars 8.7g; Fat 4.5g, of which saturates 0.7g; Cholesterol 163mg; Calcium 102mg; Fibre 0.7g; Sodium 234mg.

GOAN PRAWN CURRY WITH MANGO

THIS SWEET, SPICY, HOT-AND-SOUR CURRY COMES FROM THE SHORES OF WESTERN INDIA. IT IS SIMPLE TO MAKE, AND THE ADDITION OF MANGO AND TAMARIND PRODUCES A VERY FULL, RICH FLAVOUR. IF YOU HAVE TIME, MAKE THE SAUCE THE DAY BEFORE TO GIVE THE FLAVOURS TIME TO DEVELOP.

SERVES FOUR

INGREDIENTS
  5ml/1 tsp hot chilli powder
  15ml/1 tbsp paprika
  2.5ml/1/2 tsp ground turmeric
  4 garlic cloves, crushed
  10ml/2 tsp finely grated ginger
  30ml/2 tbsp ground coriander
  10ml/2 tsp ground cumin
  15ml/1 tbsp jaggery or palm sugar
  1 green mango
  400g/14oz can coconut milk
  10ml/2 tsp salt
  15ml/1 tbsp tamarind paste
  1kg/2¼lb large prawns (shrimp)
  chopped coriander (cilantro),
    to garnish
  steamed rice, chopped tomato, and
    cucumber and onion salad, to serve

VARIATION
Peel the prawns before cooking if you like, but be careful not to overcook.

1 Wash, stone (pit) and slice the mango and set aside. In a large bowl, combine the chilli powder, paprika, turmeric, garlic, ginger, ground coriander, ground cumin and jaggery or palm sugar. Add 400ml/14fl oz/1⅔ cups cold water to the bowl and stir to combine.

2 Pour the spice mixture into a wok and place over a high heat and bring the mixture to the boil. Cover the wok with a lid, reduce the heat to low and simmer gently for 8–10 minutes.

3 Add the mango, coconut milk, salt and tamarind paste to the wok and stir to combine. Bring to a simmer and then add the prawns.

4 Cover the wok and cook gently for 10–12 minutes, or until the prawns have turned pink and are cooked.

5 Serve the curry garnished with chopped coriander, accompanied by steamed rice and a tomato, cucumber and onion salad.

Energy 151Kcal/648kJ; Protein 22.1g; Carbohydrate 14.1g, of which sugars 14g; Fat 1.1g, of which saturates 0.5g; Cholesterol 263mg; Calcium 143mg; Fibre 1g; Sodium 2102mg.

HERB- <u>AND</u> CHILLI SEARED SCALLOPS

TENDER, SUCCULENT SCALLOPS TASTE SIMPLY DIVINE WHEN MARINATED IN FRESH CHILLI, FRAGRANT MINT AND AROMATIC BASIL, THEN QUICKLY SEARED IN A PIPING HOT WOK. IF YOU CAN'T FIND KING SCALLOPS FOR THIS RECIPE, USE TWICE THE QUANTITY OF SMALLER QUEEN SCALLOPS.

SERVES FOUR

INGREDIENTS
   20–24 king scallops, cleaned
   120ml/4fl oz/$\frac{1}{2}$ cup olive oil
   finely grated rind and juice
     of 1 lemon
   30ml/2 tbsp finely chopped mixed
     fresh mint and basil
   1 fresh red chilli, seeded and finely
     chopped
   salt and ground black pepper
   500g/1$\frac{1}{4}$lb pak choi (bok choy)

1 Place the scallops in a shallow, non-metallic bowl in a single layer. In a clean bowl, mix together half the oil, the lemon rind and juice, chopped herbs and chilli and spoon over the scallops. Season well with salt and black pepper, cover and set aside.

2 Using a sharp knife, cut each pak choi lengthways into four pieces.

VARIATION
If you can't find pak choi (bok choy) use Chinese broccoli, purple sprouting broccoli or Swiss chard instead.

3 Heat a wok over a high heat. When hot, drain the scallops (reserving the marinade) and add to the wok. Cook for 1 minute on each side, or until cooked to your liking.

4 Pour the marinade over the scallops and remove the wok from the heat. Transfer the scallops and juices to a platter and keep warm. Wipe out the wok with a piece of kitchen paper.

5 Place the wok over a high heat. When all traces of moisture have evaporated, add the remaining oil. When the oil is hot add the pak choi and stir-fry over a high heat for 2–3 minutes, until the leaves wilt.

6 Divide the greens among four warmed serving plates, then top with the reserved scallops and their juices and serve immediately.

Energy 410Kcal/1714kJ; Protein 44.5g; Carbohydrate 8.3g, of which sugars 2.1g; Fat 22.3g, of which saturates 3.5g; Cholesterol 82mg; Calcium 286mg; Fibre 3.2g; Sodium 494mg.

HOT SPICY CRAB CLAWS

CRAB CLAWS ARE USED TO DELICIOUS EFFECT IN THIS QUICK STIR-FRY (TO BE EATEN WITH THE FINGERS), BASED ON AN INDONESIAN DISH CALLED KEPITING PEDAS, OR CHILLI CRAB.

SERVES FOUR

INGREDIENTS

  24 fresh or frozen and thawed
    cooked crab claws
  8 shallots, roughly chopped
  4 fresh red chillies, seeded and
    roughly chopped
  6 garlic cloves, roughly chopped
  10ml/2 tsp grated fresh root ginger
  5 ml/ 1 tsp ground coriander
  45ml/3 tbsp groundnut oil
  80ml/6 tbsp water
  20ml/4 tsp sweet soy sauce
    (*kecap manis*)
  30 ml/6 tsp lime juice
  salt
  fresh coriander (cilantro), to garnish

1 Crack the crab claws with the back of a heavy knife to make eating them easier and set aside. In a mortar, pound the chopped shallots with the pestle until pulpy. Add the chillies, garlic, ginger and ground coriander and pound until the mixture forms a fairly coarse paste.

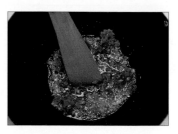

2 Heat a wok over a medium heat. Add the oil and swirl it around. When it is hot, stir in the chilli paste. Stir-fry for about 30 seconds. Increase the heat to high. Add the crab claws and stir-fry for another 3–4 minutes until the crab meat is heated through.

3 Stir in the water, soy sauce, lime juice and salt to taste. Continue to stir-fry for 1–2 minutes. Serve at once, garnished with fresh coriander.

COOK'S TIP

If whole crab claws are unavailable, look out for frozen ready-prepared crab claws. These are shelled, with just the tip of the claw attached to the whole meat. Stir-fry for about 2 minutes until hot throughout.

Energy 224kcal/933kJ; Protein 10.1g; Carbohydrate 16.9g, of which sugars 0g; Fat 12.9g, of which saturates 1.7g; Cholesterol 78mg; Calcium 62mg; Fibre 0.3g; Sodium 256mg.

QUICK-FRIED PRAWNS WITH HOT SPICES

THESE SPICY PRAWNS ARE STIR-FRIED IN MOMENTS TO MAKE A WONDERFUL DISH. EAT WITH THE
FINGERS AND SERVE WITH WARM NAAN BREAD TO MOP UP THE DELICIOUS JUICES.

SERVES FOUR

INGREDIENTS
900g/2lb large raw prawns (shrimp)
5cm/2in fresh root ginger, grated
4 garlic cloves, crushed
10ml/2 tsp hot chilli powder
10ml/2 tsp ground turmeric
20ml/4 tsp black mustard seeds
seeds from 8 green cardamom
    pods, crushed
100g/4oz/8 tbsp ghee or butter
240ml/8fl oz/ 1 cup coconut milk
salt and ground black pepper
chopped fresh coriander (cilantro),
    to garnish

1 Peel the prawns carefully, leaving the tails attached.

2 Using a small sharp knife, make a slit along the back of each prawn and remove the dark vein.

3 Rinse the prawns under cold running water, drain and pat completely dry with kitchen paper.

4 Put the ginger, garlic, chilli powder, turmeric, mustard seeds and cardamom seeds in a bowl. Add the prawns and toss to coat with the spice mixture.

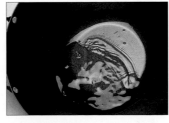

5 Heat a wok until hot. Add the ghee or butter and swirl it around until foaming.

6 Add the prawns and stir-fry for 1–1½ minutes until they are just turning pink.

7 Stir in the coconut milk and simmer for 3–4 minutes until the prawns are just cooked through. Season to taste with salt and pepper. Sprinkle over the coriander and serve at once.

Energy 388kcal/1618kJ; Protein 40.7g; Carbohydrate 5.1g, of which sugars 3.1g; Fat 22.9g, of which saturates 13.4g; Cholesterol 492mg; Calcium 248mg; Fibre 1.7g; Sodium 679mg.

CLAMS WITH CHILLI AND YELLOW BEAN SAUCE

SEAFOOD IS ABUNDANT IN THAILAND, ESPECIALLY AT ALL OF THE BEACH HOLIDAY RESORTS. THIS DELICOUS DISH, WHICH IS SIMPLE TO PREPARE, IS A THAI FAVOURITE.

SERVES FOUR TO SIX

INGREDIENTS

1kg/2¼lb fresh clams
30ml/2 tbsp vegetable oil
4 garlic cloves, finely chopped
15ml/1 tbsp grated root ginger
4 shallots, finely chopped
30ml/2 tbsp yellow bean sauce
6 red chillies, seeded and
  chopped
15ml/1 tbsp Thai fish sauce
pinch of granulated sugar
handful of basil leaves, plus extra
  to garnish

COOK'S TIP
Discard any clams that remain closed
after cooking

1 Scrub the clams. Heat the oil in a wok or large frying pan. Add the garlic and ginger and fry for 30 seconds, add the shallots and fry for a further minute.

2 Add the clams. Using a fish slice or spatula, turn them a few times to coat with the oil. Add the yellow bean sauce and half the red chillies.

3 Continue to cook, stirring often, until all the clams open, about 5–7 minutes. You may need to add a splash of water. Season with fish sauce and sugar.

4 Finally add the basil and transfer to individual bowls or a serving platter. Garnish with the remaining red chillies and basil leaves.

Energy 94kcal/393kJ; Protein 11.6g; Carbohydrate 2.4g, of which sugars 0.6g; Fat 4.3g, of which saturates 0.6g; Cholesterol 45mg; Calcium 75mg; Fibre 0.7g; Sodium 998mg.

PRAWN FU YUNG

THIS IS A VERY COLOURFUL AND POPULAR DISH THAT ORIGINATED IN AMERICAN CHINESE CUISINE. IT IS SIMPLE AND QUICK TO MAKE IN A WOK.

SERVES FOUR

INGREDIENTS

3 eggs, reserving
    5ml/1 tsp egg white
15ml/1 tbsp finely chopped
    spring onions (scallions)
45–60ml/3–4 tbsp vegetable oil
225g/8oz raw prawns
    (shrimp), peeled
5ml/1 tsp cornflour (cornstarch),
    mixed to a paste with
    10ml/2 tsp cold water
175g/6oz green peas
15ml/1 tbsp Chinese rice wine
    or dry sherry
salt

1 Beat the eggs with a pinch of salt and a few pieces of the spring onions. Heat a little oil in a preheated wok over a moderate heat. Add the egg mixture and stir to scramble. Remove the scrambled eggs and reserve.

2 Mix the prawns with salt, 5ml/1 tsp egg white and the cornflour paste. Stir-fry the peas in hot oil for 30 seconds Add the prawns and spring onions. Stir-fry for 1 minute, then stir into the egg with the wine or sherry and serve.

Energy 228kcal/948kJ; Protein 18.6g; Carbohydrate 6.2g, of which sugars 1.1g; Fat 14.3g, of which saturates 2.6g; Cholesterol 281mg; Calcium 80mg; Fibre 2.1g; Sodium 171mg.

GRIDDLED SQUID AND TOMATOES IN A TAMARIND DRESSING

THIS IS A LOVELY VIETNAMESE DISH — SWEET, CHARRED SQUID SERVED IN A TANGY DRESSING MADE WITH TAMARIND, LIME AND NUOC MAM. IT IS BEST MADE WITH BABY SQUID BECAUSE THEY ARE TENDER AND SWEET. THE TOMATOES AND HERBS ADD WONDERFUL FRESH FLAVOURS.

2 Heat a ridged griddle, wipe the pan with a little oil, and griddle the tomatoes until lightly charred on both sides. Transfer them to a board, chop into bitesize chunks, and place in a bowl.

3 Clean the griddle, then heat it up again and wipe with a little more oil. Griddle the squid for 2–3 minutes each side, pressing them down with a spatula, until nicely browned. Transfer to the bowl with the tomatoes, add the herbs and the dressing and toss well. Serve immediately.

SERVES FOUR

INGREDIENTS
   vegetable oil, for greasing
   2 large tomatoes, skinned, halved
     and seeded
   500g/1¼lb fresh baby squid
   1 bunch each fresh basil, coriander
     (cilantro) and mint, stalks removed,
     leaves chopped
For the dressing
   15ml/1 tbsp tamarind paste
   juice of half a lime
   30ml/2 tbsp *nuoc mam*
   15ml/1 tbsp raw cane sugar
   1 garlic clove, crushed
   2 shallots, halved and finely sliced
   2 Serrano chillies, seeded and sliced

1 Put the dressing ingredients in a bowl and stir until well mixed. Set aside.

VARIATION
Traditionally, the squid are steamed for this dish: you can steam them for 10–15 minutes in a wok if you prefer.

COOK'S TIPS
• To prepare squid yourself, get a firm hold of the head and pull it from the body. Reach down inside the body sac and pull out the transparent backbone, as well as any stringy parts. Rinse the body sac inside and out and pat dry. Cut the tentacles off above the eyes and add to the pile of squid you're going to cook. Discard everything else.
• Griddled scallops and prawns (shrimp) are also delicious in this tangy dressing.

Energy 165Kcal/701kJ; Protein 22g; Carbohydrate 15g, of which sugars 10g; Fat 3g, of which saturates 1g; Cholesterol 281mg; Calcium 105mg; Fibre 1g; Sodium 500mg.

PRAWN <u>AND</u> CAULIFLOWER CURRY <u>WITH</u> FENUGREEK, COCONUT <u>AND</u> LIME

THIS IS A BASIC FISHERMAN'S CURRY FROM THE SOUTHERN COAST OF VIETNAM. SIMPLE TO MAKE, IT WOULD USUALLY BE EATEN FROM A COMMUNAL BOWL, OR FROM THE WOK ITSELF, AND SERVED WITH NOODLES, RICE OR CHUNKS OF BAGUETTE TO MOP UP THE DELICIOUSLY FRAGRANT, CREAMY SAUCE.

SERVES FOUR

INGREDIENTS

   450g/1lb raw tiger prawns (jumbo
     shrimp), shelled and cleaned
   juice of 1 lime
   15ml/1 tbsp sesame or vegetable oil
   1 red onion, roughly chopped
   2 garlic cloves, roughly chopped
   2 Thai chillies, seeded and chopped
   1 cauliflower, broken into florets
   5ml/1 tsp sugar
   2 star anise, dry-fried and ground
   10ml/2 tsp fenugreek, dry-fried
     and ground
   450ml/¾ pint/2 cups coconut milk
   1 bunch fresh coriander (cilantro),
     stalks removed, leaves chopped, to
     garnish
   salt and ground black pepper

1 In a bowl, toss the prawns in the lime juice and set aside. Heat a wok or heavy pan and add the oil. Stir in the onion, garlic and chillies. As they brown, add the cauliflower. Stir-fry for 2–3 minutes.

VARIATION
Other popular combinations include prawns with butternut squash or pumpkin.

2 Toss in the sugar and spices. Add the coconut milk, stirring to make sure it is thoroughly combined. Reduce the heat and simmer for 10–15 minutes, or until the liquid has reduced and thickened a little. Add the prawns and lime juice and cook for 1–2 minutes, or until the prawns turn opaque. Season to taste, and sprinkle with coriander. Serve hot.

Energy 232Kcal/971kJ; Protein 25g; Carbohydrate 13g, of which sugars 12g; Fat 10g, of which saturates 2g; Cholesterol 219mg; Calcium 167mg; Fibre 2.2g; Sodium 500mg.

THAI FISH STIR-FRY

THIS IS A SUBSTANTIAL DISH, BEST SERVED WITH A MOUND OF PLAIN RICE, OR SOME CRUSTY BREAD FOR MOPPING UP ALL THE SPICY, CREAMY JUICES.

SERVES FOUR

INGREDIENTS

675g/1½lb mixed seafood, such as
   red snapper and cod, filleted and
   skinned, and raw prawns (shrimp)
300ml/½ pint/1¼ cups coconut milk
15ml/1 tbsp vegetable oil
salt and ground black pepper
crusty bread, to serve

For the sauce

2 large red fresh chillies
1 onion, roughly chopped
5cm/2in fresh root ginger, peeled
   and sliced
5cm/2in lemon grass stalk,
   outer leaf discarded,
   roughly sliced
5cm/2in piece galangal, peeled
   and sliced
6 blanched almonds, chopped
2.5ml/½ tsp turmeric
2.5ml/½ tsp salt

1 Cut the filleted fish into large chunks. Peel and devein the prawns, keeping their tails intact.

COOK'S TIP
Galangal is a rhizome from the same family as ginger, with a similar but milder flavour. It is peeled and sliced, chopped or grated in the same way as root ginger. It is an important spice in South-east Asian cooking.

2 To make the sauce, remove the seeds from the chillies and chop the flesh roughly. Put the chillies and the other sauce ingredients in a food processor or blender with 45ml/3 tbsp of the coconut milk. Process until smooth.

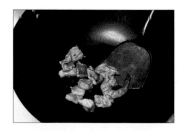

3 Heat a wok, then add the oil. When the oil is hot, stir-fry the seafood for 2–3 minutes, then remove.

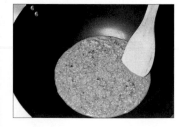

4 Add the sauce and the remaining coconut milk to the wok, then return the seafood and toss in the sauce. Bring to the boil, season well and serve with crusty bread.

Energy 207kcal/869kJ; Protein 32.3g; Carbohydrate 5.4g, of which sugars 5g; Fat 6.3g, of which saturates 0.8g; Cholesterol 78mg; Calcium 54mg; Fibre 0.6g; Sodium 186mg.

KARAHI PRAWNS AND FENUGREEK

THE BLACK-EYED BEANS, PRAWNS AND PANEER IN THIS MEAN THAT IT IS RICH IN PROTEIN. THE COMBINATION OF BOTH GROUND AND FRESH FENUGREEK MAKES THIS A VERY FRAGRANT DISH.

SERVES FOUR TO SIX

INGREDIENTS
60ml/4 tbsp corn oil
2 onions, sliced
2 medium tomatoes, sliced
7.5ml/1½ tsp crushed garlic
5ml/1 tsp chilli powder
5ml/1 tsp grated fresh root ginger
5ml/1 tsp ground cumin
5ml/1 tsp ground coriander
5ml/1 tsp salt
150g/5oz paneer, cubed
5ml/1 tsp ground fenugreek
1 bunch fresh fenugreek leaves
115g/4oz cooked prawns (shrimp)
2 fresh red chillies, sliced
30ml/2 tbsp chopped fresh
coriander (cilantro)
50g/2oz canned black-eyed
beans, drained
15ml/1 tbsp lemon juice

1 Heat the oil in a wok and fry the onions and tomatoes, stirring occasionally, for about 3 minutes.

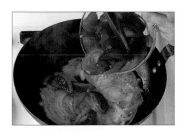

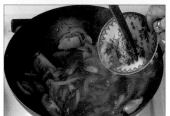

2 Add the crushed garlic, chilli powder, fresh ginger, ground cumin, ground coriander, salt, cubed paneer and the ground and fresh fenugreek.

3 Stir through to mix together, then lower the heat slightly and stir-fry for about 2 minutes.

4 Add the prawns, chillies, coriander and black-eyed beans to the wok.

5 Cook for a further 3–5 minutes, stirring occasionally, until the prawns are heated through and the liquid is slightly reduced. Finally sprinkle over the lemon juice and serve immediately.

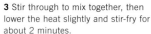

Energy 151kcal/629kJ; Protein 8.5g; Carbohydrate 10.1g, of which sugars 6.6g; Fat 8.7g, of which saturates 1.7g; Cholesterol 41mg; Calcium 72mg; Fibre 1.8g; Sodium 445mg.

GRILLED PRAWN SALAD WITH PEANUTS AND POMELO

THIS REFRESHING SALAD IS TYPICAL OF THE SALADS OF CENTRAL AND SOUTHERN VIETNAM, WHERE FRUIT, VEGETABLES, MEAT, FISH AND SHELLFISH ARE ALL TOSSED TOGETHER IN ONE DISH. THE PRAWNS CAN ALSO BE COOKED ON THE BARBECUE.

SERVES FOUR

INGREDIENTS

   16 raw tiger prawns (jumbo shrimp),
     peeled and deveined
   1 small cucumber, peeled and cut
     into matchsticks
   1 pomelo, separated into segments
     and cut into bitesize pieces
   1 carrot, peeled and cut into
     matchsticks
   1 green Serrano chilli, seeded and
     finely sliced
   30ml/2 tbsp roasted peanuts,
     roughly chopped
   juice of half a lime
   60ml/4 tbsp *nuoc cham*
   vegetable oil, for griddling
   1 small bunch fresh basil,
     stalks removed
   1 small bunch coriander (cilantro),
     stalks removed
   salt
For the marinade
   30ml/2 tbsp *nuoc mam*
   30ml/2 tbsp soy sauce
   15ml/1 tbsp groundnut (peanut) or
     sesame oil
   1 shallot, finely chopped
   1 garlic clove, crushed
   10ml/2 tsp raw cane sugar

2 Sprinkle the cucumber matchsticks with salt and leave for 15 minutes. Rinse and drain, then mix in a bowl with the pomelo, carrot, chilli peanuts, lime juice and *nuoc cham*. Toss well.

3 Heat oil in a wok and stir fry the prawns until they singe slightly.

4 Once cooked, toss the prawns into the salad with the herbs and serve.

1 In a wide bowl, combine all the marinade ingredients. Add the prawns, making sure they are coated, and set aside for 30 minutes.

Energy 219Kcal/912kJ; Protein 14g; Carbohydrate 14g, of which sugars 9g; Fat 12g, of which saturates 2g; Cholesterol 98mg; Calcium 121mg; Fibre 1.4g; Sodium 500mg.

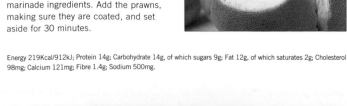

SPICED SCALLOPS AND SUGAR SNAP PEAS ON CRISPY NOODLE CAKES

TENDER, JUICY SCALLOPS AND SUGAR SNAP PEAS COOKED IN SPICES AND SERVED ON A BED OF FRIED NOODLES IS A WINNING COMBINATION. IT'S SIMPLE AND STYLISH AND MAKES A GREAT DISH FOR SPECIAL-OCCASION ENTERTAINING.

SERVES FOUR

INGREDIENTS
 45ml/3 tbsp oyster sauce
 10ml/2 tsp soy sauce
 5ml/1 tsp sesame oil
 5ml/1 tsp golden caster
  (superfine) sugar
 30ml/2 tbsp sunflower oil
 2 fresh red chillies, finely sliced
 4 garlic cloves, finely chopped
 10ml/2 tsp finely chopped fresh
  root ginger
 250g/9oz sugar snap peas, trimmed
 600g/1¼lb king scallops, cleaned,
  roes discarded and sliced in half
 3 spring onions (scallions),
  finely shredded
For the noodle cakes
 250g/9oz fresh thin egg noodles
 10ml/2 tsp sesame oil
 120ml/4fl oz/½ cup sunflower oil

1 Cook the noodles in a wok of boiling water for 1 minute, or until tender. Drain well and transfer to a bowl with the sesame oil and 15ml/1 tbsp of the sunflower oil. Spread the noodles out on a large baking sheet and leave to dry in a warm place for 1 hour.

VARIATION
Use king prawns (jumbo shrimp) instead of scallops, if you like.

2 To cook the noodles, heat 15ml/ 1 tbsp of the oil in a non-stick wok over a high heat. Divide the noodle mixture into four portions and add one portion to the wok. Using a spatula, flatten it out and shape it into a cake.

3 Reduce the heat slightly and cook the cake for about 5 minutes on each side, or until crisp and golden. Drain on kitchen paper and keep warm while you make the remaining three noodle cakes in the same way.

4 Mix together the oyster sauce, soy sauce, sesame oil and sugar in a small bowl, stirring until the sugar has dissolved completely.

5 Heat a wok over medium heat and add the sunflower oil. When hot add the chillies, garlic and ginger, and stir-fry for 30 seconds. Add the sugar snap peas and stir-fry for 1–2 minutes.

6 Add the scallops and spring onions to the wok and stir fry over high heat for 1 minute. Stir in the oyster sauce mixture and cook for a further 1 minute until warmed through.

7 To serve, place a noodle cake on each of four warmed plates and top each one with the scallop mixture. Serve immediately.

Energy 689Kcal/2888kJ; Protein 41.4g; Carbohydrate 59.9g, of which sugars 6.2g; Fat 33.3g, of which saturates 5.4g; Cholesterol 78mg; Calcium 73mg; Fibre 5g; Sodium 700mg.

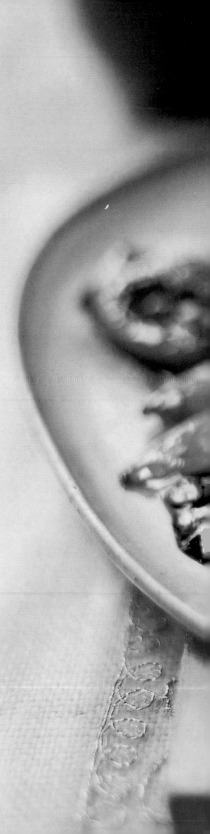

FRIED JASMINE RICE WITH PRAWNS

*STRIPS OF OMELETTE ARE USED TO GARNISH THIS RICE DISH. USE YOUR WOK FOR FRYING THE
OMELETTE – THE SLOPING SIDES MAKE IT EASY TO SPREAD THE BEATEN EGG THINLY AND THEN TO
SLIDE IT OUT, READY FOR ROLLING AND SLICING.*

SERVES FOUR TO SIX

INGREDIENTS
    45ml/3 tbsp vegetable oil
    1 egg, beaten
    1 onion, chopped
    15ml/1 tbsp chopped garlic
    15ml/1 tbsp shrimp paste
    1kg/2¼lb/4 cups cooked jasmine rice
    350g/12oz cooked shelled prawns
      (shrimp)
    50g/2oz thawed frozen peas
    oyster sauce, to taste
    2 spring onions (scallions), chopped
    15–20 Thai basil leaves, roughly
      snipped, plus an extra sprig,
      to garnish

1 Heat 15ml/1 tbsp of the oil in a wok
or frying pan. Add the beaten egg and
swirl it around to set like a thin pancake.

2 Cook the pancake (on one side only)
over a gentle heat until golden. Slide
the pancake on to a board, roll up and
cut into thin strips. Set aside.

3 Heat the remaining oil in the wok
or pan, add the onion and garlic and
stir-fry for 2–3 minutes. Stir in the
shrimp paste and mix well until
thoroughly combined.

4 Add the rice, prawns and peas and
toss and stir together, until everything is
heated through.

5 Season with oyster sauce to taste,
taking great care as the shrimp paste is
salty. Mix in the spring onions and basil
leaves. Transfer to a serving dish and
top with the strips of egg pancake.
Serve, garnished with a sprig of basil.

Energy 357Kcal/1508kJ; Protein 17.6g; Carbohydrate 54.6g, of which sugars 1.7g; Fat 9.2g, of which saturates 1.5g; Cholesterol 154mg; Calcium 111mg; Fibre 1g; Sodium 198mg.

CRAB AND TOFU STIR FRY

FOR A LIGHT MEAL SUITABLE FOR SERVING AT ANY TIME, THIS SPEEDY STIR-FRY IS THE IDEAL CHOICE.
AS YOU NEED ONLY A LITTLE CRAB MEAT — AND YOU COULD USE THE CANNED VARIETY — THIS IS A
VERY ECONOMICAL DISH. THE TOFU BOOSTS THE PROTEIN CONTENT.

SERVES TWO

INGREDIENTS
    250g/9oz silken tofu
    60ml/4 tbsp vegetable oil
    2 garlic cloves, finely chopped
    115g/4oz white crab meat
    130g/4½oz/generous 1 cup baby
      corn, halved lengthways
    2 spring onions (scallions), chopped
    1 fresh red chilli, seeded and
      finely chopped
    30ml/2 tbsp soy sauce
    15ml/1 tbsp Thai fish sauce
    5ml/1 tsp palm sugar or light
      muscovado (brown) sugar
    juice of 1 lime
    small bunch fresh coriander
      (cilantro), chopped, to garnish

1 Using a sharp knife, cut the silken tofu into 1cm/½in cubes.

2 Heat the oil in a wok or large, heavy frying pan. Add the tofu cubes and stir-fry until golden all over, taking care not to break them up. Remove the tofu with a slotted spoon and set aside.

3 Add the garlic to the wok or pan and stir-fry until golden. Add the crab meat, tofu, corn, spring onions, chilli, soy sauce, fish sauce and sugar. Cook, stirring constantly, until the vegetables are just tender. Stir in the lime juice, transfer to warmed bowls, sprinkle with the coriander and serve immediately.

Energy 365Kcal/1514kJ; Protein 23.1g; Carbohydrate 5.8g, of which sugars 4.8g; Fat 27.9g, of which saturates 3.3g; Cholesterol 41mg; Calcium 719mg; Fibre 1.2g; Sodium 2131mg.

LOBSTER AND CRAB STEAMED IN BEER

IN SPITE OF ITS APPEARANCE ON MENUS IN RESTAURANTS THAT SPECIALIZE IN THE COMPLEX AND REFINED IMPERIAL DISHES OF HUE, THIS RECIPE IS VERY EASY TO MAKE. IT MAY BE EXPENSIVE, BUT IT'S A WONDERFUL DISH FOR A SPECIAL OCCASION.

SERVES FOUR

INGREDIENTS
    4 uncooked lobsters, about
        450g/1lb each
    4 uncooked crabs, about
        225g/8oz each
    600ml/1 pint/2½ cups beer
    4 spring onions (scallions), trimmed
        and chopped into long pieces
    4cm/1½in fresh root ginger, peeled
        and finely sliced
    2 green or red Thai chillies, seeded
        and finely sliced
    3 lemon grass stalks, finely sliced
    1 bunch fresh dill, fronds chopped
    1 bunch each fresh basil and
        coriander (cilantro), stalks removed,
        leaves chopped
    about 30ml/2 tbsp *nuoc mam*, plus
        extra for serving
    juice of 1 lemon
    salt and ground black pepper

1 Clean the lobsters and crabs thoroughly and rub them with salt and pepper. Place them in a large steamer and pour the beer into the base.

2 Scatter half the spring onions, ginger, chillies, lemon grass and herbs over the lobsters and crabs, and steam for about 10 minutes, or until the lobsters turn red. Lift them on to a warmed serving dish.

3 Add the remaining flavouring ingredients to the beer with the *nuoc mam* and lemon juice, Pour into a dipping bowl and serve immediately with the hot lobsters and crabs, with extra splashes of *nuoc mam*, if you like.

COOK'S TIP
Whether you cook the lobsters and crabs at the same time depends on the number of people you are cooking for and the size of your steamer. However, they don't take long to cook so it is easy to steam them in batches. In the markets and restaurants of Vietnam, you can find crabs that are 60cm/24in in diameter, which may feed several people but require a huge steamer. Depending on the size and availability of the lobsters and crabs, you can make this recipe for as many people as you like, because the quantities are simple to adjust. For those who like their food fiery, splash a little chilli sauce into the beer broth.

VARIATION
Prawns (shrimp) and mussels are also delicious cooked this way.

Energy 264Kcal/1112kJ; Protein 48g; Carbohydrate 4g, of which sugars 1g; Fat 7g, of which saturates 1g; Cholesterol 210mg; Calcium 185mg; Fibre 0.5g; Sodium 130mg.

STEAMED SCALLOPS WITH GINGER

IT HELPS TO HAVE TWO WOKS WHEN MAKING THIS DISH. IF YOU ARE NOT DOUBLY BLESSED, BORROW AN EXTRA ONE FROM A FRIEND, OR USE A LARGE, HEAVY PAN WITH A TRIVET FOR STEAMING THE SECOND PLATE OF SCALLOPS. TAKE CARE NOT TO OVERCOOK THE TENDER SEAFOOD.

SERVES FOUR

INGREDIENTS

24 king scallops in their
  shells, cleaned
15ml/1 tbsp very finely shredded
  fresh root ginger
5ml/1 tsp very finely chopped garlic
1 large fresh red chilli, seeded and
  very finely chopped
15ml/1 tbsp light soy sauce
15ml/1 tbsp Chinese
  rice wine
a few drops of sesame oil
2–3 spring onions (scallions), very
  finely shredded
15ml/1 tbsp very finely chopped
  fresh chives
noodles or rice, to serve

1 Remove the scallops from their shells, then remove the membrane and hard white muscle from each one. Arrange the scallops on two plates. Rinse the shells, dry and set aside.

2 Fill two woks with 5cm/2in water and place a trivet in the base of each one. Bring to the boil.

3 Meanwhile, mix together the ginger, garlic, chilli, soy sauce, rice wine, sesame oil, spring onions and chives.

COOK'S TIP
Use the freshest scallops you can find. If you ask your fishmonger to shuck them, remember to ask for the shells.

4 Spoon the flavourings over the scallops. Lower a plate into each of the woks. Turn the heat to low, cover and steam for 10–12 minutes.

5 Divide the scallops among four, or eight, of the reserved shells and serve immediately with noodles or rice.

Energy 167Kcal/708kJ; Protein 29.8g; Carbohydrate 7g, of which sugars 2.6g; Fat 2g, of which saturates 0.6g; Cholesterol 59mg; Calcium 53mg; Fibre 0.8g; Sodium 496mg.

LANGOUSTINES WITH LEMON GRASS RISOTTO

THE WOK IS WONDERFUL FOR MAKING RISOTTO. FOR THIS VERSION, THE TRADITIONAL ITALIAN RISOTTO IS GIVEN A SUBTLE ASIAN TWIST WITH THE ADDITION OF FRAGRANT LEMON GRASS, ASIAN FISH SAUCE AND CHINESE CHIVES: THE PERFECT ACCOMPANIMENT TO SIMPLY STEAMED LANGOUSTINES.

SERVES FOUR

INGREDIENTS

8 fresh langoustines
30ml/2 tbsp olive oil
15ml/1 tbsp butter
1 onion, finely chopped
1 carrot, finely diced
1 celery stick, finely diced
30ml/2 tbsp very finely chopped
  lemon grass
300g/11oz/1½ cups arborio or other
  risotto rice
200ml/7fl oz/scant 1 cup
  dry white wine
1.5 litres/2½ pints/6¼ cups boiling
  vegetable stock
50ml/2fl oz/¼ cup Thai fish sauce
30ml/2 tbsp finely chopped
  Chinese chives
salt and ground black pepper

1 Place the langoustines in a baking parchment-lined bamboo steamer, cover and place over a wok of simmering water. Steam for 6–8 minutes, remove from the heat and keep warm.

2 Heat the oil and butter in a wok and add the vegetables. Cook over a high heat for 2–3 minutes. Add the lemon grass and rice and stir-fry for 2 minutes.

3 Add the wine to the wok, reduce the heat and slowly stir until the wine is absorbed. Add about two-thirds of the stock and cook gently, stirring until absorbed. Continue adding the stock, stirring until absorbed before adding more. When the rice is tender, stir in the fish sauce and Chinese chives, check the seasoning and serve immediately, topped with langoustines.

Energy 467Kcal/1949kJ; Protein 23.8g; Carbohydrate 64.2g, of which sugars 3.4g; Fat 8.9g, of which saturates 2.3g; Cholesterol 201mg; Calcium 114mg; Fibre 0.9g; Sodium 218mg.

STIR-FRIED SQUID WITH GINGER

THERE'S AN ANCIENT BELIEF THAT A WELL-LOVED WOK HOLDS THE MEMORY OF ALL THE DISHES THAT HAVE EVER BEEN COOKED IN IT. GIVE YOURS SOMETHING TO THINK ABOUT BY INTRODUCING IT TO THIS CLASSIC COMBINATION OF BABY SQUID IN SOY SAUCE, GINGER AND LEMON JUICE.

SERVES TWO

INGREDIENTS

4 ready-prepared baby squid, total
    weight about 250g/9oz
15ml/1 tbsp vegetable oil
2 garlic cloves, finely chopped
30ml/2 tbsp soy sauce
2.5cm/1in piece fresh root ginger,
    peeled and finely chopped
juice of ½ lemon
5ml/1 tsp granulated sugar
2 spring onions (scallions), chopped

VARIATIONS

This dish is often prepared with fresh galangal rather than ginger and works well with most kinds of seafood including prawns (shrimp) and scallops.

1 Rinse the squid well and pat dry with kitchen paper. Cut the bodies into rings and halve the tentacles, if necessary.

2 Heat the oil in a wok or frying pan and cook the garlic until golden brown, but do not let it burn. Add the squid and stir-fry for 30 seconds over a high heat.

3 Add the soy sauce, ginger, lemon juice, sugar and spring onions. Stir-fry for a further 30 seconds, then serve.

COOK'S TIP

Squid has an undeserved reputation for being rubbery in texture. This is always a result of overcooking it.

Energy 165Kcal/694kJ; Protein 19.7g; Carbohydrate 4.8g, of which sugars 3.2g; Fat 7.6g, of which saturates 1.2g; Cholesterol 281mg; Calcium 20mg; Fibre 0g; Sodium 1206mg.

STEAMED MUSSELS IN COCONUT MILK

MUSSELS STEAMED IN COCONUT MILK AND FRESH AROMATIC HERBS AND SPICES MAKE AN IDEAL DISH FOR INFORMAL ENTERTAINING. IT IS QUICK AND EASY TO MAKE IN A WOK, AND IS GREAT FOR A RELAXED DINNER WITH FRIENDS. SERVE WITH PLENTY OF CRUSTY BREAD.

SERVES FOUR

INGREDIENTS
  15ml/1 tbsp sunflower oil
  6 garlic cloves, roughly chopped
  15ml/1 tbsp finely chopped
    fresh root ginger
  2 large fresh red chillies, seeded
    and finely sliced
  6 spring onions (scallions),
    finely chopped
  400ml/14fl oz/1⅔ cups coconut milk
  45ml/3 tbsp light soy sauce
  2 limes
  5ml/1 tsp caster (superfine) sugar
  1.6kg/3½lb mussels, scrubbed
    and beards removed
  a large handful of chopped
    coriander (cilantro)
  salt and ground black pepper

1 Heat the wok over a high heat and then add the oil. Stir in the garlic, ginger, chillies and spring onions and stir-fry for 30 seconds. Pour in the coconut milk, then add the soy sauce.

2 Grate the zest of the limes into the coconut milk mixture and add the sugar. Stir to mix and bring to the boil.

3 Add the cleaned mussels. Return to the boil, cover and cook briskly for 5–6 minutes, or until all the mussels have opened. Discard any mussels that remain closed.

4 Remove the wok from the heat and stir the chopped coriander into the mussel mixture.

5 Season the mussels well with salt and pepper. Ladle into warmed bowls and serve immediately.

COOK'S TIP
For an informal supper with friends, take the wok straight to the table rather than serving in individual bowls. A wok makes a great serving dish, and there's something utterly irresistible about eating the mussels straight from it.

Energy 165Kcal/702kJ; Protein 21.9g; Carbohydrate 7.7g, of which sugars 7.6g; Fat 5.6g, of which saturates 1g; Cholesterol 48mg; Calcium 276mg; Fibre 0.3g; Sodium 1165mg.

Mussels Steamed with Chilli, Ginger Leaves and Lemon Grass

This dish is an Asian version of the French classic, moules marinière, and it works really well in a wok with a lid. Here the mussels are steamed open in a herb-infused stock with lemon grass and chilli instead of wine and parsley.

SERVES FOUR

INGREDIENTS

600ml/1 pint/2½ cups chicken stock
   or beer, or a mixture of the two
1 Thai chilli, seeded and chopped
2 shallots, finely chopped
3 lemon grass stalks,
   finely chopped
1 bunch ginger or basil leaves
1kg/2¼lb fresh mussels, cleaned
   and bearded
salt and ground black pepper

COOK'S TIP

Aromatic ginger leaves are hard to find outside Asia. If you can't find them, basil or coriander (cilantro) will work well.

1 Pour the stock or beer into a wok or deep pan. Add the chopped chilli, shallots, lemon grass and most of the ginger or basil leaves, retaining a few leaves for the garnish Bring to the boil. Cover and simmer for 10–15 minutes, then season to taste.

2 Discard any mussels that remain open when tapped, then add the remaining mussels to the wok or pan. Stir well, cover and cook for 2 minutes, or until the mussels have opened. Discard any that remain closed. Ladle the mussels and cooking liquid into individual bowls.

Energy 73Kcal/311kJ; Protein 11g; Carbohydrate 3g, of which sugars 1g; Fat 2g, of which saturates 0g; Cholesterol 36mg; Calcium 37mg; Fibre 0.7g; Sodium 700mg.

SHELLFISH CURRY WITH COCONUT MILK AND BASIL

THIS RECIPE IS MADE WITH PRAWNS, SQUID AND SCALLOPS BUT YOU COULD USE ANY COMBINATION OF SHELLFISH, OR EVEN ADD CHUNKS OF FILLETED FISH. SERVE WITH STEAMED RICE OR BAGUETTES BROKEN INTO CHUNKS, WITH A FEW EXTRA CHILLIES TO MUNCH ON THE SIDE.

SERVES FOUR

INGREDIENTS
 4cm/1½ in fresh root ginger, peeled
   and roughly chopped
 3 garlic cloves, roughly chopped
 45ml/3 tbsp groundnut (peanut) oil
 1 onion, finely sliced
 2 lemon grass stalks, finely sliced
 2 green or red Thai chillies, seeded
   and finely sliced
 15ml/1 tbsp raw cane sugar
 10ml/2 tsp shrimp paste
 15ml/1 tbsp *nuoc mam*
 30ml/2 tbsp curry powder or
   garam masala
 550ml/18fl oz/2½ cups coconut milk
 grated rind and juice of 1 lime
 4 medium-sized squid, cleaned
   and cut diagonally into 3 or 4
   pieces
 12 king or queen scallops, shelled
 20 large raw prawns (shrimp), shelled
   and deveined
 1 small bunch fresh basil,
   stalks removed
 1 small bunch fresh coriander
   (cilantro), stalks removed, leaves
   finely chopped, to garnish
 salt

1 Using a mortar and pestle, grind the ginger with the garlic until it almost resembles a paste. Heat the oil in a wok or heavy pan and stir in the onion. Cook until the onion begins to turn brown, then stir in the garlic and ginger paste.

2 Once the fragrant aromas begin to rise, add the sliced lemon grass, sliced chillies and raw cane sugar. Cook briefly before adding the Vietnamese or Thai shrimp paste, *nuoc mam* and curry powder or garam masala. Mix thoroughly with a wooden spoon and stir-fry gently for 1–2 minutes.

3 Add the coconut milk, lime rind and juice. Mix well and bring to the boil. Cook, stirring, for 2–3 minutes. Season to taste with salt.

4 Gently stir in the squid, scallops and prawns and bring to the boil once more. Reduce the heat and cook gently until the shellfish turns opaque. Stir in the basil leaves and sprinkle the chopped coriander over the top. Serve immediately from the pot.

COOK'S TIP
To devein the prawns, first peel off the shells, then make a shallow cut down the centre of the curved back of each prawn. Carefully pull out the black vein with a cocktail stick (toothpick) or your fingers, then rinse the deveined prawns well.

Energy 528Kcal/2225kJ; Protein 68g; Carbohydrate 24g, of which sugars 14g; Fat 18g, of which saturates 4g; Cholesterol 699mg; Calcium 250mg; Fibre 2.5g; Sodium 1300mg.

BABY SQUID STUFFED <u>WITH</u> PORK, MUSHROOMS, TIGER LILY BUDS <u>AND</u> DILL

BABY SQUID IS BEAUTIFULLY TENDER AND IS OFTEN STIR-FRIED OR STUFFED. VARIATIONS OF THIS DISH CAN BE SERVED AS AN APPETIZER OR A MAIN COURSE. THIS RECIPE CALLS FOR THE SQUID TO BE STUFFED WITH A DILL-FLAVOURED PORK MIXTURE. THE SQUID CAN BE GRILLED OR FRIED.

SERVES FOUR

INGREDIENTS
   3 dried cloud ear (wood ear)
     mushrooms
   10 dried tiger lily buds
   25g/1oz bean thread
     (cellophane) noodles
   8 baby squid
   350g/12oz minced (ground) pork
   3–4 shallots, finely chopped
   4 garlic cloves, finely chopped
   1 bunch dill fronds, finely chopped
   30ml/2 tbsp *nuoc mam*
   5ml/1 tsp palm sugar
   ground black pepper
   vegetable or groundnut (peanut) oil,
     for frying
   coriander (cilantro) leaves, to garnish
   nuoc cham, for drizzling

1 Soak the mushrooms, tiger lily buds and bean thread noodles in lukewarm water for about 15 minutes, until they have softened.

2 Meanwhile, prepare the squid one at a time. Hold the body sac in one hand, hold the head with the other and pull it off. Pull out the backbone and rinse out the body sac. Peel off the outer membrane, pat the body sac dry, and put aside. Sever the tentacles from the head. Discard the head and chop the tentacles. Repeat with the other squid.

3 Drain the soaked cloud ear mushrooms, tiger lily buds and bean thread noodles. Squeeze them in kitchen paper to get rid of any excess water, then chop them finely and put them in a bowl. Add the chopped tentacles, minced pork, shallots, garlic and three-quarters of the dill. Mix well.

COOK'S TIPS
• Instead of frying the squid, you can cook them over a charcoal or conventional grill (broiler).
• Served on a platter, these baby squid are an impressive sight at parties.

4 In a small bowl, stir the *nuoc mam* with the sugar, until it dissolves completely. Add it to the mixture in the bowl and mix well. Season with ground black pepper.

5 Using your fingers, stuff the pork mixture into each squid, packing it in firmly. Leave a little gap at the end to sew together with a needle and cotton thread or to skewer with a cocktail stick (toothpick) so that the filling doesn't spill out on cooking.

6 Heat some oil in a large wok or heavy pan, and fry the squid for about 5 minutes, turning them from time to time. Pierce each one several times to release any excess water – this will cause the oil to spit, so take care when doing this; you may wish to use a spatterproof lid. Continue cooking for a further 10 minutes, until the squid are nicely browned. Serve whole or thinly sliced, garnished with the remaining dill and coriander, and drizzled with *nuoc cham*.

LAKSA LEMAK

THIS SPICY SOUP MAKES A MARVELLOUS PARTY DISH, AND IS SUBSTANTIAL ENOUGH FOR AN ENTIRE MAIN COURSE. GUESTS SPOON NOODLES INTO WIDE SOUP BOWLS, ADD ACCOMPANIMENTS OF THEIR CHOICE, TOP UP WITH SOUP AND THEN TAKE A FEW PRAWN CRACKERS TO NIBBLE.

SERVES SIX

INGREDIENTS
675g/1½lb small clams
50g/2oz ikan bilis (dried anchovies)
2 × 400ml/14fl oz cans coconut milk
900ml/1½ pints/3¾ cups water
115g/4oz shallots, finely chopped
4 garlic cloves, chopped
6 macadamia nuts or blanched
   almonds, chopped
3 lemon grass stalks, root trimmed
90ml/6 tbsp sunflower oil
1cm/½in cube shrimp paste
25g/1oz/¼ cup mild curry powder
a few curry leaves
2–3 aubergines (eggplants), trimmed
675g/1½lb raw peeled prawns
   (shrimp)
10ml/2 tsp sugar
1 head Chinese leaves (Chinese
   cabbage), thinly sliced
115g/4oz/2 cups beansprouts, rinsed
2 spring onions (scallions), finely
   chopped
50g/2oz crispy fried onions
115g/4oz fried tofu
675g/1½lb mixed noodles
prawn (shrimp) crackers, to serve

1 Scrub the clams and then put in a large pan with 1cm/½in water. Bring to the boil, cover and steam for 3–4 minutes until all the the clams have opened. Drain.

2 Put the ikan bilis (dried anchovies) in a pan and add the water. Bring to the boil and simmer for 20 minutes.

3 Make up the coconut milk to 1.2 litres/2 pints/5 cups with water.

4 Meanwhile, put the shallots, garlic and nuts into a mortar. Cut off the lower 5cm/2in of two of the lemon grass stalks, chop finely and add to the mortar. Pound the mixture to a paste.

5 Heat the oil in a wok, add the shallot paste and fry until the mixture gives off a rich aroma. Bruise the remaining lemon grass stalk and add to the pan. Toss over the heat to release its flavour.

6 Mix the shrimp paste and curry powder to a paste with a little of the coconut milk, add to the wok and toss the mixture over the heat for 1 minute, stirring all the time, and keeping the heat low. Stir in the remaining coconut milk. Add the curry leaves and leave the mixture to simmer while you prepare the accompaniments.

7 Strain the ikan bilis, retaining the stock. Discard the ikan bilis and return the stock to the pan, bring to the boil, then add the whole aubergines. Cook for about 10 minutes or until the flesh is tender and the skins can be removed with ease.

COOK'S TIP
Dried shrimp or prawn paste, also called blachan, is sold in small blocks and is available from Asian supermarkets.

8 Lift the aubergines out of the pan of stock, peel, discard the skin, and cut the flesh into thick strips. Arrange the aubergines on a serving platter.

9 Sprinkle the prawns with sugar, add to the stock pan and cook for 2–4 minutes until they turn pink. Remove and place next to the aubergines. Gradually stir the remaining ikan bilis stock into the pan of soup and bring to the boil.

10 Place the clams, Chinese leaves, beansprouts, spring onions and crispy fried onions on the platter.

11 Rinse the fried tofu in boiling water, cool slightly and squeeze to remove excess oil. Cut each piece in half and add to the soup. Lower the heat to a very gentle simmer.

12 Cook the noodles according to the instructions, drain and pile in a dish. Remove the curry leaves and lemon grass from the soup.

13 Place the noodles, soup and the platter of seafood and vegetables on the table, along with a bowl of prawn crackers. Guests can then help themselves to what they want.

VARIATION
You could substitute mussels for clams, if you like. Scrub them thoroughly, removing any beards, and cook them in lightly salted water until they open. As when preparing the clams, discard any mussels that remain closed.

Energy 814Kcal/3432kJ; Protein 51.2g; Carbohydrate 101.8g, of which sugars 16.6g; Fat 25.2g, of which saturates 2.2g; Cholesterol 258mg; Calcium 558mg; Fibre 7.7g; Sodium 1302mg.

HANOI FRIED FISH <u>WITH</u> DILL

THE SPICY, CRISPY COATING ON THIS FRIED FISH GOES BEAUTIFULLY WITH THE LARGE QUANTITY OF LOVELY, PUNGENT FRESH HERBS, AND THE PEANUTS ADD TEXTURE AND EXTRA CRUNCH. SERVE THE HERBY FISH WITH PLAIN BOILED RICE, LIME WEDGES AND NUOC CHAM OR SOY SAUCE.

SERVES FOUR

INGREDIENTS

75g/3oz/⅔ cup rice flour
7.5ml/1½ tsp ground turmeric
500g/1¼lb white fish fillets, such as
  cod, skinned and cut into chunks
vegetable oil, for deep-frying
1 large bunch fresh dill
15ml/1 tbsp groundnut (peanut) oil
30ml/2 tbsp roasted peanuts
4 spring onions (scallions), cut into
  bitesize pieces
1 small bunch fresh basil,
  stalks removed, leaves chopped
1 small bunch fresh coriander
  (cilantro), stalks removed
cooked rice, 1 lime, cut into wedges
  and *nuoc cham*, to serve

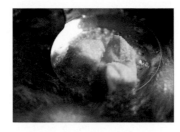

1 Mix the flour with the ground turmeric and toss the chunks of fish in it until they are well coated. Heat the oil in a wok or a large heavy pan and cook the fish in batches until crisp and golden. Use a perforated ladle to remove the fish from the oil, and drain on kitchen paper.

2 Scatter some of the dill fronds on a serving dish, arrange the fish on top and keep warm. Chop some of the remaining dill fronds and set aside for the garnish.

3 Heat the groundnut oil in a small wok or frying pan. Stir in the peanuts and cook for 1 minute, then add the spring onions, the remaining dill fronds, basil and coriander. Stir-fry for no more than 30 seconds, then spoon the herbs and peanuts over the fish. Garnish with the chopped dill and serve with lime wedges and *nuoc cham* to drizzle over the top.

Energy 350Kcal/1458kJ; Protein 27g; Carbohydrate 17g, of which sugars 1g; Fat 19g, of which saturates 3g; Cholesterol 85mg; Calcium 112mg; Fibre 1.2g; Sodium 200mg.

SOUR CARP WITH TAMARIND AND CORIANDER

THIS RIVER CARP DISH IS POPULAR THROUGHOUT CAMBODIA AND VIETNAM. IF YOU WANT TO MAKE A SLIGHTLY SIMPLER VERSION, YOU COULD JUST TOSS THE COOKED FISH IN THE HERBS AND SERVE IT WITH NOODLES OR RICE AND A SALAD.

SERVES FOUR

INGREDIENTS

    500g/1¼lb carp fillets, cut into 3
      or 4 pieces
    30ml/2 tbsp sesame or vegetable oil
    10ml/2 tsp ground turmeric
    1 small bunch each fresh
      coriander (cilantro) and basil,
      stalks removed
    20 lettuce leaves or rice wrappers
    nuoc mam or other dipping sauce,
      to serve
For the marinade
    30ml/2 tbsp tamarind paste
    15ml/1 tbsp soy sauce
    juice of 1 lime
    1 green or red Thai chilli,
      finely chopped
    2.5cm/1in galangal root, peeled
      and grated
    a few sprigs of fresh coriander
      (cilantro) leaves, finely chopped

1 Prepare the marinade by mixing together all the marinade ingredients in a bowl. Toss the fish pieces in the marinade, cover with clear film (plastic wrap) and chill in the refrigerator for at least 6 hours, or overnight.

COOK'S TIP
Any freshwater fish can be used for this recipe but, because it is stirred in a wok, you will need one with firm, thick flesh, such as catfish or barb. Allow plenty of time for the fish to marinate and soak up the flavours.

2 Lift the pieces of fish out of the marinade and lay them on a plate. Heat a wok or heavy pan, add the oil and stir in the turmeric. Working quickly, so that the turmeric doesn't burn, add the fish pieces, gently moving them around the wok for 2–3 minutes. Add any remaining marinade to the pan and cook for a further 2–3 minutes, or until the pieces of fish are cooked through.

3 To serve, divide the fish among four plates, sprinkle with the coriander and basil, and add some of the lettuce leaves or rice wrappers and a small bowl of dipping sauce to each serving. To eat, tear off a bitesize piece of fish, place it on a wrapper with a few herb leaves, fold it up into a roll, then dip it into the sauce.

Energy 298Kcal/1246kJ; Protein 24g; Carbohydrate 19g, of which sugars 5g; Fat 14g, of which saturates 2g; Cholesterol 121mg; Calcium 120mg; Fibre 0g; Sodium 300mg

FISH ᴵᴺ COCONUT CUSTARD

THIS IS A CLASSIC CAMBODIAN FISH, RICH AND SUMPTUOUS,
VARIATIONS OF IT CROP UP ALL OVER THE COUNTRY. IN PHNOM
PENH, THERE ARE RESTAURANTS THAT SPECIALIZE IN IT. THE FISH
IS STEAMED IN A CUSTARD, MADE WITH COCONUT MILK AND
FLAVOURED WITH THE CAMBODIAN HERBAL PASTE, KROEUNG.

SERVES FOUR

INGREDIENTS
   2 x 400ml/14oz cans coconut milk
   3 eggs
   80ml/3fl oz *kroeung*
   15ml/1 tbsp *tuk trey*
   10ml/2 tsp palm sugar or honey
   1 kg/2¼lb fresh, skinned white fish
      fillets
   1 small bunch chopped fresh
      coriander (cilantro), plus a few
      whole sprigs, to garnish
   jasmine rice or crusty bread and
      salad, to serve

1 With a sharp knife, cut the white fish
fillets into 8 equal pieces.

2 Half fill a wok or large pan with water.
Set a bamboo or stainless steel steamer
over it and put the lid on. Bring the
water to the boil.

3 In a bowl, beat the coconut milk with
the eggs, *kroeung*, *tuk trey* and sugar or
honey, until it is well blended and the
sugar has dissolved.

4 Place the fish pieces in a heatproof
dish that will fit in the steamer.

VARIATION
If you don't have a big enough steamer,
this dish can be cooked in the oven in a
bain marie. Cook at 160°C/325°F/Gas 3
for about 50 minutes.

5 Pour the coconut milk and egg
mixture over the fish making sure that
the tops of the pieces of fish have a
covering of the custard.

6 Place the dish in the steamer. Put the
lid back on the steamer and reduce the
heat so that the water is simmering. The
custard should cook slowly and gently
so that it doesn't curdle.

7 Steam over gently simmering water
until the fish is cooked. Top up the wok
with boiling water from the kettle if
necessary.

8 When the fish is opaque, remove the
dish from the steamer. Garnish with
coriander and serve immediately with
jasmine rice or crusty bread and salad.

Energy 309Kcal/1304kJ; Protein 51.1g; Carbohydrate 12.4g, of which sugars 12.4g; Fat 6.5g, of which saturates 1.8g;
Cholesterol 258mg; Calcium 103mg; Fibre 0g; Sodium 400mg.

SPICY TUNA WITH WARM CUCUMBER, GARLIC AND GINGER DRESSING

TUNA IS A GREAT FISH TO COOK IN THE WOK BECAUSE IT IS PERFECTLY SUITED TO THE QUICK HEAT THE WOK CAN PROVIDE, TUNA IS DELICIOUS PAN-SEARED AND SERVED A LITTLE RARE, SO GET YOUR WOK GOOD AND HOT BEFORE YOU SEAR, AND DON'T LEAVE IT COOKING TOO LONG.

SERVES FOUR

INGREDIENTS
  1 small cucumber
  10ml/2 tsp sesame oil
  2 garlic cloves, crushed
  4 tuna steaks
For the dressing
  4cm/1½in fresh root ginger, peeled
    and roughly chopped
  1 garlic clove, roughly chopped
  2 green Thai chillies, seeded and
    roughly chopped
  45ml/3 tbsp raw cane sugar
  45ml/3 tbsp *nuoc mam*
  juice of 1 lime
  60ml/4 tbsp water

1 To make the dressing, grind the ginger, garlic and chillies to a pulp with the sugar, using a mortar and pestle. Stir in the *nuoc mam*, lime juice and water, and mix well. Leave the dressing to stand for 15 minutes.

2 Cut the cucumber in half lengthways and remove the seeds. Cut the flesh into long, thin strips. Toss the cucumber in the dressing and leave to soak for at least 15 minutes.

3 Wipe a wok with the oil and rub the garlic around it, then drizzle a little more oil into the wok, heat, and add the tuna steaks. Sear for a few minutes on both sides, so that the outside is slightly charred. Lift the steaks on to a warm serving dish. Arrange the cucumber strips around the steaks. Pour the dressing into the hot wok, stir it quickly, then pour it, sizzling, onto the tuna steaks. Serve immediately.

Energy 262Kcal/1103kJ; Protein 31g; Carbohydrate 16g, of which sugars 13g; Fat 8g, of which saturates 2g; Cholesterol 35mg; Calcium 44mg; Fibre 0.5g; Sodium 150mg.

EEL BRAISED ᴵᴺ ᴬ CARAMEL SAUCE ᵂᴵᵀᴴ BUTTERNUT SQUASH

EEL IS VERY POPULAR IN VIETNAM, THIS IS A TRADITIONAL NORTHERN DISH AND IT IS THERE, IN THE HIGHLANDS, THAT IT IS BEST SAMPLED. THE EELS ARE CAUGHT IN THE RED, BLACK AND SONG MA RIVERS, AND THE LOCAL NAME OF THE DISH IS "THREE RIVERS EEL".

SERVES FOUR

INGREDIENTS
  45ml/3 tbsp raw cane sugar
  30ml/2 tbsp soy sauce
  45ml/3 tbsp *nuoc mam*
  2 garlic cloves, crushed
  2 dried chillies
  2–3 star anise
  4–5 black peppercorns
  350g/12oz eel on the bone, skinned,
    cut into 2.5cm/1in-thick chunks
  200g/7oz butternut squash, cut into
    bitesize chunks
  4 spring onions (scallions), cut into
    bitesize pieces
  30ml/2 tbsp sesame or vegetable oil
  5cm/2in fresh root ginger, peeled
    and cut into matchsticks
  salt
  cooked rice or noodles,
    to serve

2 Add the eel chunks, squash and spring onions, making sure the fish is well coated in the sauce, and season with salt. Reduce the heat, cover the pan and simmer gently for about 20 minutes, until the eel and vegetables are tender.

3 Meanwhile, heat a small wok, pour in the oil and stir fry the ginger until crisp and golden. Remove and drain on kitchen paper.

4 Serve with rice or noodles, with the crispy ginger sprinkled on top.

1 Put the sugar in a wok or heavy pan with 30ml/2 tbsp water, and gently heat it until it turns golden. Remove the pan from the heat and stir in the soy sauce and *nuoc mam* with 120ml/4fl oz/½ cup water. Add the garlic, chillies, star anise and peppercorns and return to the heat.

COOK'S TIP
If you can't find eel, use mackerel for this dish. The fat rendered from these fish melts into the caramel sauce, making it deliciously velvety. It is often served with chopped fresh coriander (cilantro) on top.

Energy 204Kcal/857kJ; Protein 11g; Carbohydrate 20g, of which sugars 14g; Fat 10g, of which saturates 1g; Cholesterol 0mg; Calcium 76mg; Fibre 1g; Sodium 110mg.

SOTONG SAMBAL

SQUID IS READILY AVAILABLE THESE DAYS, AND IT NOW COMES CLEANED, WHICH IS A DEFINITE BONUS.
WASH THOROUGHLY INSIDE THE POCKET TO MAKE SURE THAT ALL THE QUILL HAS BEEN REMOVED.

SERVES TWO

INGREDIENTS
   8 small squid, each about 10cm/4in
      long, total weight about 350g/12oz
   lime juice (optional)
   salt
   boiled rice, to serve
For the stuffing
   175g/6oz white fish fillets, such as
      sole or plaice, skinned
   2.5cm/1in piece fresh root ginger,
      peeled and finely sliced
   2 spring onions (scallions), finely
      chopped
   50g/2oz peeled cooked prawns
      (shrimp), roughly chopped
For the sambal sauce
   4 macadamia nuts or
      blanched almonds
   1cm/$\frac{1}{2}$in piece fresh galangal,
      peeled, or 5ml/1 tsp drained
      bottled galangal
   2 lemon grass stalks, root trimmed
   1cm/$\frac{1}{2}$in cube shrimp paste
   4 fresh red chillies, or to taste,
      seeded and roughly chopped
   175g/6oz small onions, roughly
      chopped
   60–90ml/4–6 tbsp vegetable oil
   400ml/14fl oz can coconut milk

1 Clean the squid, leaving them whole.
Set aside with the tentacles.

2 To make the stuffing, put the fish,
ginger and spring onions in a mortar.
Add a little salt and pound to a paste.
Use a food processor to grind the
mixture, if you like, but retain a little
texture and don't overprocess.

3 Transfer the fish mixture to a bowl
and stir in the prawns.

4 Divide the filling among the squid,
using a spoon or a forcing bag fitted
with a plain tube to fill them. Tuck the
tentacles into the stuffing and secure
the top of each squid with a cocktail
stick, to stop the filling escaping.

5 Make the sauce. Put the macadamia
nuts or almonds and galangal in a food
processor. Cut off the lower 5cm/2in
from the lemon grass stalks, chop them
roughly and add them to the processor
with the shrimp paste, chillies and
onions. Process to a paste.

6 Heat the oil in a wok and fry the
mixture to bring out the full flavours.
Bruise the remaining lemon grass and
add it to the wok with the coconut milk.
Stir constantly until the sauce comes to
the boil, then lower the heat and
simmer the sauce for 5 minutes.

7 Arrange the squid in the sauce, and
cook for 15–20 minutes. Taste and
season with salt and lime juice, if liked.
Serve with boiled rice.

Energy 538Kcal/2253kJ; Protein 50.4g; Carbohydrate 19.6g, of which sugars 15.4g; Fat 29.4g, of which saturates 4g; Cholesterol 483mg; Calcium 148mg; Fibre 1.8g; Sodium 517mg.

DEEP-FRIED PLAICE

IN THIS DISH THE FLESH OF THE FISH AND ALSO THE SKELETON IS DEEP-FRIED IN A WOK TO SUCH CRISPNESS THAT YOU CAN EAT THE BONES, TAILS AND HEADS, IF YOU LIKE.

SERVES FOUR

INGREDIENTS
    4 small plaice or flounder, about
        500–675g/1¼–1½lb total weight,
        gutted, not trimmed
    60ml/4 tbsp cornflour (cornstarch)
    vegetable oil, for deep-frying
    salt
For the condiment
    130g/4½oz mooli (daikon), peeled
    4 dried chillies, seeded
    1 bunch of chives, finely chopped
        (to make 50ml/2fl oz/¼ cup)
For the sauce
    20ml/4 tsp rice vinegar
    20ml/4 tsp shoyu

1 Wash the fish under running water and put on a chopping board. Use a very sharp knife to make deep cuts around the gills and across the tail.

2 Cut through the skin from the head down to the tail along the centre of the fish. Slide the knife under the cut near the head and cut the fillet from the bone. Fold the fillet with your hand as you cut as if peeling from the bone. Keep the knife horizontal to the fish.

3 Repeat for the other half, then turn the fish over and do the same to get four fillets from each fish. Place in a dish and sprinkle with a little salt on both sides. Keep the bony skeletons.

4 Pierce the mooli with a skewer or a chopstick in four places to make holes, then insert the chillies. After 15 minutes grate finely.

5 Squeeze out the moisture by hand. Scoop a quarter of the grated mooli and chilli into an egg cup, then press with your fingers. Turn out the cup on to a plate. Make three more mounds.

6 Mix the rice vinegar and shoyu and put in a bowl.

7 Cut the fish fillets into four slices crossways and put into a plastic bag with the cornflour. Shake gently to coat. Heat the oil in a wok or pan to 175°C/347°F. Deep-fry the fillets, two to three at a time, until light golden brown.

8 Raise the temperature to 180°C/350°F. Dust the skeletons with cornflour and slide into the oil.

9 Cook until golden, drain on a wire rack for 5 minutes, then fry again until very crisp. Drain and sprinkle with salt.

10 Arrange the skeletons and fried fish on the plates. Put the mooli and chives to one side on each plate. Have small plates for the sauce. To eat, mix the condiment with the sauce and dip the fillets and bones into the sauce.

Energy 331Kcal/1378kJ; Protein 19.7g; Carbohydrate 16.2g, of which sugars 1.2g; Fat 21.2g, of which saturates 2.6g; Cholesterol 0mg; Calcium 120mg; Fibre 1.2g; Sodium 640mg.

SWEET AND SOUR FISH

WHEN FISH SUCH AS RED MULLET OR SNAPPER IS DEEP-FRIED IN OIL THE SKIN BECOMES CRISP, WHILE THE FLESH INSIDE REMAINS MOIST AND JUICY. THE SWEET AND SOUR SAUCE IN THIS DISH, WITH ITS COLOURFUL CHERRY TOMATOES, PERFECTLY COMPLEMENTS THE FISH.

SERVES FOUR TO SIX

INGREDIENTS
1 large or 2 medium fish, such as snapper or mullet, cleaned with heads removed
20ml/4 tsp cornflour (cornstarch)
120ml/4fl oz/½ cup vegetable oil
15ml/1 tbsp chopped garlic
15ml/1 tbsp chopped fresh ginger
30ml/2 tbsp chopped shallots
225g/8oz cherry tomatoes
30ml/2 tbsp red wine vinegar
30ml/2 tbsp granulated sugar
30ml/2 tbsp tomato ketchup
15ml/1 tbsp Thai fish sauce
45ml/3 tbsp water
salt and ground black pepper
coriander (cilantro) leaves and shredded spring onions (scallions), to garnish

1 Rinse and dry the fish. Score the skin diagonally on both sides, then coat the fish lightly all over with 15ml/1 tbsp of the cornflour. Shake off any excess.

2 Heat the oil in a wok or large frying pan. Add the fish and cook over a medium heat for 6–7 minutes. Turn the fish over and cook for 6–7 minutes more, until it is crisp and brown.

3 Remove the fish with a metal spatula or fish slice and place on a large platter. Pour off all but 30ml/2 tbsp of the oil from the wok or pan and reheat. Add the garlic, ginger and shallots and cook over a medium heat, stirring occasionally, for 3–4 minutes, until golden.

4 Add the cherry tomatoes and cook until they burst open. Stir in the vinegar, sugar, tomato ketchup and fish sauce. Lower the heat and simmer gently for 1–2 minutes, then taste and adjust the seasoning, adding more vinegar, sugar and/or fish sauce, if necessary.

5 In a cup, mix the remaining 5ml/1 tsp cornflour to a paste with the water. Stir into the sauce. Heat, stirring, until it thickens. Pour the sauce over the fish, garnish with coriander leaves and shredded spring onions and serve.

Energy 245Kcal/1023kJ; Protein 16.2g; Carbohydrate 14.8g, of which sugars 10.6g; Fat 13.8g, of which saturates 1.6g; Cholesterol 38mg; Calcium 27mg; Fibre 1.1g; Sodium 138mg.

STEAMED FISH WITH CHILLI SAUCE

*A LARGE WOK IS IDEAL FOR STEAMING FISH. BY LEAVING THE FISH WHOLE AND ON THE BONE,
MAXIMUM FLAVOUR IS RETAINED AND THE FLESH REMAINS BEAUTIFULLY MOIST. THE BANANA LEAF IS
BOTH AUTHENTIC AND ATTRACTIVE, BUT YOU CAN USE BAKING PARCHMENT INSTEAD.*

SERVES FOUR

INGREDIENTS

    1 large or 2 medium firm fish such
      as sea bass or grouper, scaled
      and cleaned
    30ml/2 tbsp rice wine
    3 fresh red chillies, seeded and
      thinly sliced
    2 garlic cloves, finely chopped
    2cm/¾in piece fresh root ginger,
      peeled and finely shredded
    2 lemon grass stalks, crushed and
      finely chopped
    2 spring onions
      (scallions), chopped
    30ml/2 tbsp Thai fish sauce
    juice of 1 lime
    1 fresh banana leaf
For the chilli sauce
    10 fresh red chillies, seeded
      and chopped
    4 garlic cloves, chopped
    60ml/4 tbsp Thai fish sauce
    15ml/1 tbsp granulated sugar
    75ml/5 tbsp fresh lime juice

1 Thoroughly rinse the fish under cold
running water. Pat it dry with kitchen
paper. With a sharp knife, slash the skin
of the fish a few times on both sides.

2 Mix together the rice wine, chillies,
garlic, shredded ginger, lemon grass
and spring onions in a non-metallic
bowl. Add the fish sauce and lime juice
and mix to a paste. Place the fish on
the banana leaf and spread the spice
paste evenly over it, rubbing it in well
where the skin has been slashed.

3 Put a rack or a small upturned plate
in the base of a wok. Pour in boiling
water to a depth of 5cm/2in. Lift the
banana leaf, together with the fish, and
place it on the rack or plate. Cover with
a lid and steam for 10–15 minutes, or
until the fish is cooked.

4 Meanwhile, make the sauce. Place all
the ingredients in a food processor and
process until smooth. If the mixture
seems to be too thick, add a little cold
water. Scrape into a serving bowl.

5 Serve the fish hot, on the banana leaf
if you like, with the sweet chilli sauce to
spoon over the top.

Energy 228Kcal/960kJ; Protein 35.2g; Carbohydrate 12g, of which sugars 10.1g; Fat 4.7g, of which saturates 0.7g; Cholesterol 140mg; Calcium 254mg; Fibre 1.6g; Sodium 392mg.

SEA BASS STEAMED IN COCONUT MILK

THIS IS A DELICIOUS RECIPE FOR ANY WHOLE WHITE FISH, SUCH AS SEA BASS OR COD, OR FOR LARGE CHUNKS OF TROUT OR SALMON. YOU WILL NEED A STEAMER LARGE ENOUGH.

SERVES FOUR

INGREDIENTS

200ml/7fl oz coconut milk
10ml/2 tsp raw cane or muscovado
   (molasses) sugar
about 15ml/1 tbsp vegetable oil
2 garlic cloves, finely chopped
1 red Thai chilli, seeded and
   finely chopped
4cm/1½in fresh root ginger, peeled
   and grated
750g/1lb 10oz sea bass, gutted and
   skinned on one side
1 star anise, ground
1 bunch fresh basil, stalks removed
30ml/2 tbsp cashew nuts
sea salt and ground black pepper
rice and salad, to serve

1 Heat the coconut milk with the sugar in a small pan, stirring until the sugar dissolves, then remove from the heat.

2 Heat the oil in a small frying pan and stir in the garlic, chilli and ginger. Cook until they begin to brown, then add the mixture to the coconut milk and mix well to combine.

3 Place the fish, skin side down, on a wide piece of foil and tuck up the sides to form a boat-shaped container.

4 Using a sharp knife, cut several diagonal slashes into the flesh on the top and rub with the ground star anise.

5 Season with salt and pepper and spoon the coconut milk over the top, making sure that the fish is well coated.

6 Scatter half the basil leaves over the top of the fish and pull the foil packet almost closed. Lay the packet in a steamer. Cover the steamer, bring the water to the boil, reduce the heat and simmer for 20–25 minutes, or until just cooked. Alternatively, place the foil packet on a baking tray and cook in a preheated oven at 180°C/350°F/Gas 4.

7 Roast the cashew nuts in the frying pan, adding extra oil if necessary. Drain the nuts on kitchen paper, then grind them to crumbs. When the fish is cooked, lift it out of the foil and transfer it to a serving dish. Spoon the cooking juices over, sprinkle with the cashew nut crumbs and garnish with the remaining basil leaves. Serve with rice and a salad.

Energy 235Kcal/983kJ; Protein 26g; Carbohydrate 8g, of which sugars 6g; Fat 11g, of which saturates 2g; Cholesterol 100mg; Calcium 217mg; Fibre 0.3g; Sodium 300mg.

BRAISED FISH FILLET <u>WITH</u> MUSHROOMS

THIS IS THE CHINESE STIR-FRIED VERSION OF THE FRENCH FILETS DE SOLE BONNE FEMME (SOLE COOKED WITH MUSHROOMS AND WINE SAUCE).

SERVES FOUR

INGREDIENTS
    450g/1lb lemon sole or
        plaice fillets
    5ml/1 tsp salt
    1/2 egg white
    10ml/2 tsp cornflour (cornstarch)
    about 600ml/1 pint/2½ cups
        vegetable oil
    15ml/1 tbsp finely chopped
        spring onions (scallions)
    2.5ml/½ tsp finely chopped fresh
        root ginger
    115g/4oz white mushrooms,
        thinly sliced
    5ml/1 tsp light brown sugar
    15ml/1 tbsp light soy sauce
    30ml/2 tbsp Chinese rice wine or
        dry sherry
    15ml/1 tbsp brandy
    about 120ml/4fl oz/½ cup fish or
        light chicken stock
    few drops sesame oil

2 Heat the oil to medium-hot and deep-fry the fish for about 1 minute, stirring gently. Remove the fish and drain. Pour off all but about 30ml/2 tbsp oil.

3 Stir-fry the spring onions, ginger and mushrooms for 1 minute. Add the sugar, soy sauce, rice wine or sherry, brandy and stock. Bring to the boil.

4 Return the fish to the wok and braise for 1 minute. Stir in the remaining cornflour paste to thicken the sauce and sprinkle with sesame oil.

1 Trim off the soft bones along the edge of the fish, but leave the skin on. Cut each fillet into bite-sized pieces. Blend the cornflour with 30ml/2tbsp cold water to make a paste. Mix the fish with a little salt, the egg white and about half of the cornflour paste.

COOK'S TIP
You could substitute straw mushrooms, so called because they are grown on beds of rice straw. They have a subtle flavour and a slightly slippery texture.

Energy 241kcal/1003kJ; Protein 19.8g; Carbohydrate 1.7g, of which sugars 1.6g; Fat 15.5g, of which saturates 1.9g; Cholesterol 47mg; Calcium 55mg; Fibre 0.4g; Sodium 145mg.

FRAGRANT RED SNAPPER IN BANANA LEAVES

SHINY, DARK GREEN BANANA LEAVES MAKE A REALLY GOOD
WRAPPING FOR FISH THAT IS STEAMED IN THE WOK. HERE, WHOLE
SNAPPERS ARE INFUSED WITH A DELIGHTFUL MIX OF COCONUT
CREAM, MINT, CORIANDER, KAFFIR LIME LEAVES, LEMON GRASS AND
CHILLI TO MAKE AN IMPRESSIVE MAIN COURSE.

SERVES FOUR

INGREDIENTS
 4 small red snapper, grouper, tilapia
   or red bream, gutted and cleaned
 4 large squares of banana leaf
   (approximately 30cm/12in square)
 50ml/2fl oz/¼ cup coconut cream
 90ml/6 tbsp chopped coriander
   (cilantro)
 90ml/6 tbsp chopped mint
 juice of 3 limes
 3 spring onions (scallions),
   finely sliced
 4 kaffir lime leaves, finely shredded
 2 red chillies, seeded and finely
   sliced
 4 lemon grass stalks, split lengthways
 salt and ground black pepper
 steamed rice and steamed Asian
   greens, to serve

1 Using a small sharp knife, score the fish diagonally on each side. Half fill a wok with water and bring to the boil.

2 Dip each square of banana leaf into the boiling water in the wok for 15–20 seconds so they become pliable. Lift out carefully, rinse under cold water and dry with kitchen paper.

3 Place the coconut cream, chopped herbs, lime juice, spring onions, lime leaves and chillies in a bowl and stir well. Season with salt and pepper.

4 Lay each banana leaf out flat on a work surface and place a fish and a split lemon grass stalk in the centre of each of them. Spread the herb mixture over each fish.

5 Wrap the banana leaf around each one to form four neat parcels. Secure each parcel tightly with a bamboo skewer or a cocktail stick (toothpick).

6 Place the parcels in a single layer in one or two tiers of a large bamboo steamer and place over a wok of simmering water. Cover tightly and steam for 15–20 minutes, or until the fish is cooked through.

7 Remove the fish from the steamer and serve immediately, still in their banana-leaf wrappings, with steamed rice and steamed Asian greens.

COOK'S TIP
When you spread the spicy coconut cream mixture over the fish, work the mixture into the cuts that you have made. This allows the flavours to penetrate the flesh and gives the finished dish a fabulous flavour. If you have time, leave the fish to stand for about half an hour before steaming. Swap the steamer baskets over halfway through cooking, so each gets similar exposure to maximum heat.

Energy 185Kcal/781kJ; Protein 39.4g; Carbohydrate 0.9g, of which sugars 0.8g; Fat 2.7g, of which saturates 0.6g; Cholesterol 74mg; Calcium 87mg; Fibre 0.1g; Sodium 168mg.

Deep-fried Skate Wings with Wasabi

Whole skate wings dipped in a tempura batter and deep-fried until crisp and golden look stunning and taste wonderful. The creamy, zesty mayonnaise flavoured with soy sauce, fiery wasabi paste and spring onions makes a great accompaniment.

SERVES FOUR

INGREDIENTS

4 x 250g/9oz skate wings
65g/2½oz/9 tbsp cornflour
　(cornstarch)
65g/2½oz/9 tbsp plain
　(all-purpose) flour
5ml/1 tsp salt
5ml/1 tsp Chinese five-spice powder
15ml/1 tbsp sesame seeds
200ml/7fl oz/scant 1 cup ice-cold
　soda water
sunflower oil, for frying
For the mayonnaise
200ml/7fl oz/scant 1 cup mayonnaise
15ml/1 tbsp light soy sauce
finely grated rind and juice of 1 lime
5ml/1 tsp wasabi
15ml/1 tbsp finely chopped spring
　onion (scallion)

1 Using kitchen scissors, trim away the frill from the edges of the skate wings and discard. Set aside.

2 In a large mixing bowl combine the cornflour, plain flour, salt, five-spice powder and sesame seeds. Gradually pour in the soda water and stir to mix. (It will be quite lumpy.)

3 Fill a large wok one-third full of sunflower oil and heat to 190°C/375°F or until a cube of bread, dropped into the oil, browns in 40 seconds.

4 One at a time, dip the skate wings in the batter, then lower them carefully into the wok and deep-fry for 4–5 minutes, until the skate is fully cooked and crispy. Drain on kitchen paper. Set aside and keep warm.

5 Meanwhile, mix together all the mayonnaise ingredients and divide among four small bowls. Serve immediately with the skate wings.

COOK'S TIP
Look for packets of tempura batter mix at health food stores and Asian markets. It doesn't take long to make your own batter, but sometimes seconds count.

Energy 705Kcal/2921kJ; Protein 31.9g; Carbohydrate 11.7g, of which sugars 1.2g; Fat 59.3g, of which saturates 11g; Cholesterol 38mg; Calcium 112mg; Fibre 0.5g; Sodium 792mg.

FISH MOOLIE

THIS IS A VERY POPULAR SOUTH-EAST ASIAN FISH CURRY IN A COCONUT SAUCE, WHICH IS TRULY DELICIOUS. CHOOSE A FIRM-TEXTURED FISH SO THAT THE PIECES STAY INTACT DURING THE BRIEF COOKING PROCESS. HALIBUT AND COD WORK EQUALLY WELL.

SERVES FOUR

INGREDIENTS

500g/1¼lb monkfish or other firm-
  textured fish fillets, skinned and cut
  into 2.5cm/1in cubes
2.5ml/½ tsp salt
50g/2oz/⅔ cup desiccated (dry
  unsweetened shredded) coconut
6 shallots or small onions, chopped
6 blanched almonds
2–3 garlic cloves, roughly chopped
2.5cm/1in piece fresh root ginger,
  peeled and sliced
2 lemon grass stalks, trimmed
10ml/2 tsp ground turmeric
45ml/3 tbsp vegetable oil
2 × 400ml/14fl oz cans coconut milk
1–3 fresh chillies, seeded and sliced
salt and ground black pepper
fresh chives, to garnish
boiled rice, to serve

1 Spread out the pieces of fish in a shallow dish and sprinkle them with the salt. Dry-fry the coconut in a wok or large frying pan over medium heat, stirring constantly until it is crisp. Put in a food processor, process to an oily paste and transfer to a bowl.

2 Add the shallots or onions, almonds, garlic and ginger to the food processor. Chop the lower 5cm/2in of the lemon grass stalks and add to the processor. Process the mixture to a paste. Add the turmeric and process briefly to mix. Bruise the remaining lemon grass and set the stalks aside.

3 Heat the oil in a wok. Add the onion mixture and cook for a few minutes without browning. Stir in the coconut milk and bring to the boil, stirring constantly to prevent curdling.

4 Add the fish, most of the sliced chilli and the bruised lemon grass stalks. Cook for 3–4 minutes. Stir in the coconut paste and cook for a further 2–3 minutes only. Do not overcook the fish. Taste and adjust the seasoning.

5 Remove the lemon grass. Transfer to a hot serving dish and sprinkle with the remaining chilli. Garnish with chives and serve with boiled rice.

Energy 319Kcal/1335kJ; Protein 22.4g; Carbohydrate 16.7g, of which sugars 14.9g; Fat 18.6g, of which saturates 8.3g; Cholesterol 18mg; Calcium 96mg; Fibre 3g; Sodium 249mg.

HALIBUT AND TOMATO CURRY WITH GINGER

THE CHUNKY CUBES OF WHITE FISH CONTRAST VISUALLY WITH THE RICH RED SPICY TOMATO SAUCE AND TASTE JUST AS GOOD AS THEY LOOK. HALIBUT IS USED HERE, BUT YOU CAN USE ANY TYPE OF FIRM WHITE FISH FOR THIS RECIPE.

SERVES FOUR

INGREDIENTS
- 1 lemon
- 60ml/4 tbsp rice wine vinegar
- 30ml/2 tbsp cumin seeds
- 5ml/1 tsp ground turmeric
- 5ml/1 tsp chilli powder
- 5ml/1 tsp salt
- 750g/1lb 11oz thick halibut
  fillets, skinned and cubed
- 60ml/4 tbsp sunflower oil
- 1 onion, finely chopped
- 3 garlic cloves, finely grated
- 30ml/2 tbsp finely grated
  fresh root ginger
- 10ml/2 tsp black mustard seeds
- 2 x 400g/14oz cans
  chopped tomatoes
- 5ml/1 tsp sugar
- chopped coriander (cilantro)
  and sliced fresh green chilli,
  to garnish
- natural (plain) yogurt,
  to drizzle (optional)
- basmati rice, pickles and
  poppadums, to serve

1 Squeeze the lemon and pour 60ml/ 4 tbsp of the juice into a shallow glass bowl. Add the vinegar, cumin, turmeric, chilli powder and salt.

2 Add the cubed fish to the bowl and coat evenly. Cover the bowl with clear film (plastic wrap) and refrigerate for 25–30 minutes.

3 Meanwhile, heat a wok over a high heat and add the oil. When hot, add the onion, garlic, ginger and mustard seeds. Reduce the heat to low and cook very gently for about 10 minutes, stirring occasionally.

4 Add the tomatoes and sugar to the wok, bring to the boil, reduce the heat, cover and cook gently for 15–20 minutes, stirring occasionally.

5 Add the fish and its marinade to the wok, stir gently to mix, then cover and simmer gently for 15–20 minutes, or until the fish is cooked through and flakes easily with a fork.

6 Ladle the curry into shallow bowls, garnish with fresh coriander and green chillies, and drizzle over some natural yogurt if you like. Serve with basmati rice, pickles and poppadums.

COOK'S TIP
Halibut is quite a dense fish, so will take about 15 minutes to cook, especially if the cubes are thick. It is important not to overcook the fish, so if you choose a different type, or buy fillets that are relatively thin, check after 5 minutes. As soon as the flesh becomes opaque and the fish flakes easily when prodded with a fork or the tip of a knife, it is ready.

Energy 335Kcal/1409kJ; Protein 41.9g; Carbohydrate 8.4g, of which sugars 8.1g; Fat 15.2g, of which saturates 2.1g; Cholesterol 66mg; Calcium 73mg; Fibre 2.2g; Sodium 622mg.

SEAFOOD BALTI WITH VEGETABLES

THE SPICY SEAFOOD IS COOKED SEPARATELY AND COMBINED WITH VEGETABLES AT THE LAST MINUTE.

SERVES FOUR

INGREDIENTS
  225g/8oz firm white fish such as cod
  225g/8 oz peeled, cooked prawns
    (shrimp)
  6 crab sticks, halved lengthwise
  15ml/1 tbsp lemon juice
  5ml/1 tsp ground coriander
  5ml/1 tsp chilli powder
  5ml/1 tsp salt
  5ml/1 tsp ground cumin
  60ml/4 tbsp cornflour (cornstarch)
  150ml/¼ pint/⅔ cup corn oil
For the vegetables
  150ml/¼ pint/⅔ cup corn oil
  2 onions, chopped
  5ml/1 tsp onion seeds
  ½ cauliflower, cut into florets
  115g/4oz green beans, cut into
    2.5cm/1in lengths
  175g/6oz corn kernels
  5ml/1 tsp shredded fresh root ginger
  5ml/1 tsp chilli powder
  5ml/1 tsp salt
  4 fresh green chillies, sliced
  30ml/2 tbsp chopped fresh
    coriander (cilantro)
  lime slices, to garnish (optional)

1 Skin the fish and cut into small cubes. Put it into a mixing bowl with the prawns and crab sticks.

2 In a separate bowl, mix together the lemon juice, ground coriander, chilli powder, salt and ground cumin. Pour this mixture over the seafood and mix everything together thoroughly using your hands.

3 Sprinkle on the cornflour and mix again until the seafood is well coated. Set aside in the refrigerator for about 1 hour to allow the flavours to blend and develop fully.

4 To make the vegetable mixture, heat the oil in a preheated wok. Add the onions and the onion seeds and stir-fry until lightly browned.

5 Add the cauliflower, green beans, corn, ginger, chilli powder, salt, green chillies and fresh coriander. Stir-fry for about 7–10 minutes over a medium heat, making sure that the cauliflower florets retain their shape.

6 Spoon the fried vegetables around the edge of a shallow serving dish, leaving a space in the middle for the seafood, and keep warm.

7 Wash and dry the pan, then heat the oil to fry the seafood. Fry the seafood pieces in two or three batches, until golden brown. Remove with a slotted spoon and drain on kitchen paper.

8 Arrange each batch of seafood in the middle of the dish of vegetables and keep warm while you fry the remaining batches. Garnish with lime slices and serve immediately.

COOK'S TIP
Raita makes a delicious accompaniment to this seafood dish. Whisk 300ml/ ½ pint/1¼ cups natural yogurt, then whisk in 120ml/4 fl oz/½ cup water. Stir in 5ml/1 tsp salt, 30ml/2 tbsp chopped fresh coriander (cilantro) and 1 finely chopped green chilli. Garnish with slices of cucumber and one or two sprigs of mint.

Energy 454kcal /1894kJ; protein 24.5g; carbohydrate 30.9g, of which sugars 9.1g; fat 26.7g, of which saturates 3.2g; cholesterol 141mg; calcium 84mg; fibre 2.3g; sodium 372mg.

BALTI FISH FILLETS ᴵᴺ COCONUT SAUCE

USE FRESH FISH TO MAKE THIS DISH IF YOU CAN, AS IT HAS MUCH MORE FLAVOUR THAN FROZEN.

SERVES FOUR

INGREDIENTS

30ml/2 tbsp corn oil
5ml/1 tsp onion seeds
4 dried red chillies
3 garlic cloves, sliced
1 onion, sliced
2 tomatoes, sliced
30ml/2 tbsp desiccated (dry
  unsweetened shredded) coconut
5ml/1 tsp salt
5ml/1 tsp ground coriander
4 flatfish fillets, such as plaice,
  sole or flounder, each weighing
  about 75g/3oz
150ml/¼ pint/⅔ cup water
15ml/1 tbsp lime juice
15ml/1 tbsp chopped fresh
  coriander (cilantro)
boiled rice, to serve

1 Heat a wok or a large, heavy-based frying pan and add the oil.

2 Lower the heat slightly and add the onion seeds, dried red chillies, garlic slices and onion. Cook for 3–4 minutes, stirring once or twice.

3 Add the tomatoes, coconut, salt and coriander to the wok and stir thoroughly.

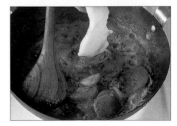

4 Cut each fish fillet into three pieces. Drop the fish pieces into the mixture and turn them over gently until they are well coated.

5 Cook for 5–7 minutes, lowering the heat if necessary. Add the water, lime juice and fresh coriander and cook for a further 3–5 minutes until most of the water has evaporated. Serve immediately with rice.

Energy 177kcal/737kJ; Protein 14g; Carbohydrate 4.3g, of which sugars 3.9g; Fat 11.6g, of which saturates 5g; Cholesterol 32mg; Calcium 70mg; Fibre 2.6g; Sodium 595mg.

STEAMED FISH SKEWERS ON RICE NOODLES

FRESH TROUT IS PERFECT FOR SUMMER ENTERTAINING. IN THIS RECIPE, SUCCULENT FILLETS ARE MARINATED IN A TANGY CITRUS SPICE BLEND, THEN SKEWERED AND STEAMED IN THE WOK BEFORE SERVING ON A BED OF FRAGRANT HERB NOODLES, FLAVOURED WITH CHILLI AND SPRING ONIONS.

SERVES FOUR

INGREDIENTS

   4 trout fillets, skinned
   2.5ml/½ tsp turmeric
   15ml/1 tbsp mild curry paste
   juice of 2 lemons
   15ml/1 tbsp sunflower oil
   salt and ground black pepper
   45ml/3 tbsp chilli-roasted peanuts,
     roughly chopped
   chopped fresh mint, to garnish
For the noodles
   300g/11oz rice noodles
   15ml/1 tbsp sunflower oil
   1 red chilli, seeded
     and finely sliced
   4 spring onions (scallions),
     cut into slivers
   60ml/4 tbsp roughly chopped
     fresh mint
   60ml/4 tbsp roughly chopped
     fresh sweet basil

3 Thread 2 bamboo skewers through each trout fillet and arrange in two tiers of a bamboo steamer lined with baking parchment.

4 Cover the steamer and place over a wok of simmering water (making sure the water doesn't touch the steamer). Steam the fish skewers for 5–6 minutes, or until the fish is just cooked through.

5 Meanwhile, in a clean wok heat the oil. Add the chilli, spring onions and drained noodles and stir-fry for about 2 minutes and then stir in the chopped herbs. Season with salt and ground black pepper and divide among four bowls or plates.

6 Top each bowl of noodles with a steamed fish skewer and scatter over the chilli-roasted peanuts. Garnish with chopped mint and serve immediately.

VARIATION
You can grill (broil) these fillets instead of steaming. Soak the bamboo skewers in cold water for at least 30 minutes before threading them through the trout fillets to prevent them burning.

1 Trim each fillet and place in a large bowl. Mix together the turmeric, curry paste, lemon juice and oil and pour over the fish. Season with salt and black pepper and toss to mix well.

2 Place the rice noodles in a bowl and pour over enough boiling water to cover. Leave to soak for 3–4 minutes and then drain. Refresh in cold water, drain and set aside.

Energy 555Kcal/2317kJ; Protein 36g; Carbohydrate 62.8g, of which sugars 1g; Fat 16.6g, of which saturates 1.6g; Cholesterol 0mg; Calcium 52mg; Fibre 1.3g; Sodium 97mg.

MALAYSIAN FISH CURRY

FISH GENTLY COOKED IN COCONUT MILK MAKES A CREAMY, DELICATELY FLAVOURED CURRY. SERVE IT WITH A FIERY RELISH AND PLAIN RICE TO ABSORB THE DELICIOUS SAUCE.

SERVES FOUR TO SIX

INGREDIENTS
  675g/1½lb monkfish, hokey or
    red snapper fillet
  salt, to taste
  45ml/3 tbsp grated fresh coconut
  30ml/2 tbsp vegetable oil
  2.5cm/1in galangal or fresh root
    ginger, peeled and thinly sliced
  2 small red chillies, seeded and
    finely chopped
  2 cloves garlic, crushed
  5cm/2in lemon grass stalk, shredded
  1 piece shrimp paste, 1cm/½in
    square, or 15ml/1 tbsp fish sauce
  400g/14oz canned coconut milk
  600ml/1 pint/2½ cups chicken stock
  2.5ml/½ tsp turmeric
  15ml/1 tbsp sugar
  juice of 1 lime, or ½ lemon
  lime slices and fresh coriander
    (cilantro), to garnish

1 Remove any skin and bones from the fish and cut into large chunks. Season with salt and set aside.

COOK'S TIP
Sambal, a fiery hot relish, is traditionally served with this curry. Mix together 2 skinned and chopped tomatoes, 1 finely chopped onion, 1 finely chopped green chilli and 30ml/2 tbsp lime juice. Season to taste with salt and pepper and sprinkle over 30ml/2 tbsp grated coconut.

2 Dry-fry the coconut in a large wok until evenly brown. Add the vegetable oil, galangal or ginger, chillies, garlic and lemon grass and fry briefly. Stir in the shrimp paste or fish sauce. Strain the coconut milk through a sieve into the wok, and reserve the thick part.

3 Add the chicken stock, turmeric, sugar, a little salt and the lime or lemon juice. Simmer for 10 minutes. Add the fish and simmer for 6–8 minutes. Stir in the thick part of the coconut milk and simmer to thicken. Garnish with coriander and lime slices.

Energy 176kcal/739kJ; Protein 24.4g; Carbohydrate 8.5g, of which sugars 8.1g; Fat 5.1g, of which saturates 0.8g; Cholesterol 59mg; Calcium 74mg; Fibre 0.7g; Sodium 236mg.

VINEGAR FISH

COOKING FISH IN THIS SPICY MIXTURE THAT INCLUDES CHILLIES, GINGER AND VINEGAR IS AN INDONESIAN SPECIALITY. IT IS WELL SUITED TO STRONG-FLAVOURED, OILY FISH SUCH AS MACKEREL.

SERVES TWO TO THREE

INGREDIENTS
2–3 mackerel, filleted
2–3 red chillies, seeded
4 macadamia nuts or 8 almonds
1 red onion, quartered
2 garlic cloves, crushed
1cm/½in piece fresh root ginger,
   peeled and sliced
5ml/1 tsp ground turmeric
45ml/3 tbsp coconut or vegetable oil
45ml/3 tbsp wine vinegar
150ml/¼ pint/⅔ cup water
salt
deep-fried onions and finely chopped
   chilli, to garnish
boiled or coconut rice,
   to serve

COOK'S TIP
To make coconut rice, put 400g/14oz washed long grain rice in a heavy pan with 2.5ml/½ tsp salt, a 5cm/2in piece of lemon grass and 25g/1oz creamed coconut or 100ml/3½fl oz/scant ½ cup coconut cream. Add 750ml/1¼ pints/3 cups boiling water and stir once to prevent the grains sticking together. Simmer over a medium heat for 10–12 minutes. Remove the pan from the heat, cover and set aside for 5 minutes. Fluff the rice with a fork before serving.

1 Rinse the mackerel fillets in cold water and dry well on kitchen paper. Set aside.

2 Put the chillies, macadamia nuts or almonds, onion, garlic, ginger, turmeric and 15ml/1 tbsp of the oil in a food processor and process to form a paste. Alternatively, grind the mixture by hand in a pestle and mortar.

3 Heat the remaining oil in a wok. When it is hot, add the paste and cook for 1–2 minutes without browning. Stir in the vinegar and water and season with salt to taste. Bring to the boil, then lower the heat.

4 Lower the mackerel fillets into the sauce in a single layer and cook gently for 8–10 minutes, or under the fish is cooked through.

5 Transfer the fish to a warm serving dish. Bring the sauce to a boil and cook for 1 minute or until it has reduced slightly.

6 Pour the sauce over the fish, garnish with deep-fried onions and chopped chilli and serve with rice.

Energy 624kcal/2589kJ; Protein 40.4g; Carbohydrate 1.4g, of which sugars 0.6g; Fat 50.8g, of which saturates 8.5g; Cholesterol 108mg; Calcium 65mg; Fibre 1.4g; Sodium 135mg.

MACKEREL WITH MUSHROOMS AND BLACK BEANS

EARTHY-TASTING SHIITAKE MUSHROOMS, ZESTY FRESH GINGER AND PUNGENT SALTED BLACK BEANS ARE THE PERFECT PARTNERS FOR ROBUSTLY FLAVOURED MACKEREL FILLETS. THE STRIKING FLAVOURS ALL COME TOGETHER BEAUTIFULLY IN THIS COMBINATION.

SERVES FOUR

INGREDIENTS

8 x 115g/4oz mackerel fillets
20 dried shiitake mushrooms
15ml/1 tbsp finely julienned fresh
   root ginger
3 star anise
45ml/3 tbsp dark soy sauce
15ml/1 tbsp Chinese rice wine
15ml/1 tbsp salted black beans
6 spring onions (scallions), finely
   shredded
30ml/2 tbsp sunflower oil
5ml/1 tsp sesame oil
4 garlic cloves, very thinly sliced
sliced cucumber and steamed
   basmati rice, to serve

1 Divide the mackerel fillets between two lightly oiled heatproof plates, with the skin-side up. Using a small, sharp knife, make 3–4 diagonal slits in each one, then set aside.

2 Place the dried shiitake mushrooms in a large bowl and pour over enough boiling water to cover. Leave to soak for 20–25 minutes. Drain, reserving the soaking liquid, discard the stems and slice the caps thinly.

3 Place a trivet or a steamer rack in a large wok and pour in 5cm/2in of the mushroom liquid (top up with water if necessary). Add half the ginger and the star anise.

COOK'S TIP
If the mackerel has been cleaned but you need to fillet it, this is very easy to do. Just open the fish up like a book, lay it on a board with the skin side uppermost, and press down firmly with your fingers all along the backbone. Turn the fish over and the backbone will come away easily. Remove any stray bones with tweezers and cut off the tail.

4 Push the remaining ginger strips into the slits in the fish and scatter over the sliced mushrooms. Bring the liquid in the wok to a boil and lower one of the prepared plates on to the trivet.

5 Cover the wok, reduce the heat and steam for 10–12 minutes, or until the mackerel is cooked. Remove the plate and repeat with the second plate of fish, adding liquid to the wok if necessary.

6 Transfer the steamed fish to a serving platter and keep warm. Ladle 105ml/ 7 tbsp of the steaming liquid into a clean wok with the soy sauce, wine and black beans, place over a gentle heat and bring to a simmer. Spoon over the fish and sprinkle over the spring onions.

7 Wipe out the wok with a piece of kitchen paper and place over a medium heat. Add the oils and garlic and stir-fry for a few minutes until lightly golden. Pour over the fish and serve with sliced cucumber and steamed basmati rice.

Energy 573Kcal/2378kJ; Protein 43.9g; Carbohydrate 3.2g, of which sugars 1.1g; Fat 42.7g, of which saturates 8.2g; Cholesterol 122mg; Calcium 37mg; Fibre 1.2g; Sodium 678mg.

VEGETARIAN MAIN DISHES

The recipes in this section are exciting and innovative without being overly intricate. Aromatic Okra and Coconut Stir-fry, for instance, tastes spectacular, is easy to cook at home, and only takes about 10 minutes. Other unusual offerings are Sweet Pumpkin and Peanut Curry, Thai Noodles with Chinese Chives, and Marinated Tofu and Broccoli with Crispy Fried Shallots. Salad Rolls with Pumpkin, Tofu, Peanuts and Basil — a traditional Vietnamese favourite, which guests assemble for themselves at the table.

DEEP-FRIED BEAN CURD ROLLS STUFFED <u>WITH</u> SPICED VEGETABLES

BEAN CURD SHEETS ARE MADE FROM BOILED SOYA MILK; THE SKIN THAT FORMS ON THE TOP IS LIFTED OFF AND DRIED IN SHEETS. THEY ARE AVAILABLE IN ASIAN SUPERMARKETS AND NEED TO BE DUNKED BRIEFLY IN WATER BEFORE THEY CAN BE USED.

SERVES FOUR

INGREDIENTS
30ml/2 tbsp groundnut (peanut) oil
50g/2oz fresh enokitake mushrooms,
    finely chopped
1 garlic clove, crushed
5ml/1 tsp grated fresh root ginger
4 spring onions (scallions),
    finely shredded
1 small carrot, cut into thin
    matchsticks
115g/4oz bamboo shoots,
    cut into thin matchsticks
15ml/1 tbsp light soy sauce
5ml/1 tsp chilli sauce
5ml/1 tsp sugar
15ml/1 tbsp cornflour (cornstarch)
8 bean curd sheets (approximately
    18 x 23cm/7 x 9in each)
sunflower oil, for deep-frying
crisp salad leaves, to serve

1 Heat the groundnut oil in a wok over a high heat and add the chopped mushrooms, garlic, ginger, spring onions, carrot and bamboo shoots. Stir-fry for 2–3 minutes and add the soy sauce, chilli sauce and sugar and toss to mix thoroughly.

2 Remove the vegetables from the heat and place in a sieve to drain the juices. Set aside to cool.

3 In a small bowl, mix the cornflour with 60ml/4 tbsp of cold water to form a smooth paste. Soak the bean curd sheets in a bowl of warm water for 10–15 seconds and then lay them out on a clean work surface and pat dry with kitchen paper.

4 Brush the edges of one of the bean curd sheets with the cornflour paste and place 30–45ml/2–3 tbsp of the vegetable mixture at one end of the sheet. Fold the edges over towards the centre and roll up tightly to form a neat roll. Repeat with the remaining bean curd sheets and filling.

5 Place the filled rolls on a baking parchment-lined baking sheet or tray, cover and chill for 3–4 hours.

6 To cook, fill a wok one-third full with sunflower oil and heat to 180°C/350°F or until a cube of bread, dropped into the oil, browns in 45 seconds.

7 Working in batches, deep-fry the rolls for 2–3 minutes, or until they are crisp and golden. Drain on kitchen paper and serve immediately with crisp salad leaves.

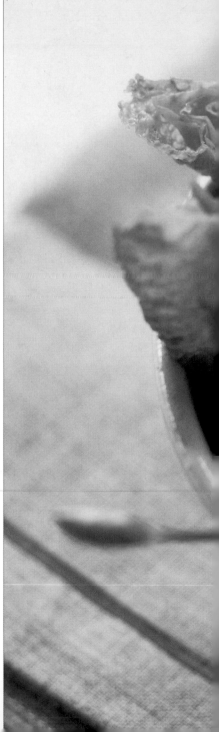

Energy 288Kcal/1190kJ; Protein 9.5g; Carbohydrate 3.2g, of which sugars 2.2g; Fat 26.5g, of which saturates 3.2g; Cholesterol 0mg; Calcium 524mg; Fibre 1g; Sodium 10mg.

SWEET PUMPKIN AND PEANUT CURRY

A HEARTY, SOOTHING CURRY PERFECT FOR AUTUMN OR WINTER EVENINGS. ITS CHEERFUL COLOUR ALONE WILL RAISE THE SPIRITS — AND THE COMBINATION OF PUMPKIN AND PEANUTS TASTES GREAT.

SERVES FOUR

INGREDIENTS

30ml/2 tbsp vegetable oil
4 garlic cloves, crushed
4 shallots, finely chopped
30ml/2 tbsp yellow curry paste
600ml/1 pint/2½ cups
  vegetable stock
2 kaffir lime leaves, torn
15ml/1 tbsp chopped fresh galangal
450g/1lb pumpkin, peeled, seeded
  and diced
225g/8oz sweet potatoes, diced
90g/3½ oz/scant 1 cup unsalted,
  roasted peanuts, chopped
300ml/½ pint/1¼ cups coconut milk
90g/3½ oz/1½ cups chestnut
  mushrooms, sliced
30ml/2 tbsp soy sauce
50g/2oz/⅓ cup pumpkin
  seeds, toasted, and fresh green
  chilli flowers, to garnish

1 Heat the oil in a wok. Add the garlic and shallots and cook over a medium heat, stirring occasionally, for 10 minutes, until softened and golden. Do not let them burn.

2 Add the yellow curry paste and stir-fry over medium heat for 30 seconds, until fragrant, then add the stock, lime leaves, galangal, pumpkin and sweet potatoes. Bring to the boil, stirring frequently, then reduce the heat to low and simmer gently for 15 minutes.

3 Add the peanuts, coconut milk and mushrooms. Stir in the soy sauce and simmer for 5 minutes more. Spoon into warmed individual serving bowls, garnish with the pumpkin seeds and chillies and serve.

COOK'S TIP
The well-drained vegetables from any of these curries would make a very tasty filling for a pastry or pie. This may not be a Thai tradition, but it is a good example of fusion food.

Energy 285Kcal/1189kJ; Protein 8.5g; Carbohydrate 24.8g, of which sugars 12.8g; Fat 17.5g, of which saturates 3g; Cholesterol 0mg; Calcium 94mg; Fibre 4.9g; Sodium 535mg.

TOFU AND GREEN BEAN RED CURRY

RED CURRY PASTE IS ONE OF THE AUTHENTIC FLAVOURINGS OF THAI COOKING, AND WORKS JUST AS WELL IN VEGETARIAN DISHES AS IT DOES IN MEAT-BASED RECIPES.

SERVES FOUR TO SIX

INGREDIENTS
   600ml/1 pint/2½ cups coconut milk
   15ml/1 tbsp Thai red curry paste
   45ml/3 tbsp mushroom ketchup
   10ml/2 tsp palm sugar or light
     muscovado (brown) sugar
   225g/8oz/3¼ cups button
     (white) mushrooms
   115g/4oz/scant 1 cup green
     beans, trimmed
   175g/6oz firm tofu, rinsed, drained
     and cut in 2cm/¾in cubes
   4 kaffir lime leaves, torn
   2 fresh red chillies, sliced
   fresh coriander (cilantro) leaves,
     to garnish

1 Pour about one-third of the coconut milk into a wok. Cook until it starts to separate and an oily sheen appears on the surface.

2 Add the red curry paste and mushroom ketchup and sugar to the wok. Mix thoroughly, then add the mushrooms. Stir and cook for 1 minute.

3 Stir in the remaining coconut milk. Bring back to the boil, then add the green beans and tofu cubes. Simmer gently for 4–5 minutes more.

4 Stir in the kaffir lime leaves and sliced red chillies. Spoon the curry into a serving dish, garnish with the coriander leaves and serve immediately.

Energy 79Kcal/333kJ; Protein 3.9g; Carbohydrate 8.2g, of which sugars 7.8g; Fat 3.6g, of which saturates 0.6g; Cholesterol 0mg; Calcium 189mg; Fibre 0.8g; Sodium 647mg.

THAI YELLOW VEGETABLE CURRY

THIS HOT AND SPICY CURRY MADE WITH COCONUT MILK HAS A CREAMY RICHNESS THAT CONTRASTS WONDERFULLY WITH THE HEAT OF CHILLI AND THE BITE OF LIGHTLY COOKED VEGETABLES.

SERVES FOUR

INGREDIENTS

30ml/2 tbsp sunflower oil
200ml/7fl oz/scant 1 cup
  coconut cream
300ml/½ pint/1¼ cups coconut milk
150ml/¼ pint/⅔ cup vegetable
  stock
200g/7oz snake beans, cut into
  2cm/¾in lengths
200g/7oz baby corn
4 baby courgettes (zucchini), sliced
1 small aubergine (eggplant), cubed
  or sliced
10ml/2 tsp palm sugar
fresh coriander (cilantro) leaves,
  to garnish
noodles or rice, to serve
For the curry paste
10ml/2 tsp hot chilli powder
10ml/2 tsp ground coriander
10ml/2 tsp ground cumin
5ml/1 tsp ground turmeric
15ml/1 tbsp chopped fresh
  galangal
10ml/2 tsp finely grated garlic
30ml/2 tbsp finely chopped
  lemon grass
4 red Asian shallots, finely
  chopped
5ml/1 tsp finely chopped lime rind

3 Add the coconut milk, stock and vegetables and cook gently for 8–10 minutes, until the vegetables are just tender. Stir in the palm sugar, garnish with coriander leaves and serve with noodles or rice.

COOK'S TIP
To make your own curry paste you will need a good food processor or blender, preferably one with an attachment for processing smaller quantities. Alternatively, you can use a large mortar and pestle, but be warned – it will be hard work. Store any remaining curry paste in a screw-top jar in the refrigerator for up to a week.

1 Make the curry paste. Place the spices, galangal, garlic, lemon grass, shallots and lime rind in a small food processor and blend with 30–45ml/2–3 tbsp of cold water to make a smooth paste. Add a little more water if the paste seems too dry.

2 Heat a large wok over a medium heat and add the sunflower oil. When hot add 30–45ml/2–3 tbsp of the curry paste and stir-fry for 1–2 minutes. Add the coconut cream and cook gently for 8–10 minutes, or until the mixture starts to separate.

Energy 126Kcal/528kJ; Protein 4.7g; Carbohydrate 12.7g, of which sugars 11.9g; Fat 6.7g, of which saturates 1.1g; Cholesterol 5mg; Calcium 90mg; Fibre 2.5g; Sodium 752mg.

CORN AND CASHEW NUT CURRY

A SUBSTANTIAL CURRY, DUE TO THE POTATOES AND CORN, THIS COMBINES ALL THE ESSENTIAL FLAVOURS OF SOUTHERN THAILAND. IT IS DELICIOUSLY AROMATIC, BUT THE FLAVOUR IS FAIRLY MILD.

SERVES FOUR

INGREDIENTS
30ml/2 tbsp vegetable oil
4 shallots, chopped
90g/3½oz/scant 1 cup cashew nuts
5ml/1 tsp Thai red curry paste
400g/14oz potatoes, peeled and cut into chunks
1 lemon grass stalk, finely chopped
200g/7oz can chopped tomatoes
600ml/1 pint/2½ cups boiling water
200g/7oz/generous 1 cup drained canned whole kernel corn
4 celery sticks, sliced
2 kaffir lime leaves, rolled into cylinders and thinly sliced
15ml/1 tbsp tomato ketchup
15ml/1 tbsp light soy sauce
5ml/1 tsp palm sugar or light muscovado (brown) sugar
4 spring onions (scallions), thinly sliced
small bunch fresh basil, chopped

COOK'S TIP
Rolling the lime leaves into cylinders before slicing with a sharp knife produces very fine strips – a technique known as cutting *en chiffonnade*. Remove the central rib from the leaves before cutting them.

1 Heat the oil in a wok. Add the shallots and stir-fry over a medium heat for 2–3 minutes, until softened. Add the cashew nuts and stir-fry for a few minutes until they are golden.

2 Stir in the red curry paste. Stir-fry for 1 minute, then add the potatoes, lemon grass, tomatoes and boiling water.

3 Bring back to the boil, then reduce the heat to low, cover and simmer gently for 15–20 minutes, or until the potatoes are tender.

4 Stir the corn, celery, lime leaves, ketchup, soy sauce, sugar and spring onions into the pan or wok. Simmer for a further 5 minutes, until heated through, then spoon into warmed serving bowls. Sprinkle with the sliced spring onions and basil and serve.

Energy 401Kcal/1681kJ; Protein 9.9g; Carbohydrate 51.7g, of which sugars 16.3g; Fat 18.6g, of which saturates 3.2g; Cholesterol 0mg; Calcium 41mg; Fibre 3.9g; Sodium 698mg.

Salad Rolls with Pumpkin, Tofu, Peanuts and Basil

This is one of the best Vietnamese "do-it-yourself" dishes. You place all the ingredients on the table with the rice wrappers for everyone to assemble their own rolls. In towns all over southern Vietnam, bo bia (salad roll) carts come out in the warm weather.

SERVES FOUR TO FIVE

INGREDIENTS

30ml/2 tbsp groundnut (peanut) or
  sesame oil
175g/6oz tofu, rinsed and
  patted dry
4 shallots, halved and sliced
2 garlic cloves, finely chopped
350g/12oz pumpkin flesh,
  cut into thin slices
1 carrot, cut into thin slices
15ml/1 tbsp soy sauce
4 green Thai chillies, seeded
  and finely sliced
1 small, crisp lettuce,
  leaves separated
1 bunch fresh basil, stalks removed
115g/4oz/⅔ cup roasted peanuts,
  chopped
100ml/3½fl oz/scant ½ cup
  hoisin sauce
20 dried rice wrappers
salt
nuoc cham, to serve (optional)

1 In a wok or heavy frying pan, heat half of the oil. Place the block of tofu in the wok and sear on all sides. Transfer to a plate and cut into thin strips.

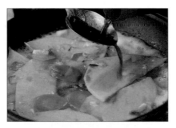

2 Heat the remaining oil in the pan and stir in the shallots and garlic. Add the pumpkin and carrot, then pour in the soy sauce and 120ml/4fl oz/½ cup water. Add salt to taste and cook gently until the vegetables have softened.

3 Meanwhile, arrange the tofu, chillies, lettuce, basil, roasted peanuts and hoisin sauce in separate dishes and put them on the table.

4 Fill a bowl with hot water and place it in the middle of the table, or fill a small bowl for each person. Place the stack of rice wrappers beside it. Spoon the vegetable mixture into a dish and add to the bowls of ingredients on the table.

5 To eat, take a rice wrapper and dip it in the water for a few seconds to soften. Lay the wrapper flat on the table or on a plate and, just off-centre, spread a few strips of lettuce, followed by the pumpkin mixture, some tofu, a sprinkling of chillies, a drizzle of hoisin sauce, some basil leaves and peanuts, layering the ingredients in a neat stack.

6 Pull the shorter edge of the wrapper (the side with filling on it) up over the stack, tuck in the sides and roll into a tight cylinder. Dip the roll into *nuoc cham*.

VARIATIONS
Squash, courgette (zucchini) or aubergine (eggplant) could be used in the filling, and cured Chinese sausage is often used instead of tofu.

Energy 402Kcal/1669kJ; Protein 14g; Carbohydrate 29g, of which sugars 13g; Fat 26g, of which saturates 5g; Cholesterol 0mg; Calcium 321mg; Fibre 4.1g; Sodium 400mg.

VEGETARIAN STIR-FRY WITH PEANUT SAUCE

STIR-FRIED VEGETABLES ARE POPULAR THROUGHOUT SOUTH-EAST ASIA. WHEREVER YOU GO, THERE WILL BE SOME VARIATION ON THE THEME. IN CAMBODIA, THE VEGETABLES ARE SOMETIMES DRIZZLED IN A PEANUT SAUCE LIKE THIS ONE, PARTICULARLY AMONG THE BUDDHIST COMMUNITIES.

SERVES FOUR TO SIX

INGREDIENTS
  6 Chinese black mushrooms (dried
    shiitake), soaked in lukewarm water
    for 20 minutes
  20 tiger lily buds, soaked in
    lukewarm water for 20 minutes
  225g/8oz tofu
  60ml/4 tbsp sesame or groundnut
    (peanut) oil
  1 large onion, halved and
    finely sliced
  1 large carrot, finely sliced
  300g/11oz pak choi (bok choy),
    the leaves separated from
    the stems
  225g/8oz can bamboo shoots,
    drained and rinsed
  50ml/2fl oz/¼ cup soy sauce
  10ml/2 tsp sugar
For the peanut sauce
  15ml/1 tbsp groundnut (peanut) or
    sesame oil
  2 garlic cloves, finely chopped
  2 red chillies, seeded and
    finely chopped
  90g/3½oz/generous ½ cup unsalted
    roasted peanuts, finely chopped
  150ml/5fl oz/⅔ cup coconut milk
  30ml/2 tbsp hoisin sauce
  15ml/1 tbsp soy sauce
  15ml/1 tbsp sugar

1 To make the sauce, heat the oil in a small wok or heavy pan. Stir in the garlic and chillies, stir-fry until they begin to colour, then add all the peanuts except 15ml/1 tbsp. Stir-fry for a few minutes until the natural oil from the peanuts begins to weep.

VARIATION
The popular piquant peanut sauce is delicious served hot with stir-fried, deep-fried or steamed vegetables. Alternatively, leave it to cool, garnish with a little chopped mint and coriander (cilantro) and serve it as a dip for raw vegetables, such as strips of carrot, cucumber and celery.

2 Add the remaining ingredients and bring to the boil. Reduce the heat and cook gently until the sauce thickens a little and specks of oil appear on the surface. Put aside.

3 Drain the mushrooms and lily buds and squeeze out any excess water. Cut the mushroom caps into strips and discard the stalks. Trim off the hard ends of the lily buds and tie a knot in the centre of each one. Put the mushrooms and lily buds aside.

4 Cut the tofu into slices. Heat 30ml/2 tbsp of the oil in a wok or heavy pan and brown the tofu on both sides. Drain on kitchen paper and cut it into strips.

5 Heat a wok or heavy pan and add the remaining oil. Stir in the onion and carrot and stir-fry for a minute. Add the pak choi stems and stir-fry for 2 minutes. Add the mushrooms, lily buds, tofu and bamboo shoots and stir-fry for a minute more. Toss in the pak choi leaves, followed by the soy sauce and sugar. Stir-fry until heated through.

6 Heat up the peanut sauce and drizzle over the vegetables in the wok and spoon the vegetables into individual bowls and top with a little sauce. Garnish with the remaining peanuts and serve.

Energy 252Kcal/1045kJ; Protein 10g; Carbohydrate 12g, of which sugars 8.5g; Fat 18g, of which saturates 3g; Cholesterol 0mg; Calcium 319mg; Fibre 3.6g; Sodium 1055mg.

AROMATIC OKRA AND COCONUT STIR-FRY

STIR-FRIED OKRA SPICED WITH MUSTARD, CUMIN AND RED CHILLIES AND SPRINKLED WITH FRESHLY GRATED COCONUT MAKES A GREAT QUICK SUPPER. IT IS THE PERFECT WAY TO ENJOY THESE SUCCULENT PODS, WITH THE SWEETNESS OF THE COCONUT COMPLEMENTING THE WARM SPICES.

SERVES FOUR

INGREDIENTS
  600g/1lb 6oz okra
  60ml/4 tbsp sunflower oil
  1 onion, finely chopped
  15ml/1 tbsp mustard seeds
  15ml/1 tbsp cumin seeds
  2–3 dried red chillies
  10–12 curry leaves
  2.5ml/½ tsp ground turmeric
  90g/3½oz freshly grated coconut
  salt and ground black pepper
  poppadums, rice or naan, to serve

1 With a sharp knife, cut each of the okra diagonally into 1cm/½in lengths. Set aside. Heat the wok and add the sunflower oil.

2 When the oil is hot add the chopped onion and stir-fry over a medium heat for about 5 minutes until softened.

3 Add the mustard seeds, cumin seeds, red chillies and curry leaves to the onions and stir-fry over a high heat for about 2 minutes.

4 Add the okra and turmeric to the wok and continue to stir-fry over a high heat for 3–4 minutes.

5 Remove the wok from the heat, sprinkle over the coconut and season well with salt and ground black pepper. Serve immediately with poppadums, steamed rice or naan bread.

COOK'S TIP
Fresh okra is widely available from most supermarkets and Asian stores. Choose fresh, firm, green specimens and avoid any that are limp or turning brown.

Energy 211Kcal/873kJ; Protein 5g; Carbohydrate 6.3g, of which sugars 5.2g; Fat 18.7g, of which saturates 7.1g; Cholesterol 0mg; Calcium 246mg; Fibre 7.6g; Sodium 15mg.

STIR-FRIED SEEDS AND VEGETABLES

THE CONTRAST BETWEEN THE CRUNCHY SEEDS AND VEGETABLES AND THE RICH, SAVOURY SAUCE IS WHAT MAKES THIS DISH SO DELICIOUS. SUPER-SPEEDY WHEN TOSSED TOGETHER IN THE WOK, IT CAN BE SERVED ON ITS OWN, OR WITH RICE OR NOODLES.

SERVES FOUR

INGREDIENTS

30ml/2 tbsp vegetable oil
30ml/2 tbsp sesame seeds
30ml/2 tbsp sunflower seeds
30ml/2 tbsp pumpkin seeds
2 garlic cloves, finely chopped
2.5cm/1in piece fresh root ginger, peeled and finely chopped
2 large carrots, cut into batons
2 large courgettes (zucchini), cut into batons
90g/3½oz/1½ cups oyster mushrooms, broken in pieces
150g/5oz watercress or spinach leaves, coarsely chopped
small bunch fresh mint or coriander (cilantro), leaves and stems chopped
60ml/4 tbsp black bean sauce
30ml/2 tbsp light soy sauce
15ml/1 tbsp palm sugar or light muscovado (brown) sugar
30ml/2 tbsp rice vinegar

1 Heat the oil in a wok. Add the seeds. Toss over a medium heat for 1 minute, then add the garlic and ginger and continue to stir-fry until the ginger is aromatic and the garlic is golden. Do not let the spices or garlic burn or they will taste bitter.

2 Add the carrot and courgette batons and the mushroom pieces to the wok and stir-fry over a medium heat for a further 5 minutes, or until all the vegetables are crisp-tender and are golden at the edges.

3 Add the watercress or spinach with the fresh herbs. Toss over the heat for 1 minute, then stir in the black bean sauce, soy sauce, sugar and vinegar. Stir-fry for 1–2 minutes, until combined and hot. Serve immediately.

COOK'S TIP
Oyster mushrooms have acquired their name because of their texture, rather than flavour, which is quite superb. They are delicate, so it is usually better to tear them into pieces along the lines of the gills, rather than slice them with a knife.

Energy 205Kcal/849kJ; Protein 6.9g; Carbohydrate 9.7g, of which sugars 7.7g; Fat 15.6g, of which saturates 2g; Cholesterol 0mg; Calcium 159mg; Fibre 3.4g; Sodium 294mg.

STUFFED SWEET PEPPERS

THIS IS AN UNUSUAL RECIPE IN THAT THE STUFFED PEPPERS ARE STEAMED RATHER THAN BAKED, BUT THE RESULT IS LIGHT AND TENDER. THE FILLING OF LIGHTLY CURRIED MUSHROOMS LOOKS ATTRACTIVE AND TASTES WONDERFUL. CREAMY YOGURT WOULD MAKE A GOOD ACCOMPANIMENT.

SERVES FOUR

INGREDIENTS

    3 garlic cloves, finely chopped
    2 coriander (cilantro) roots,
      finely chopped
    400g/14oz/3 cups
      mushrooms, quartered
    5ml/1 tsp Thai red curry paste
    1 egg, lightly beaten
    15ml/1 tbsp mushroom ketchup
    15ml/1 tbsp light soy sauce
    2.5ml/½ tsp granulated sugar
    3 kaffir lime leaves, finely chopped
    4 yellow (bell) peppers, halved
      lengthways and seeded

1 In a mortar or spice grinder pound or grind the garlic with the coriander roots. Scrape into a bowl.

2 Put the mushrooms in a food processor and pulse briefly until they are finely chopped. Add to the garlic mixture, then stir in the curry paste, egg, sauces, sugar and lime leaves.

3 Place the pepper halves in a single layer in a steamer basket. Spoon the mixture loosely into the pepper halves. Do not pack the mixture down tightly or the filling will dry out too much. Bring the water in the wok to the boil, then lower the heat to a simmer. Steam the peppers for 15 minutes, or until the flesh is tender. Serve hot.

Energy 103Kcal/429kJ; Protein 6.1g; Carbohydrate 14.4g, of which sugars 12g; Fat 2.7g, of which saturates 0.7g; Cholesterol 48mg; Calcium 30mg; Fibre 4.4g; Sodium 297mg.

STIR-FRIED CRISPY TOFU

THE ASPARAGUS GROWN IN THE PART OF ASIA WHERE THIS RECIPE ORIGINATED TENDS TO HAVE SLENDER STALKS. LOOK FOR IT IN THAI MARKETS OR SUBSTITUTE THE THIN ASPARAGUS POPULARLY KNOWN AS SPRUE. IF YOU USE THICKER ASPARAGUS, YOU MAY NEED TO COOK IT FOR LONGER.

SERVES TWO

INGREDIENTS

250g/9oz fried tofu cubes
30ml/2 tbsp groundnut (peanut) oil
15ml/1 tbsp Thai green curry paste
30ml/2 tbsp light soy sauce
2 kaffir lime leaves, rolled into
  cylinders and thinly sliced
30ml/2 tbsp granulated sugar
150ml/¼ pint/⅔ cup vegetable stock
250g/9oz Asian asparagus, trimmed
  and sliced into 5cm/2in lengths
30ml/2 tbsp roasted peanuts,
  finely chopped

VARIATION

Substitute slim carrot sticks or broccoli florets for the asparagus.

1 Preheat the grill (broiler) to medium. Place the tofu cubes in a grill pan and grill (broil) for 2–3 minutes, then turn them over and continue to cook until they are crisp and golden brown all over. Watch them carefully; they must not be allowed to burn.

2 Heat the oil in a wok or heavy frying pan. Add the green curry paste and cook over a medium heat, stirring constantly, for 1–2 minutes, until it gives off its aroma.

3 Stir the soy sauce, lime leaves, sugar and vegetable stock into the wok or pan and mix well. Bring to the boil, then reduce the heat to low so that the mixture is just simmering.

4 Add the asparagus and simmer gently for 5 minutes. Meanwhile, chop each piece of tofu into four, then add to the pan with the peanuts.

5 Toss to coat all the ingredients in the sauce, then spoon into a warmed dish and serve immediately.

Energy 287Kcal/1195kJ; Protein 14.3g; Carbohydrate 20.3g, of which sugars 19.5g; Fat 17g, of which saturates 2.1g; Cholesterol 0mg; Calcium 682mg; Fibre 2.2g; Sodium 1075mg.

MARINATED TOFU AND BROCCOLI WITH CRISPY FRIED SHALLOTS

THIS MELTINGLY TENDER TOFU FLAVOURED WITH A FRAGRANT BLEND OF SPICES AND SERVED WITH TENDER YOUNG STEMS OF BROCCOLI MAKES A PERFECT LIGHT SUPPER OR LUNCH. YOU CAN BUY THE CRISPY FRIED SHALLOTS FROM ASIAN SUPERMARKETS, BUT THEY ARE VERY EASY TO MAKE YOURSELF.

SERVES FOUR

INGREDIENTS

500g/1¼lb block of firm tofu,
  drained
45ml/3 tbsp kecap manis
30ml/2 tbsp sweet chilli sauce
45ml/3 tbsp soy sauce
5ml/1 tsp sesame oil
5ml/1 tsp finely grated fresh
  root ginger
400g/14oz tenderstem broccoli,
  halved lengthways
45ml/3 tbsp roughly chopped
  coriander (cilantro)
30ml/2 tbsp toasted sesame seeds
30ml/2 tbsp crispy fried shallots
steamed rice or noodles,
  to serve
For the crispy fried shallots
10 Thai shallots, sliced into paper
  thin rings and separated
oil for deep-frying

1 Make the crispy shallots. Add the shallot rings to a wok one-third full of hot oil, then lower the heat and stir constantly until crisp. Spread on kitchen paper to drain.

2 Cut the tofu into 4 triangular pieces: slice the block in half widthways, then diagonally. Place in a heatproof dish.

3 In a small bowl, combine the kecap manis, chilli sauce, soy sauce, sesame oil and ginger, then pour over the tofu. Leave the tofu to marinate for at least 30 minutes, turning occasionally.

4 Place the broccoli on a heatproof plate and place on a trivet or steamer rack in the wok. Cover and steam for 4–5 minutes, until just tender. Remove and keep warm.

5 Place the dish of tofu on the trivet or steamer rack in the wok, cover and steam for 4–5 minutes. Divide the broccoli among four warmed serving plates and top each one with a triangle of tofu.

6 Spoon the remaining juices over the tofu and broccoli, then sprinkle over the coriander, sesame seeds and crispy shallots. Serve immediately with steamed rice or noodles.

Energy 202Kcal/840kJ; Protein 16.5g; Carbohydrate 6.9g, of which sugars 5.6g; Fat 12.1g, of which saturates 1.7g; Cholesterol 0mg; Calcium 750mg; Fibre 3.5g; Sodium 938mg.

NOODLES <u>AND</u> VEGETABLES <u>IN</u> COCONUT SAUCE

WHEN EVERYDAY VEGETABLES ARE LIVENED UP WITH THAI SPICES AND FLAVOURS, THE RESULT IS A DELECTABLE DISH THAT EVERYONE WILL ENJOY. NOODLES ADD BULK AND A WELCOME CONTRAST IN TEXTURE, AND THE RED CURRY AND COCONUT SAUCE MARRIES EVERYTHING TOGETHER PERFECTLY.

SERVES FOUR TO SIX

INGREDIENTS
   30ml/2 tbsp sunflower oil
   1 lemon grass stalk, finely chopped
   15ml/1 tbsp Thai red curry paste
   1 onion, thickly sliced
   3 courgettes (zucchini), thickly sliced
   115g/4oz Savoy cabbage,
     thickly sliced
   2 carrots, thickly sliced
   150g/5oz broccoli, stem thickly
     sliced and head separated
     into florets
   2 × 400ml/14fl oz cans coconut milk
   475ml/16fl oz/2 cups vegetable stock
   150g/5oz dried egg noodles
   30ml/2 tbsp soy sauce
   60ml/4 tbsp chopped fresh
     coriander (cilantro)
   coriander sprigs, to garnish

1 Heat the oil in a wok. Add the lemon grass and red curry paste and stir-fry for 2–3 seconds.

2 Add the onion to the wok and continue to stir fry over medium heat, stirring occasionally, until the onion has softened but not browned.

3 Add the courgettes, cabbage, carrots and slices of broccoli stem to the onion and curry paste mixture, and toss until all the vegetable pieces are coated.

4 Reduce the heat to low and cook gently, stirring occasionally, for a further 5 minutes.

5 Increase the heat to medium, stir in the coconut milk and vegetable stock and bring to the boil.

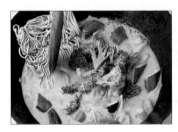

6 Add the broccoli florets and the noodles to the wok, lower the heat and simmer gently for 20 minutes.

7 Stir the soy sauce and chopped coriander into the noodle mixture. Spoon on to the platter, garnish with coriander sprigs and serve.

Energy 192Kcal/808kJ; Protein 5.6g; Carbohydrate 29.4g, of which sugars 11.5g; Fat 6.6g, of which saturates 1.4g;
Cholesterol 8mg; Calcium 83mg; Fibre 2.4g; Sodium 554mg.

SWEET AND SOUR VEGETABLES WITH TOFU

Big, bold and beautiful, this is a hearty stir-fry that will satisfy the hungriest guests. Stir-fries are always a good choice when entertaining, because you can prepare the ingredients ahead of time and then cook them incredibly quickly in the wok.

SERVES FOUR

INGREDIENTS
4 shallots
3 garlic cloves
30ml/2 tbsp groundnut (peanut) oil
250g/9oz Chinese leaves (Chinese
  cabbage), shredded
8 baby corn cobs, sliced on
  the diagonal
2 red (bell) peppers, seeded and
  thinly sliced
200g/7oz/1¾ cups mangetouts
  (snow peas), trimmed and sliced
250g/9oz tofu, rinsed, drained and
  cut in 1cm/½ in cubes
60ml/4 tbsp vegetable stock
30ml/2 tbsp light soy sauce
15ml/1 tbsp granulated sugar
30ml/2 tbsp rice vinegar
2.5ml/½ tsp dried chilli flakes
small bunch coriander
  (cilantro), chopped

1 Slice the shallots thinly using a sharp knife. Finely chop the garlic.

2 Heat the oil in a wok or large frying pan and cook the shallots and garlic for 2–3 minutes over a medium heat, until golden. Do not let the garlic burn or it will taste bitter.

3 Add the shredded cabbage, toss over the heat for 30 seconds, then add the corn cobs and repeat the process.

4 Add the red peppers, mangetouts and tofu in the same way, each time adding a single ingredient and tossing it over the heat for about 30 seconds before adding the next ingredient.

5 Pour in the stock and soy sauce. Mix together the sugar and vinegar in a small bowl, stirring until the sugar has dissolved, then add to the wok or pan. Sprinkle over the chilli flakes and coriander, toss to mix well and serve.

Energy 478Kcal/2010kJ; Protein 16.8g; Carbohydrate 64.2g, of which sugars 5.1g; Fat 18.9g, of which saturates 3.2g; Cholesterol 86mg; Calcium 323mg; Fibre 2.9g; Sodium 466mg.

THAI NOODLES WITH CHINESE CHIVES

*THIS RECIPE REQUIRES A LITTLE TIME FOR PREPARATION, BUT THE COOKING TIME IS VERY FAST.
EVERYTHING IS COOKED IN A HOT WOK AND SHOULD BE EATEN IMMEDIATELY. THIS IS A FILLING
AND TASTY VEGETARIAN DISH, IDEAL FOR A WEEKEND LUNCH.*

SERVES FOUR

INGREDIENTS

    350g/12oz dried rice noodles
    1cm/½in piece fresh root ginger,
      peeled and grated
    30ml/2 tbsp light soy sauce
    45ml/3 tbsp vegetable oil
    225g/8oz Quorn (mycoprotein), cut
      into small cubes
    2 garlic cloves, crushed
    1 large onion, cut into thin wedges
    115g/4oz fried tofu, thinly sliced
    1 fresh green chilli, seeded and
      thinly sliced
    175g/6oz/3 cups beansprouts
    2 large bunches garlic chives, total
      weight about 115g/4oz, cut into
      5cm/2in lengths
    50g/2oz/½ cup roasted
      peanuts, ground
    30ml/2 tbsp dark soy sauce
    30ml/2 tbsp chopped fresh coriander
      (cilantro), and 1 lemon, cut into
      wedges, to garnish

1 Place the noodles in a bowl, cover
with warm water and leave to soak for
30 minutes. Drain and set aside.

2 Mix the ginger, light soy sauce and
15ml/1 tbsp of the oil in a bowl. Add the
Quorn, then set aside for 10 minutes.
Drain, reserving the marinade.

3 Heat 15ml/1 tbsp of the remaining oil
in a wok and cook the garlic for a few
seconds. Add the Quorn and stir-fry for
3–4 minutes. Using a slotted spoon,
transfer to a plate and set aside.

4 Heat the remaining oil in the wok and
stir-fry the onion for 3–4 minutes, until
softened and tinged with brown. Add
the tofu and chilli, stir-fry briefly and
then add the noodles. Stir-fry over a
medium heat for 4–5 minutes.

5 Stir in the beansprouts, garlic chives
and most of the ground peanuts,
reserving a little for the garnish. Stir
well, then add the Quorn, the dark soy
sauce and the reserved marinade.

6 When hot, spoon on to serving plates
and garnish with the remaining ground
peanuts, the coriander and lemon.

Energy 584Kcal/2435kJ; Protein 19.7g; Carbohydrate 82.9g, of which sugars 7.5g; Fat 18.2g, of which saturates 2.6g; Cholesterol 0mg; Calcium 242mg; Fibre 5.8g; Sodium 984mg.

TOFU STIR-FRY

THE TOFU HAS A PLEASANT CREAMY TEXTURE, WHICH CONTRASTS DELIGHTFULLY WITH THE CRUNCHY STIR-FRIED VEGETABLES. THIS RECIPE CALLS FOR FIRM TOFU, WHICH IS EASY TO CUT NEATLY.

SERVES FOUR

INGREDIENTS
115g/4oz hard white cabbage
2 green chillies
450g/1lboz firm tofu
45ml/3 tbsp vegetable oil
2 cloves garlic, crushed
3 spring onions (scallions), chopped
175g/6oz green beans, topped
  and tailed
175g/6oz baby corn, halved
115g/4oz beansprouts
45ml/3 tbsp smooth peanut butter
25ml/1½ tbsp dark soy sauce
300ml/½ pint/1¼ cups coconut milk

1 Shred the white cabbage. Carefully remove the seeds from the chillies and chop finely. Wear rubber gloves to protect your hands, if necessary.

2 Cut the tofu into thin strips. Heat the wok, then add 30ml/2 tbsp of the oil. When the oil is hot, add the tofu, stir-fry for 3 minutes and remove. Set aside. Wipe out the wok with kitchen paper.

3 Add the remaining oil. When it is hot, add the garlic, spring onions and chillies and stir-fry for 1 minute. Add the green beans, corn and beansprouts and stir-fry for a further 2 minutes.

4 Add the peanut butter and soy sauce to the wok. Stir well to coat the vegetables. Add the tofu to the wok.

5 Pour the coconut milk over the vegetables. Simmer for 3 minutes to blend the flavours and reduce the sauce slightly. Serve immediately.

COOK'S TIP
There are hundreds of varieties of chilli. The "heat factor" of chillies is measured in Scoville units, with sweet peppers at 0 at the bottom of the scale and Mexican habanero chillies at 300,000, the hottest, at the top. Indonesian and Thai dishes can be very fiery, but Chinese recipes tend to use mild varieties.

Energy 242kcal/1004kJ; Protein 11g; Carbohydrate 11.2g, of which sugars 8.9g; Fat 17.3g, of which saturates 2.9g; Cholesterol 0mg; Calcium 356mg; Fibre 3.4g; Sodium 1072mg.

BLACK BEAN AND VEGETABLE STIR-FRY

WHEN STIR-FRYING A MIXTURE OF VEGETABLES, THE INGREDIENTS NEED TO BE ADDED TO THE WOK IN THE RIGHT ORDER SO THAT LARGER PIECES HAVE A LONGER COOKING TIME THAN THE SMALLER ONES.

SERVES FOUR

INGREDIENTS
  8 spring onions (scallions)
  225g/8oz button (white) mushrooms
  1 red (bell) pepper
  1 green (bell) pepper
  2 large carrots
  60ml/4 tbsp sesame oil
  2 garlic cloves, crushed
  60ml/4 tbsp black bean sauce
  90ml/6 tbsp warm water
  225g/8oz beansprouts
  salt and ground black pepper

1 Thinly slice the spring onions and button mushrooms.

2 Cut the peppers and carrots into fine strips of equal size.

COOK'S TIP
Black bean sauce is quite a thick paste and readily available in jars, bottles and cans from large supermarkets and Asian food stores. Store the sauce in the refrigerator after opening.

3 Heat the oil in a large preheated wok until very hot. Add the spring onions and garlic and stir-fry for 30 seconds.

4 Add the mushrooms, peppers and carrots. Stir-fry for 5–6 minutes over a high heat until the vegetables are just beginning to soften.

5 Mix the black bean sauce with the water. Add the mixture to the wok and cook for 3–4 minutes.

6 Stir in the beansprouts and cook for 1 minute more, until all the vegetables are coated in the sauce. Season to taste, then serve at once.

Energy 196kcal/817kJ; Protein 6.5g; Carbohydrate 16.1g, of which sugars 9.4g; Fat 12.2g, of which saturates 1.9g; Cholesterol 0mg; Calcium 45mg; Fibre 4.6g; Sodium 19mg.

NOODLE
DISHES

Noodles are the Asian equivalent of pasta, and are just as versatile and quick to prepare. With the addition of a few fresh ingredients, or even some bottled or canned standbys, you can produce delicious and satisfying one-dish meals in a very short time. A wok is the essential utensil for this kind of meal: you can speedily stir-fry meat, fish or vegetables, create a spicy sauce and then add cooked noodles, with plenty of room to toss everything together. Noodles are made from wheat, rice, buckwheat or beans; dried noodles need to be briefly boiled, fresh ones can be added straight to the wok.

NOODLES WITH CRAB AND CLOUD EAR MUSHROOMS

THIS IS A DISH OF CONTRASTING FLAVOURS. IN VIETNAM IT IS COOKED WHILE ONE HAND GENTLY TURNS THE NOODLES AND THE OTHER TAKES CHUNKS OF CRAB MEAT AND DROPS THEM IN.

SERVES FOUR

INGREDIENTS

25g/1oz dried cloud ear (wood ear) mushrooms, soaked in warm water for 20 minutes
115g/4oz dried cellophane (bean thread noodles, soaked in warm water for 20 minutes
30ml/2 tbsp vegetable or sesame oil
3 shallots, halved and thinly sliced
2 garlic cloves, crushed
2 green or red Thai chillies, seeded and sliced
1 carrot, peeled and cut into thin diagonal rounds
5ml/1 tsp sugar
45ml/3 tbsp oyster sauce
15ml/1 tbsp soy sauce
400ml/14fl oz/1⅔ cups water or chicken stock
225g/8oz fresh, raw crabmeat, cut into bite-sized chunks
ground black pepper
fresh coriander (cilantro) leaves, to garnish

1 Remove the centres from the soaked cloud ear mushrooms and cut the mushrooms in half. Drain the soaked noodles and cut them into 30cm/12in pieces and put aside.

2 Heat a wok or pan and add 15ml/1 tbsp of the oil. Stir in the shallots, garlic and chillies, and cook until fragrant. Add the carrot rounds and cook for 1 minute, then add the mushrooms.

3 Stir in the sugar with the oyster and soy sauces, followed by the cellophane noodles. Pour in the water or stock, cover the wok or pan and cook for about 5 minutes, or until the noodles are soft and have absorbed most of the sauce.

4 Meanwhile, heat the remaining oil in a heavy pan. Add the crabmeat and cook until it is nicely pink and tender. Season well with black pepper. Arrange the noodles and crab meat on a serving dish and garnish with coriander.

Energy 252kcal/1051kJ; Protein 12.9g; Carbohydrate 35.7g, of which sugars 10.3g; Fat 6.3g, of which saturates 0.7g; Cholesterol 41mg; Calcium 97mg; Fibre 1.6g; Sodium 770mg.

EGG NOODLES WITH TUNA AND TOMATO SAUCE

RAID THE STORECUPBOARD, ADD A FEW FRESH INGREDIENTS AND YOU CAN PRODUCE A SCRUMPTIOUS MAIN MEAL IN MOMENTS.

SERVES FOUR

INGREDIENTS
   45ml/3 tbsp olive oil
   2 garlic cloves, finely chopped
   2 dried red chillies, seeded
   and chopped
   1 large red onion, finely sliced
   175g/6oz canned tuna, drained
   115g/4oz pitted black olives
   400g/14oz can chopped tomatoes
   30ml/2 tbsp chopped parsley
   350g/12oz medium egg noodles
   salt and freshly ground black pepper

1 Heat the oil in a wok and fry the garlic and chillies for a few seconds before adding the sliced onion. Fry, stirring, for about 5 minutes until the onion softens.

2 Add the tuna and black olives to the pan and stir until well mixed. Stir in the tomatoes and any juices. Bring to the boil, season with salt and pepper, add the parsley, then lower the heat and leave to simmer gently for about 15 minutes, stirring occasionally.

3 Meanwhile, bring a pan of salted water to the boil and cook the noodles for about 4 minutes, until just tender, following the directions on the packet. Drain well. Adjust the seasoning of the sauce if necessary, toss the noodles with the sauce and serve at once.

Energy 518kcal/2182kJ; Protein 22.8g; Carbohydrate 67.4g, of which sugars 5.9g; Fat 19.4g, of which saturates 3.9g; Cholesterol 49mg; Calcium 77mg; Fibre 5g; Sodium 958mg.

NOODLES WITH SUN-DRIED TOMATOES AND PRAWNS

THIN JAPANESE WHEAT NOODLES AND AN INTENSE, PIQUANT SAUCE OF SUN DRIED TOMATOES MAKE AN INTERESTING CONTRAST WITH THE LUSCIOUS PRAWNS.

SERVES FOUR

INGREDIENTS

    350g/12oz somen noodles
    45ml/3 tbsp olive oil
    20 uncooked king prawns (jumbo
      shrimp), peeled and deveined
    2 garlic cloves, finely chopped
    45–60ml/3–4 tbsp sun-dried
      tomato paste
    salt and freshly ground black pepper
For the garnish
    handful of basil leaves
    30ml/2 tbsp sun-dried tomatoes in
      oil, drained and cut into strips

1 Cook the noodles in a large pan of boiling water until tender. Drain.

2 Heat half the oil in a wok or large frying pan, add the prawns and garlic and fry over a medium heat for 3–5 minutes, until the prawns turn pink and are firm. Stir in 15ml/1 tbsp of the sun-dried tomato paste. Transfer the prawns to a bowl and keep hot.

3 Add the remaining oil and sun-dried tomato paste to the pan. Add a spoonful of water if the mixture is very thick.

4 When the mixture starts to sizzle, toss in the noodles. Add salt and pepper to taste and mix well.

5 Return the prawns to the pan and toss to combine. Serve garnished with basil and strips of sun-dried tomatoes.

COOK'S TIP
Ready-made sun-dried tomato paste is readily available, but you can make your own simply by processing bottled sun-dried tomatoes with their oil.

Energy 481kcal/2026kJ; Protein 19.2g; Carbohydrate 67.4g, of which sugars 2.9g; Fat 16.8g, of which saturates 1.6g; Cholesterol 98mg; Calcium 62mg; Fibre 2.8g; Sodium 99mg.

BUCKWHEAT NOODLES WITH SMOKED TROUT AND PAK CHOI

THE LIGHT, CRISP TEXTURE OF THE PAK CHOI BALANCES THE EARTHY FLAVOURS OF THE MUSHROOMS, THE BUCKWHEAT NOODLES AND THE SMOKINESS OF THE TROUT

SERVES FOUR

INGREDIENTS

350g/12oz buckwheat noodles
30ml/2 tbsp vegetable oil
115g/4oz fresh shiitake
  mushrooms, quartered
2 garlic cloves, finely chopped
15ml/1 tbsp grated fresh
  root ginger
225g/8oz pak choi (bok choy)
1 spring onion (scallion), finely
  sliced diagonally
15ml/1 tbsp dark sesame oil
30ml/2 tbsp mirin
30ml/2 tbsp soy sauce
2 smoked trout, skinned and
  boned, flaked into bite-size pieces
salt and freshly ground black pepper
30ml/2 tbsp coriander (cilantro)
  leaves, to garnish
10ml/2 tsp sesame seeds, toasted,
  to garnish

1 Bring a large pan of water to the boil and cook the buckwheat noodles for about 7–10 minutes or until just tender, following the directions on the packet.

2 Meanwhile heat the oil in a wok or a large frying pan. Add the shiitake mushrooms and stir-fry over a medium heat for 3 minutes.

3 Add the garlic, ginger and pak choi, and continue to stir-fry for 2 minutes.

4 Drain the noodles and add them to the mushroom mixture with the spring onion, sesame oil, mirin and soy sauce. Toss and season with salt and pepper.

5 Arrange the noodles on individual serving plates and place the smoked trout on top. Garnish with coriander and sesame seeds and serve at once.

Energy 343kcal/1443kJ; Protein 16.3g; Carbohydrate 47.9g, of which sugars 3.8g; Fat 10.9g, of which saturates 1.2g; Cholesterol 10mg; Calcium 29mg; Fibre 3.5g; Sodium 814mg.

FRIED NOODLES <u>WITH</u> SPICY PEANUT SATAY, BEEF <u>AND</u> FRAGRANT HERBS

IF YOU LIKE CHILLIES AND PEANUTS, THIS DELICIOUS DISH MAKES THE PERFECT CHOICE. THE STRINGY RICE STICKS ARE FIDDLY TO STIR-FRY AS THEY HAVE A TENDENCY TO CLING TO ONE ANOTHER, SO WORK QUICKLY. THIS DISH IS USUALLY SERVED WITH A TABLE SALAD OR PICKLES.

SERVES FOUR

INGREDIENTS

15–30ml/1–2 tbsp vegetable oil
300g/11oz beef sirloin, cut against the grain into thin slices
225g/8oz dried rice sticks (vermicelli), soaked in warm water for 20 minutes
225g/8oz/1 cup beansprouts
5–10ml/1–2 tsp *nuoc mam*
1 small bunch each of fresh basil and mint, stalks removed, leaves shredded, to garnish
pickles, to serve

For the satay

4 dried Serrano chillies, seeded
60ml/4 tbsp groundnut (peanut) oil
4–5 garlic cloves, crushed
5–10ml/1–2 tsp curry powder
40g/1½oz/⅓ cup roasted peanuts, finely ground

1 To make the satay, grind the Serrano chillies in a mortar with a pestle. Heat the oil in a heavy pan and stir in the garlic until it begins to colour. Add the chillies, curry powder and the peanuts and stir over a low heat, until the mixture forms a paste. Remove the pan from the heat and leave the mixture to cool.

2 Heat a wok or heavy pan, and pour in 15ml/1 tbsp of the oil. Add the sliced beef and cook for 1–2 minutes, and stir in 7.5ml/1½ tsp of the spicy peanut satay. Tip the beef on to a clean plate and set aside. Drain the rice sticks.

VARIATION
Although it is quite similar to *pad Thai*, one of the national noodle dishes of Thailand, the addition of *nuoc mam*, basil and mint give this fragrant dish a distinctly Vietnamese flavour. There are many similar versions throughout Southeast Asia, made with prawns (shrimp), pork and chicken.

3 Add 7.5ml/1½ tsp oil to the wok and add the rice sticks and 15ml/1 tbsp saté. Toss the noodles until coated in the sauce and cook for 4–5 minutes, or until tender. Toss in the beef for 1 minute, then add the beansprouts with the *nuoc mam*. Place the noodles on a serving dish and sprinkle with the basil and mint. Serve with pickles.

Energy 603Kcal/2507kJ; Protein 26g; Carbohydrate 52g, of which sugars 2g; Fat 32g, of which saturates 6g; Cholesterol 38mg; Calcium 73mg; Fibre 2.2g; Sodium 200mg.

CAMBODIAN WHEAT NOODLES
WITH STIR-FRIED PORK

WHEAT NOODLES ARE POPULAR IN CAMBODIA. SOLD DRIED, IN STRAIGHT BUNDLES LIKE STICKS, THEY ARE VERSATILE AND ROBUST. NOODLES DRYING IN THE OPEN AIR, HANGING FROM BAMBOO POLES, ARE COMMON IN THE MARKETS. THIS SIMPLE RECIPE COMES FROM A NOODLE STALL IN PHNOM PENH.

SERVES FOUR

INGREDIENTS
  225g/8oz pork loin, cut into thin strips
  225g/8oz dried wheat noodles, soaked
    in lukewarm water for 20 minutes
  15ml/1 tbsp groundnut (peanut) oil
  2 garlic cloves, finely chopped
  2–3 spring onions (scallions),
    trimmed and cut into bitesize pieces
  45ml/3 tbsp *kroeung*
  15ml/1 tbsp *tuk trey*
  30ml/2 tbsp unsalted roasted
    peanuts, finely chopped
  chilli oil, for drizzling
For the marinade
  30ml/2 tbsp *tuk trey*
  30ml/2 tbsp soy sauce
  15ml/1 tbsp peanut oil
  10ml/2 tsp sugar

1 In a bowl, combine the ingredients for the marinade, stirring constantly until the sugar dissolves.

2 Toss in the strips of pork, making sure it is well coated in the marinade. Put aside for 30 minutes.

3 Drain the wheat noodles. Bring a large pan of water to the boil. Drop in the noodles, untangling them with chopsticks, if necessary. Cook for 4–5 minutes, until tender. Allow the noodles to drain thoroughly, then divide them among individual serving bowls. Keep the noodles warm until the dish is ready to serve.

4 Meanwhile, heat a wok. Add the oil and stir-fry the garlic and spring onions, until fragrant. Add the pork, tossing it around the wok for 2 minutes. Stir in the *kroeung* and *tuk trey* for 2 minutes – add a splash of water if the wok gets too dry – and place the pork on top of the noodles. Sprinkle the peanuts on top and drizzle with chilli oil to serve.

Energy 357Kcal/1494kJ; Protein 17g; Carbohydrate 51g, of which sugars 4.8g; Fat 9g, of which saturates 2g; Cholesterol 35mg; Calcium 21mg; Fibre 0.7g; Sodium 495mg.

SHANGHAI NOODLES WITH LAP CHEONG

LAP CHEONG ARE FIRM, CURED WAXY PORK SAUSAGES, AVAILABLE FROM CHINESE FOOD MARKETS.
SWEET AND SAVOURY, THEY CAN BE STEAMED WITH RICE, CHICKEN OR PORK, ADDED TO AN OMELETTE
OR STIR-FRIED WITH VEGETABLES.

SERVES SIX

INGREDIENTS
    30ml/2 tbsp vegetable oil
    115g/4oz rindless back bacon, cut
      into bite-size pieces
    2 lap cheong, rinsed in warm water,
      drained and finely sliced
    2 garlic cloves, finely chopped
    2 spring onions (scallions),
      roughly chopped
    225g/8oz Chinese leaves (Chinese
      cabbage) or fresh spinach leaves,
      cut into 5cm/2in pieces
    450g/1lb fresh Shanghai noodles
    30ml/2 tbsp oyster sauce
    30ml/2 tbsp soy sauce
    freshly ground black pepper

1 Heat half the oil in a wok or large frying pan. Add the bacon and lap cheong with the chopped garlic and spring onions. Stir-fry for a few minutes until golden. Using a slotted spoon, remove the mixture from the wok or pan and keep warm.

2 Add the remaining oil to the wok or pan. Stir-fry the Chinese greens or spinach for about 3 minutes until it just starts to wilt. Add the noodles and the lap cheong mixture. Season with oyster sauce, soy sauce and pepper. Stir-fry until the noodles are heated through.

Energy 485kcal/2042kJ; Protein 30.5g; Carbohydrate 60.7g, of which sugars 5.3g; Fat 14.9g, of which saturates 2.8g; Cholesterol 63mg; Calcium 46mg; Fibre 3.2g; Sodium 440mg.

SPECIAL CHOW MEIN

SLICES OF LAP CHEONG ADD A PIQUANT NOTE TO THIS DELECTABLE MIXTURE, SETTING OFF THE SWEETNESS OF THE SUCCULENT LARGE PRAWNS. IF THESE SAUSAGES ARE NOT AVAILABLE, HOWEVER, YOU CAN SUBSTITUTE ANOTHER SPICY CURED SAUSAGE SUCH AS CHORIZO OR SALAMI.

SERVES FOUR TO SIX

INGREDIENTS
450g/1lb egg noodles
45ml/3 tbsp vegetable oil
2 garlic cloves, sliced
5ml/1 tsp finely chopped fresh
    root ginger
2 red chillies, chopped
2 lap cheong, about 75g/3oz, rinsed
    and sliced
1 boneless chicken breast,
    thinly sliced
16 uncooked tiger prawns (jumbo
    shrimp), peeled, tails left intact,
    and deveined
115g/4oz green beans
225g/8oz beansprouts
50g/2oz garlic chives
30ml/2 tbsp soy sauce
15ml/1 tbsp oyster sauce
salt and freshly ground black pepper
15ml/1 tbsp sesame oil
2 spring onions (scallions), shredded,
    to garnish
15ml/1 tbsp coriander (cilantro)
    leaves, to garnish

1 Bring a pan of salted water to the boil and cook the noodles for about 4 minutes, until just tender. Drain well.

2 Heat 15ml/1 tbsp of the oil in a wok or large frying pan and fry the garlic, ginger and chillies. Add the lap cheong, chicken, prawns and beans. Stir-fry for about 2 minutes over a high heat or until the chicken and prawns are cooked. Transfer the mixture to a bowl and set aside.

3 Heat the rest of the oil in the same wok. Add the beansprouts and garlic chives. Stir fry for 1–2 minutes.

4 Add the noodles and toss and stir to mix. Season with soy sauce, oyster sauce, salt and pepper.

5 Return the prawn mixture to the wok. Reheat and mix well with the noodles. Stir in the sesame oil. Serve garnished with spring onions and coriander leaves.

Energy 359kcal/1516kJ; Protein 19.6g; Carbohydrate 47.6g, of which sugars 2.9g; Fat 11.4g, of which saturates 2.3g; Cholesterol 106mg; Calcium 53mg; Fibre 2.3g; Sodium 1102mg.

CHICKEN CHOW MEIN

CHOW MEIN IS ARGUABLY THE BEST-KNOWN CHINESE NOODLE DISH IN THE WEST. THE NOODLES ARE QUICKLY STIR-FRIED WITH MEAT, SEAFOOD OR VEGETABLES.

3 Heat half the vegetable oil in a wok or large frying pan over a high heat. When it starts smoking, add the chicken mixture. Stir-fry for 2 minutes until the chicken is cooked through, then transfer to a plate and keep hot.

4 Wipe the wok clean and heat the remaining oil. Stir in the garlic, mange-touts, beansprouts and ham, stir-fry for another minute or so, then add the cooked noodles.

5 Continue to stir-fry until the noodles are heated through. Add the remaining soy sauce to taste and season with salt and pepper.

6 Return the chicken and any juices to the noodle mixture, add the chopped spring onions and give the mixture a final stir. Serve at once.

SERVES FOUR

INGREDIENTS
  350g/12oz medium egg noodles
  225g/8oz skinless, boneless
    chicken breasts
  45ml/3 tbsp soy sauce
  15ml/1 tbsp Chinese rice wine
    or dry sherry
  15ml/1 tbsp dark sesame oil
  60ml/4 tbsp vegetable oil
  2 garlic cloves, finely chopped
  50g/2oz mangetouts (snow peas),
    topped and tailed
  115g/4oz beansprouts
  50g/2oz ham, finely shredded
  4 spring onions (scallions),
    finely chopped
  salt and freshly ground black pepper

1 Cook the noodles in a saucepan of boiling water until tender. Drain, rinse under cold water and drain well.

2 Slice the chicken into fine shreds about 5cm/2in in length. Place in a bowl with 10ml/2 tsp of the soy sauce, the rice wine or sherry and sesame oil.

COOK'S TIP
This is a very flexible dish that can be made with different ingredients. Try using pork instead of chicken, or make a vegetarian version using mushrooms and peppers or tofu.

Energy 593kcal/2494kJ; Protein 31.1g; Carbohydrate 69.7g, of which sugars 4.4g; Fat 22.6g, of which saturates 2.7g; Cholesterol 44mg; Calcium 44mg; Fibre 3.4g; Sodium 995mg.

RICE NOODLES, BEEF AND BLACK BEAN SAUCE

THIS IS AN EXCELLENT COMBINATION — TENDER STRIPS OF BEEF IN A CHILLI SAUCE ARE TOSSED WITH SILKY SMOOTH RICE NOODLES.

SERVES FOUR

INGREDIENTS

450g/1lb fresh rice noodles
60ml/4 tbsp vegetable oil
1 onion, finely sliced
2 garlic cloves, finely chopped
2 slices fresh root ginger,
  finely chopped
225g/8oz mixed (bell) peppers,
  seeded and cut into strips
350g/12oz rump steak, finely sliced
  across the grain
45ml/3 tbsp fermented black beans,
  rinsed in warm water, drained
  and chopped
30ml/2 tbsp soy sauce
30ml/2 tbsp oyster sauce
15ml/1 tbsp chilli black bean sauce
15ml/1 tbsp cornflour (cornstarch)
120ml/4fl oz/½ cup stock or water
2 spring onions (scallions), finely
  chopped, and 2 red chillies, seeded
  and finely sliced, to garnish

1 Rinse the noodles under hot water; drain well. Heat half the oil in a wok or large frying pan, swirling it around.

2 Add the onion, garlic, ginger and mixed pepper strips. Stir-fry for 3–5 minutes, then remove with a slotted spoon and keep hot.

3 Add the remaining oil to the wok. When hot, add the sliced beef and fermented black beans and stir-fry over a high heat for 5 minutes or until the beef is cooked.

4 In a small bowl, blend the soy sauce, oyster sauce and chilli black bean sauce with the cornflour and stock or water until smooth.

5 Add the mixture to the wok, then return the onion mixture to the wok and cook, stirring, for 1 minute.

6 Add the noodles and mix lightly. Stir over a medium heat until the noodles are heated through. Adjust the seasoning if necessary.

7 Serve at once, garnished with the chopped spring onions and chillies.

Energy 567kcal/2376kJ; Protein 25.8g; Carbohydrate 100.4g, of which sugars 4.7g; Fat 5.5g, of which saturates 1.7g; Cholesterol 52mg; Calcium 29mg; Fibre 1.2g; Sodium 338mg.

CHIANG MAI NOODLES

AN INTERESTING NOODLE DISH FROM THAILAND THAT COMBINES SOFT, BOILED NOODLES WITH CRISP DEEP-FRIED ONES AND ADDS THE CLASSIC THAI CONTRAST OF SWEET, HOT AND SOUR FLAVOURS.

SERVES FOUR

INGREDIENTS
250ml/8fl oz/1 cup coconut cream
15ml/1 tbsp magic paste
5ml/1 tsp Thai red curry paste
450g/1lb chicken thigh meat,
   chopped into small pieces
30ml/2 tbsp dark soy sauce
2 red (bell) peppers, seeded and
   finely diced
600ml/1 pint/2½ cups chicken or
   vegetable stock
90g/3½ oz fresh or dried rice noodles
For the garnishes
vegetable oil, for deep-frying
90g/3½ oz fine dried rice noodles
2 pickled garlic cloves, chopped
small bunch fresh coriander
   (cilantro), chopped
2 limes, cut into wedges

1 Pour the coconut cream into a large wok and bring to the boil over a medium heat. Continue to boil, stirring frequently, for 8–10 minutes, until the milk separates and an oily sheen appears on the surface.

2 Add the magic paste and red curry paste and cook, stirring constantly, for 3–5 seconds, until fragrant.

3 Add the chicken and toss over the heat until sealed on all sides. Stir in the soy sauce and the diced peppers and stir-fry for 3–4 minutes. Pour in the stock. Bring to the boil, then lower the heat and simmer for 10–15 minutes, until the chicken is fully cooked.

4 Meanwhile, make the noodle garnish. Heat the oil in a wok to 190°C/375°F or until a cube of bread, added to the oil, browns in 40 seconds. Break all the noodles in half, then divide them into four portions. Add one portion at a time to the hot oil. They will puff up on contact. As soon as they are crisp, lift the noodles out with a slotted spoon and drain on kitchen paper.

5 Bring a large pan of water to the boil and cook the fresh or dried noodles until tender, following the instructions on the packet. Drain well, divide among four warmed individual dishes, then spoon the curry sauce over them. Top each portion with a cluster of fried noodles. Sprinkle the chopped pickled garlic and coriander over the top and serve immediately, offering lime wedges for squeezing.

COOK'S TIP
Magic paste is a commercial product sold in jars in Asian stores. It is a blend of garlic, coriander (cilantro) root and white pepper. This combination of flavours is widely used in Thai home cooking. When mixed with red curry paste, magic paste gives a great flavour to this combination of chicken, red (bell) peppers and noodles.

Energy 245Kcal/1034kJ; Protein 29.4g; Carbohydrate 27.6g, of which sugars 9g; Fat 1.8g, of which saturates 0.6g; Cholesterol 79mg; Calcium 35mg; Fibre 1.4g; Sodium 677mg.

CURRIED NOODLES

CHICKEN OR PORK CAN BE USED IN THIS TASTY DISH. IT IS SO QUICK AND EASY TO PREPARE AND COOKS IN NEXT TO NO TIME, MAKING IT THE PERFECT SNACK FOR BUSY PEOPLE.

SERVES TWO

INGREDIENTS

30ml/2 tbsp vegetable oil
10ml/2 tsp magic paste
1 lemon grass stalk, finely chopped
5ml/1 tsp Thai red curry paste
90g/3½oz skinless chicken breast
  fillets or pork fillet (tenderloin),
  sliced into slivers
30ml/2 tbsp light soy sauce
400ml/14fl oz/1⅔ cups coconut milk
2 kaffir lime leaves, rolled into
  cylinders and thinly sliced
250g/9oz dried medium egg noodles
90g/3½oz Chinese leaves (Chinese
  cabbage), shredded
90g/3½oz spinach or watercress,
  shredded
juice of 1 lime
small bunch fresh coriander
  (cilantro), chopped

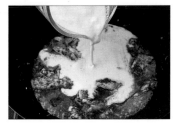

1 Heat the oil in a wok or large, heavy frying pan. Add the magic paste and lemon grass and stir-fry over a low to medium heat for 4–5 seconds, until they give off their aroma.

2 Stir in the curry paste, then add the chicken or pork. Stir-fry over a medium to high heat for 2 minutes, until the chicken or pork is coated in the paste and seared on all sides.

3 Add the soy sauce, coconut milk and sliced lime leaves. Bring to a simmer, then add the noodles. Simmer gently for 4 minutes, tossing the mixture occasionally to make sure that the noodles cook evenly.

4 Add the Chinese leaves and the spinach or watercress. Stir well. Add the lime juice. Spoon into a warmed bowl, sprinkle with the coriander and serve.

Energy 709Kcal/2989kJ; Protein 29.5g; Carbohydrate 102.1g, of which sugars 14.6g; Fat 23.1g, of which saturates 4.8g; Cholesterol 69mg; Calcium 251mg; Fibre 5.5g; Sodium 1666mg.

SPICY FRIED NOODLES

THIS IS A WONDERFULLY VERSATILE DISH BECAUSE YOU CAN ADAPT IT TO INCLUDE YOUR FAVOURITE INGREDIENTS, OR WHATEVER YOU HAPPEN TO HAVE IN THE REFRIGERATOR — JUST AS LONG AS YOU KEEP A BALANCE OF FLAVOURS, TEXTURES AND COLOURS.

SERVES FOUR

INGREDIENTS

225g/8oz egg thread noodles
60ml/4 tbsp vegetable oil
2 garlic cloves, finely chopped
175g/6oz pork fillet (tenderloin),
  sliced into thin strips
1 skinless, boneless chicken breast
  portion, sliced into thin strips
115g/4oz/1 cup cooked peeled
  prawns (shrimp)
juice of half a lemon
45ml/3 tbsp Thai fish sauce
30ml/2 tbsp soft light brown sugar
2 eggs, beaten
½ fresh red chilli, seeded and
  finely chopped
50g/2oz/⅔ cup beansprouts
60ml/4 tbsp roasted
  peanuts, chopped
3 spring onions (scallions), cut into
  5cm/2in lengths and shredded
45ml/3 tbsp chopped fresh
  coriander (cilantro)

1 Bring a large pan of water to the boil. Add the noodles, remove the pan from the heat and leave for 5 minutes.

2 Meanwhile, heat 45ml/3 tbsp of the oil in a wok or large frying pan, add the garlic and cook for 30 seconds. Add the pork and chicken and stir-fry until lightly browned, then add the prawns and stir-fry for 2 minutes.

3 Add the lemon juice, then add the fish sauce and sugar. Stir-fry until the sugar has dissolved.

4 Drain the noodles and add to the wok or pan with the remaining 15ml/1 tbsp oil. Toss all the ingredients together.

5 Pour the beaten eggs over the noodles and stir-fry until almost set, then add the chilli and beansprouts.

6 Divide the roasted peanuts, spring onions and coriander leaves into two equal portions, add one portion to the pan and stir-fry for about 2 minutes.

7 Turn the noodles on to a serving plate. Sprinkle on the remaining roasted peanuts, spring onions and chopped coriander and serve immediately.

COOK'S TIP
Store beansprouts in the refrigerator and use within a day of purchase, as they tend to lose their crispness and become slimy and unpleasant quite quickly. The most commonly used beansprouts are sprouted mung beans, but you could use other types of beansprouts instead.

Energy 597Kcal/2504kJ; Protein 39.3g; Carbohydrate 50.8g, of which sugars 10.3g; Fat 27.8g, of which saturates 5.5g; Cholesterol 226mg; Calcium 76mg; Fibre 2.9g; Sodium 250mg.

CRISPY THAI NOODLE SALAD

RICE NOODLES PUFF UP AND BECOME LIGHT AND CRISPY WHEN DEEP-FRIED AND MAKE A LOVELY BASE FOR THIS TANGY, FRAGRANT SALAD. SERVE AS A SNACK OR LIGHT MEAL, AND ENJOY THE HEADY COMBINATION OF SPICY CHILLIES, FRAGRANT PORK AND PRAWNS, AND CRISPY NOODLES.

SERVES FOUR

INGREDIENTS
sunflower oil, for deep-frying
115g/4oz rice vermicelli
45ml/3 tbsp groundnut (peanut) oil
2 eggs, lightly beaten with 15ml/
  1 tbsp water
30ml/2 tbsp palm sugar
30ml/2 tbsp Thai fish sauce
15ml/1 tbsp rice wine vinegar
30ml/2 tbsp tomato ketchup
1 fresh red chilli, thinly sliced
3 garlic cloves, crushed
5ml/1 tsp finely grated fresh
  root ginger
200g/7oz minced (ground) pork
400g/14oz cooked peeled tiger
  prawns (shrimp)
4 spring onions (scallions),
  finely shredded
60ml/4 tbsp chopped coriander
  (cilantro) leaves

1 Fill a wok one-third full of sunflower oil and heat to 180°C/350°F or until a cube of bread, dropped into the oil, browns in 45 seconds. Working in batches, deep-fry the vermicelli, for 10–20 seconds, or until puffed up. Remove from the wok with a slotted spoon and drain on kitchen paper.

2 Carefully discard the oil and wipe out the wok. Heat 15ml/1 tbsp of the groundnut oil in the wok. Add half the egg mixture and swirl the wok to make a thin omelette. Cook gently for 2–3 minutes, until the egg has just set and then carefully transfer to a board.

3 Repeat with a further 15ml/1 tbsp of groundnut oil and the remaining egg mixture to make a second omelette. Place the second omelette on top of the first and roll up into a cylinder. Using a sharp knife, cut the cylinder crossways to make thin strips, then set the strips aside on a plate.

4 Mix together the palm sugar, fish sauce, rice wine vinegar, tomato ketchup, chilli, garlic and ginger. Stir half this mixture into the pork and mix.

5 Heat the remaining groundnut oil in the wok. When hot, add the pork mixture and stir-fry for 4–5 minutes until cooked through. Add the prawns and stir-fry for 1–2 minutes.

6 Remove the wok from the heat and add the remaining palm sugar mixture, fried vermicelli, spring onions and coriander and toss to combine.

7 Divide the mixture among four warmed plates and top with the shredded omelette. Serve immediately.

Energy 508Kcal/2118kJ; Protein 35.1g; Carbohydrate 33.1g, of which sugars 10.5g; Fat 26.4g, of which saturates 5g; Cholesterol 371mg; Calcium 142mg; Fibre 0.8g; Sodium 405mg.

SINGAPORE NOODLES

THE VIETNAMESE HAVE PUT THEIR OWN DELICIOUS STAMP ON
SINGAPORE NOODLES, WHICH ARE POPULAR THROUGHOUT SOUTH-
EAST ASIA. IN HO CHI MINH CITY, THE NOODLES ARE STANDARD
STREET AND CAFÉ FOOD, AN IDEAL FAST FOOD SNACK.

SERVES FOUR

INGREDIENTS

30ml/2 tbsp sesame oil
1 onion, finely chopped
3 garlic cloves, finely chopped
3–4 green or red Thai chillies,
   seeded and finely chopped
4cm/1½in fresh root ginger,
   peeled and finely chopped
6 spring onions (scallions),
   finely chopped
1 skinless chicken breast fillet,
   cut into bitesize strips
90g/3½oz pork, cut into bitesize
   strips
90g/3½oz prawns (shrimp), shelled
2 tomatoes, skinned, seeded
   and chopped
30ml/2 tbsp tamarind paste
15ml/1 tbsp *nuoc mam*
grated rind and juice of 1 lime
10ml/2 tsp sugar
150ml/¼ pint/⅔ cup water or
   fish stock
225g/8oz fresh rice sticks
   (vermicelli)
salt and ground black pepper
1 bunch each fresh basil and mint,
   stalks removed, and *nuoc cham*,
   to serve

2 Add the tomatoes, followed by the tamarind paste, *nuoc mam*, lime rind and juice, and sugar. Pour in the water or fish stock, and cook gently for 2–3 minutes. Bubble up the liquid to reduce it.

3 Meanwhile, toss the noodles in a large pan of boiling water and cook for a few minutes until tender.

4 Drain the noodles and add to the chicken and prawn mixture. Season with salt and ground black pepper.

5 Serve immediately, with basil and mint leaves scattered over the top, and drizzled with spoonfuls of *nuoc cham*.

COOK'S TIP

It's important to serve this dish immediately once the noodles have been added, otherwise they will go soft.

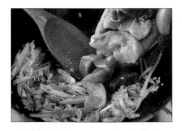

1 Heat a wok and add the oil. Stir in the onion, garlic, chillies and ginger, and cook until they begin to colour. Add the spring onions and cook for 1 minute, add the chicken and pork, and cook for 1–2 minutes, then stir in the prawns.

Energy 420Kcal/1756kJ; Protein 23g; Carbohydrate 59g, of which sugars 9g; Fat 10g, of which saturates 2g; Cholesterol 86mg; Calcium 119mg; Fibre 1.3g; Sodium 500mg.

STIR-FRIED RICE NOODLES <u>WITH</u> CHICKEN <u>AND</u> PRAWNS

SHELLFISH HAVE A NATURAL AFFINITY WITH BOTH MEAT AND POULTRY. THIS THAI-STYLE RECIPE COMBINES CHICKEN WITH PRAWNS AND HAS THE CHARACTERISTIC SWEET, SOUR AND SALTY FLAVOUR.

3 Add the chicken and prawns to the wok and stir-fry for 3–4 minutes.

4 Push the chicken and prawn mixture in the wok out to the sides. Break the egg into the centre, then stir to break up the yolk and cook over a medium heat until the egg is lightly scrambled.

5 Add the drained noodles to the wok together with the fish sauce mixture. Mix together well.

6 Add half the crushed peanuts to the wok and cook, stirring frequently, until the noodles are soft and most of the liquid has been absorbed.

7 Add the spring onions and half of the beansprouts. Cook, stirring, for 1 minute more, until the spring onions are slightly wilted, and the beansprouts are heated through.

8 Spoon on to a serving dish. Sprinkle with the remaining peanuts and beansprouts. Garnish with the coriander and lime wedges and serve.

SERVES FOUR

INGREDIENTS

  225g/8oz dried flat rice noodles
  120ml/4fl oz/½ cup water
  60ml/4 tbsp Thai fish sauce
  15ml/1 tbsp sugar
  15ml/1 tbsp fresh lime juice
  5ml/1 tsp paprika
  pinch of cayenne pepper
  45ml/3 tbsp oil
  2 garlic cloves, finely chopped
  1 skinless, boneless chicken breast,
    finely sliced
  8 raw prawns (shrimp), peeled,
    deveined and cut in half
  1 egg
  50g/2oz roasted peanuts,
    coarsely crushed
  3 spring onions (scallions), cut into
    short lengths
  175g/6oz beansprouts
  coriander (cilantro) leaves and 1
    lime, cut into wedges, to garnish

1 Place the rice noodles in a large bowl, cover with warm water and soak for 30 minutes until soft. Drain.

2 Combine the water, fish sauce, sugar, lime juice, paprika and cayenne in a small bowl. Set aside until required. Heat the oil in a wok. Add the garlic and stir-fry for 30 seconds until brown.

Energy 388kcal/1625kJ; Protein 22.5g; Carbohydrate 54.3g, of which sugars 5.9g; Fat 8.4g, of which saturates 1.7g; Cholesterol 113mg; Calcium 76mg; Fibre 2.4g; Sodium 105mg.

STIR-FRIED NOODLES <u>WITH</u> WILD MUSHROOMS

THE GREATER THE VARIETY OF WILD MUSHROOMS YOU HAVE AVAILABLE, THE MORE INTERESTING THIS DISH WILL BE. OF COURSE, A MIXTURE OF CULTIVATED MUSHROOMS CAN BE USED INSTEAD.

SERVES SIX

INGREDIENTS
   350g/12oz broad flat egg noodles
   45ml/3 tbsp vegetable oil
   115g/4oz rindless back or streaky
      bacon, cut into small pieces
   225g/8oz wild mushrooms, trimmed
      and cut in half
   115g/4oz garlic chives, snipped
   225g/8oz beansprouts
   15ml/1 tbsp oyster sauce
   15ml/1 tbsp soy sauce
   salt and freshly ground black pepper

1 Cook the noodles in a large pan of boiling water for about 3–4 minutes or until just tender. Drain, rinse under cold water and drain well.

2 Heat 15ml/1 tbsp of the oil in a wok or large frying pan. Add the bacon and fry until browned and crisp.

3 Using a slotted spoon, transfer the cooked bacon to a small bowl and set aside until needed. Add the rest of the oil to the wok or pan. When the oil is hot, add the mushrooms and stir-fry for 3 minutes.

4 Add the garlic chives and beansprouts to the wok and fry for another 3 minutes, then add the drained noodles.

5 Season with salt, pepper, oyster sauce and soy sauce. Continue to stir-fry until the noodles are thoroughly heated through. Sprinkle the crispy bits of bacon on top and serve.

Energy 310kcal/1307kJ; Protein 10.1g; Carbohydrate 47.9g, of which sugars 6.6g; Fat 10g, of which saturates 2.1g; Cholesterol 8mg; Calcium 26mg; Fibre 3.2g; Sodium 173mg.

FRESH RICE NOODLES

A VARIETY OF DRIED NOODLES IS AVAILABLE IN ASIAN SUPERMARKETS, BUT FRESH ONES ARE QUITE DIFFERENT AND NOT THAT DIFFICULT TO MAKE. THE FRESHLY-MADE NOODLE SHEETS CAN BE SERVED AS A SNACK DIPPED INTO A SAVOURY SAUCE, OR CUT INTO WIDE STRIPS AND GENTLY STIR-FRIED.

SERVES FOUR

INGREDIENTS
225g/8oz/2 cups rice flour
600ml/1 pint/2½ cups water
a pinch of salt
15ml/1 tbsp vegetable oil, plus extra
   for brushing
slivers of red chilli and fresh root
   ginger, and coriander (cilantro)
   leaves, to garnish (optional)

1 Place the flour in a bowl and stir in some of the water to form a paste. Pour in the rest of the water, beating it to make a lump-free batter. Add the salt and oil and leave to stand for 15 minutes.

COOK'S TIP
You may need to top up the water through one of the slits and tighten the cloth.

2 Meanwhile, fill a wide pan with water. Cut a piece of smooth cotton cloth a little larger than the diameter of the pan. Stretch it over the top of the pan, pulling the edges tautly down over the sides, then wind a piece of string around the edge, to secure. Using a sharp knife, make three small slits, about 2.5cm/1in from the edge of the cloth, at regular intervals.

3 Bring the water to the boil. Stir the batter and ladle 30–45ml/2–3 tbsp on to the cloth, swirling it to form a 13–15cm/5–6in wide circle. Cover with a domed lid, such as a wok lid, and steam for 1 minute, or until the noodle sheet is translucent.

4 Carefully insert a spatula or knife under the noodle sheet and prise it off the cloth. (If it doesn't peel off easily, you may need to steam it a little longer.) Transfer the noodle sheet to a lightly oiled baking tray, brush lightly with oil, and cook the remaining batter in the same way.

VARIATION
Fresh noodles are delicious cut into strips and stir-fried with garlic, ginger, chillies and *nuoc cham* or soy sauce.

Energy 251Kcal/1046kJ; Protein 4g; Carbohydrate 45g, of which sugars 0g; Fat 5g, of which saturates 1g; Cholesterol 0mg; Calcium 24mg; Fibre 1.1g; Sodium 200mg.

CRISPY NOODLES WITH MIXED VEGETABLES

IN THIS DISH, RICE VERMICELLI NOODLES ARE DEEP FRIED, THEN TOSSED INTO A COLOURFUL SELECTION OF STIR-FRIED VEGETABLES. FRY THE NOODLES IN SMALL BATCHES AND DRAIN ON KITCHEN PAPER TO KEEP THEM CRISP.

SERVES FOUR

INGREDIENTS
- 2 large carrots
- 2 courgettes (zucchini)
- 4 spring onions (scallions)
- 115g/4oz yard-long beans or green beans
- 115g/4oz dried vermicelli rice noodles or cellophane (bean thread) noodles
- groundnut oil, for deep frying
- 2.5cm/1in fresh root ginger, shredded
- 1 fresh red chilli, sliced
- 115g/4oz fresh shiitake or button mushrooms, thickly sliced
- few Chinese cabbage leaves, roughly shredded
- 75g/3oz beansprouts
- 30ml/2 tbsp light soy sauce
- 30ml/2 tbsp Chinese rice wine or dry sherry
- 5ml/1 tsp sugar
- 30ml/2 tbsp roughly torn fresh coriander (cilantro) leaves

4 Reheat the oil. When hot, add the beans and stir-fry for 2–3 minutes.

5 Add the ginger, red chilli, mushrooms, carrots and courgettes and stir-fry for 1–2 minutes. Add the Chinese cabbage, beansprouts and spring onions. Stir-fry for 1 minute, then add the soy sauce, rice wine or sherry and sugar. Cook, stirring, for about 30 seconds.

6 Add the noodles and coriander and toss, taking care not to crush the noodles too much. Serve at once.

COOK'S TIP
Vermicelli rice noodles, which are thin and brittle, look like a bundle of white hair. They cook almost instantly in hot liquid, provided they have first been soaked in warm water. Rice noodles can also be deep fried.

1 Cut the carrots and courgettes into fine sticks. Shred the spring onions into similar-sized pieces. Trim the beans and cut them into short lengths.

2 Break the noodles into pieces about 7.5cm/3in long. Half-fill a wok with oil and heat it to 180°C/350°F.

3 Deep-fry the raw noodles, a handful at a time, for 1–2 minutes until puffed and crispy. Drain on kitchen paper. Pour off all but 30ml/2 tbsp of the oil.

Energy 230kcal/964kJ; Protein 7.9g; Carbohydrate 44.6g, of which sugars 5.4g; Fat 2.4g, of which saturates 0.3g; Cholesterol 0mg; Calcium 52mg; Fibre 2.8g; Sodium 623mg.

VEGETARIAN FRIED NOODLES

WHEN MAKING THIS DISH FOR NON-VEGETARIANS, ADD A SMALL CHUNK OF BLACAN (COMPRESSED SHRIMP PASTE) TO ADD A DELICIOUSLY RICH, AROMATIC FLAVOUR.

3 Heat the oil in a wok or large frying pan. Fry the onion until soft, then reduce the heat and add the chilli paste, sliced chillies and soy sauce. Fry for 2–3 minutes.

4 Add the potatoes and fry for about 2 minutes until beginning to brown, mixing well with the chillies. Add the tofu, then the beansprouts, green beans and noodles.

SERVES FOUR

INGREDIENTS

2 eggs
5ml/1 tsp chilli powder
5ml/1 tsp turmeric
60ml/4 tbsp vegetable oil
1 large onion, finely sliced
2 red chillies, seeded and
  finely sliced
15ml/1 tbsp soy sauce
2 large cooked potatoes, cut into
  small cubes
6 pieces fried tofu, sliced
225g/8oz beansprouts
115g/4oz green beans, blanched
350g/12oz fresh thick egg noodles
salt and freshly ground black pepper
sliced spring onions (scallions),
  to garnish

COOK'S TIP
Be very careful when handling chillies. Keep your hands away from your eyes as chillies will sting them. Wash your hands thoroughly after touching chillies.

1 Beat the eggs lightly, then strain them into a bowl. Heat a lightly greased omelette pan. Pour in half of the egg to cover the bottom of the pan thinly. When the egg is just set, turn the omelette over and fry the other side briefly. Slide on to a plate, blot with kitchen paper, roll up and cut into narrow strips. Make a second omelette in the same way and slice. Set the omelette strips aside for the garnish.

2 In a cup, mix together the chilli powder and turmeric. Form a paste by stirring in a little water.

5 Gently stir-fry until the noodles are evenly coated and heated through. Take care not to break up the potatoes or the tofu. Season with salt and pepper. Serve hot, garnished with the reserved omelette strips and spring onion slices.

Energy 696kcal/2923kJ; Protein 28.3g; Carbohydrate 83g, of which sugars 8.2g; Fat 30.3g, of which saturates 4.2g; Cholesterol 121mg; Calcium 813mg; Fibre 5g; Sodium 476mg.

MIXED RICE NOODLES

A DELICIOUS NOODLE DISH MADE EXTRA SPECIAL BY THE ADDITION OF AVOCADO AND A GARNISH OF PRAWNS. TAHINI AND PEANUT BUTTER ENRICH THE SIMPLE SAUCE.

SERVES FOUR

INGREDIENTS

15ml/1 tbsp sunflower oil
2.5cm/1in fresh root ginger, peeled
  and grated
2 cloves garlic, crushed
45ml/3 tbsp dark soy sauce
225g/8oz peas, thawed if frozen
450g/1lb rice noodles
450g/1lb spinach, stalks removed
30ml/2 tbsp smooth peanut butter
30ml/2 tbsp tahini
150ml/¼ pint/⅔ cup milk
1 ripe avocado, peeled and stoned
  (pitted)
roasted peanuts and peeled, cooked
  prawns (shrimp), to garnish

1 Heat the wok, then add the oil. When the oil is hot, stir-fry the ginger and garlic for 30 seconds. Add 15ml/1 tbsp of the soy sauce and 150ml/¼ pint/⅔ cup boiling water.

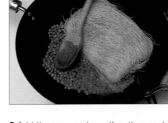

2 Add the peas and noodles, then cook for 3 minutes. Stir in the spinach. Remove the vegetables and noodles, drain and keep warm.

3 Stir the peanut butter, remaining soy sauce, tahini and milk together in the wok, and simmer for 1 minute.

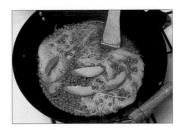

4 Add the vegetables and noodles, slice in the avocado and toss together gently to avoid breaking the avocado slices.

5 Serve the noodles piled on individual plates. Spoon some sauce over each portion and garnish with roasted peanuts and prawns.

Energy 648kcal/2698kJ; Protein 16.5g; Carbohydrate 102.3g, of which sugars 4.5g; Fat 17.7g, of which saturates 3.2g; Cholesterol 0mg; Calcium 275mg; Fibre 6.9g; Sodium 1002mg.

NOODLES WITH A CREAMY ASPARAGUS AND SAFFRON SAUCE

A RATHER ELEGANT SUMMERY DISH WITH A CREAMY SAUCE COLOURED WITH FRAGRANT SAFFRON.

SERVES FOUR

INGREDIENTS

- 450g/1lb young asparagus
- pinch of saffron threads
- 25g/1oz butter
- 2 shallots, finely chopped
- 30ml/2 tbsp white wine
- 250ml/8fl oz/1 cup double (heavy) cream
- grated rind and juice of ½ lemon
- 115g/4oz peas
- 350g/12oz somen noodles
- ½ bunch chervil, roughly chopped
- salt and freshly ground black pepper
- grated Parmesan cheese (optional)

1 Cut off the asparagus tips (about 5cm/2in in length), then slice the remaining spears into short rounds. Steep the saffron in 30ml/2 tbsp boiling water in a cup.

2 Melt the butter in a small pan, add the shallots and cook over a low heat for 3 minutes until soft. Add the white wine, cream and saffron infusion.

3 Bring to the boil, reduce the heat and simmer gently for 5 minutes or until the sauce thickens to a coating consistency. Add the grated lemon rind and juice, with salt and pepper to taste.

4 Bring a large pan of lightly salted water to the boil. Blanch the asparagus tips, scoop them out and add them to the sauce, then cook the peas and short asparagus rounds in the boiling water until just tender. Scoop them out and add to the sauce.

5 Cook the somen noodles in the same water until just tender, following the directions on the packet. Drain, place in a wide pan and pour the sauce over the top.

6 Toss the noodles with the sauce and vegetables, adding the chervil and more salt and pepper if needed. Finally, sprinkle with the grated Parmesan, if using, and serve hot.

Energy 738kcal/3060kJ; Protein 11.1g; Carbohydrate 79.5g, of which sugars 5.1g; Fat 40.1g, of which saturates 24.3g; Cholesterol 99mg; Calcium 108mg; Fibre 4.1g; Sodium 69mg.

FRIED NOODLES <u>WITH</u> BEANSPROUTS <u>AND</u> ASPARAGUS

SOFT FRIED NOODLES CONTRAST BEAUTIFULLY WITH CRISP BEANSPROUTS AND ASPARAGUS.

SERVES SIX

INGREDIENTS

115g/4oz medium-thick dried
  egg noodles
60ml/4 tbsp vegetable oil
1 small onion, chopped
2.5cm/1in fresh root ginger, peeled
  and grated
2 garlic cloves, crushed
175g/6oz young asparagus
  spears, trimmed
115g/4oz beansprouts
4 spring onions (scallions),
  sliced diagonally
45ml/3 tbsp soy sauce
salt and freshly ground
  black pepper

1 Bring a pan of salted water to the boil. Add the noodles and cook for 2–3 minutes, until tender. Drain and toss them in 30ml/2 tbsp of the oil.

2 Heat the remaining oil in a preheated wok until very hot. Add the onion, ginger and garlic and stir-fry for 2–3 minutes. Add the asparagus and stir-fry for a further 2–3 minutes.

3 When the asparagus is almost tender, but still retains a little crunch, add the noodles and beansprouts to the wok and stir-fry for 2 minutes until the noodles are heated through.

4 Stir in the spring onions and soy sauce. Season to taste, adding salt sparingly as the soy sauce will add quite a salty flavour. Stir-fry for 1 minute, then serve at once.

Energy 157kcal/654kJ; Protein 3.7g; Carbohydrate 15.9g, of which sugars 2.2g; Fat 9.1g, of which saturates 1.3g; Cholesterol 6mg; Calcium 20mg; Fibre 1.3g; Sodium 570mg.

SWEET AND HOT VEGETABLE NOODLES

THIS NOODLE DISH HAS THE COLOUR OF FIRE, BUT ONLY THE MILDEST SUGGESTION OF HEAT. GINGER AND PLUM SAUCE GIVE IT ITS FRUITY FLAVOUR, WHILE LIME JUICE AND TAMARIND PASTE ADD A DELICIOUS TANG TO THE AROMATIC STIR-FRIED VEGETABLES AND CHOPPED CORIANDER.

SERVES FOUR

INGREDIENTS

   130g/4½oz dried rice noodles
   30ml/2 tbsp groundnut (peanut) oil
   2.5cm/1in piece fresh root ginger,
     sliced into thin batons
   1 garlic clove, crushed
   130g/4½oz drained canned bamboo
     shoots, sliced into thin batons
   2 medium carrots, sliced into batons
   130g/4½oz/1½ cups beansprouts
   1 small white cabbage, shredded
   10ml/2 tsp tamarind paste
   30ml/2 tbsp soy sauce
   30ml/2 tbsp plum sauce
   10ml/2 tsp sesame oil
   15ml/1 tbsp palm sugar or light
     muscovado (brown) sugar
   juice of ½ lime
   90g/3½oz mooli (daikon), sliced into
     thin batons
   small bunch fresh coriander
     (cilantro), chopped
   60ml/4 tbsp sesame seeds, toasted

1 Cook the noodles in a large pan of boiling water, following the instructions on the packet. Meanwhile, heat the oil in a wok or large frying pan and stir-fry the ginger and garlic for 2–3 minutes over a medium heat, until golden. Drain the noodles and set them aside.

2 Add the bamboo shoots to the wok, increase the heat to high and stir-fry for 5 minutes. Add the carrots, beansprouts and cabbage and stir-fry for a further 5 minutes, until they are beginning to char on the edges.

3 Stir in the tamarind paste, soy and plum sauces, sesame oil, sugar and lime juice. Add the mooli and coriander, toss to mix, then spoon into a warmed bowl, sprinkle with toasted sesame seeds and serve immediately.

COOK'S TIP
Use a large, sharp knife for shredding cabbage. Remove any tough outer leaves, if necessary, then cut the cabbage into quarters. Cut off and discard the hard core from each quarter, place flat side down, then shred the cabbage thinly.

Energy 321Kcal/1333kJ; Protein 7.1g; Carbohydrate 37.8g, of which sugars 9.8g; Fat 15.4g, of which saturates 2.1g; Cholesterol 0mg; Calcium 142mg; Fibre 4.3g; Sodium 413mg.

VEGETABLE NOODLES <u>WITH</u> BEAN SAUCE

YELLOW BEAN SAUCE ADDS A DISTINCTIVE CHINESE FLAVOUR TO THIS WONDERFULLY SIMPLE DISH OF SPICY VEGETABLES AND NOODLES. THE SAUCE IS MADE FROM FERMENTED YELLOW BEANS AND HAS A MARVELLOUS TEXTURE AND SPICY, AROMATIC FLAVOUR, IF USED IN THE RIGHT PROPORTION.

SERVES FOUR

INGREDIENTS
    150g/5oz thin egg noodles
    200g/7oz baby leeks, sliced
        lengthways
    200g/7oz baby courgettes (zucchini),
        halved lengthways
    200g/7oz sugarsnap
        peas, trimmed
    200g/7oz peas
    15ml/1 tbsp sunflower oil
    5 garlic cloves, sliced
    45ml/3 tbsp yellow bean sauce
    45ml/3 tbsp sweet chilli sauce
    30ml/2 tbsp sweet soy sauce
    roasted cashew nuts, to garnish

1 Cook the noodles according to the packet instructions, drain and set aside.

2 Line a large bamboo steamer with perforated baking parchment and place the leeks, courgettes and both types of peas in it.

3 Cover the steamer and suspend it over a wok of simmering water. Steam the vegetables for about 5 minutes, then remove and set aside.

4 Pour the water from the wok and wipe dry with kitchen paper. Pour the sunflower oil into the wok and place over a medium heat. Add the sliced garlic and stir-fry for 1–2 minutes.

5 In a separate bowl, mix together the yellow bean, sweet chilli and soy sauces, then pour into the wok. Stir to mix with the garlic, then add the steamed vegetables and the noodles and toss together to combine.

6 Cook the vegetables and noodles for 2–3 minutes, stirring frequently, until heated through.

7 To serve, divide the noodles among four warmed serving bowls and scatter over the cashew nuts to garnish.

Energy 296Kcal/1241kJ; Protein 14.2g; Carbohydrate 44.9g, of which sugars 7.4g; Fat 7.8g, of which saturates 1.6g; Cholesterol 11mg; Calcium 61mg; Fibre 8.2g; Sodium 209mg.

CANTONESE FRIED NOODLES

CHOW MEIN IS HUGELY POPULAR WITH THE THRIFTY CHINESE, WHO BELIEVE IN TURNING LEFTOVERS INTO TASTY DISHES. FOR THIS DELICIOUS DISH, BOILED NOODLES ARE FRIED TO FORM A CRISPY CRUST, WHICH IS TOPPED WITH A SAVOURY SAUCE CONTAINING WHATEVER TASTES GOOD AND NEEDS EATING UP.

SERVES TWO TO THREE

INGREDIENTS
    225g/8oz can bamboo shoots, drained
    1 leek, trimmed
    150g/5oz Chinese leaves (Chinese
      cabbage)
    25g/1oz Chinese dried mushrooms,
      soaked for 30 minutes in 120ml/
      4fl oz/½ cup warm water
    450g/1lb cooked egg noodles
      (225g/8oz dried), drained well
    90ml/6 tbsp vegetable oil
    30ml/2 tbsp dark soy sauce
    15ml/1 tbsp cornflour (cornstarch)
    15ml/1 tbsp rice wine or sherry
    5ml/1 tsp sesame oil
    5ml/1 tsp sugar
    salt and ground black pepper

1 Slice the bamboo shoots and leek into matchsticks. Cut the Chinese leaves into 2.5cm/1in diamond-shaped pieces and sprinkle with salt.

2 Drain the mushrooms, reserving 90ml/6 tbsp of the soaking water. Cut off and discard the stems, then slice the caps finely. Pat the noodles dry with kitchen paper. Divide into three piles.

3 Heat a third of the oil in a large wok or frying pan and sauté one pile of noodles. After turning it over once, press the noodles evenly against the bottom of the pan with a wooden spatula until they form a flat, even cake. Cook over medium heat for about 4 minutes or until the noodles at the bottom have become crisp.

4 Turn the noodle cake over with a spatula or fish slice or invert on to a large plate and slide back into the wok. Cook for 3 minutes more, then slide on to a heated plate. Keep warm. Repeat with the other two piles of noodles.

5 Heat 30ml/2 tbsp of the remaining oil in the wok. Add the strips of leek, and stir-fry for 10–15 seconds. Sprinkle over half of the the soy sauce and then add the bamboo shoots and the mushrooms, with salt and pepper to taste. Toss over the heat for 1 minute, then transfer this mixture to a plate and set aside.

6 Heat the remaining oil in the wok and sauté the Chinese leaves for 1 minute. Return the vegetable mixture to the wok and sauté with the leaves for 30 seconds, stirring constantly.

7 Mix the cornflour with the reserved mushroom water. Stir into the wok along with the rice wine or sherry, sesame oil, sugar and remaining soy sauce. Cook for 15 seconds to thicken. Divide the noodles among 2–3 serving dishes and pile the vegetables on top.

Energy 481Kcal/2006kJ; Protein 24.4g; Carbohydrate 28.9g, of which sugars 7.8g; Fat 30.5g, of which saturates 5.7g; Cholesterol 53mg; Calcium 67mg; Fibre 4.4g; Sodium 791mg.

SICHUAN NOODLES WITH SESAME SAUCE

NOODLES AND ASIAN VEGETABLES SEEM MADE FOR EACH OTHER, AND WHEN THE MARRIAGE TAKES PLACE IN A WOK, WITH A FINE SAUCE TO GUARANTEE HARMONY, THE RESULTS ARE INEVITABLY EXCELLENT. ROASTED NUTS ADD TEXTURE WHILE BOOSTING THE NUTRITIONAL VALUE OF THIS DISH.

SERVES THREE TO FOUR

INGREDIENTS

450g/1lb fresh or 225g/8oz dried
  egg noodles
1/2 cucumber, sliced lengthways,
  seeded and diced
4–6 spring onions (scallions)
a bunch of radishes, about 115g/4oz
225g/8oz mooli (daikon), peeled
115g/4oz/2 cups beansprouts,
  rinsed then left in iced water
  and drained
60ml/4 tbsp groundnut (peanut) oil
  or sunflower oil
2 garlic cloves, crushed
45ml/3 tbsp toasted sesame paste
15ml/1 tbsp sesame oil
15ml/1 tbsp light soy sauce
5–10ml/1–2 tsp chilli sauce, to taste
15ml/1 tbsp rice vinegar
120ml/4fl oz/1/2 cup chicken stock
  or water
5ml/1 tsp sugar, or to taste
salt and ground black pepper
roasted peanuts or cashew nuts,
  to garnish

1 If using fresh noodles, cook them in boiling water for 1 minute then drain well. Rinse the noodles in fresh water and drain again. Cook dried noodles according to the instructions on the packet, draining and rinsing them as for fresh noodles.

2 Sprinkle the cucumber with salt, leave for 15 minutes, rinse well, then drain and pat dry on kitchen paper. Place in a large salad bowl.

3 Cut the spring onions into fine shreds. Cut the radishes in half and slice finely. Coarsely grate the mooli using a mandolin or a food processor. Add all the vegetables to the cucumber and toss gently.

4 Heat half the oil in a wok or frying pan and stir-fry the noodles for about 1 minute. Using a slotted spoon, transfer the noodles to a large serving bowl and keep warm. Add the remaining oil to the wok. When it is hot, fry the garlic to flavour the oil.

COOK'S TIP
When warming through the sauce, it is important not to heat it too much or too quickly to avoid it over-thickening.

5 Remove from the heat and stir in the sesame paste, with the sesame oil, soy and chilli sauces, vinegar and stock or water. Add a little sugar and season to taste. Warm through over a gentle heat. Pour the sauce over the noodles and toss well. Garnish with the nuts and serve with the vegetables.

Energy 440Kcal/1838kJ; Protein 11g; Carbohydrate 44.6g, of which sugars 4.6g; Fat 25.4g, of which saturates 4.1g; Cholesterol 17mg; Calcium 128mg; Fibre 4.2g; Sodium 384mg.

MEE KROB

THE NAME OF THIS DISH MEANS "DEEP-FRIED NOODLES" AND IT IS VERY POPULAR IN THAILAND. THE TASTE IS A STUNNING COMBINATION OF SWEET AND HOT, SALTY AND SOUR, WHILE THE TEXTURE CONTRIVES TO BE BOTH CRISP AND CHEWY. TO SOME WESTERN PALATES, IT MAY SEEM RATHER UNUSUAL, BUT THIS DELICIOUS DISH IS WELL WORTH MAKING.

SERVES TWO

INGREDIENTS
vegetable oil, for deep-frying
130g/4½oz rice vermicelli noodles
For the sauce
   30ml/2 tbsp vegetable oil
   130g/4½oz fried tofu, cut into
     thin strips
   2 garlic cloves, finely chopped
   2 small shallots, finely chopped
   15ml/1 tbsp light soy sauce
   30ml/2 tbsp palm sugar or light
     muscovado (brown) sugar
   60ml/4 tbsp vegetable stock
   juice of 1 lime
   2.5ml/½ tsp dried chilli flakes
For the garnish
   15ml/1 tbsp vegetable oil
   1 egg, lightly beaten with
     15ml/1 tbsp cold water
   25g/1oz/⅓ cup beansprouts
   1 spring onion (scallion),
     thinly shredded
   1 fresh red chilli, seeded and
     finely chopped
   1 whole head pickled garlic, sliced
     across the bulb so each slice looks
     like a flower

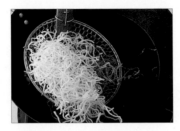

1 Heat the oil for deep-frying in a wok or large pan to 190°C/375°F or until a cube of bread, added to the oil, browns in about 40 seconds. Add the noodles and deep-fry until golden and crisp. Drain on kitchen paper and set aside.

2 Make the sauce. Heat the oil in a wok, add the fried tofu and cook over a medium heat until crisp. Using a slotted spoon, transfer it to a plate.

3 Add the garlic and shallots to the wok and cook until golden brown. Stir in the soy sauce, sugar, stock, lime juice and chilli flakes. Cook, stirring, until the mixture begins to caramelize.

4 Add the reserved tofu and stir until it has soaked up some of the liquid. Remove the wok from the heat and set aside.

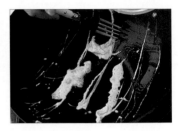

5 Prepare the egg garnish. Heat the oil in a wok or frying pan. Pour in the egg in a thin stream to form trails. As soon as it sets, lift it out with a fish slice or metal spatula and place on a plate.

6 Crumble the noodles into the tofu sauce, mix well, then spoon into warmed serving bowls. Sprinkle with the beansprouts, spring onion, fried egg strips, chilli and pickled garlic "flowers" and serve immediately.

COOK'S TIP
Successful deep-frying depends, to a large extent, on the type of oil used and the temperature to which it is heated. A bland-tasting oil, such as sunflower, will not alter the flavour of the food. All fats have a "smoke point" – the temperature at which they begin to decompose. Most vegetable oils have a high smoke point, with groundnut (peanut) oil the highest of all and so also the safest.

Energy 497Kcal/2075kJ; Protein 10.2g; Carbohydrate 70.2g, of which sugars 18.3g; Fat 19.95g, of which saturates 2.8g; Cholesterol 104.5mg; Calcium 51mg; Fibre .7g; Sodium 583.5mg.

RICE
DISHES

Rice is known to have been cultivated in China for at least 7,000 years; it is a staple food all over south and east Asia and an important feature of the cuisines of many countries. There are numerous different varities, including aromatic Indian Basmati and Thai jasmine rice. Plain boiled long-grain rice is the ideal accompaniment to most of the meat, fish and vegetable stir-fries in this book, but there are also plenty of ways in which rice can be dressed and combined with other ingredients to become one of the starring features of a meal.

SPICY FRIED RICE STICKS <u>WITH</u> PRAWNS

THIS WELL-KNOWN RECIPE IS BASED ON THE CLASSIC THAI NOODLE DISH CALLED PAD THAI.
POPULAR ALL OVER THAILAND, IT IS ENJOYED MORNING, NOON AND NIGHT.

SERVES FOUR

INGREDIENTS
15g/½ oz dried shrimps
15ml/1 tbsp tamarind pulp
45ml/3 tbsp Thai fish sauce
15ml/1 tbsp sugar
2 garlic cloves, chopped
2 fresh red chillies, seeded
    and chopped
45ml/3 tbsp groundnut
    (peanut) oil
2 eggs, beaten
225g/8oz dried rice sticks
225g/8oz cooked, peeled king
    prawns (jumbo shrimp)
3 spring onions (scallions) cut into
    2.5cm/1in lengths
75g/3oz beansprouts
30ml/2 tbsp roughly chopped
    unsalted peanuts, roasted or
    dry-fried until golden
30ml/2 tbsp chopped fresh coriander
    (cilantro) leaves
lime slices, to garnish

1 Soak the rice sticks in warm water for
30 minutes, then refresh under cold
running water and drain and set aside
until required.

2 Put the dried shrimps in a small bowl
and pour over enough warm water to
cover. Leave to soak for 30 minutes
until soft, then drain.

3 Put the tamarind pulp in a bowl with
60ml/4 tbsp hot water. Blend together.

4 Press the tamarind through a sieve to
extract thick tamarind water. Mix 30ml/
2 tbsp tamarind water with the fish
sauce and sugar.

5 Using a mortar and pestle, pound the
garlic and chillies together to form a
thick paste, or process together in a
food processor.

6 Heat a wok over a medium heat and
add 15ml/1 tbsp of the oil. When the oil
is hot add the beaten eggs and stir for
1–2 minutes until the eggs are cooked.

7 Remove the cooked egg from the wok
into a small bowl and set aside. Wipe
the wok clean.

8 Reheat the wok until hot, add the
remaining oil, then the chilli paste and
the reconstituted dried shrimps and
stir-fry for 1 minute.

COOK'S TIP
For a vegetarian dish, omit the dried
shrimps and replace the king prawns
with cubes of deep-fried tofu.

9 Add the rice sticks and tamarind
mixture to the wok and stir-fry together
for 3–4 minutes.

10 Add the scrambled eggs, prawns,
spring onions, beansprouts, peanuts
and coriander, then stir-fry for 2
minutes until well mixed. Serve at once,
garnishing each portion with lime slices.

Energy 436kcal/1819kJ; Protein 21.1g; Carbohydrate 52.1g, of which sugars 5.4g; Fat 15.3g, of which saturates 2.5g; Cholesterol 224mg; Calcium 151mg; Fibre 1.5g; Sodium 318mg.

STIR-FRIED RICE <u>WITH</u> CHINESE SAUSAGE

TRADITIONAL VIETNAMESE STIR-FRIED RICE INCLUDES CHINESE PORK SAUSAGE, OR STRIPS OF PORK COMBINED WITH PRAWNS OR CRAB. PREPARED THIS WAY, THE DISH CAN BE EATEN AS A SNACK, OR AS PART OF THE MEAL WITH GRILLED AND ROASTED MEATS ACCOMPANIED BY A VEGETABLE DISH OR SALAD.

SERVES FOUR

INGREDIENTS
    25g/1oz dried cloud ear (wood ear)
    mushrooms, soaked for 20 minutes
    15ml/1 tbsp vegetable or sesame oil
    1 onion, sliced
    2 green or red Thai chillies, seeded
    and finely chopped
    2 Chinese sausages (15cm/6in long),
    each sliced into 10 pieces
    175g/6oz prawns (shrimp), shelled
    and deveined
    30ml/2 tbsp *nuoc mam*, plus extra
    for drizzling
    10ml/2 tsp five-spice powder
    1 bunch of fresh coriander (cilantro),
    stalks removed, leaves finely
    chopped
    450g/1lb/4 cups cold steamed rice
    ground black pepper

1 Drain the soaked cloud ear mushrooms and cut them into strips. Heat a wok or heavy pan and add the oil. Add the onion and chillies. Fry until they begin to colour, then stir in the mushrooms.

COOK'S TIP
The rice used in these stir-fries is usually made the day before and added cold to the dish.

2 Add the sausage slices, moving them around the wok or pan until they begin to brown. Add the prawns and move them around until they turn opaque. Stir in the *nuoc mam*, the five-spice powder and 30ml/2 tbsp of the coriander.

3 Season well with pepper, then quickly add the rice, making sure it doesn't stick to the pan. As soon as the rice is heated through, sprinkle with the remainder of the coriander and serve with *nuoc mam* to drizzle over it.

Energy 398Kcal/1673kJ; Protein 19g; Carbohydrate 44g, of which sugars 4g; Fat 18g, of which saturates 5g; Cholesterol 116mg; Calcium 158mg; Fibre 2g; Sodium 800mg

SPECIAL FRIED RICE

SPECIAL FRIED RICE IS SO SUBSTANTIAL AND TASTY THAT IT IS ALMOST A MEAL IN ITSELF. IN CHINA, FRIED RICE IS USUALLY SERVED AT THE END OF A MEAL, NOT AS AN ACCOMPANIMENT, AND IS OFTEN COOKED IN ORDER TO USE UP LEFT OVER BOILED RICE FROM THE DAY BEFORE.

SERVES FOUR

INGREDIENTS
50g/2oz peeled, cooked
    prawns (shrimp)
50g/2oz cooked ham
115g/4oz green peas
3 eggs
5ml/1 tsp salt
2 spring onions (scallions),
    finely chopped
60ml/4 tbsp vegetable oil
15ml/1 tbsp light soy sauce
15ml/1 tbsp Chinese rice wine or
    dry sherry
450g/1lb cooked, cold rice

1 Pat dry the prawns with kitchen paper. Cut the ham into small dice about the same size as the peas.

2 In a bowl, lightly beat the eggs with a pinch of the salt and a few pieces of the spring onions.

3 Heat a wok or a very large, heavy-based frying pan on a medium flame. When the wok is hot, add half the oil.

4 When the oil is hot, stir-fry the peas, prawns and ham together for 1 minute, then add the soy sauce and rice wine or sherry. Remove the mixture from the pan and keep warm.

5 Heat the remaining oil in the pan and lightly scramble the eggs.

6 Add the rice to the scrambled egg, and stir to make sure that each grain of rice is separated.

7 Add the remaining salt, spring onions and the prawn, ham and pea mixture. Blend well and serve either hot or cold.

Energy 343kcal/1434kJ; Protein 20.2g; Carbohydrate 40.5g, of which sugars 4.2g; Fat 11.2g, of which saturates 1.6g; Cholesterol 124mg; Calcium 91mg; Fibre 2.4g; Sodium 632mg.

FRAGRANT HARBOUR FRIED RICE

THE CHINESE NAME FOR HONG KONG IS FRAGRANT HARBOUR, AND IT IS THE CROSSROADS FOR MANY STYLES OF COOKING. COOK THE RICE THE DAY BEFORE IF POSSIBLE.

SERVES FOUR

INGREDIENTS

225g/8oz/generous 1 cup long
   grain rice
about 90ml/6 tbsp vegetable oil
2 eggs, beaten
4 Chinese dried mushrooms, soaked
   for 30 minutes in warm water to cover
8 shallots or 2 small onions, sliced
115g/4oz peeled cooked prawns
   (shrimp), thawed if frozen
3 garlic cloves, crushed
115g/4oz cooked pork, cut into
   thin strips
115g/4oz Chinese sausage, cooked
   and sliced at an angle
30ml/2 tbsp light soy sauce
115g/4oz/1 cup frozen peas, thawed
2 spring onions (scallions), shredded
1–2 fresh or dried red chillies,
   seeded (optional)
salt and ground black pepper
coriander (cilantro) leaves, to garnish

1 Bring a large pan of lightly salted water to the boil. Add the rice and cook for 12–15 minutes until just tender. Drain and cool quickly. Tip into a bowl and chill. Ideally use the next day.

2 Heat about 15ml/1 tbsp of the oil in a wok over a medium heat, pour in the beaten eggs and allow to set without stirring. Slide the omelette on to a plate, roll it up and with a sharp knife cut into fine strips. Set aside.

3 Drain the mushrooms, cut off and discard the stems and slice the caps finely. Heat a wok, add 15ml/1 tbsp of the remaining oil and, when hot, stir-fry the shallots or onions until crisp and golden brown. Remove with a slotted spoon and set aside.

4 Add the prawns and garlic to the wok, with a little more oil if needed, and fry for 1 minute.

5 Remove the prawns and garlic from the wok and set aside. Add 15ml/1 tbsp more oil to the wok.

6 Stir-fry the shredded pork and the mushrooms for 2 minutes; add the cooked Chinese sausage slices and heat for a further 2 minutes. Lift out from the wok and keep warm.

7 Wipe the wok, reheat with the remaining oil and stir-fry the rice, adding more oil if needed so the grains are coated. Stir in the soy sauce, salt and pepper, plus half the cooked ingredients.

8 Add the peas and half the spring onions and toss over the heat until the peas are cooked.

9 Pile the fried rice on a heated platter and arrange the remaining cooked ingredients on top, with the remaining spring onions. Add the chilli, if using, and the coriander leaves, to garnish.

COOK'S TIP
There are many theories on the best way to cook rice. This method gives excellent results every time: Put 225g/8oz/ generous 1 cup long grain rice in a sieve and rinse thoroughly in cold water. Place in a large bowl, add salt to taste and pour in just under 600ml/1 pint/2½ cups boiling water. Cover with microwave film, leaving a gap, and cook in a 675 watt microwave on full power for 10 minutes. Leave to stand for 5 minutes more. Cool, then stir with a chopstick.

Energy 450Kcal/1872kJ; Protein 14.5g; Carbohydrate 51g, of which sugars 4.4g; Fat 20.9g, of which saturates 3.1g; Cholesterol 113mg; Calcium 48mg; Fibre 1.1g; Sodium 58mg.

NASI GORENG

ONE OF THE MOST POPULAR AND BEST-KNOWN DISHES FROM INDONESIA, THIS IS A MARVELLOUS WAY TO USE UP LEFTOVER RICE, AND MEATS SUCH AS PORK AND CHICKEN.

SERVES FOUR TO SIX

INGREDIENTS

350g/12oz/1¾ cups basmati rice
   (dry weight), cooked and cooled
2 eggs
30ml/2 tbsp water
105ml/7 tbsp sunflower oil
225g/8oz pork fillet (tenderloin)
2–3 fresh red chillies
10ml/2 tsp shrimp paste
2 garlic cloves, crushed
1 onion, sliced
115g/4oz cooked, peeled prawns
   (shrimp)
225g/8oz cooked chicken, chopped
30ml/2 tbsp dark soy sauce
salt and ground black pepper
Deep-fried Onions, to serve

1 Separate the grains of the cooked rice with a fork. Cover and set aside. Beat the eggs with the water and seasoning.

2 Heat 15ml/1 tbsp of the oil in a frying pan or wok, pour in about half the egg mixture and cook until set, without stirring. Roll up the omelette, slide it on to a plate, cut into strips and set aside. Make another omelette in the same way.

3 Cut the pork or beef fillet into neat strips. Finely shred one of the chillies and set aside.

4 Put the shrimp paste into a food processor, add the remaining chilli, garlic and onion. Process to a paste.

5 Heat the remaining oil in a wok. Fry the paste, without browning, until it gives off a spicy aroma.

6 Add the strips of pork or beef and toss the meat over the heat, to seal in the juices. Cook the meat in the wok for about 2 minutes, stirring constantly.

7 Add the prawns, cook for 2 minutes, then add the chicken, rice, and soy sauce, with salt and pepper to taste, stirring constantly. Serve in individual bowls, garnished with omelette strips, shredded chilli and Deep-fried Onions.

Energy 463Kcal/1929kJ; Protein 27.3g; Carbohydrate 49.4g, of which sugars 2.1g; Fat 17.1g, of which saturates 2.7g; Cholesterol 151mg; Calcium 49mg; Fibre 0.5g; Sodium 288mg.

FRIED RICE WITH BEEF

ONE OF THE JOYS OF WOK COOKING IS THE EASE AND SPEED WITH WHICH A REALLY GOOD MEAL CAN BE PREPARED. THIS DELECTABLE BEEF AND RICE STIR-FRY CAN BE ON THE TABLE IN 15 MINUTES.

SERVES FOUR

INGREDIENTS

200g/7oz beef steak, chilled
15ml/1 tbsp vegetable oil
2 garlic cloves,
   finely chopped
1 egg
250g/9oz/2¼ cups cooked
   jasmine rice
½ medium head broccoli,
   coarsely chopped
30ml/2 tbsp dark soy sauce
15ml/1 tbsp light soy sauce
5ml/1 tsp palm sugar or light
   muscovado (brown) sugar
15ml/1 tbsp Thai fish sauce
ground black pepper
chilli sauce, to serve

1 Trim the steak and cut into very thin strips with a sharp knife.

2 Heat the oil in a wok or frying pan and cook the garlic over a low to medium heat until golden. Do not let it burn. Increase the heat to high, add the steak and stir-fry for 2 minutes.

3 Move the pieces of beef to the edges of the wok or pan and break the egg into the centre. When the egg starts to set, stir-fry it with the meat.

4 Add the rice and toss all the contents of the wok together, scraping up any residue on the base, then add the broccoli, soy sauces, sugar and fish sauce and stir-fry for 2 minutes more. Season to taste with pepper and serve immediately with chilli sauce.

COOK'S TIP
Soy sauce is made from fermented soya beans. The first extraction is sold as light soy sauce and has a delicate, "beany" fragrance. Dark soy sauce has been allowed to mature for longer.

Energy 385Kcal/1606kJ; Protein 20.7g; Carbohydrate 52.7g, of which sugars 2.5g; Fat 9.8g, of which saturates 2.8g; Cholesterol 81mg; Calcium 59mg; Fibre 1.6g; Sodium 590mg.

FRIED RICE WITH PORK

THIS IS GREAT FOR USING UP LAST NIGHT'S LEFTOVER RICE, BUT FOR SAFETY'S SAKE, IT MUST HAVE BEEN COOLED QUICKLY AND KEPT IN THE REFRIGERATOR, THEN FRIED UNTIL THOROUGHLY HEATED.

SERVES FOUR TO SIX

INGREDIENTS

45ml/3 tbsp vegetable oil
1 onion, chopped
15ml/1 tbsp chopped garlic
115g/4oz pork, cut into small cubes
2 eggs, beaten
1kg/2¼lb/4 cups cooked rice
30ml/2 tbsp Thai fish sauce
15ml/1 tbsp dark soy sauce
2.5ml/½ tsp caster (superfine) sugar
4 spring onions (scallions),
  finely sliced, sliced fresh red
  chillies, and 1 lime, cut into
  wedges, to serve

COOK'S TIP
To make 1kg/2¼lb/4 cups cooked rice,
you will need approximately 400g/14oz/
2 cups uncooked rice.

1 Heat the oil in a wok or large frying pan. Add the onion and garlic and cook for about 2 minutes until softened.

2 Add the pork to the softened onion and garlic. Stir-fry until the pork changes colour and is cooked.

3 Add the eggs and cook until scrambled into small lumps.

4 Add the rice and continue to stir and toss, to coat it with the oil and prevent it from sticking.

5 Add the fish sauce, soy sauce and sugar and mix well. Continue to fry until the rice is thoroughly heated. Spoon into warmed individual bowls and serve, with sliced spring onions, chillies and lime wedges.

Energy 343Kcal/1448kJ; Protein 11.2g; Carbohydrate 54.3g, of which sugars 2.2g; Fat 10.6g, of which saturates 2g; Cholesterol 82mg; Calcium 51mg; Fibre 0.6g; Sodium 220mg.

CURRIED CHICKEN AND RICE

THIS SIMPLE ONE-WOK MEAL IS PERFECT FOR CASUAL ENTERTAINING. IT CAN BE MADE USING VIRTUALLY ANY TENDER PIECES OF MEAT OR STIR-FRY VEGETABLES THAT YOU HAVE TO HAND.

SERVES FOUR

INGREDIENTS
   60ml/4 tbsp vegetable oil
   4 garlic cloves, finely chopped
   1 chicken (about 1.5kg/3–3½ lb)
     or chicken pieces, skinned and
     boned and cut into bite size pieces
   5ml/1 tsp garam masala
   450g/1lb/2⅔ cups jasmine rice,
     rinsed and drained
   10ml/2 tsp salt
   1 litre/1¾ pints/4 cups
     chicken stock
   small bunch fresh coriander
     (cilantro), chopped, to garnish

COOK'S TIP
You will probably need to brown the chicken in batches, so don't be tempted to add too much chicken at once.

1 Heat the oil in a wok or flameproof casserole, which has a lid. Add the garlic and cook over a low to medium heat until golden brown. Add the chicken, increase the heat and brown the pieces on all sides (see Cook's Tip).

2 Add the garam masala, stir well to coat the chicken all over in the spice, then tip in the drained rice. Add the salt and stir to mix.

3 Pour in the stock, stir well, then cover the wok or casserole and bring to the boil. Reduce the heat to low and simmer gently for 10 minutes, until the rice is cooked and tender.

4 Lift the wok or casserole off the heat, leaving the lid on, and leave for 10 minutes. Fluff up the rice grains with a fork and spoon on to a platter. Sprinkle with the coriander and serve immediately.

Energy 715Kcal/2994kJ; Protein 56.3g; Carbohydrate 89.8g, of which sugars 0g; Fat 13.8g, of which saturates 1.9g; Cholesterol 140mg; Calcium 32mg; Fibre 0g; Sodium 1103mg.

THAI FRIED RICE

THIS SUBSTANTIAL AND TASTY DISH IS BASED ON THAI JASMINE RICE COOKED IN COCONUT MILK.
DICED CHICKEN, RED PEPPER AND CORN KERNELS ADD COLOUR AND EXTRA FLAVOUR.

SERVES FOUR

INGREDIENTS
475ml/16fl oz/2 cups water
50g/2oz/½ cup coconut milk powder
350g/12oz/1¾ cups Thai jasmine
 rice, rinsed
30ml/2 tbsp groundnut (peanut) oil
2 garlic cloves, chopped
1 small onion, finely chopped
2.5cm/1in piece fresh root ginger,
 peeled and grated
225g/8oz skinned chicken breast
 fillets, cut into 1cm/½in pieces
1 red (bell) pepper, seeded
 and sliced
115g/4oz/1 cup drained canned
 whole kernel corn
5ml/1 tsp chilli oil
5ml/1 tsp hot curry powder
2 eggs, beaten
salt
spring onion (scallion) shreds,
 to garnish

1 Pour the water into a pan and whisk in the coconut milk powder. Add the rice and bring to the boil. Reduce the heat, cover and cook for 12 minutes, or until the rice is tender and the liquid has been absorbed. Spread the rice on a baking sheet and leave until cold.

2 Heat the oil in a wok, add the garlic, onion and ginger and stir-fry over a medium heat for 2 minutes.

COOK'S TIP
It is important that the rice is completely cold before being fried.

3 Push the onion mixture to the sides of the wok, add the chicken to the centre and stir-fry for 2 minutes. Add the rice and toss well. Stir-fry over a high heat for about 3 minutes more, until the chicken is cooked through.

4 Stir in the sliced red pepper, corn, chilli oil and curry powder, with salt to taste. Toss over the heat for 1 minute. Stir in the beaten eggs and cook for 1 minute more. Garnish with the spring onion shreds and serve.

Energy 563Kcal/2358kJ; Protein 26.7g; Carbohydrate 88.9g, of which sugars 13.9g; Fat 11.2g, of which saturates 2.1g; Cholesterol 139mg; Calcium 77mg; Fibre 1.8g; Sodium 284mg.

FRAGRANT RICE WITH CHICKEN AND MINT

FROM THE NORTH OF VIETNAM, THIS REFRESHING DISH CAN BE SERVED SIMPLY, DRIZZLED WITH NUOC CHAM, OR AS PART OF A CELEBRATORY MEAL THAT MIGHT INCLUDE FISH OR CHICKEN, EITHER GRILLED OR ROASTED WHOLE, AND ACCOMPANIED BY PICKLES AND A TABLE SALAD.

3 Put the rice in a heavy pan and stir in the stock. When the rice settles, check that the stock sits roughly 2.5cm/1in above the rice; if not, top it up. Bring the liquid to the boil, cover the pan and cook for about 25 minutes, or until all the water has been absorbed.

4 Remove the pan from the heat and, using a fork, add the shredded chicken, shallots and mint. Cover the pan again and leave the flavours to mingle for 10 minutes. Tip the rice into bowls, or on to a serving dish, garnish with the remaining spring onions, and serve with the *nuoc cham*.

SERVES FOUR

INGREDIENTS

15ml/1 tbsp vegetable or groundnut (peanut) oil
2–3 shallots, halved and finely sliced
1 bunch of fresh mint, stalks removed, leaves finely shredded
2 spring onions (scallions), finely sliced
350g/12oz/1¾ cups long grain rice
nuoc cham, to serve
For the stock
2 meaty chicken legs
1 onion, peeled and quartered
4cm/1½in fresh root ginger, peeled and coarsely chopped
15ml/1 tbsp *nuoc mam*
3 black peppercorns
1 bunch of fresh mint
sea salt

1 To make the stock, put the chicken and other stock ingredients into a deep pan, and pour in 1 litre/1¾ pints/4 cups water. Bring the water to the boil, skim off any foam, then reduce the heat and simmer gently with the lid on for 1 hour. Remove the lid, increase the heat and simmer for a further 30 minutes to reduce the stock. Skim off any fat, strain the stock and season with salt. Measure 750ml/1¼ pints/3 cups stock. Remove the chicken meat from the bone and shred.

2 Heat a wok and add a drizzle of oil. Stir fry the sliced shallots together with half of the spring onion, retain the rest for garnishing. When the shallots are golden, toss in the chicken and the mint, then remove from the heat.

Energy 370Kcal/1569kJ; Protein 12g; Carbohydrate 79g, of which sugars 1g; Fat 3g, of which saturates 0g; Cholesterol 26mg; Calcium 41mg; Fibre 0.8g; Sodium 200mg

RICE PORRIDGE

In Cambodia, a steaming bowl of thick rice porridge or BOBOR *is a nourishing and satisfying breakfast. Usually made with long grain rice, it can be made plain, or with the addition of chicken, pork, fish or prawns.*

SERVES SIX

INGREDIENTS

15ml/1 tbsp vegetable or groundnut
(peanut) oil
25g/1oz fresh root ginger, shredded
115g/4oz/generous 1 cup long grain
rice, rinsed and drained
1.2 litres/2 pints/5 cups chicken
stock or water
30–45ml/2–3 tbsp *tuk trey*
10ml/2 tsp sugar
450g/1lb fresh fish fillets, boned
(any fish will do)
sea salt and ground black pepper
For the garnish
15ml/1 tbsp vegetable or groundnut
(peanut) oil
2 garlic cloves, finely chopped
1 lemon grass stalk, trimmed and
finely sliced
25g/1oz fresh root ginger, shredded
a few coriander (cilantro) leaves

1 In a heavy pan heat the oil and stir in the ginger and rice for 1 minute. Pour in the stock and bring it to the boil. Reduce the heat and simmer, partially covered, for 20 minutes, until the rice is tender and the soup is thick. Stir the *tuk trey* and sugar into the soupy porridge. Season and keep the porridge hot.

2 Meanwhile, fill a wok a third of the way with water. Fit a covered bamboo steamer on top and bring the water to the boil so that the steam rises. Season the fish fillets, place them on a plate and put them inside the steamer. Cover and steam the fish until cooked.

3 For the garnish, heat the oil in small wok or heavy pan. Add the chopped garlic, lemon grass and ginger and stir-fry until golden and fragrant. Add chillies to the mixture, if you like.

4 Ladle the rice porridge into bowls. Tear off pieces of steamed fish fillet to place on top. Sprinkle with the stir-fried garlic, lemon grass and ginger, and garnish with a few coriander leaves.

Energy 152Kcal/636kJ; Protein 15g; Carbohydrate 17g, of which sugars 1.7g; Fat 2g, of which saturates 0.3g; Cholesterol 35mg; Calcium 11mg; Fibre 0g; Sodium 45mg

FRIED RICE WITH TURKEY

TURKEY IS GREAT FOR A STIR-FRY AS IT COOKS SO QUICKLY. USE FILLETS FROM THE BREAST FOR THIS DISH, OR YOU CAN ALSO USE CHICKEN IF YOU PREFER. GARNISH THE FINISHED DISH WITH FINE STRIPS OF OMELETTE JUST BEFORE SERVING, IF YOU WISH.

3 Add the rice and continue to stir and toss, to coat it with the oil and prevent it from sticking.

4 Add the fish sauce, soy sauce and sugar and mix well. Continue to fry until the rice is thoroughly heated.

5 Garnish with sliced spring onion, red chillies and lime wedges. Top with a few strips of omelette, if you like.

SERVES FOUR TO SIX

INGREDIENTS
    45ml/3 tbsp vegetable oil
    1 onion, chopped
    15ml/1 tbsp chopped garlic
    115g/4oz turkey breast fillet, cut
        into small cubes
    2 eggs, beaten
    1kg/2¼lb/4 cups cooked long-grain
        rice, cooled
    30ml/2 tbsp Thai fish sauce
    15ml/1 tbsp dark soy sauce
    2.5 ml/½ tsp caster (superfine) sugar
    4 spring onions (scallions), finely
        sliced, to garnish
    2 red chillies, sliced, to garnish
    1 lime, cut into wedges, to garnish
    strips of omelette, to garnish
        (optional)

1 Heat the oil in a wok or large frying pan. Add the onion and garlic and cook for about 2 minutes until softened.

2 Add the turkey to the softened onion and garlic. Stir-fry until the meat is cooked and evenly browned. Add the eggs and cook until scrambled into small lumps.

Energy 343kcal/1448kJ; Protein 11.3g; Carbohydrate 54.3g, of which sugars 2.2g; Fat 10.6g, of which saturates 2g; Cholesterol 82mg; Calcium 51mg; Fibre 0.6g; Sodium 220mg.

COCONUT RICE

ORIGINALLY FROM INDIA AND THAILAND, COCONUT RICE IS POPULAR IN CAMBODIA AND SOUTHERN VIETNAM. RICH AND NOURISHING, IT IS OFTEN SERVED WITH A TANGY FRUIT AND VEGETABLE SALAD, SUCH AS THE ONES MADE WITH GREEN PAPAYA OR GREEN MANGO.

SERVES FOUR TO SIX

INGREDIENTS
- 400ml/14fl oz/1⅔ cups unsweetened coconut milk
- 400ml/14fl oz/1⅔ cups seasoned chicken stock
- 225g/8oz/generous 1 cup long grain rice, rinsed in several bowls of water and drained
- 115g/4oz fresh coconut, grated

COOK'S TIP
As the coconut shells are often halved and used as bowls, they make a perfect serving vessel for this rice, garnished with fresh or roasted coconut or crispy-fried ginger. In the street, this rice is often served on a banana leaf.

1 Pour the coconut milk and stock into a heavy pan and stir well to combine. Bring the liquid to the boil and stir in the rice. Stir once, reduce the heat and cover the pan. Simmer gently for about 25 minutes, until the rice has absorbed all the liquid. Remove from the heat and leave the rice to sit for 10 minutes.

2 Meanwhile, heat a small, heavy pan. Stir in the fresh coconut and roast it until it turns golden with a nutty aroma. Tip the roasted coconut into a bowl.

3 Fluff up the rice with a fork and spoon it into bowls. Scatter the roasted coconut over the top and serve.

Energy 175Kcal/731kJ; Protein 3g; Carbohydrate 33.5g, of which sugars 3.5g; Fat 3g, of which saturates 2g; Cholesterol 0mg; Calcium 28mg; Fibre 0.6g; Sodium 75mg

JEWELLED VEGETABLE RICE WITH CRISPY FRIED EGGS

INSPIRED BY THE TRADITIONAL INDONESIAN DISH NASI GORENG,
THIS VIBRANT, COLOURFUL STIR-FRY MAKES A TASTY LIGHT MEAL.
ALTERNATIVELY, SERVE IT AS AN ACCOMPANIMENT TO SIMPLY
GRILLED MEAT OR FISH. TO MAKE AN EXTRA-HEALTHY OPTION, USE
BROWN BASMATI RICE IN PLACE OF THE WHITE RICE.

SERVES FOUR

INGREDIENTS
  2 fresh corn on the cob
  60ml/4 tbsp sunflower oil
  2 garlic cloves, finely chopped
  4 red Asian shallots, thinly sliced
  1 small fresh red chilli, finely sliced
  90g/3½oz carrots, cut into
    thin matchsticks
  90g/3½oz fine green beans,
    cut into 2cm/¾in lengths
  1 red (bell) pepper, seeded and
    cut into 1cm/½in dice
  90g/3½oz baby button
    (white) mushrooms
  500g/1¼lb cooked long grain rice,
    completely cooled
  45ml/3 tbsp light soy sauce
  10ml/2 tsp green Thai curry paste
  4 eggs
  crisp green salad leaves and
    lime wedges, to serve

3 Add the carrots, green beans, corn, red pepper and mushrooms to the wok and stir-fry for 3–4 minutes. Add the cooked, cooled rice and stir-fry for a further 4–5 minutes.

4 Mix together the light soy sauce and curry paste and add to the wok. Toss to mix well and stir-fry for 2–3 minutes until piping hot.

5 Meanwhile, fry the eggs one at a time in a clean wok. Make sure that the oil is sizzling hot before you pour the egg in, as this will give the white a lovely crispy edge. When the egg is cooked, remove it from the wok and keep warm until the others are fried.

6 Ladle the rice into four bowls or plates and top each portion with a crispy fried egg. Serve with crisp green salad leaves and wedges of lime to squeeze over.

1 First shuck the corn cobs. Remove all the papery leaves, and the silky threads, then with a sharp knife cut at the base of the kernels right down the length of the cob.

2 Heat 30ml/2 tbsp of the sunflower oil in a wok over a high heat. When hot, add the garlic, shallots and chilli. Stir-fry for about 2 minutes.

COOK'S TIP
When making this dish, it is better to use cold cooked rice rather than hot, freshly cooked rice. Hot boiled rice tends to clump together when stir-frying, whereas the grains of cooled rice will remain separate.

Energy 392Kcal/1648kJ; Protein 13.6g; Carbohydrate 51.4g, of which sugars 8.2g; Fat 16.1g, of which saturates 3.6g; Cholesterol 261mg; Calcium 79mg; Fibre 2.1g; Sodium 968mg.

SAVOURY FRIED RICE

*THE TITLE MAKES THIS SOUND LIKE RATHER AN ORDINARY DISH, BUT IT IS NOTHING OF THE KIND.
CHILLI, NUTS AND TOASTED COCONUT GIVE THE MIXTURE OF RICE AND BEANS AND WILTED GREENS
PLENTY OF FLAVOUR, AND THE EGG THAT IS STIRRED IN PROVIDES THE PROTEIN CONTENT.*

SERVES TWO

INGREDIENTS

30ml/2 tbsp vegetable oil
2 garlic cloves, finely chopped
1 small fresh red chilli, seeded and
finely chopped
50g/2oz/½ cup cashew nuts, toasted
50g/2oz/⅔ cup desiccated
(dry unsweetened shredded)
coconut, toasted
2.5ml/½ tsp palm sugar or light
muscovado (brown) sugar
30ml/2 tbsp light soy sauce
15ml/1 tbsp rice vinegar
1 egg
115g/4oz/1 cup green beans, sliced
½ spring cabbage or 115g/4oz spring
greens (collards) or pak choi (bok
choy), shredded
90g/3½oz jasmine rice, cooked
lime wedges, to serve

1 Heat the oil in a wok or large, heavy frying pan. Add the garlic and cook over a medium to high heat until golden. Do not let it burn or it will taste bitter.

2 Add the red chilli, cashew nuts and toasted coconut to the wok or pan and stir-fry briefly, taking care to prevent the coconut from scorching. Stir in the sugar, soy sauce and rice vinegar. Toss over the heat for 1–2 minutes.

3 Push the stir-fry to one side of the wok or pan and break the egg into the empty side. When the egg is almost set, stir it into the garlic and chilli mixture with a wooden spatula or spoon.

4 Add the green beans, greens and cooked rice. Stir over the heat until the greens have just wilted, then spoon into a dish to serve. Offer the lime wedges separately, for squeezing over the rice.

Energy 570Kcal/2366kJ; Protein 16.1g; Carbohydrate 30.5g, of which sugars 8.7g; Fat 43.6g, of which saturates 18.2g; Cholesterol 95mg; Calcium 187mg; Fibre 8.5g; Sodium 1196mg.

RICE CONGEE

ORIGINATING IN CHINA, THIS DISH HAS NOW SPREAD THROUGHOUT THE WHOLE OF SOUTH-EAST ASIA AND IS LOVED FOR ITS COMFORTING BLANDNESS. IT IS INVARIABLY TEAMED WITH A FEW STRONGLY FLAVOURED ACCOMPANIMENTS TO PROVIDE CONTRASTING TASTES AND TEXTURES.

SERVES TWO

INGREDIENTS
    900ml/1½ pints/3¾ cups
        vegetable stock
    200g/7oz cooked rice
    15ml/1 tbsp Thai fish sauce, or
        mushroom ketchup
    2 heads pickled garlic,
        finely chopped (see Cook's Tip)
    1 celery stick, finely diced
    salt and ground black pepper
To garnish
    30ml/2 tbsp groundnut (peanut) oil
    4 garlic cloves, thinly sliced
    4 small red shallots, finely sliced

1 Make the garnishes by heating the groundnut oil in a wok and cooking the garlic and shallots over a low heat until brown. Drain on kitchen paper and reserve for the soup.

2 Pour the stock into a large pan. Bring to the boil and add the rice.

3 Stir in the sauce and pickled garlic and simmer for 10 minutes to let the flavours develop. Stir in the celery.

4 Serve the rice congee in individual warmed bowls. Sprinkle the prepared garlic and shallots on top and season with plenty of ground pepper.

COOK'S TIP
Pickled garlic has a distinctive flavour and is available from Asian food stores.

Energy 509Kcal/2126kJ; Protein 27.3g; Carbohydrate 37.2g, of which sugars 0.8g; Fat 29g, of which saturates 6.3g; Cholesterol 74mg; Calcium 39mg; Fibre 1.8g; Sodium 86mg.

FRIED RICE WITH SPICES

THIS MILDLY SPICED RICE MAKES A GOOD ACCOMPANIMENT TO ANY CURRIED DISH. WHOLE SPICES ARE USED TO FLAVOUR IT, AND THESE ARE NOT, OF COURSE, INTENDED TO BE EATEN.

2 Put the rice, salt and 600ml/1 pint/ 2½ cups water in a heavy pan. Bring to the boil, then cover tightly and simmer for about 10 minutes. The rice should be just cooked but still retain a little bite to it. Drain off any excess water, fluff up the grains with a fork or chopsticks, then spread the rice out on a tray and set aside to cool.

3 Heat a wok or large frying pan and add the ghee or butter. Wait until it is foaming, then add the whole spices and stir-fry for 1 minute.

SERVES THREE TO FOUR

INGREDIENTS
    175g/6oz basmati rice
    2.5ml/½ tsp salt
    15ml/1 tbsp ghee or butter
    8 whole cloves
    4 green cardamom pods, bruised
    1 bay leaf
    7.5cm/3in cinnamon stick
    5ml/1 tsp black peppercorns
    5ml/1 tsp cumin seeds
    5ml/1 tsp coriander seeds

COOK'S TIP
You could add 2.5ml/½ tsp ground turmeric to the rice in step 2 of the recipe to colour it yellow.

1 Put the rice in a colander and wash it under cold running water, or dunk into a bowl of cold water, until the water clears. Put in a bowl and pour 600ml/ 1 pint/2½ cups fresh water over the rice. Leave the rice to soak for 20 minutes; then drain thoroughly.

4 Add the cooled rice to the wok and stir-fry for 3–4 minutes until warmed through and thoroughly coated in the spiced butter. Serve at once.

Energy 248kcal/1036kJ; Protein 6.7g; Carbohydrate 42.8g, of which sugars 2.3g; Fat 5.4g, of which saturates 0.7g; Cholesterol 0mg; Calcium 94mg; Fibre 0.5g; Sodium 25mg.

THAI FRIED RICE

THIS HOT AND SPICY DISH IS EASY TO PREPARE AND MAKES A COMPLETE MEAL IN ITSELF AS IT
INCLUDES CHUNKS OF CHICKEN AND STIR-FRIED EGGS.

SERVES FOUR

INGREDIENTS
225g/8oz Thai fragrant rice
45ml/3 tbsp vegetable oil
1 onion, chopped
1 small red (bell) pepper, cut into
  2cm/¾in cubes
350g/12oz skinless,
  chicken breast fillets, cut into
  2cm/¾in cubes
1 garlic clove, crushed
15ml/1 tbsp mild curry paste
2.5ml/1/2 tsp paprika
2.5ml/1/2 tsp ground turmeric
30ml/2 tbsp Thai fish sauce
2 eggs, beaten
salt and ground black pepper
fried basil leaves, to garnish

3 Add the chicken, garlic, curry paste and spices and stir-fry for 2–3 minutes.

4 Reduce the heat to medium, add the cooled rice, fish sauce and seasoning. Stir-fry for 2–3 minutes until the rice is very hot.

5 Make a well in the centre and add the remaining oil. When hot, add the beaten eggs, leave to cook for about 2 minutes until lightly set, then stir into the rice.

6 Scatter the fried basil leaves over the rice and serve at once.

1 Put the rice in a sieve and wash well under cold running water. Put in a heavy pan with 1.5 litres/2½ pints/6¼ cups boiling water. Return to the boil, then simmer, uncovered, for 8–10 minutes; drain well. Spread out the grains on a tray and leave to cool.

2 Heat a wok and add 30ml/2 tbsp of the oil. Stir-fry the onion and red pepper for 1 minute.

COOK'S TIP
Among the various types of rice available, Thai fragrant rice is one of the more popular, especially in Thai, Vietnamese and some other South-east Asian recipes. It does, in fact, have a particularly special fragrance and is generally served on feast days and other important occasions.

Energy 508kcal/2127kJ; Protein 24.7g; Carbohydrate 83.9g, of which sugars 8.7g; Fat 8g, of which saturates 1.6g; Cholesterol 135mg; Calcium 57mg; Fibre 1.3g; Sodium 204mg.

GARLIC AND GINGER RICE WITH CORIANDER

IN VIETNAM AND CAMBODIA, WHEN RICE IS SERVED ON THE SIDE, IT IS USUALLY STEAMED AND PLAIN, OR FRAGRANT WITH THE FLAVOURS OF GINGER AND HERBS. THE COMBINATION OF GARLIC AND GINGER IS POPULAR IN BOTH COUNTRIES AND COMPLIMENTS ALMOST ANY VEGETABLE, FISH OR MEAT DISH.

SERVES FOUR TO SIX

INGREDIENTS

- 15ml/1 tbsp vegetable or groundnut (peanut) oil
- 2–3 garlic cloves, finely chopped
- 25g/1oz fresh root ginger, finely chopped
- 225g/8oz/generous 1 cup long grain rice, rinsed in several bowls of water and drained
- 900ml/1½ pints/3¾ cups chicken stock
- a bunch of fresh coriander (cilantro) leaves, finely chopped
- a bunch of fresh basil and mint, (optional), finely chopped

1 Heat the oil in a clay pot or heavy pan. Stir in the garlic and ginger and fry until golden. Stir in the rice and allow it to absorb the flavours for 1–2 minutes. Pour in the stock and stir to make sure the rice doesn't stick. Bring the stock to the boil, then reduce the heat.

2 Scatter the coriander over the surface of the stock, cover the pan, and leave to cook gently for 20–25 minutes, until the rice has absorbed all the liquid. Turn off the heat and gently fluff up the rice to mix in the coriander. Cover and leave to infuse for 10 minutes before serving.

Energy 151Kcal/632kJ; Protein 3g; Carbohydrate 30g, of which sugars 0g; Fat 2g, of which saturates 0.3g; Cholesterol 0mg; Calcium 9mg; Fibre 0.1g; Sodium 124mg

SAIGON SOUTHERN-SPICED CHILLI RICE

ALTHOUGH PLAIN STEAMED RICE IS SERVED AT ALMOST EVERY MEAL, MANY SOUTHERN FAMILIES LIKE TO SNEAK IN A LITTLE SPICE TOO. A BURST OF CHILLI FOR FIRE, TURMERIC FOR COLOUR, AND CORIANDER FOR ITS COOLING FLAVOUR, ARE ALL THAT'S NEEDED.

SERVES FOUR

INGREDIENTS
  15ml/1 tbsp vegetable oil
  2–3 green or red Thai chillies,
    seeded and finely chopped
  2 garlic cloves, finely chopped
  2.5cm/1in fresh root ginger, chopped
  5ml/1 tsp sugar
  10–15ml/2–3 tsp ground turmeric
  225g/8oz/generous 1 cup long
    grain rice
  30ml/2 tbsp *nuoc mam*
  600ml/1 pint/2½ cups water or stock
  1 bunch of fresh coriander
    (cilantro), stalks removed, leaves
    finely chopped
  salt and ground black pepper

1 Heat the oil in a heavy pan. Stir in the chillies, garlic and ginger with the sugar. As they begin to colour, stir in the turmeric. Add the rice, coating it well, then pour in the *nuoc mam* and the water or stock – the liquid should sit about 2.5cm/1in above the rice.

2 Tip the rice on to a serving dish. Add some of the coriander and lightly toss together using a fork. Garnish with the remaining coriander.

COOK'S TIP
This rice goes well with grilled and stir-fried fish and shellfish dishes, but you can serve it as an alternative to plain rice. Add extra chillies, if you like.

3 Season with salt and ground black pepper and bring the liquid to the boil. Reduce the heat, cover and simmer for about 25 minutes, or until the water has been absorbed. Remove from the heat and leave the rice to steam for a further 10 minutes.

Energy 252Kcal/1066kJ; Protein 5g; Carbohydrate 51g, of which sugars 1g; Fat 5g, of which saturates 1g; Cholesterol 0mg; Calcium 24mg; Fibre 0.3g; Sodium 500mg

STEAMED RICE

LONG GRAIN RICE IS THE MOST FREQUENTLY EATEN GRAIN IN VIETNAM — FRESHLY STEAMED AND SERVED AT ALMOST EVERY MEAL. IF THE MAIN DISH DOESN'T INCLUDE NOODLES, THEN A BOWL OF STEAMED RICE — COM — OR RICE WRAPPERS WILL PROVIDE THE STARCH FOR THE MEAL.

SERVES FOUR

INGREDIENTS

   225g/8oz/generous 1 cup long grain
     rice, rinsed and drained
   a pinch of salt

1 Put the rice into a heavy pan or clay pot. Add 600ml/1 pint/2½ cups water to cover the rice by 2.5cm/1in. Add the salt, and then bring the water to the boil.

VARIATION
Jasmine rice is delicious and readily available from Asian stores.

2 Reduce the heat, cover the pan and cook gently for about 20 minutes, or until all the water has been absorbed. Remove the pan from the heat and leave to steam, still covered, for a further 5–10 minutes.

3 To serve, simply fluff up with a fork.

Energy 203Kcal/864kJ; Protein 4g; Carbohydrate 49g, of which sugars 0g; Fat 1g, of which saturates 0g; Cholesterol 0mg; Calcium 2mg; Fibre 0.3g; Sodium 0mg

BAMBOO-STEAMED STICKY RICE

VIETNAMESE STICKY RICE, OR GLUTINOUS RICE, CALLED XOI NEP, *REQUIRES A LONG SOAK IN WATER BEFORE BEING COOKED IN A BAMBOO STEAMER. IT IS USED FOR SAVOURY AND SWEET RICE CAKES, SUCH AS* BANH CHUNG *AND* HUE COM SEN.

SERVES FOUR

INGREDIENTS
350g/12oz/1¾ cups sticky rice

1 Put the rice into a large bowl and fill the bowl with cold water. Leave the rice to soak for at least 6 hours, then drain, rinse thoroughly, and drain again.

2 Fill a wok or heavy pan one-third full with water. Place a bamboo steamer, with the lid on, over the wok or pan and bring the water to the boil.

3 Place a dampened piece of muslin (cheesecloth) into the steamer. Tip the rice into the middle and spread it out. Fold the muslin over the rice, cover and steam for 25 minutes until the rice is tender but firm.

VARIATION
Sticky rice is enjoyed as a sweet, filling snack mixed with sugar and coconut milk and then rolled into little balls. It can also be served with dipping sauces, light dishes and vegetarian meals.

Energy 314Kcal/1314kJ; Protein 7g; Carbohydrate 66g, of which sugars 0g; Fat 1g, of which saturates 0g; Cholesterol 0mg; Calcium 14mg; Fibre 0g; Sodium 0mg

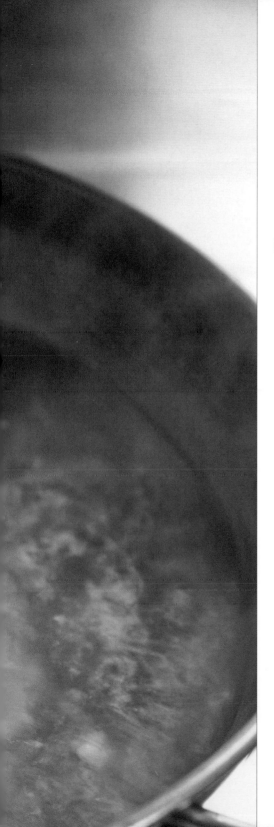

SALADS, VEGETABLE DISHES AND CONDIMENTS

Although it is perfectly possible to cook an entire meal in a wok it can also be a very useful utensil for making side dishes. A vegetable stir-fry may not be the first dish that comes to mind for serving with the Sunday roast, but why not? The crisp, clean flavours would be an ideal contrast to more classic accompaniments, and the colours would look lovely on the plate. A wok is great for making a warm salad, too, whether you simply use it for dry-roasting rice, as in Bamboo Shoot Salad, or let it take a leading role in a dish such as Spicy Chickpeas with Spinach.

SEARED BEEF SALAD ^{IN A} LIME DRESSING

*THIS DISH, GOI BO, IS AN INDO-CHINESE FAVOURITE AND
VERSIONS OF IT ARE ENJOYED IN VIETNAM, THAILAND, CAMBODIA
AND LAOS. IT IS ALSO ONE OF THE TRADITIONAL DISHES THAT
APPEAR IN THE BO BAY MON — BEEF SEVEN WAYS FEAST — IN
WHICH SEVEN DIFFERENT BEEF DISHES ARE SERVED.*

SERVES FOUR

INGREDIENTS
    about 7.5ml/1½ tsp vegetable oil
    450g/1lb beef fillet (tenderloin), cut
      into steaks 2.5cm/1in thick
    115g/4oz/½ cup beansprouts
    1 bunch each fresh basil and mint,
      stalks removed, leaves shredded
    1 lime, cut into slices, to serve
For the dressing
    grated and juice (about 80ml/3fl oz)
      of 2 limes
    30ml/2 tbsp *nuoc mam*
    30ml/2 tbsp raw cane sugar
    2 garlic cloves, crushed
    2 lemon grass stalks, finely sliced
    2 red Serrano chillies, seeded and
      finely sliced

1 To make the dressing, beat the lime
rind, juice and *nuoc mam* in a bowl
with the sugar, until the sugar dissolves.
Stir in the garlic, lemon grass and
chillies and set aside.

2 Pour a little oil into a heavy pan and
rub it over the base with a piece of
kitchen paper. Heat the pan and sear
the steaks for 1–2 minutes each side,
depending on how thick it is.

3 Transfer the steaks to a board and
leave to cool a little. Using a sharp
knife, cut the meat into very thin slices.
Toss the slices in the dressing, cover
and leave to marinate for 1–2 hours.

4 Drain the meat of any excess juice
and transfer it to a wide serving bowl.
Add the beansprouts and herbs and
toss it all together. Serve with lime slices
to squeeze over.

COOK'S TIP
It is worth buying an excellent-quality
piece of tender fillet steak for this recipe
as the meat is only just seared.

Energy 233Kcal/979kJ; Protein 26g; Carbohydrate 12g, of which sugars 9g; Fat 9g, of which saturates 3g; Cholesterol
69mg; Calcium 74mg; Fibre 0.5g; Sodium 400mg

CAMBODIAN RAW FISH SALAD

SWEET-FLESHED FRESHWATER FISH AND SHELLFISH ARE OFTEN EATEN RAW IN CAMBODIA, PLUCKED STRAIGHT FROM THE WATER, OR TOSSED IN A MARINADE. WRAPPED IN A LETTUCE LEAF WITH EXTRA LEAFY HERBS, OR SERVED WITH NOODLES, THIS CAMBODIAN SALAD, KOY PA, IS LIGHT AND DELICIOUS.

SERVES FOUR TO SIX

INGREDIENTS

450g/1lb white fish fillets, boned
  and finely sliced
juice of 4 limes
30ml/2 tbsp *tuk trey*
4 spring onions (scallions),
  finely sliced
2 garlic cloves, finely sliced
1 fresh red chilli, seeded and
  finely sliced
1 small bunch fresh coriander
  (cilantro), stalks removed
lettuce leaves, to serve

1 Place the sliced fish in a large bowl. Pour over the juice of 3 limes and toss well, making sure all the fish is coated Cover and chill in the refrigerator for 24 hours.

2 Drain the fish and place in a clean bowl with the juice of the remaining lime, the *tuk trey*, spring onions, garlic, chilli and coriander. Toss well and serve with lettuce leaves.

Energy 66Kcal/280kJ; Protein 14g; Carbohydrate 1.2g, of which sugars 1.1g; Fat 0.6g, of which saturates 0.1g; Cholesterol 35mg; Calcium 11mg; Fibre 0.2g; Sodium 402mg

BANANA BLOSSOM SALAD <u>WITH</u> PRAWNS

BANANA BLOSSOM IS VERY POPULAR — THE PURPLISH-PINK SHEATHS ARE USED FOR PRESENTATION, THE PETALS AS A GARNISH, AND THE POINTED, CREAMY YELLOW HEART IS TOSSED IN SALADS, WHERE IT IS COMBINED WITH LEFTOVER GRILLED CHICKEN OR PORK, STEAMED OR GRILLED PRAWNS, OR TOFU.

SERVES FOUR

INGREDIENTS
  2 banana blossom hearts
  juice of 1 lemon
  225g/8oz prawns (shrimp), cooked
    and shelled
  30ml/2 tbsp roasted peanuts, finely
    chopped, fresh basil leaves and
    lime slices, to garnish
For the dressing
  juice of 1 lime
  30ml/2 tbsp white rice vinegar
  60ml/4 tbsp *nuoc mam* or *tuk trey*
  45ml/3 tbsp palm sugar
  3 red Thai chillies, seeded and
    finely sliced
  2 garlic cloves, peeled and
    finely chopped

2 To make the dressing, beat the lime juice, vinegar, and *nuoc mam* or *tuk trey* with the sugar in a small bowl, until it has dissolved. Stir in the chillies and garlic and set aside.

3 Drain the sliced banana blossom and put it in a bowl. Add the prawns and pour over the dressing. Toss well and garnish with the roasted peanuts, basil leaves and lime slices.

1 Cut the banana blossom hearts into quarters lengthways and then slice them very finely crossways. To prevent them discolouring, tip the slices into a bowl of cold water mixed with the lemon juice and leave to soak for about 30 minutes.

COOK'S TIP
Banana blossom doesn't actually taste of banana. Instead, it is mildly tannic, similar to an unripe persimmon – a taste and texture that complements chillies, lime and the local fish sauce.

VARIATION
If you cannot find banana blossom hearts in Asian supermarkets, you can try this recipe with raw, or lightly steamed or roasted, fresh artichoke hearts.

Energy 103Kcal/438kJ; Protein 11g; Carbohydrate 15g, of which sugars 13g; Fat 0.5g, of which saturates 0.1g; Cholesterol 110mg; Calcium 54mg; Fibre 0.7g; Sodium 109mg

CAMBODIAN RAW BEEF SALAD <u>WITH</u> PEANUTS

THERE ARE MANY RECIPES FOR RAW BEEF SALADS THROUGHOUT SOUTH-EAST ASIA, SUCH AS THE VIETNAMESE GOI BO, BUT THIS CAMBODIAN RECIPE, PLEAH SAIKO, IS QUITE DISTINCTIVE AS IT USES THE FLAVOURSOME FISH EXTRACT, TUK PRAHOC, AND ROASTED PEANUTS.

SERVES FOUR

INGREDIENTS
- 450g/1lb beef fillet (tenderloin)
- 45ml/3 tbsp *tuk prahoc*
- juice of 3 limes
- 45ml/3 tbsp palm sugar
- 2 lemon grass stalks, trimmed and finely sliced
- 2 shallots, peeled and finely sliced
- 2 garlic cloves, finely chopped
- 1 red chilli, seeded and finely sliced
- 50g/2oz roasted, unsalted peanuts, finely chopped or crushed
- 1 small bunch fresh coriander (cilantro), finely chopped, plus extra leaves, to garnish

1 With a very sharp knife, slice the beef very thinly. This is easier to do if the steak is chilled first.

2 In a bowl, beat 30ml/2 tbsp *tuk prahoc* with the juice of 2 limes and 30ml/2 tbsp of the sugar, until the sugar has dissolved. Add the lemon grass, shallots and garlic and mix well.

3 Toss the slices of beef into the marinade, cover and place in the refrigerator for at least 2 hours.

4 Meanwhile, in a small bowl, beat the remaining *tuk prahoc* with the juice of the third lime. Stir in the remaining sugar, until it dissolves, and put aside.

5 Put the beef slices, drained of any remaining liquid, in a clean bowl. Add the chilli, peanuts and coriander. Toss with the dressing, garnish with coriander leaves and serve immediately.

Energy 321Kcal/1343kJ; Protein 29g; Carbohydrate 15g, of which sugars 14g; Fat 16g, of which saturates 5g; Cholesterol 65mg; Calcium 48mg; Fibre 1.6g; Sodium 78mg

CAMBODIAN SOYA BEANSPROUT SALAD

HIGH IN PROTEIN AND FAT, SOYA BEANSPROUTS ARE PARTICULARLY FAVOURED IN CAMBODIA. UNLIKE MUNG BEANSPROUTS, THEY ARE SLIGHTLY POISONOUS WHEN RAW AND NEED TO BE PARBOILED BEFORE USING. TOSSED IN A SALAD, THEY ARE OFTEN EATEN WITH NOODLES AND RICE.

SERVES FOUR

INGREDIENTS
    450g/1lb fresh soya beansprouts
    2 spring onions (scallions), finely
      sliced
    1 small bunch fresh coriander
      (cilantro), stalks removed
For the dressing
    15ml/1 tbsp sesame oil
    30ml/2 tbsp *tuk trey*
    15ml/1 tbsp white rice vinegar
    10ml/2 tsp palm sugar
    1 red chilli, seeded and finely sliced
    15g/½oz fresh young root ginger,
      finely shredded

1 First make the dressing. In a bowl, beat the oil, *tuk trey* and rice vinegar with the sugar, until it dissolves. Stir in the chilli and ginger and leave to stand for 30 minutes to allow the flavours to develop.

2 Bring a pan of salted water to the boil. Drop in the beansprouts and blanch for a minute only. Drain and refresh under cold water until cool. Drain again and put them into a clean dishtowel. Shake out the excess water.

3 Put the beansprouts into a bowl with the spring onions. Pour over the dressing and toss well. Garnish with coriander leaves and serve.

Energy 76Kcal/317kJ; Protein 3.4g; Carbohydrate 8.6g, of which sugars 6.5g; Fat 3.3g, of which saturates 0.5g; Cholesterol 0mg; Calcium 27mg; Fibre 1.8g; Sodium 6mg

CHICKEN AND SHREDDED CABBAGE SALAD

IN SOME VIETNAMESE AND CAMBODIAN HOUSEHOLDS, A WHOLE CHICKEN IS COOKED IN WATER WITH HERBS AND FLAVOURINGS TO MAKE A BROTH. THE CHICKEN IS THEN SHREDDED. SOME OF THE MEAT GOES BACK INTO THE BROTH, THE REST IS TOSSED IN A SALAD.

SERVES FOUR TO SIX

INGREDIENTS
450g/1lb chicken, cooked and torn into thin strips
1 white Chinese leaves (Chinese cabbage), trimmed and shredded
2 carrots, finely shredded or grated
a small bunch fresh mint, stalks removed, finely shredded
1 small bunch fresh coriander (cilantro) leaves, to garnish
For the dressing
30ml/2 tbsp vegetable or groundnut (peanut) oil
30ml/2 tbsp white rice vinegar

45ml/3 tbsp *nuoc mam* or *tuk trey*
juice of 2 limes
30ml/2 tbsp palm sugar
2 red Thai chillies, seeded and finely chopped
25g/1oz fresh young root ginger, sliced
3 garlic cloves, crushed
2 shallots, finely chopped

1 First make the dressing. In a bowl, beat the oil, vinegar, *nuoc mam* or *tuk trey*, and lime juice with the sugar, until it has dissolved. Stir in the other ingredients and leave to stand for about 30 minutes to let the flavours mingle.

2 Put the cooked chicken strips, cabbage, carrots and mint in a large bowl. Pour over the dressing and toss well. Garnish with coriander leaves and serve.

Energy 142Kcal/597kJ; Protein 19; Carbohydrate 5.7g, of which sugars 5.1g; Fat 4.8g, of which saturates 0.7g; Cholesterol 53mg; Calcium 53mg; Fibre 1.9g; Sodium 57mg

BAMBOO SHOOT SALAD

GRAINS OF GLUTINOUS RICE THAT HAVE BEEN DRY-ROASTED IN THE WOK, THEN GROUND TO FINE CRUMBS, MAKE AN INTERESTING ADDITION TO THIS COLOURFUL AND UNUSUAL SALAD. THE CRUNCH THEY PROVIDE MAKES A GOOD CONTRAST TO THE SILKY SMOOTHNESS OF THE BAMBOO SHOOTS.

SERVES FOUR

INGREDIENTS

    400g/14oz canned bamboo shoots, in
      large pieces
    25g/1oz/about 3 tbsp Thai sticky
      rice, cooked
    30ml/2 tbsp chopped shallots
    15ml/1 tbsp chopped garlic
    45ml/3 tbsp chopped spring
      onions (scallions)
    30ml/2 tbsp Thai fish sauce
    30ml/2 tbsp fresh lime juice
    5ml/1 tsp sugar
    2.5ml/½ tsp dried chilli flakes
    20–25 small fresh mint leaves
    15ml/1 tbsp toasted sesame seeds

1 Rinse the bamboo shoots under cold running water, then drain them and pat them thoroughly dry with kitchen paper and set them aside.

2 Dry-roast the rice in a wok until it is golden brown. Leave to cool slightly, then grind to find crumbs in a mortar.

3 Transfer the rice to a bowl and add the shallots, garlic, spring onions, fish sauce, lime juice, sugar, chilli flakes and half the mint leaves. Mix well.

4 Add the bamboo shoots to the bowl and toss to mix. Serve sprinkled with the toasted sesame seeds and mint.

Energy 85Kcal/357kJ; Protein 4.2g; Carbohydrate 11.3g, of which sugars 4.1g; Fat 2.7g, of which saturates 0.4g; Cholesterol 0mg; Calcium 51mg; Fibre 2g; Sodium 6mg.

NOODLE, TOFU AND SPROUTED BEAN SALAD

BEAN THREAD NOODLES LOOK LIKE SPUN GLASS ON THIS STUNNING SALAD, WHICH OWES ITS GOODNESS TO FRESH BEANSPROUTS, DICED TOMATO AND CUCUMBER IN A SWEET-SOUR DRESSING. THE SALAD TAKES ONLY MINUTES TO TOSS TOGETHER.

SERVES FOUR

INGREDIENTS

    25g/1oz bean thread noodles
    500g/1¼lb mixed sprouted beans
       and pulses (aduki, chickpea, mung,
       red lentil)
    4 spring onions (scallions), finely
       shredded
    115g/4oz firm tofu, diced
    1 ripe plum tomato, seeded and
       diced
    ½ cucumber, peeled, seeded and
       diced
    60ml/4 tbsp chopped fresh coriander
       (cilantro)
    45ml/3 tbsp chopped fresh mint
    60ml/4 tbsp rice vinegar
    10ml/2 tsp caster (superfine) sugar
    10ml/2 tsp sesame oil
    5ml/1 tsp chilli oil
    salt and ground black pepper

1 Place the bean thread noodles in a bowl and pour over enough boiling water to cover. Leave to soak for 12–15 minutes.

2 Drain the noodles and then refresh them under cold, running water and drain again. Using a pair of scissors, cut the noodles into roughly 7.5cm/3in lengths and transfer to a bowl.

3 Fill a wok one-third full of boiling water and place over high heat. Add the sprouted beans and pulses and blanch for 1 minute. Drain, transfer to the noodle bowl and add the spring onions, tofu, tomato, cucumber and herbs.

4 Combine the rice vinegar, sugar, sesame oil and chilli oil and toss into the noodle mixture. Transfer to a serving dish and chill for 30 minutes before serving.

COOK'S TIP

If you leave the salad to stand for half an hour to an hour, the flavours will improve as they develop and fuse together.

Energy 113Kcal/475kJ; Protein 6.8g; Carbohydrate 14.1g, of which sugars 6.6g; Fat 3.5g, of which saturates 0.5g; Cholesterol 0mg; Calcium 184mg; Fibre 2.4g; Sodium 11mg.

FRAGRANT MUSHROOMS IN LETTUCE LEAVES

THIS QUICK AND EASY VEGETABLE DISH IS SERVED ON LETTUCE LEAF "SAUCERS" SO CAN BE EATEN WITH THE FINGERS — A GREAT TREAT FOR CHILDREN AND FUN FOR ADULTS TOO.

SERVES TWO

INGREDIENTS
  30ml/2 tbsp vegetable oil
  2 garlic cloves, finely chopped
  2 baby cos or romaine lettuces,
    or 2 Little Gem (Bibb) lettuces
  1 lemon grass stalk, finely chopped
  2 kaffir lime leaves, rolled in
    cylinders and thinly sliced
  200g/7oz/3 cups oyster or chestnut
    mushrooms, sliced
  1 small fresh red chilli, seeded
    and finely chopped
  juice of ½ lemon
  30ml/2 tbsp light soy sauce
  5ml/1 tsp palm sugar or light
    muscovado (brown) sugar
  small bunch fresh mint leaves

1 Heat the oil in a wok or frying pan. Add the garlic and cook over a medium heat, stirring occasionally, until golden. Do not let it burn or it will taste bitter.

2 Meanwhile, separate the individual lettuce leaves. Wash and dry them, then set them aside in a bowl.

3 Increase the heat under the wok or pan and add the lemon grass, lime leaves and sliced mushrooms. Stir-fry for about 2 minutes.

4 Add the chilli, lemon juice, soy sauce and sugar to the wok or pan. Toss the mixture over the heat to combine the ingredients together, then stir-fry for a further 2 minutes.

5 Arrange the lettuce on a plate. Spoon a small amount of mushroom mixture on to each leaf and top with a mint leaf.

Energy 154Kcal/641kJ; Protein 3.9g; Carbohydrate 7.1g, of which sugars 6.8g; Fat 12.5g, of which saturates 1.6g; Cholesterol 0mg; Calcium 66mg; Fibre 2.9g; Sodium 1079mg.

CABBAGE SALAD

THIS IS A SIMPLE AND DELICIOUS WAY OF SERVING A SOMEWHAT MUNDANE VEGETABLE. THE WOK COMES IN HANDY FOR STIR-FRYING THE AROMATIC VEGETABLES THAT FLAVOUR THE CABBAGE.

SERVES FOUR TO SIX

INGREDIENTS
    30ml/2 tbsp vegetable oil
    2 large fresh red chillies, seeded and
        cut into thin strips
    6 garlic cloves, thinly sliced
    6 shallots, thinly sliced
    1 small cabbage, shredded
    30ml/2 tbsp coarsely chopped
        roasted peanuts, to garnish
For the dressing
    30ml/2 tbsp Thai fish sauce
    grated rind of 1 lime
    30ml/2 tbsp fresh lime juice
    120ml/4fl oz/½ cup coconut milk

VARIATION
Other vegetables, such as cauliflower, broccoli and Chinese leaves (Chinese cabbage), can be cooked in this way.

1 Make the dressing by mixing the fish sauce, lime rind and juice and coconut milk in a bowl. Whisk until thoroughly combined, then set aside.

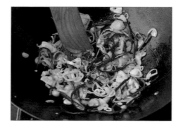

2 Heat the oil in a wok. Stir-fry the chillies, garlic and shallots over a medium heat for 3–4 minutes, until the shallots are brown and crisp. Remove with a slotted spoon and set aside.

3 Bring a large pan of lightly salted water to the boil. Add the cabbage and blanch for 2–3 minutes. Tip it into a colander, drain well and put into a bowl.

4 Whisk the dressing again, add it to the warm cabbage and toss to mix. Transfer the salad to a serving dish. Sprinkle with the fried shallot mixture and the peanuts. Serve immediately.

Energy 96Kcal/400kJ; Protein 2.7g; Carbohydrate 7.7g, of which sugars 6.6g; Fat 6.2g, of which saturates 0.9g; Cholesterol 0mg; Calcium 50mg; Fibre 2.2g; Sodium 147mg.

SWEET-AND-SOUR CUCUMBER WITH CHILLIES

SHORT, FAT CUCUMBERS ARE A COMMON SIGHT IN THE MARKETS OF VIETNAM. THIS SALAD IS A GREAT ADDITION TO A SUMMER BARBECUE OR THE SALAD TABLE, AND IS A DELIGHTFUL ACCOMPANIMENT TO ANY MEAT, POULTRY AND SEAFOOD DISHES.

SERVES FOUR TO SIX

INGREDIENTS
2 cucumbers
30ml/2 tbsp sugar
100ml/3½fl oz/½ cup rice vinegar
juice of half a lime
2 green Thai chillies, seeded and
   finely sliced
2 shallots, halved and finely sliced
1 small bunch each fresh coriander
   (cilantro) and mint, stalks removed,
   leaves finely chopped
salt
fresh coriander leaves, to garnish

COOK'S TIP
Decorate the dish with edible flowers, such as nasturtiums, to add colour.

1 Use a vegetable peeler to remove strips of the cucumber peel. Halve the cucumbers lengthways and cut into slices. Place the slices on a plate and sprinkle with a little salt.

2 Leave the cucumber slices to stand for 15 minutes. Rinse well, drain and pat them dry with kitchen paper.

3 In a bowl, mix the sugar with the vinegar until it has dissolved, then stir in the lime juice and a little salt to taste. Add the chillies, shallots, herbs and cucumber to the dressing and leave to stand for 15–20 minutes. Garnish with coriander leaves and a flower, if you like.

Energy 59Kcal/248kJ; Protein 2g; Carbohydrate 12g, of which sugars 11g; Fat 0g, of which saturates 0g; Cholesterol 0mg; Calcium 63mg; Fibre 0.8g; Sodium 200mg

VIETNAMESE TABLE SALAD

WHEN THIS VIETNAMESE TABLE SALAD IS SERVED ON ITS OWN, THE VEGETABLES AND FRUIT ARE USUALLY FOLDED INTO LITTLE PACKETS USING LETTUCE LEAVES OR RICE WRAPPERS, AND THEN DIPPED IN A SAUCE, OR ADDED BIT BY BIT TO BOWLS OF RICE OR NOODLES.

SERVES FOUR TO SIX

INGREDIENTS
1 crunchy lettuce, leaves separated
half a cucumber, peeled and
  thinly sliced
2 carrots, peeled and finely sliced
200g/7oz/scant 1 cup beansprouts
2 unripe star fruit, finely sliced
2 green bananas, finely sliced
1 firm papaya, cut in half, seeds
  removed, peeled and finely sliced
1 bunch each fresh mint and basil,
  stalks removed
juice of 1 lime
dipping sauce, to serve

1 Arrange the salad ingredients attractively on a large plate, with the lettuce leaves placed on one side so that they can be used as wrappers.

2 Squeeze the lime juice over the sliced fruits, particularly the bananas to help them retain their colour, and place the salad in the middle of the table. Serve with a dippping sauce.

Energy 108Kcal/455kJ; Protein 4g; Carbohydrate 21g, of which sugars 12g; Fat 1g, of which saturates 0g; Cholesterol 0mg; Calcium 110mg; Fibre 42g; Sodium 20mg

GREEN MANGO SALAD

ALTHOUGH THE ORANGE AND YELLOW MANGOES AND PAPAYAS ARE DEVOURED IN VAST QUANTITIES WHEN RIPE AND JUICY, THEY ARE ALSO POPULAR WHEN GREEN. THEIR TART FLAVOUR AND CRUNCHY TEXTURE MAKE THEM IDEAL FOR SALADS AND STEWS.

SERVES FOUR

INGREDIENTS
   450g/1lb green mangoes
   grated rind and juice of 2 limes
   30ml/2 tbsp sugar
   30ml/2 tbsp *nuoc mam*
   2 green Thai chillies, seeded and
      finely sliced
   1 small bunch fresh coriander
      (cilantro), stalks removed,
      finely chopped
   salt

1 Peel, halve and stone (pit) the green mangoes, and slice them into thin strips.

2 In a bowl, mix together the lime rind and juice, sugar and *nuoc mam*. Add the mango strips with the chillies and coriander. Add salt to taste and leave to stand for 20 minutes to allow the flavours to mingle before serving.

Energy 92Kcal/391kJ; Protein 1g; Carbohydrate 22g, of which sugars 15g; Fat 0g; Cholesterol 0mg; Calcium 32mg; Fibre 33g; Sodium 0.5g

LOTUS STEM SALAD <u>WITH</u> SHALLOTS

YOU MAY BE LUCKY ENOUGH TO FIND FRESH LOTUS STEMS IN AN ASIAN MARKET, OR, AS HERE, YOU CAN USE THE ONES PRESERVED IN BRINE. ALTERNATIVELY, TRY THIS RECIPE WITH FRESHLY STEAMED, CRUNCHY ASPARAGUS TIPS.

SERVES FOUR

INGREDIENTS
    half a cucumber
    225g/8oz jar preserved lotus stems,
        drained and cut into 5cm/2in strips
    2 shallots, finely sliced
    25g/1oz/½ cup fresh basil
        leaves, shredded
    salt
    fresh coriander (cilantro) leaves,
        to garnish
For the dressing
    juice of 1 lime
    30ml/2 tbsp *nuoc mam*
    1 red Thai chilli, seeded and chopped
    1 garlic clove, crushed
    15ml/1 tbsp sugar

1 Mix together the dressing ingredients in a bowl and set aside.

2 Peel the cucumber and cut it into 5cm/2in batons. Soak the batons in cold salted water for 20 minutes.

3 Put the lotus stems into a bowl of water. Using a pair of chopsticks, stir the water so that the loose fibres of the stems wrap around the sticks.

4 Drain the lotus stems and put them in a bowl. Drain the cucumber batons and add to the bowl, then add the sliced shallots, shredded basil leaves and the prepared dressing.

5 Leave the salad to marinate for 20 minutes before serving. Garnish with fresh coriander leaves.

Energy 43Kcal/181kJ; Protein 1g; Carbohydrate 9g, of which sugars 6g; Fat 0g, of which saturates 0g; Cholesterol 0mg; Calcium 40mg; Fibre 0.5g; Sodium 300mg

HERB AND CHILLI AUBERGINES

PLUMP AND JUICY AUBERGINES ARE DELICIOUS STEAMED IN THE WOK UNTIL TENDER AND THEN TOSSED IN A FRAGRANT MINTY DRESSING WITH CORIANDER AND CRUNCHY PEANUTS AND WATER CHESTNUTS. THE COMBINATION OF TEXTURES AND FLAVOURS IS ABSOLUTELY SENSATIONAL.

SERVES FOUR

INGREDIENTS

500g/1¼lb firm, baby aubergines
 (eggplants)
30ml/2 tbsp sunflower oil
6 garlic cloves, very finely chopped
15ml/1 tbsp very finely chopped
 fresh root ginger
8 spring onions (scallions), cut
 diagonally into 2.5cm/1in lengths
2 fresh red chillies, seeded and
 thinly sliced
45ml/3 tbsp light soy sauce
15ml/1 tbsp Chinese rice wine
15ml/1 tbsp golden caster
 (superfine) sugar or palm sugar
a handful of fresh mint leaves
30–45ml/2–3 tbsp roughly chopped
 fresh coriander (cilantro) leaves
115g/4oz water chestnuts
50g/2oz/½ cup roasted peanuts,
 roughly chopped
steamed egg noodles or rice, to serve

1 Cut the aubergines in half lengthways and place on a heatproof plate.

2 Place a steamer rack in a wok and add 5cm/2in of water. Bring the water to the boil and lower the plate on to the rack and reduce the heat to low.

3 Cover and steam the aubergines for 25–30 minutes, until they are cooked through. (Check the water level regularly, adding more if necessary.) Set the aubergines aside to cool.

4 Place the oil in a clean, dry wok and place over a medium heat. When hot, add the garlic, ginger, spring onions and chillies and stir-fry for 2–3 minutes. Remove from the heat and stir in the soy sauce, rice wine and sugar.

5 Add the mint leaves, chopped coriander, water chestnuts and peanuts to the aubergine and toss. Pour the garlic-ginger mixture evenly over the vegetables, toss gently and serve with steamed egg noodles or rice.

Energy 177Kcal/739kJ; Protein 6.2g; Carbohydrate 12.1g, of which sugars 9g; Fat 12g, of which saturates 1.9g; Cholesterol 0mg; Calcium 46mg; Fibre 4.4g; Sodium 823mg.

STEAMED VEGETABLES WITH CHILLI DIP

AN INEXPENSIVE BAMBOO STEAMER IS A GREAT WOK ACCESSORY, MAKING IT POSSIBLE TO COOK VEGETABLES QUICKLY AND EASILY SO THAT THEY RETAIN MAXIMUM NUTRIENTS AND KEEP THEIR COLOUR. MIX IN FRESH VEGETABLES, ADD A SPICY DIP AND YOU HAVE A HEALTHY AND TASTY DISH.

SERVES FOUR

INGREDIENTS
  1 head broccoli, divided
    into florets
  130g/4½ oz/1 cup green
    beans, trimmed
  130g/4½ oz asparagus, trimmed
  ½ head cauliflower, divided
    into florets
  8 baby corn cobs
  130g/4½ oz mangetouts (snow peas)
    or sugar snap peas
  salt
For the dip
  1 fresh green chilli, seeded
  4 garlic cloves, peeled
  4 shallots, peeled
  2 tomatoes, halved
  5 pea aubergines (eggplants)
  30ml/2 tbsp lemon juice
  30ml/2 tbsp soy sauce
  2.5ml/½ tsp salt
  5ml/1 tsp granulated sugar

COOK'S TIP
Cauliflower varieties with pale green curds have a more delicate flavour than those with white curds. Look out for baby brassicas – miniature cauliflowers and heads of broccoli – for serving whole.

1 Place the broccoli, green beans, asparagus and cauliflower in a bamboo steamer and steam over boiling water in a wok for about 4 minutes, until just tender but still with a "bite". Transfer to a bowl and add the corn cobs and mangetouts or sugar snap peas. Season to taste with a little salt. Toss to mix.

2 Make the dip. Preheat the grill (broiler). Wrap the chilli, garlic cloves, shallots, tomatoes and aubergines in a foil package. Grill (broil) for 10 minutes, until the vegetables have softened, turning the package over once or twice.

3 Unwrap the foil and tip its contents into a mortar or food processor. Add the lemon juice, soy sauce, salt and sugar. Pound with a pestle or process to a fairly liquid paste.

4 Scrape the dip into a serving bowl or four individual bowls. Serve, surrounded by the steamed and raw vegetables.

VARIATIONS
You can use a combination of other vegetables if you like. Use pak choi (bok choy) instead of the cauliflower or substitute raw baby carrots for the corn cobs and mushrooms in place of the mangetouts (snow peas).

Energy 129Kcal/541kJ; Protein 13.3g; Carbohydrate 13.3g, of which sugars 11.3g; Fat 2.8g, of which saturates 0.6g; Cholesterol 0mg; Calcium 138mg; Fibre 8.5g; Sodium 772mg.

STEAMED AUBERGINES WITH SESAME SAUCE

THIS JAPANESE RECIPE REPRESENTS A TYPICAL ZEN TEMPLE COOKING STYLE. FRESH SEASONAL VEGETABLES ARE CHOSEN AND SIMPLY COOKED WITH CARE. THEN A SAUCE MADE OF CAREFULLY BALANCED FLAVOURS IS ADDED. THIS DISH IS ALSO DELICIOUS COLD.

SERVES FOUR

INGREDIENTS
 2 large aubergines (eggplants)
 400ml/14fl oz/1⅔ cups second dashi
  stock made using water and instant
  dashi powder
 25ml/1½ tbsp caster (superfine)
  sugar
 15ml/1 tbsp shoyu
 15ml/1 tbsp sesame seeds, finely
  ground
 15ml/1 tbsp sake
 15ml/1 tbsp cornflour (cornstarch)
 salt
For the accompanying vegetables
 130g/4½oz shimeji mushrooms
 115g/4oz/¾ cup fine green beans
 100ml/3fl oz/scant ½ cup second
  dashi stock, made using water and
  instant dashi powder
 25ml/1½ tbsp caster (superfine)
  sugar
 15ml/1 tbsp sake
 1.5ml/¼ tsp salt
 dash of shoyu

1 Peel the aubergines and cut them in quarters lengthways. Prick all over with a skewer, then plunge into a bowl of salted water for 30 minutes.

2 Drain the aubergine wedges and place them side by side in a bamboo steamer basket. Place the basket on a trivet, on top of a wok containing boiling water. Cover and steam for 20 minutes. Do not let the water touch the bottom of the steamer basket.

3 Mix the dashi stock, sugar, shoyu and 1.5ml/¼ tsp salt together in a large pan. Gently transfer the aubergines to this pan, then cover and cook over a low heat for a further 15 minutes. Take a few tablespoonfuls of stock from the pan and mix with the ground sesame seeds. Add this mixture to the pan.

4 Thoroughly mix the sake with the cornflour, add to the pan with the aubergines and stock and shake the pan gently, but quickly. When the sauce becomes quite thick, remove the pan from the heat.

5 While the aubergines are cooking, prepare and cook the accompanying vegetables. Cut off the hard base part of the mushrooms and separate the large block into smaller chunks with your fingers. Trim the green beans and cut them in half.

6 Mix the stock with the sugar, sake, salt and shoyu in a shallow pan. Add the green beans and mushrooms and cook for 7 minutes until just tender. Serve the aubergines and their sauce in individual bowls with the accompanying vegetables over the top.

Energy 127Kcal/536kJ; Protein 3.3g; Carbohydrate 20.9g, of which sugars 16.8g; Fat 3.1g, of which saturates 0.5g; Cholesterol 0mg; Calcium 60mg; Fibre 4.3g; Sodium 8mg.

SPICY CHICKPEAS WITH SPINACH

THIS RICHLY FLAVOURED DISH MAKES A GREAT ACCOMPANIMENT TO A DRY CURRY, OR WITH A RICE-BASED STIR FRY. IT IS PARTICULARLY GOOD SERVED DRIZZLED WITH A LITTLE PLAIN YOGURT — THE SHARP, CREAMY FLAVOUR COMPLEMENTS THE COMPLEX SPICES PERFECTLY.

SERVES FOUR

INGREDIENTS

200g/7oz dried chickpeas
30ml/2 tbsp sunflower oil
2 onions, halved and thinly sliced
10ml/2 tsp ground coriander
10ml/2 tsp ground cumin
5ml/1 tsp hot chilli powder
2.5ml/½ tsp ground turmeric
15ml/1 tbsp medium curry powder
400g/14oz can chopped tomatoes
5ml/1 tsp caster (superfine) sugar
salt and ground black pepper
30ml/2 tbsp chopped mint leaves
115g/4oz baby leaf spinach
steamed rice or bread, to serve

1 Soak the chickpeas in cold water overnight. Drain, rinse and place in a large pan. Cover with water and bring to the boil. Reduce the heat and simmer for 45 minutes, or until just tender. Drain and set aside.

2 Heat the oil in a wok, add the onions and cook over a low heat for 15 minutes, until lightly golden. Add the ground coriander and cumin, chilli powder, turmeric and curry powder and stir-fry for 1–2 minutes.

COOK'S TIP
You can save time and effort by using canned chickpeas. Tip the contents of two 400g/14oz cans of chickpeas into a colander, rinse gently under cold water and drain before adding to the spicy tomato sauce in the wok. Reheat gently before stirring in the mint.

3 Add the tomatoes, sugar and 105ml/7 tbsp water to the wok and bring to the boil. Cover, reduce the heat and simmer gently for 15 minutes.

4 Add the chickpeas to the wok, season well and cook gently for 8–10 minutes. Stir in the chopped mint.

5 Divide the spinach leaves between shallow bowls, top with the chickpea mixture and serve with some steamed rice or bread.

Energy 267Kcal/1122kJ; Protein 13.3g; Carbohydrate 35.5g, of which sugars 10.2g; Fat 9g, of which saturates 1.1g; Cholesterol 0mg; Calcium 170mg; Fibre 8.2g; Sodium 83mg.

CARROT <u>IN</u> SWEET VINEGAR

FOR THIS JAPANESE SIDE DISH CARROT STRIPS ARE MARINATED IN RICE VINEGAR, SHOYU AND MIRIN. IT IS A GOOD ACCOMPANIMENT FOR RICH DISHES SUCH AS FRIED AUBERGINE WITH MISO SAUCE BELOW.

SERVES FOUR

INGREDIENTS
2 large carrots, peeled
5ml/1 tsp salt
30ml/2 tbsp sesame seeds
For the sweet vinegar marinade
75ml/5 tbsp rice vinegar
30ml/2 tbsp shoyu (use the pale
awakuchi soy sauce if available)
45ml/3 tbsp mirin

COOK'S TIP
This marinade is called *san bai zu*, and is one of the essential basic sauces in Japanese cooking. Dilute the marinade with 15ml/1 tbsp second dashi stock, then add sesame seeds and a few dashes of sesame oil for a very tasty and healthy salad dressing.

1 Cut the carrots into thin matchsticks, 5cm/2in long. Put the carrots and salt into a mixing bowl, and mix well with your hands. After 25 minutes, rinse the wilted carrot in cold water, then drain.

2 In another bowl, mix together the marinade ingredients. Add the carrots, and leave to marinate for 3 hours.

3 Put a wok on a high heat, add the sesame seeds and toss constantly until the seeds start to pop. Remove from the heat and cool.

4 Chop the sesame seeds with a large, sharp knife on a large chopping board. Place the carrots in a bowl, sprinkle with the sesame seeds and serve cold.

FRIED AUBERGINE <u>WITH</u> MISO SAUCE

THIS WELL-FLAVOURED STIR-FRIED AUBERGINE IS COATED IN A RICH MISO SAUCE. MAKE SURE THE OIL IS SMOKING HOT WHEN ADDING THE AUBERGINE PIECES, SO THEY DO NOT ABSORB TOO MUCH OIL.

SERVES FOUR

INGREDIENTS
2 large aubergines (eggplants)
1–2 dried red chillies
45ml/3 tbsp sake
45ml/3 tbsp mirin
45ml/3 tbsp caster (superfine) sugar
30ml/2 tbsp shoyu
45ml/3 tbsp red miso (use either the
dark red aka miso or even darker
hatcho miso)
90ml/6 tbsp sesame oil
salt

VARIATION
Sweet (bell) peppers could also be used for this dish instead of the aubergines (eggplants). Take 1 red, 1 yellow and 2 green peppers. Remove the seeds and chop them into 1cm/½in strips, then follow the rest of the recipe.

1 Cut the aubergines into bitesize pieces and place in a large colander, sprinkle with some salt and leave for 30 minutes to remove the bitter juices. Squeeze the aubergine pieces by hand. Remove the seeds from the chillies and chop the chillies into thin rings.

2 Mix the sake, mirin, sugar and shoyu in a cup. In a separate bowl, mix the red miso with 45ml/3 tbsp water to make a loose paste.

3 Heat the oil in a wok and add the chilli. When you see pale smoke rising from the oil, add the aubergine, and stir-fry for about 8 minutes, or until the aubergine pieces are tender. Lower the heat to medium.

4 Add the sake mixture to the pan, and stir for 2–3 minutes. If the sauce starts to burn, lower the heat. Add the miso paste to the pan and cook, stirring, for another 2 minutes. Serve hot.

Energy 66Kcal/272kJ; Protein 1.9g; Carbohydrate 4.6g, of which sugars 4.3g; Fat 4.5g, of which saturates 0.7g; Cholesterol 0mg; Calcium 64mg; Fibre 1.8g; Sodium 1039mg.
Energy 94Kcal/397kJ; Protein 1.8g; Carbohydrate 16.8g, of which sugars 16.4g; Fat 1.4g, of which saturates 0.3g; Cholesterol 0mg; Calcium 24mg; Fibre 3g; Sodium 806mg.

PAK CHOI <u>WITH</u> LIME DRESSING

THE LIME DRESSING FOR THIS THAI SPECIALITY IS TRADITIONALLY MADE USING FISH SAUCE, BUT VEGETARIANS COULD USE MUSHROOM SAUCE INSTEAD. THIS IS A WOK DISH THAT PACKS A FIERY PUNCH; USE FEWER CHILLIES IF YOU PREFER, OR REMOVE THE SEEDS BEFORE STIR-FRYING.

SERVES FOUR

INGREDIENTS
30ml/2 tbsp oil
3 fresh red chillies, cut into
  thin strips
4 garlic cloves, thinly sliced
6 spring onions (scallions),
  sliced diagonally
2 pak choi (bok choy), shredded
15ml/1 tbsp crushed peanuts
For the dressing
30ml/2 tbsp fresh lime juice
15–30ml/1–2 tbsp Thai fish sauce
250ml/8fl oz/1 cup coconut milk

1 Make the dressing. Put the lime juice and fish sauce in a bowl and mix well together, then gradually whisk in the coconut milk until combined.

2 Heat the oil in a wok and stir-fry the chillies for 2–3 minutes, until crisp. Transfer to a plate using a slotted spoon. Add the garlic to the wok and stir-fry for 30–60 seconds, until golden brown. Transfer to the plate.

3 Stir-fry the white parts of the spring onions for about 2–3 minutes, then add the green parts and stir-fry for 1 minute more. Transfer to the plate.

4 Bring a large pan of lightly salted water to the boil and add the pak choi. Stir twice, then drain immediately.

5 Place the pak choi in a large bowl, add the dressing and toss to mix. Spoon into a large serving bowl and sprinkle with the crushed peanuts and the stir-fried ingredients. Serve warm or cold.

Energy 93Kcal/384kJ; Protein 2.9g; Carbohydrate 6.2g, of which sugars 5.7g; Fat 6.4g, of which saturates 0.9g; Cholesterol 0mg; Calcium 157mg; Fibre 2.1g; Sodium 354mg.

HOT AND SPICY YAM

THE YAM OF THE TITLE ISN'T THE VEGETABLE THAT RESEMBLES SWEET POTATO, BUT IS RATHER A NAME GIVEN TO A SPICY SAUCE BASED ON COCONUT MILK AND MUSHROOMS. IT IS EASY TO MAKE IN THE WOK AND TASTES GOOD WITH STEAMED GREENS, BEANSPROUTS, BEANS AND BROCCOLI.

SERVES FOUR

INGREDIENTS

    90g/3½oz Chinese leaves (Chinese
      cabbage), shredded
    90g/3½oz/scant 2 cups beansprouts
    90g/3½oz/scant 1 cup green
      beans, trimmed
    90g/3½oz broccoli, preferably the
      purple sprouting variety, divided
      into florets
    15ml/1 tbsp sesame seeds, toasted
For the yam
    60ml/4 tbsp coconut cream
    5ml/1 tsp Thai red curry paste
    90g/3½oz/1¼ cups oyster
      mushrooms or field
      (portabello) mushrooms, sliced
    60ml/4 tbsp coconut milk
    5ml/1 tsp ground turmeric
    5ml/1 tsp thick tamarind juice, made
      by mixing tamarind paste with
      warm water
    juice of ½ lemon
    60ml/4 tbsp light soy sauce
    5ml/1 tsp palm sugar or light
      muscovado (brown) sugar

1 Steam the shredded Chinese leaves, beansprouts, green beans and broccoli separately or blanch them in boiling water for 1 minute per batch. Drain, place in a serving bowl and leave to cool.

2 Make the yam. Pour the coconut cream into a wok or frying pan and heat gently for 2–3 minutes, until it separates. Stir in the red curry paste. Cook over a low heat for 30 seconds.

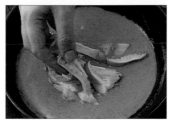

3 Increase the heat to high and add the mushrooms to the wok or pan. Cook for a further 2–3 minutes.

4 Pour in the coconut milk and add the ground turmeric, tamarind juice, lemon juice, soy sauce and sugar to the wok or pan. Mix thoroughly.

5 Pour the yam mixture over the prepared vegetables in the serving bowl and toss well so they are all coated with the sauce. Sprinkle with the toasted sesame seeds and serve immediately.

COOK'S TIPS
• There's no need to buy coconut cream especially for this dish. Use a carton or can of coconut milk. Skim the cream off the top and cook 60ml/4 tbsp of it before adding the curry paste. Add the measured coconut milk later, as described in the recipe.
• Oyster mushrooms may have fawn, peacock-blue or yellow caps, depending on the variety.

Energy 66Kcal/277kJ; Protein 3.9g; Carbohydrate 6.6g, of which sugars 5.8g; Fat 2.9g, of which saturates 0.5g; Cholesterol 0mg; Calcium 74mg; Fibre 2.4g; Sodium 752mg.

SICHUAN-SPICED AUBERGINE

*THIS STRAIGHTFORWARD YET VERSATILE VEGETARIAN DISH CAN BE SERVED HOT, WARM OR COLD,
AS THE OCCASION DEMANDS. TOPPED WITH A SPRINKLING OF TOASTED SESAME SEEDS, IT IS EASY
TO PREPARE, COOKS QUICKLY IN THE WOK, AND TASTES ABSOLUTELY DELICIOUS.*

SERVES FOUR TO SIX

INGREDIENTS
    2 aubergines (eggplants), total weight
       about 600g/1lb 6oz, cut into large
       chunks
    15ml/1 tbsp salt
    5ml/1 tsp chilli powder or to taste
    75–90ml/5–6 tbsp sunflower oil
    15ml/1 tbsp rice wine or
       medium-dry sherry
    100ml/3½fl oz/scant ½ cup water
    75ml/5 tbsp chilli bean sauce
       (see Cook's Tip)
    salt and ground black pepper
    a few toasted sesame seeds,
       to garnish

1 Place the aubergine chunks on a
plate, sprinkle them with the salt and
leave to stand for 15–20 minutes. Rinse
well, drain and dry thoroughly on
kitchen paper. Toss the aubergine
cubes in the chilli powder.

2 Heat a wok and add the oil. When the
oil is hot, add the aubergine chunks,
with the rice wine or sherry. Stir
constantly until the aubergine chunks
start to turn a little brown. Stir in the
water, cover the wok and steam for
2–3 minutes. Add the chilli bean sauce
and cook for 2 minutes. Season to
taste, then spoon on to a serving dish,
scatter with sesame seeds and serve.

COOK'S TIP
If you can't get hold of chilli bean sauce,
use 15–30ml/1–2 tbsp chilli paste mixed
with 2 crushed garlic cloves, 15ml/
1 tbsp each of dark soy sauce and rice
vinegar, and 10ml/2 tsp light soy sauce.

KAN SHAO GREEN BEANS

*A PARTICULAR STYLE OF COOKING FROM SICHUAN, KAN SHAO MEANS "DRY-COOKED" – IN OTHER WORDS
USING NO STOCK OR WATER. THE SLIM GREEN BEANS AVAILABLE ALL THE YEAR ROUND FROM SUPERMARKETS
ARE IDEAL FOR USE IN THIS QUICK AND TASTY RECIPE.*

SERVES SIX

INGREDIENTS
    175ml/6fl oz/¾ cup sunflower oil
    450g/1lb fresh green beans, topped,
       tailed and cut in half
    5 × 1cm/2 × ½in piece fresh
       root ginger, peeled and cut
       into matchsticks
    5ml/1 tsp sugar
    10ml/2 tsp light soy sauce
    salt and ground black pepper

1 Heat the oil in a wok. When the oil
is very hot and just beginning to smoke,
carefully add the beans and fry them,
stirring constantly, for 1–2 minutes until
they are just tender.

2 Lift out the green beans on to a plate
lined with kitchen paper. Using a ladle,
carefully remove all but 30ml/2 tbsp oil
from the wok. Reheat the remaining oil,
add the ginger and stir-fry for a minute
or two to flavour the oil.

3 Return the green beans to the wok,
stir in the sugar, soy sauce and salt and
pepper, and toss together quickly to
ensure the green beans are well coated. Pile
up the glazed beans on a serving plate
and serve at once.

VARIATION
This simple recipe works just as well
with other fresh green vegetables, such
as asparagus spears and okra. Vegetables
that can be piled on a serving plate look
the most dramatic.

Energy 108Kcal/448kJ; Protein 1.5g; Carbohydrate 3.7g, of which sugars 2.2g; Fat 9.6g, of which saturates 1.2g; Cholesterol 0mg; Calcium 13mg; Fibre 2.5g; Sodium 3mg.
Energy 170Kcal/698kJ; Protein 1.5g; Carbohydrate 3.2g, of which sugars 2.6g; Fat 16.9g, of which saturates 2.1g; Cholesterol 0mg; Calcium 28mg; Fibre 1.7g; Sodium 119mg.

SLOW-COOKED SHIITAKE <u>WITH</u> SHOYU

SHIITAKE COOKED SLOWLY ARE SO RICH AND FILLING, THAT SOME PEOPLE CALL THEM "VEGETARIAN STEAK". MUSHROOMS COOKED IN THIS MANNER WILL KEEP FOR SEVERAL DAYS IN THE REFRIGERATOR, AND CAN BE EATEN AS THEY ARE OR USED TO FLAVOUR OTHER DISHES.

SERVES FOUR

INGREDIENTS
  20 dried shiitake mushrooms
  45ml/3 tbsp vegetable oil
  30ml/2 tbsp shoyu
  25ml/1½ tbsp caster (superfine)
    sugar
  15ml/1 tbsp toasted sesame oil

VARIATION
To make shiitake rice, cut the slow-cooked shiitake into thin strips. Mix with 600g/1lb 6oz/5¼ cups cooked rice and 15ml/1 tbsp finely chopped chives. Serve in individual rice bowls and sprinkle with toasted sesame seeds.

1 Start soaking the dried shiitake the day before. Put them in a large bowl almost full of water. Cover the shiitake with a plate or lid to stop them floating to the surface of the water. Leave to soak overnight.

2 Measure 120ml/4fl oz/½ cup liquid from the bowl. Drain the shiitake into a sieve. Remove and discard the stalks.

3 Heat the oil in a wok or a large pan. Stir-fry the shiitake over a high heat for 5 minutes, stirring continuously.

4 Reduce the heat to the lowest setting, then add the measured liquid, the shoyu and sugar. Cook until there is almost no moisture left, stirring frequently. Add the sesame oil and remove from the heat.

5 Leave to cool, then slice and arrange the shiitake on a large plate.

Energy 133Kcal/553kJ; Protein 1.2g; Carbohydrate 7.4g, of which sugars 7.2g; Fat 11.2g, of which saturates 1.4g; Cholesterol 0mg; Calcium 8mg; Fibre 0.6g; Sodium 537mg.

NEW POTATOES COOKED IN DASHI STOCK

THIS IS A SIMPLE YET SCRUMPTIOUS JAPANESE DISH, INVOLVING LITTLE MORE THAN NEW SEASON'S POTATOES AND ONION COOKED IN DASHI STOCK. AS THE STOCK EVAPORATES, THE ONION BECOMES MELTINGLY SOFT AND CARAMELIZED, MAKING A WONDERFUL SAUCE THAT COATS THE POTATOES.

SERVES FOUR

INGREDIENTS
15ml/1 tbsp toasted sesame oil
1 small onion, thinly sliced
1kg/2¼lb baby new potatoes, unpeeled
200ml/7fl oz/scant 1 cup second dashi stock, made using water and instant dashi powder
45ml/3 tbsp shoyu

COOK'S TIP
Japanese chefs use toasted sesame oil for its distinctive strong aroma. If the smell is too strong, use a mixture of half sesame and half vegetable oil.

1 Heat the sesame oil in a wok or large pan. Add the onion slices and stir-fry for 30 seconds, then add the potatoes. Stir constantly until all the potatoes are well coated in sesame oil.

2 Pour on the dashi stock and shoyu and reduce the heat to the lowest setting. Cover and cook for 15 minutes, turning the potatoes every 5 minutes so that they are evenly cooked.

3 Uncover the wok or pan for a further 5 minutes to reduce the liquid. If there is already very little liquid remaining, remove the wok or pan from the heat, cover and leave to stand for 5 minutes. Check that the potatoes are cooked, then remove from the heat.

4 Transfer the potatoes and onions to a deep serving bowl. Pour the sauce over the top and serve immediately.

Energy 207Kcal/876kJ; Protein 4.6g; Carbohydrate 41.8g, of which sugars 4.4g; Fat 3.5g, of which saturates 0.7g; Cholesterol 0mg; Calcium 20mg; Fibre 2.7g; Sodium 295mg.

MORNING GLORY WITH FRIED SHALLOTS

OTHER NAMES FOR MORNING GLORY INCLUDE WATER SPINACH, WATER CONVOLVULUS AND SWAMP CABBAGE. IT IS A GREEN LEAFY VEGETABLE WITH LONG JOINTED STEMS AND ARROW-SHAPED LEAVES. THE STEMS REMAIN CRUNCHY WHILE THE LEAVES WILT LIKE SPINACH WHEN COOKED.

SERVES FOUR

INGREDIENTS
  2 bunches morning glory, total weight
    about 250g/9oz, trimmed and
    coarsely chopped into 2.5cm/
    1in lengths
  30ml/2 tbsp vegetable oil
  4 shallots, thinly sliced
  6 large garlic cloves, thinly sliced
  sea salt
  1.5ml/¼ tsp dried chilli flakes

VARIATIONS
Use spinach instead of morning glory, or
substitute young spring greens (collards),
sprouting broccoli or Swiss chard.

1 Place the morning glory in a steamer and steam over a pan of boiling water for 30 seconds, until just wilted. If necessary, cook it in batches. Place the leaves in a bowl or spread them out on a large serving plate.

2 Heat the oil in a wok and stir-fry the shallots and garlic over a medium to high heat until golden. Spoon the mixture over the morning glory, sprinkle with a little sea salt and the chilli flakes and serve immediately.

Energy 77Kcal/316kJ; Protein 2.4g; Carbohydrate 3.2g, of which sugars 1.9g; Fat 6.1g, of which saturates 0.7g; Cholesterol 0mg; Calcium 111mg; Fibre 1.8g; Sodium 88mg.

STIR-FRIED PINEAPPLE WITH GINGER

*THIS DISH MAKES AN INTERESTING ACCOMPANIMENT TO GRILLED MEAT OR STRONGLY FLAVOURED FISH
SUCH AS TUNA OR SWORDFISH. IF THE IDEA SEEMS STRANGE, THINK OF IT AS RESEMBLING A FRESH
MANGO CHUTNEY, BUT WITH PINEAPPLE AS THE PRINCIPAL INGREDIENT.*

SERVES FOUR

INGREDIENTS
  1 pineapple
  15ml/1 tbsp vegetable oil
  2 garlic cloves, finely chopped
  2 shallots, finely chopped
  5cm/2in piece fresh root ginger,
    peeled and finely shredded
  30ml/2 tbsp light soy sauce
  juice of ½ lime
  1 large fresh red chilli, seeded and
    finely shredded

VARIATION
This also tastes excellent if peaches or
nectarines are substituted for the diced
pineapple. Use three or four, depending
on their size.

1 Trim and peel the pineapple. Cut out
the core and dice the flesh.

2 Heat the oil in a wok or frying pan.
Stir-fry the garlic and shallots over a
medium heat for 2–3 minutes, until
golden. Do not let the garlic burn or the
dish will taste bitter.

3 Add the pineapple. Stir-fry for about
2 minutes, or until the pineapple cubes
start to turn golden on the edges.

4 Add the ginger, soy sauce, lime juice
and shredded chilli. Toss together until
well mixed. Cook over a low heat for a
further 2 minutes, then serve.

Energy 115Kcal/490kJ; Protein 1.2g; Carbohydrate 22g, of which sugars 21.6g; Fat 3.2g, of which saturates 0.3g; Cholesterol 0mg; Calcium 41mg; Fibre 2.6g; Sodium 539mg.

MIXED VEGETABLES IN COCONUT MILK

A MOST DELICIOUS WAY OF COOKING VEGETABLES, AS THE STIR-FRYING INTENSIFIES THEIR FLAVOUR WHILE THE COCONUT MILK FORMS A CREAMY SAUCE. IF YOU DON'T LIKE HIGHLY SPICED FOOD, USE FEWER RED CHILLIS IN THE SPICE MIXTURE.

SERVES FOUR TO SIX

INGREDIENTS

    8 red chillies, seeded
    2 stalks lemon grass, chopped
    4 kaffir lime leaves, torn
    450g/1lb mixed vegetables, such
      as aubergines (eggplants), baby
      corn, carrots, snake beans
      and patty pan squash
    30ml/2 tbsp vegetable oil
    250ml/8fl oz/1 cup coconut milk
    30ml/2 tbsp Thai fish sauce
    salt
    15–20 Thai basil leaves, to garnish

1 Put the red chillies, lemon grass and kaffir lime leaves in a mortar and grind together with a pestle.

2 Cut all the vegetables into small pieces of similar size and shape using a sharp knife.

3 Heat the oil in a wok or large deep frying pan. Add the chilli mixture and fry for 2–3 minutes.

4 Stir the coconut milk into the spice mixture and bring to the boil. Add the vegetables and cook for about 5 minutes or until they are just tender.

5 Season with the fish sauce and salt, garnish with basil leaves and serve the dish immediately.

Energy 80kcal/335kJ; Protein 1.2g; Carbohydrate 5.5g, of which sugars 5.3g; Fat 6.1g, of which saturates 0.9g; Cholesterol 0mg; Calcium 29mg; Fibre 2.3g; Sodium 71mg.

ASIAN-STYLE COURGETTE FRITTERS

*THIS IS A TWIST ON JAPANESE TEMPURA, USING INDIAN SPICES AND GRAM FLOUR IN THE BATTER.
ALSO KNOWN AS BESAN, GRAM FLOUR IS MORE COMMONLY USED IN INDIAN COOKING AND GIVES A
WONDERFULLY CRISP TEXTURE, WHILE THE COURGETTE BATON INSIDE BECOMES MELTINGLY TENDER.*

SERVES FOUR

INGREDIENTS
  90g/3½oz/¾ cup gram flour
  5ml/1 tsp baking powder
  2.5ml/½ tsp ground turmeric
  10ml/2 tsp ground coriander
  5ml/1 tsp ground cumin
  5ml/1 tsp chilli powder
  250ml/8fl oz/1 cup beer
  600g/1lb 6oz courgettes (zucchini),
    cut into batons
  sunflower oil, for deep-frying
  salt
  steamed basmati rice, natural (plain)
    yogurt and pickles, to serve

1 Sift the gram flour, baking powder, turmeric, coriander, cumin and chilli powder into a large bowl. Stir lightly to mix through. Season with salt.

2 Gradually add the beer, mixing gently as you pour it in, to make a thick batter.

3 Fill a large wok, one-third full with sunflower oil and heat to 180°C/350°F or until a cube of bread, dropped into the oil, browns in 45 seconds. Working in batches, dip the courgette batons in the spiced batter and then deep-fry for 1–2 minutes, or until crisp and golden. Lift out of the wok with a slotted spoon.

4 Drain the courgette fritters on kitchen paper and keep warm. Serve the courgettes immediately with steamed basmati rice, yogurt and pickles.

Energy 241Kcal/999kJ; Protein 7.3g; Carbohydrate 15.3g, of which sugars 4.6g; Fat 15.6g, of which saturates 1.9g; Cholesterol 0mg; Calcium 83mg; Fibre 3.8g; Sodium 15mg.

FRIED VEGETABLES <u>WITH</u> CHILLI SAUCE

A WOK MAKES THE IDEAL PAN FOR FRYING SLICES OF AUBERGINE, BUTTERNUT SQUASH AND COURGETTE BECAUSE THEY BECOME BEAUTIFULLY TENDER AND SUCCULENT. THE BEATEN EGG IN THIS RECIPE GIVES A SATISFYINGLY SUBSTANTIAL BATTER.

SERVES FOUR

INGREDIENTS

3 large (US extra large) eggs
1 aubergine (eggplant), halved
   lengthways and cut into long,
   thin slices
½ small butternut squash,
   peeled, seeded and cut into
   long, thin slices
2 courgettes (zucchini),
   trimmed and cut into long,
   thin slices
105ml/7 tbsp vegetable or
   sunflower oil
salt and ground black pepper
sweet chilli sauce, to serve

1 Beat the eggs in a large bowl. Season the egg mixture with salt and pepper. Add the slices of aubergine, butternut squash and courgette. Toss the vegetables slices until they are coated all over in the egg.

2 Have a warmed dish ready lined with kitchen paper. Heat the oil in a wok. When it is hot, add the vegetables, one strip at a time, making sure that each strip has plenty of egg clinging to it.

3 Do not cook more than eight strips of vegetable at a time or the oil will cool down too much.

4 As each strip turns golden and is cooked, lift it out, using a wire basket or slotted spoon, and transfer to the plate. Keep hot while cooking the remaining vegetables. Serve with the sweet chilli sauce as a dip.

Energy 281Kcal/1162kJ; Protein 8.8g; Carbohydrate 5.7g, of which sugars 4.8g; Fat 25.1g, of which saturates 3.9g; Cholesterol 171mg; Calcium 92mg; Fibre 3.2g; Sodium 65mg.

INDIAN-STYLE SPICED RED LENTIL DHAL

A KARAHI IS THE INDIAN EQUIVALENT OF THE WOK. HERE IT IS USED TO GREAT EFFECT TO MAKE WHAT CAN ONLY BE DESCRIBED AS CLASSIC COMFORT FOOD. THERE'S NOTHING LIKE A BOWL OF DHAL SPICED WITH MUSTARD SEEDS, CUMIN AND CORIANDER TO CLEAR AWAY THE BLUES.

SERVES FOUR

INGREDIENTS

- 30ml/2 tbsp sunflower oil
- 1 fresh green chilli, halved
- 2 red onions, halved
  and thinly sliced
- 10ml/2 tsp crushed garlic
- 10ml/2 tsp finely grated fresh
  root ginger
- 10ml/2 tsp black mustard seeds
- 15ml/1 tbsp cumin seeds
- 10ml/2 tsp crushed coriander seeds
- 10 curry leaves
- 250g/9oz/generous 1 cup red lentils
- 2.5ml/½ tsp ground turmeric
- 2 plum tomatoes
- salt
- coriander (cilantro) leaves and crispy
  fried onion, to garnish (optional)
- yogurt, poppadums and griddled
  flatbread or naans, to serve

1 Heat a karahi or wok and add the sunflower oil. When it is hot add the green chilli and onions, stir to combine, lower the heat and cook gently for 10–12 minutes, until softened.

2 Increase the heat slightly and add the garlic, ginger, mustard seeds, cumin seeds, coriander seeds and curry leaves and stir-fry for 2–3 minutes.

3 Rinse the lentils in cold water, drain, then add to the wok with 700ml/1 pint 2fl oz/scant 3 cups cold water. Stir in the turmeric and season with salt. Bring to the boil.

4 Chop the tomatoes and add to the wok. Reduce the heat and cook gently for 25–30 minutes, stirring occasionally.

5 Check the seasoning, then garnish with coriander leaves and crispy fried onion, if liked, and serve with yogurt, poppadums and flatbread or naans.

VARIATION
If you prefer, you can use yellow split peas in place of the lentils. Like red lentils, these only need to be rinsed, not soaked, before cooking.

Energy 284Kcal/1198kJ; Protein 16.1g; Carbohydrate 42.7g, of which sugars 7.3g; Fat 6.6g, of which saturates 0.8g; Cholesterol 0mg; Calcium 54mg; Fibre 4.6g; Sodium 29mg.

PICKLED VEGETABLES

ASIAN FOOD IS OFTEN ACCOMPANIES BY PICKLES, CONSISTING OF CUCUMBER, DAIKON AND CARROT —
GREEN, WHITE AND ORANGE IN COLOUR. THEY ARE SERVED FOR NIBBLING ON, AS PART OF THE TABLE
SALAD, OR AS AN ACCOMPANIMENT TO GRILLED MEATS AND SHELLFISH.

SERVES FOUR TO SIX

INGREDIENTS
  300ml/½ pint/1¼ cups white
    rice vinegar
  90g/3½oz/½ cup sugar
  450g/1lb carrots, cut into 5cm/2in
    matchsticks
  450g/1lb mooli (daikon), halved
    lengthways, and sliced thinly
  600g/1lb 6oz cucumber, partially
    peeled in strips and cut into
    5cm/2in matchsticks
  15ml/1 tbsp salt

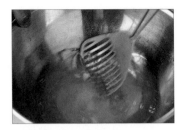

1 In a large bowl, whisk the vinegar with
the sugar, until it dissolves.

2 Add the carrots and moolie to the
vinegar mixture and toss well to coat.
Cover them and place in the refrigerator
for 24 hours, turning them occasionally.

3 Put the cucumber on a plate and
sprinkle with the salt. Leave for 30
minutes, then rinse under cold water
and drain well. Add to the carrot and
mooli and toss well in the pickling
liquid. Cover and refrigerate as before.

4 Lift the vegetables out of the pickling
liquid to serve, or spoon them into a jar
and store in the refrigerator.

Energy 104Kcal/438kJ; Protein 2g; Carbohydrate 24g, of which sugars 24g; Fat 0.5g, of which saturates 0.2g; Cholesterol 0mg; Calcium 59mg; Fibre 3.1g; Sodium 1013mg

PICKLED GINGER

WARMING, GOOD FOR THE HEART, AND BELIEVED TO AID DIGESTION, GINGER FINDS ITS WAY INTO MANY ASIAN RECIPES, IN SALADS, SOUPS, STIR-FRIES AND PUDDINGS. CHINESE IN ORIGIN, PICKLED GINGER IS OFTEN SERVED AS A CONDIMENT WITH BROTHS, NOODLES AND RICE.

SERVES FOUR TO SIX

INGREDIENTS

   225g/8oz fresh young ginger, peeled
   10ml/2 tsp salt
   200ml/7fl oz/1 cup white rice vinegar
   50g/2oz/¼ cup sugar

1 Place the ginger in a bowl and sprinkle with salt. Cover and place in the refrigerator for 24 hours.

COOK'S TIP
Juicy and tender with a pinkish-yellow skin, young ginger is less fibrous than the mature rhizome. When pickled in vinegar, the flesh turns pale pink.

2 Drain off any liquid and pat the ginger dry with a clean dishtowel. Slice each knob of ginger very finely along the grain, like thin rose petals, and place them in a clean bowl or a sterilized jar suitable for storing.

3 In a small bowl beat the vinegar and 50ml/2fl oz/¼ cup water with the sugar, until it has dissolved. Pour the pickling liquid over the ginger and cover or seal. Store in the refrigerator or a cool place for about a week.

Energy 36Kcal/151kJ; Protein 0.2g; Carbohydrate 9.1g, of which sugars 9.1g; Fat 0.1g, of which saturates 0g; Cholesterol 0mg; Calcium 20mg; Fibre 0.4g; Sodium 678mg

SPRING ONION OIL

MANY DISHES CALL FOR A FLAVOURED OIL TO BE DRIZZLED OVER NOODLES, OR BRUSHED ON GRILLED MEAT. IN VIETNAM, SPRING ONION OIL IS ALMOST ALWAYS AT HAND, READY TO BE SPLASHED INTO SOUPS, AND OVER MANY NOODLE AND STIR-FRIED DISHES.

MAKES ABOUT 250ML/8FL OZ/1 CUP

INGREDIENTS
    250ml/8fl oz/1 cup vegetable or
      groundnut (peanut) oil
    15 spring onions (scallions), trimmed
      and finely sliced

COOK'S TIP
It is important not to fry the spring
onions for too long: they should be
golden and sweet. If they become dark
brown, they will have a bitter taste. Many
South-east Asian cooks prepare batches
of this garnish to keep at hand for the
week's cooking. Refrigerate after making
up a batch. They will keep for 2 weeks.

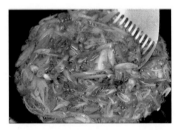

1 Heat the oil, stir in the spring onions
and fry until golden. Pour the oil into a
heatproof jug (pitcher) and leave to cool.

2 Pour the oil into a glass bottle or jar,
seal tightly, and store in a cool place.

Energy 1698Kcal/6985kJ; Protein 3g; Carbohydrate 4g, of which sugars 4g; Fat 186g, of which saturates 22g; Cholesterol 0mg; Calcium 59mg; Fibre 2.3g; Sodium 11mg

FRIED SHALLOTS

SHALLOTS FRIED WITH A COMBINATION OF GINGER, SPRING ONIONS AND GARLIC, OR JUST ONE OR TWO OF THESE FLAVOURINGS, LEND A CRUNCH AND A SWEETNESS TO FINISHED DISHES. SERVED AS GARNISHES OR CONDIMENTS, THEY ARE FOUND THROUGHOUT SOUTH-EAST ASIA.

TO GARNISH THREE TO FOUR DISHES

INGREDIENTS
   150ml/¼ pint/⅔ cup vegetable or
     groundnut (peanut) oil
   6 shallots, halved lengthways and
     sliced along the grain
   50g/2oz fresh root ginger, peeled and
     cut into fine strips
   6 spring onions (scallions), trimmed,
     cut into 2.5cm/1in pieces and
     halved lengthways
   3 garlic cloves, halved lengthways
     and cut into thin strips

1 Heat the oil in a wok or small pan. Stir in the shallots, ginger, spring onions and garlic. Stir-fry until golden, but not brown. Remove with a slotted spoon and drain on kitchen paper.

2 Leave to cool and store in a jar in the refrigerator for up to 1 week. Use as a garnish or put it on the table as a condiment. The leftover, flavoured oil can be used for stir-fries.

Energy 471Kcal/1942kJ; Protein 4g; Carbohydrate 14g, of which sugars 9g; Fat 44.7g, of which saturates 5.2g; Cholesterol 0mg; Calcium 77mg; Fibre 3.7g; Sodium 38mg

NUOC CHAM

THERE ARE MANY VERSIONS OF THIS POPULAR CHILLI DIPPING SAUCE, VARYING IN DEGREES OF SWEETNESS, SOURNESS AND HEAT. SOME PEOPLE ADD RICE VINEGAR TO THE MIX.

MAKES ABOUT 200ML/7FL OZ/SCANT 1 CUP

INGREDIENTS
    4 garlic cloves, roughly chopped
    2 red Thai chillies, seeded and
        roughly chopped
    15ml/1 tbsp sugar
    juice of 1 lime
    60ml/4 tbsp *nuoc mam*

1 Using a mortar and pestle, pound the garlic with the chillies and sugar and grind to make a paste.

2 Squeeze in the lime juice, add the *nuoc mam* and then stir in 60–75ml/ 4–5 tbsp water to taste. Blend well.

HOT PEANUT SAUCE

THIS HOT PEANUT DIPPING SAUCE IS POPULAR THROUGHOUT VIETNAM. ADJUST THE PROPORTIONS OF CHILLI, SUGAR OR LIQUID, ADDING MORE OR LESS ACCORDING TO TASTE. THIS IS ESPECIALLY GOOD SERVED WITH STEAMED, STIR-FRIED OR DEEP-FRIED VEGETABLES.

MAKES ABOUT 300ML/10FL OZ/2¼ CUPS

INGREDIENTS
    15ml/1 tbsp vegetable oil
    2 garlic cloves, finely chopped
    2 red Thai chillies, seeded
        and chopped
    115g/4oz/⅔ cup unsalted roasted
        peanuts, finely chopped
    150ml/¼ pint/⅔ cup chicken stock
    60ml/4 tbsp coconut milk
    15ml/1 tbsp hoisin sauce
    15ml/1 tbsp *nuoc mam*
    15ml/1 tbsp sugar

2 Simmer until the sauce thickens and oil appears on the surface.

1 Heat the oil in a small wok and stir in the garlic and chillies. Stir-fry until they begin to colour, then add all but 15ml/ 1 tbsp of the peanuts. Stir-fry for a few minutes until the oil from the peanuts begins to weep. Add the remaining ingredients and bring to the boil.

COOK'S TIP
If you don't use it in one sitting, this sauce will keep in the refrigerator for about one week.

3 Transfer the sauce to a serving dish and garnish with the reserved peanuts.

Energy 140Kcal/593kJ; Protein 5.; Carbohydrate 30g, of which sugars 24g; Fat 0.4g, of which saturates 0.1g; Cholesterol 0mg; Calcium 30mg; Fibre 2.4g; Sodium 4277mg
Energy 848Kcal/3525kJ; Protein 31g; Carbohydrate 39g, of which sugars 31g; Fat 64g, of which saturates 11g; Cholesterol 0mg; Calcium 104mg; Fibre 8g; Sodium 2498mg

CHILLI AND SOY DIPPING SAUCE

THIS LEMON GRASS, CHILLI AND SOY DIPPING SAUCE MAKES A GREAT ACCOMPANIMENT TO FISH DISHES OR FRIED TOFU. IT IS ALSO GOOD WITH ROASTED MEATS.

MAKES 100ML/3½FL OZ/SCANT ½ CUP

INGREDIENTS
30ml/2 tbsp vegetable oil
1 lemon grass stalk, outer leaves removed, finely chopped
1 garlic clove, crushed
2 spring onions (scallions), finely sliced
2 red Thai chillies, seeded and finely sliced
75ml/5 tbsp soy sauce

1 Heat the oil in a small wok or heavy pan and stir in the lemon grass, garlic, spring onions and chillies.

2 Stir-fry until the lemon grass turns golden, then quickly stir in the soy sauce. Remove from the heat and pour the *nuoc xa ot* into a serving bowl.

COOK'S TIP
This dipping sauce will keep in the refrigerator for two weeks, store in a screw-top jar.

GINGER SAUCE

THIS INTENSELY FLAVOURED GINGER SAUCE CAN BE SERVED AS AN ACCOMPANIMENT TO GRILLED OR ROASTED POULTRY AND FISH DISHES. IT IS ALSO DRIZZLED OVER PLAIN NOODLES OR RICE TO GIVE THEM A LITTLE EXTRA SPIKE, AND IS A GOOD SAUCE TO SERVE WITH VIETNAMESE BEEF FONDUE.

MAKES ABOUT 150ML/¼ PINT/⅔ CUP

INGREDIENTS
15ml/1 tbsp *nuoc mam*
juice of 1 lime
5ml/1 tsp honey
75g/3oz fresh root ginger, peeled and grated
2 red Thai chillies, seeded and finely chopped
100ml/3½fl oz/scant ½ cup sesame or groundnut (peanut) oil

1 In a bowl, mix the *nuoc mam* with the lime juice, honey, ginger and chillies.

2 Add the oil, mix well and leave to stand for at least 30 minutes to let the flavours develop.

Energy 279Kcal/1156kJ; Protein 6g; Carbohydrate 14g, of which sugars 8g; Fat 22g, of which saturates 3g; Cholesterol 0mg; Calcium 33mg; Fibre 2.3g; Sodium 5345mg
Energy 763Kcal/3147kJ; Protein 1g; Carbohydrate 17g, of which sugars 16.3g; Fat 77g, of which saturates 9g; Cholesterol 0mg; Calcium 38mg; Fibre 1.6g; Sodium 1117mg

SWEET DISHES AND DESSERTS

It may surprise you to discover just how many sweet dishes can be cooked in the wok, from steamed custards to sweet rice vermicelli. It is a practical pan for deep-fried treats such as fritters and crispy wontons, since less oil is needed than for conventional deep-frying, yet the inverted bowl shape gives you a good surface area. The wok can also be used for poaching fruit, such as Vanilla, Honey and Saffron Pears, or cooking desserts such as Caramelized Pineapple with Lemon Grass. If you use a wok for poaching fruit, make sure it has a non-stick surface, or the acidity may react with the metal and cause discoloration.

PANCAKES FILLED <u>WITH</u> SWEET COCONUT

TRADITIONALLY, THE PALE GREEN COLOUR IN THE BATTER FOR DADAR GULUNG *WAS OBTAINED FROM THE JUICE SQUEEZED FROM* PANDAN *LEAVES — A REAL LABOUR OF LOVE. GREEN FOOD COLOURING CAN BE USED AS THE MODERN ALTERNATIVE TO THIS LENGTHY PROCESS.*

<u>MAKES TWELVE TO FIFTEEN PANCAKES</u>

INGREDIENTS
  175g/6oz dark brown sugar
  450ml/15fl oz/scant 2 cups water
  1 pandan leaf, stripped through with
    a fork and tied into a knot
  175g/6oz desiccated (dry
    unsweetened shredded) coconut
  oil for frying
  salt
For the pancake batter
  225g/8oz plain (all-purpose) flour,
    sifted
  2 eggs, beaten
  2 drops of green food colouring
  few drops of vanilla extract
  450ml/15fl oz/scant 2 cups water
  45ml/3 tbsp groundnut (peanut) oil

1 Put the sugar in a pan with the water and the pandan leaf, and set over gentle heat, stirring all the time, until the sugar dissolves. Increase the heat and allow to boil gently for 3–4 minutes, until the mixture just becomes syrupy. Do not let it caramelize.

2 Put the coconut into a wok with a pinch of salt. Pour over the prepared sugar syrup and cook over a very gentle heat, stirring from time to time, until the mixture becomes almost dry; this will take 5–10 minutes. Remove from the heat and set aside until required.

3 To make the batter, blend together the flour, eggs, food colouring, vanilla extract, water and oil either by hand or in a food processor.

4 Brush an 18cm/7in frying pan with oil and cook 12–15 pancakes. Keep the pancakes warm. Fill each pancake with a generous spoonful of the coconut mixture, roll up and serve immediately.

Energy 200kcal/836kJ; Protein 2.6g; Carbohydrate 21.9g, of which sugars 8.8g; Fat 11.7g, of which saturates 4.4g; Cholesterol 24mg; Calcium 33mg; Fibre 1.3g; Sodium 49mg.

MANGO AND COCONUT STIR-FRY

CHOOSE A MANGO THAT IS RIPE BUT NOT TOO SOFT FOR THIS RECIPE. IF YOU BUY ONE THAT IS A LITTLE UNDER-RIPE, LEAVE IT IN A WARM PLACE FOR A DAY OR TWO BEFORE USING. COOKING GIVES THE FRUIT A WONDERFULLY INTENSE FLAVOUR.

SERVES FOUR

INGREDIENTS
¼ coconut
1 large, ripe mango
juice of 2 limes
rind of 2 limes, finely grated
15ml/1 tbsp sunflower oil
15g/½ oz butter
30ml/2 tbsp clear honey
crème fraîche, to serve

1 To prepare the coconut, pierce the end and drain out the milk. Crack the shell using a hammer, extract the flesh and shave it into thin slivers using a vegetable peeler.

2 Peel the mango. Cut the stone (pit) out and slice the flesh. Place the mango in a bowl and pour over the lime juice and rind, to marinate them.

3 Meanwhile heat a wok, then add 10ml/2 tsp of the oil. When the oil is hot, add the butter. When the butter has melted, stir in the coconut flakes. Stir-fry for 1–2 minutes until the coconut is golden brown.

4 Remove and drain on kitchen paper. Wipe out the wok. Strain the mango slices, reserving the juice.

5 Heat the wok and add the remaining oil. When the oil is hot, add the mango and stir-fry for 1–2 minutes, then add the juice and allow to bubble and reduce for 1 minute. Stir the honey into the mango, sprinkle on the coconut flakes and serve with crème fraîche.

COOK'S TIP
To prepare the coconut, pierce the two ends with a sharp nail or skewer to drain the coconut milk. Then crack the shell with a hammer, preferably with the nut inside a plastic bag. An alternative method is to drain the milk first and then heat the nut briefly in the oven until it cracks. Whichever method you choose, it is then fairly easy to extract the flesh and chop or shave it.

Energy 301kcal/1243kJ; Protein 2.4g; Carbohydrate 7.7g, of which sugars 7.6g; Fat 29.2g, of which saturates 22.4g; Cholesterol 8mg; Calcium 14mg; Fibre 6.1g; Sodium 34mg.

SWEET RICE DUMPLINGS IN GINGER SYRUP

OFTEN COOKED FOR TET AND OTHER VIETNAMESE CELEBRATIONS, THESE RICE DUMPLINGS ARE FILLED WITH THE TRADITIONAL MUNG BEAN PASTE AND THEN SIMMERED IN A GINGER-INFUSED SYRUP. THE DOUGH IS MADE WITH GLUTINOUS RICE FLOUR TO ATTAIN THE DESIRED SPRINGY, CHEWY TEXTURE.

SERVES FOUR TO SIX

INGREDIENTS

For the syrup
  25g/1oz fresh root ginger, peeled and
    finely shredded
  115g/4oz/generous ½ cup sugar
  400ml/14fl oz/1⅔ cups water
For the filling
  40g/1½oz dried split mung beans,
    soaked for 6 hours and drained
  25g/1oz/2 tbsp sugar
For the dough
  225g/8oz/2 cups sticky glutinous
    rice flour
  175ml/6fl oz/¾ cup boiling water

1 To make the syrup, stir the ginger and sugar in a heavy pan over a low heat, until the sugar begins to brown. Take the pan off the heat to stir in the water – it will bubble and spit. Return the pan to the heat and bring to the boil, stirring all the time. Reduce the heat and simmer for 5 minutes.

2 To make the filling, put the soaked mung beans in a pan with the sugar and pour in enough water to cover. Bring to the boil, stirring all the time until the sugar has dissolved. Reduce the heat and simmer for 15–20 minutes until the mung beans are soft – you may need to add more water if the beans are getting dry.

COOK'S TIP
These dumplings are popular at Vietnamese weddings. Coloured red with food dye, they represent good fortune.

3 Once soft enough and when all the water has been absorbed, pound to a smooth paste and leave to cool.

4 Using your fingers, pick up teaspoon-sized portions of the filling and roll them into small balls – there should be roughly 16–20.

5 To make the dough, put the flour in a bowl. Make a well in the centre and gradually pour in the water, drawing in the flour from the sides. Mix to form a dough, then cover and leave to stand until cool enough to handle. Dust a surface with flour and knead the dough for a few minutes, until soft, smooth and springy.

6 Divide the dough in half and roll each half into a sausage, about 25cm/10in long. Divide each sausage into 8–10 pieces, and roll each piece into a ball. Take a ball of dough and flatten it in the palm of your hand. Place a ball of the mung bean filling in the centre of the dough and seal it by pinching and rolling the dough. Repeat with the remaining balls.

7 Bring a deep pan of water to the boil. Drop in the filled dumplings and cook for a few minutes, until they rise to the surface. Once cooked, drain the dumplings in a colander. Heat the syrup in a heavy pan, drop in the cooked dumplings, and simmer for 2–3 minutes. Leave to cool and serve at room temperature, or chilled.

VARIATIONS
• For a spicy version, the syrup can be flavoured with a mixture of ginger, cloves, aniseed and cinnamon sticks.
• The dumplings can be filled with a sweetened purée of cooked sweet potato, mashed banana or even a mixture of chopped dried fruits.

Energy 231Kcal/975kJ; Protein 2.7g; Carbohydrate 54.7g, of which sugars 24.5g; Fat 0.3g, of which saturates 0g; Cholesterol 0mg; Calcium 23mg; Fibre 0.9g; Sodium 4mg.

STEAMED CUSTARD ᴵᴺ NECTARINES

STEAMING NECTARINES OR PEACHES IN THE WOK BRINGS OUT THEIR NATURAL COLOUR AND SWEETNESS, SO THIS IS A GOOD WAY OF MAKING THE MOST OF FRUIT THAT ISN'T QUITE AS RIPE AS IT COULD BE, OR WHICH NEEDS A FLAVOUR BOOST.

SERVES FOUR TO SIX

INGREDIENTS
    6 nectarines
    1 large (US extra large) egg
    45ml/3 tbsp palm sugar or light
        muscovado (brown) sugar
    30ml/2 tbsp coconut milk

COOK'S TIP
Palm sugar, also known as jaggery, is made from the sap of certain Asian palm trees, such as coconut and palmyrah. It is available from Asian food stores. If you buy it as a cake or large lump, you need to grate it before use. Muscovado sugar makes a good substitute as it has a similar, toffee-like flavour.

1 Cut the nectarines in half. Using a teaspoon, scoop out the stones (pits) and a little of the surrounding flesh.

2 Lightly beat the egg, then add the sugar and the coconut milk. Beat until the sugar has dissolved.

3 Transfer the nectarines to steamer tiers and carefully fill the cavities three-quarters full with the custard mixture. Steam over a pan of simmering water for 5–10 minutes. Remove from the heat and leave to cool completely before transferring to plates and serving.

Energy 213Kcal/897kJ; Protein 12.6g; Carbohydrate 21.6g, of which sugars 21.6g; Fat 9.4g, of which saturates 2.6g; Cholesterol 317mg; Calcium 64mg; Fibre 1.8g; Sodium 124mg.

MANGO WONTONS WITH RASPBERRY SAUCE

THESE CRISP, GOLDEN PARCELS FILLED WITH MELTINGLY SWEET, HOT MANGO ARE PERFECT FOR A CASUAL SUPPER OR A SOPHISTICATED DINNER. THE SWEET RASPBERRY SAUCE LOOKS STUNNING DRIZZLED OVER THE WONTONS AND TASTES EVEN BETTER. SERVE ANY EXTRA SAUCE IN A BOWL.

SERVES FOUR

INGREDIENTS
2 firm, ripe mangoes
24 fresh wonton wrappers
   (approximately 7.5cm/3in square)
oil, for deep-frying
icing (confectioners') sugar, to dust
For the sauce
400g/14oz/3½ cups raspberries
45ml/3 tbsp icing
   (confectioners') sugar
a squeeze of lemon juice

1 First make the sauce. Place the raspberries and icing sugar in a food processor and blend until smooth.

2 Press the raspberry purée through a sieve (strainer) to remove the seeds, then stir a squeeze of lemon juice into the sauce. Cover and place in the refrigerator until ready to serve.

3 Peel the mangoes, then carefully slice the flesh away from one side of the flat stone (pit). Repeat on the second side, then trim off any remaining flesh from around the stone. Cut the mango flesh into 1cm/½in dice.

4 Lay 12 wonton wrappers on a clean work surface and place 10ml/2 tsp of the chopped mango in the centre of each one. Brush the edges with water and top with the remaining wonton wrappers. Press the edges to seal.

5 Heat the oil in a wok to 180°C/350°F or until a cube of bread, dropped into the oil, browns in 45 seconds. Deep-fry the wontons, 2–3 at a time, for about 2 minutes, or until crisp and golden.

6 Remove the cooked wontons from the oil using a slotted spoon and drain on kitchen paper. Dust with icing sugar and serve on individual plates drizzled with the raspberry sauce.

VARIATION
This also tastes good with apricot sauce. Simply poach ready-to-eat dried apricots in water or apple juice until soft, then blitz in a blender.

COOK'S TIP
To check that a mango is ripe, cup it gently in your hand and give it a sniff. A ripe mango will yield to the touch and smell fragrant. Slightly unripe mangoes will ripen if placed in a paper bag with a banana for a day or two.

Energy 314Kcal/1331kJ; Protein 5.5g; Carbohydrate 56.1g, of which sugars 27.3g; Fat 9.2g, of which saturates 1.2g; Cholesterol 0mg; Calcium 93mg; Fibre 5.6g; Sodium 6mg.

SWEET <u>AND</u> SPICY RICE FRITTERS

THESE DELICIOUS LITTLE GOLDEN BALLS OF RICE ARE SCENTED WITH SWEET, WARM SPICES AND WILL FILL THE KITCHEN WITH WONDERFUL AROMAS WHILE YOU'RE COOKING. TO ENJOY THEM AT THEIR BEST, SERVE PIPING HOT, AS SOON AS YOU'VE DUSTED THEM WITH SUGAR.

SERVES FOUR

INGREDIENTS

175g/6oz cooked basmati rice
2 eggs, lightly beaten
60ml/4 tbsp caster (superfine) sugar
a pinch of nutmeg
2.5ml/½ tsp ground cinnamon
a pinch of ground cloves
10ml/2 tsp vanilla extract
50g/2oz/½ cup plain
  (all-purpose) flour
10ml/2 tsp baking powder
a pinch of salt
25g/1oz desiccated (dry unsweetened
  shredded) coconut
sunflower oil, for deep-frying
icing (confectioners') sugar,
  to dust

1 Place the cooked rice, eggs, sugar, nutmeg, cinnamon, cloves and vanilla extract in a large bowl and whisk together to combine.

2 Sift in the flour, baking powder and salt and add the coconut. Mix well until thoroughly combined.

3 Fill a wok one-third full of the oil and heat to 180ºC/350ºF or until a cube of bread, dropped into the oil, browns in 45 seconds.

4 Very gently, drop tablespoonfuls of the mixture into the oil, one at a time, and fry for 2–3 minutes, or until golden. Carefully remove the fritters from the wok using a slotted spoon and drain well on kitchen paper.

5 Divide the fritters into four portions, or simply pile them up on a single large platter. Dust them with icing sugar and serve immediately.

Energy 316Kcal/1321kJ; Protein 6.6g; Carbohydrate 45.8g, of which sugars 16.3g; Fat 12.4g, of which saturates 4.8g;
Cholesterol 95mg; Calcium 46mg; Fibre 1.3g; Sodium 38mg.

VIETNAMESE FRIED BANANAS

WHEREVER YOU GO IN VIETNAM, YOU WILL FIND FRIED BANANAS. THEY ARE EATEN HOT, STRAIGHT FROM THE PAN, AS A QUICK AND TASTY SNACK. FOR A MORE INDULGENT TREAT, THEY MIGHT BE COMBINED WITH ONE OF THE LOVELY FRENCH-STYLE ICE CREAMS.

SERVES FOUR

INGREDIENTS

 4 ripe but firm bananas
 vegetable oil, for deep-frying
 caster (superfine) sugar, for sprinkling
For the batter
 115g/4oz/1 cup rice flour or plain
   (all-purpose) flour
 2.5ml/½ tsp baking powder
 45ml/3 tbsp caster (superfine) sugar
 150ml/¼ pint/⅔ cup water
 150ml/¼ pint/⅔ cup beer

1 To make the batter, sift the flour with the baking powder into a bowl. Add the sugar and beat in a little of the water and beer to make a smooth paste. Gradually beat in the rest of the water and beer to form a thick batter. Leave to stand for 20 minutes.

2 Peel the bananas and cut them in half crossways, then in half again lengthways. Heat enough vegetable oil for deep-frying in a wok or a large, heavy pan.

3 Cook the bananas in batches, so they don't stick together in the pan. Dip each one into the beer batter, making sure it is well coated, and carefully slip it into the hot oil. Use tongs or chopsticks for turning and make sure each piece is crisp and golden all over.

4 Drain the fried bananas on kitchen paper and sprinkle them with sugar. Serve immediately and eat hot.

Energy 290Kcal/1211kJ; Protein 3g; Carbohydrate 48g, of which sugars 22g; Fat 9g, of which saturates 1g; Cholesterol 0mg; Calcium 22mg; Fibre 1.7g; Sodium 600mg

DEEP-FRIED MUNG BEAN DUMPLINGS

SWEET AND SAVOURY RICE DUMPLINGS ARE POPULAR SNACKS IN VIETNAM. IN THIS DISH, DAU XANH VUNG, *THE POTATO AND RICE-FLOUR DUMPLINGS ARE STUFFED WITH THE CLASSIC VIETNAMESE FILLING OF SWEETENED MUNG BEAN PASTE AND THEN ROLLED IN SESAME SEEDS.*

SERVES SIX

INGREDIENTS
100g/3½oz/scant ½ cup split
  mung beans, soaked for 6 hours
  and drained
115g/4oz/generous ½ cup caster
  (superfine) sugar
300g/10½oz/scant 3 cups glutinous
  rice flour
50g/2oz/½ cup rice flour
1 medium potato, boiled in its skin,
  peeled and mashed
75g/3oz/6 tbsp sesame seeds
vegetable oil, for deep-frying

1 Put the mung beans in a large pan with half the caster sugar and pour in 450ml/¾ pint/scant 2 cups water. Bring to the boil, stirring constantly until all the sugar has dissolved. Reduce the heat and simmer gently for 15–20 minutes until the mung beans are soft. You may need to add more water if the beans are becoming dry, otherwise they will burn on the bottom of the pan.

2 Once the mung beans are soft and all the water has been absorbed, reduce the beans to a smooth paste in a mortar and pestle or food processor and leave to cool.

3 In a large bowl, beat the flours and remaining sugar into the mashed potato. Add about 200ml/7fl oz/scant 1 cup water to bind the mixture into a moist dough. Divide the dough into 24 pieces, roll each one into a small ball, then flatten with the heel of your hand to make a disc and lay out on a lightly floured board.

VARIATION
These little fried dumplings may also be filled with a sweetened red bean paste, sweetened taro root or, as in China, a lotus paste. Alternatively, the dumplings can be steamed and then soaked in syrup. Both versions are very popular throughout Vietnam.

4 Divide the mung bean paste into 24 small portions. Place one portion of mung bean paste in the centre of a dough disc. Fold over the edges of the dough and then shape into a ball. Repeat for the remaining dumplings.

5 Spread the sesame seeds on a plate and roll the dumplings in them until evenly coated. Heat enough oil for deep-frying in a wok or heavy pan. Fry the balls in batches until golden. Drain on kitchen paper and serve warm.

Energy 321Kcal/1346kJ; Protein 7g; Carbohydrate 40g, of which sugars 21g; Fat 16g, of which saturates 2g; Cholesterol 0mg; Calcium 104mg; Fibre 3.1g; Sodium 0mg

CHINESE-STYLE TOFFEE APPLES

This classic dessert will make a great end to any meal. Wedges of crisp apple are encased in a light batter, then dipped in crispy caramel to make a sweet, sticky dessert that is guaranteed to get stuck in your teeth! You can use baby bananas in place of the apples.

SERVES FOUR

INGREDIENTS
115g/4oz/1 cup plain
  (all-purpose) flour
10ml/2 tsp baking powder
60ml/4 tbsp cornflour (cornstarch)
4 firm apples
sunflower oil, for deep-frying
200g/7oz/1 cup caster
  (superfine) sugar

1 In a large mixing bowl, combine the flour, baking powder, cornflour and 175ml/6fl oz/¾ cup water. Stir to make a smooth batter and set aside.

2 Peel and core the apples, then cut each one into 8 thick wedges.

3 Fill a wok one-third full of sunflower oil and heat to 180°C/350°F or until a cube of bread, dropped into the oil, browns in 45 seconds.

4 Working quickly, in batches, dip the apple wedges in the batter, drain off any excess and deep-fry for 2 minutes, or until golden brown. Remove with a slotted spoon and place on kitchen paper to drain.

5 Reheat the oil to 180°C/350°F and fry the wedges for a second time, again giving them about 2 minutes. Drain well on kitchen paper and set aside.

6 Very carefully, pour off all but 30ml/ 2 tbsp of the oil from the wok and stir in the sugar. Heat gently until the sugar melts and starts to caramelize. When the mixture is light brown, add a few pieces of apple at a time and toss to coat evenly.

7 Fill a large bowl with ice cubes and chilled water. Plunge the coated apple pieces briefly into the iced water to harden the caramel, then remove with a slotted spoon and serve immediately.

COOK'S TIP
Don't cook the apples in advance or the caramel will soften.

Energy 643Kcal/2688kJ; Protein 6.7g; Carbohydrate 71g, of which sugars 69.3g; Fat 38.9g, of which saturates 19.6g; Cholesterol 270mg; Calcium 100mg; Fibre 0.4g; Sodium 115mg.

ORANGE AND DATE BUTTERMILK PANCAKES

SERVE THESE SWEET, STICKY, GOLDEN PANCAKES FOR BREAKFAST, BRUNCH OR DESSERT. THEY'RE BURSTING WITH THE FLAVOUR OF ZESTY ORANGE AND SWEET JUICY DATES AND ARE UTTERLY MOREISH. MEDJOOL DATES HAVE AN INTENSELY SWEET FLESH AND WILL GIVE THE BEST RESULTS.

SERVES FOUR

INGREDIENTS
  150g/5oz/1¼ cups self-raising
    (self-rising) flour
  2.5ml/½ tsp baking powder
  a pinch of salt
  250ml/8fl oz/1 cup buttermilk
  3 eggs
  15ml/1 tbsp caster
    (superfine) sugar
  200g/7oz/1¼ cup Medjool
    dates, stoned
  finely grated rind and juice
    from 1 small orange
  50g/2oz/¼ cup unsalted (sweet)
    butter, melted
  sunflower oil, for greasing
  clear honey, to drizzle
  natural (plain) yogurt,
    to serve

1 Sift the flour and baking soda into a large bowl with a pinch of salt. Whisk in the buttermilk, eggs, sugar, dates, orange rind and juice and melted butter. Leave to stand for 15 minutes.

2 Brush a wok with a little oil and heat over a medium heat. When hot, pour a small ladleful of the mixture into the wok. Cook for 2–3 minutes until just set.

3 Cook the second side for 35–45 seconds. Transfer to a plate and keep warm while you cook the remaining batter in the same way. (You should make about 16 pancakes in total.)

4 To serve, divide the pancakes among four warmed plates, piling them up in a stack. Drizzle honey over each stack and top with a dollop of yogurt.

Energy 373Kcal/1569kJ; Protein 11.2g; Carbohydrate 51.5g, of which sugars 23g; Fat 15.2g, of which saturates 7.8g; Cholesterol 172mg; Calcium 166mg; Fibre 2.1g; Sodium 161mg.

COCONUT <u>AND</u> MANDARIN CUSTARDS

These scented custards have a fabulous melt-in-the-mouth texture and are best served warm. However, they are also delicious served chilled, making them perfect for hassle-free entertaining. The praline can be made a few days in advance and stored in an airtight container.

SERVES FOUR

INGREDIENTS
   200ml/7fl oz/scant 1 cup
     coconut cream
   200ml/7fl oz/scant 1 cup double
     (heavy) cream
   2.5ml/½ tsp finely ground star anise
   75ml/5 tbsp golden caster
     (superfine) sugar
   15ml/1 tbsp very finely grated
     mandarin or orange rind
   4 egg yolks
For the praline
   175g/6oz/scant 1 cup caster
     (superfine) sugar
   50g/2oz/½ cup roughly chopped
     mixed nuts (cashews, almonds and
     peanuts)

1 Make the praline. Place the sugar in a non-stick wok with 15–30ml/1–2 tbsp water. Cook over a medium heat until the sugar dissolves and turns light gold.

2 Remove the syrup from the heat and pour on to a baking sheet lined with baking parchment. Spread out using the back of a spoon, then sprinkle the chopped nuts evenly over the top and leave to harden.

3 Meanwhile place the coconut cream, double cream, star anise, sugar, mandarin or orange rind and egg yolks in a large bowl. Whisk to combine and pour the mixture into 4 lightly greased ramekins or small, heatproof bowls.

4 Place the ramekins or cups in a large steamer, cover and place in a wok and steam over gently simmering water for 12–15 minutes, or until the custards are just set.

5 Carefully lift the custards from the steamer and leave to cool slightly for about 10 minutes.

6 To serve, break up the praline into rough pieces and serve on top of, or alongside, the custards.

Energy 643kcal/2688kJ; Protein 6.7g; Carbohydrate 71g, of which sugars 69.3g; Fat 38.9g, of which saturates 19.6g; Cholesterol 270mg; Calcium 100mg; Fibre 0.4g; Sodium 115mg.

VANILLA, HONEY AND SAFFRON PEARS

THESE SWEET JUICY PEARS, POACHED IN A HONEY SYRUP INFUSED WITH VANILLA, SAFFRON AND LIME, MAKE A TRULY ELEGANT DESSERT. FOR A LOW-FAT VERSION YOU CAN EAT THEM ON THEIR OWN, BUT FOR A REALLY LUXURIOUS, INDULGENT TREAT, SERVE WITH CREAM OR ICE CREAM.

SERVES FOUR

INGREDIENTS
   150g/5oz/3/4 cup caster
      (superfine) sugar
   105ml/7 tbsp clear honey
   5ml/1 tsp finely grated lime rind
   a large pinch of saffron
   2 vanilla pods (beans)
   4 large, firm ripe dessert pears
   single (light) cream or ice cream,
      to serve

COOK'S TIP
For the best results use firm varieties of dessert pears, such as comice or conference, that are well ripened.

1 Place the caster sugar and honey in a medium, non-stick wok, then add the lime rind and the saffron. Using a small, sharp knife, split the vanilla pods in half and scrape the seeds into the wok, then add the vanilla pods as well.

2 Pour 500ml/17fl oz/scant 2¼ cups water into the wok and bring the mixture to the boil. Reduce the heat to low and simmer, stirring occasionally, while you prepare the pears.

3 Peel the pears, then add to the wok and gently turn in the syrup to coat evenly. Cover the wok and simmer gently for 12–15 minutes, turning the pears halfway through cooking, until they are just tender.

4 Lift the pears from the syrup using a slotted spoon and transfer to four serving bowls. Set aside.

5 Bring the syrup back to the boil and cook gently for about 10 minutes, or until reduced and thickened. Spoon the syrup over the pears and serve either warm or chilled with single cream or ice cream.

VARIATIONS
You can try using different flavourings in the syrup. Use 10ml/2 tsp chopped fresh root ginger and 1 or 2 star anise in place of the saffron and vanilla, or 1 cinnamon stick, 3 cloves and 105ml/7tbsp maple syrup in place of the spices and honey. If the syrup seems too sweet for your taste, sharpen it with a little lemon or lime juice.

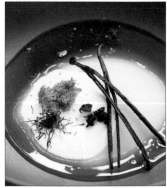

Energy 283Kcal/1207kJ; Protein 0.8g; Carbohydrate 74.3g, of which sugars 74.3g; Fat 0.2g, of which saturates 0g; Cholesterol 0mg; Calcium 38mg; Fibre 3.3g; Sodium 10mg.

CARAMELIZED PINEAPPLE WITH LEMON GRASS

THIS STUNNING DESSERT, GARNISHED WITH JEWEL-LIKE POMEGRANATE SEEDS, IS SUPERB FOR ENTERTAINING. THE TANGY, ZESTY FLAVOURS OF LEMON GRASS AND MINT BRING OUT THE EXQUISITE SWEETNESS OF THE PINEAPPLE TO CREATE A TRULY LUSCIOUS COMBINATION.

SERVES FOUR

INGREDIENTS

30ml/2 tbsp very finely chopped lemon grass, and 2 lemon grass stalks, halved lengthways
350g/12oz/1¾ cups caster (superfine) sugar
10ml/2 tsp chopped fresh mint leaves
2 small, ripe pineapples, about 600g/1lb 5oz each
15ml/1 tbsp sunflower oil
60ml/4 tbsp pomegranate seeds
crème fraîche, to serve

1 Place the chopped lemon grass, 250g/9oz of the sugar and the mint leaves in a non-stick wok. Pour over 150ml/¼ pint/⅔ cup of water and bring to the boil over medium heat.

2 Reduce the heat under the wok and simmer the mixture for 10–15 minutes, until thickened. Strain into a glass bowl, reserving the halved lemon grass stalks, then set aside.

3 Using a sharp knife, peel and core the pineapples and cut into 1cm/½in-thick slices, then sprinkle the slices with the remaining sugar.

4 Brush a large non-stick wok with the oil and place over a medium heat. Working in batches, cook the sugared pineapple slices for 2–3 minutes until they are lightly caramelised, then turn over and cook the other side for another 2–3 minutes.

5 Transfer the pineapple slices to a flat serving dish and scatter over the pomegranate seeds.

6 Pour the lemon grass syrup over the fruit and garnish with the reserved stalks. Serve hot or at room temperature with crème fraîche.

COOK'S TIP
To remove pomegranate seeds, halve the fruit and hold it over a bowl, cut side down. Tap all over with a wooden spoon and the seeds should drop out.

Energy 493Kcal/2101kJ; Protein 1.6g; Carbohydrate 121.7g, of which sugars 121.7g; Fat 3.4g, of which saturates 0.3g; Cholesterol 0mg; Calcium 101mg; Fibre 3.6g; Sodium 11mg.

LEMON ᴬᴺᴰ GINGER STEAMED PUDDINGS

THESE DECADENTLY MOIST LITTLE DESSERTS FLAVOURED WITH LEMON AND GINGER AND SERVED WITH A LUSCIOUS CARDAMOM-SPICED SYRUP WILL DEFINITELY BECOME A FIRM FAMILY FAVOURITE.

SERVES FOUR

INGREDIENTS
  150g/5oz/10 tbsp butter
  150g/5oz/¾ cup golden caster
    (superfine) sugar
  10ml/2 tsp ground ginger
  2 eggs
  150g/5oz/1¼ cups self-raising
    (self-rising) flour
  a pinch of salt
  115g/4oz/1 cup finely chopped
    pistachio nuts
  shredded lemon rind, pistachio nuts
    and chopped preserved stem ginger,
    to garnish
For the syrup
  150g/5oz/¾ cup golden caster
    (superfine) sugar
  1.5ml/¼ tsp crushed cardamom
    seeds
  5ml/1 tsp ground ginger
  10ml/2 tsp finely grated lemon rind
    and juice of 2 lemons
  5ml/1 tsp arrowroot powder

1 Make the syrup. Place the sugar, cardamom seeds and ginger in a non-stick wok and pour in 150ml/¼ pint/⅔ cup water. Heat gently until the sugar has dissolved completely, then add the lemon rind and juice. Bring to the boil and cook for 3–4 minutes.

2 Mix the arrowroot with 30ml/2 tbsp cold water and whisk into the syrup. Simmer gently for 2 minutes, or until the syrup has thickened slightly. Transfer to a bowl and set aside.

3 Grease 4 x 200ml/7fl oz/scant 1 cup heatproof bowls and set aside.

4 Whisk together the butter and sugar until pale and fluffy. Add the ginger and beat in the eggs, one at a time. Sift in the flour and salt, add the chopped nuts, and mix thoroughly to combine.

5 Spoon 20ml/4 tsp of the syrup into the base of each greased bowl (reserving the remaining syrup) and swirl to coat the sides. Spoon in the pudding mixture and level the tops. Cover tightly with greaseproof (waxed) paper or foil and secure with string.

6 Place the puddings in a bamboo steamer. Pour about 5cm/2in boiling water into a wok and place the steamer over it. Cover and steam for 1 hour and 15 minutes (replenishing the water when necessary), until the puddings have risen and are firm to the touch.

7 Reheat the remaining syrup, then carefully unmould the puddings on to individual plates and spoon over the syrup. Decorate with the lemon rind, nuts and stem ginger and serve.

Energy 868Kcal/3630kJ; Protein 12.4g; Carbohydrate 98.4g, of which sugars 69.1g; Fat 50g, of which saturates 22.5g; Cholesterol 175mg; Calcium 139mg; Fibre 2.9g; Sodium 420mg.

CALAS

THESE SWEET RICE FRITTERS ARE AN AMERICAN/CREOLE SPECIALITY, SOLD BY "CALAS" WOMEN ON THE STREETS OF THE FRENCH QUARTER OF NEW ORLEANS TO RESIDENTS AND OFFICE WORKERS, FOR WHOM THEY MAKE A POPULAR AND TASTY BREAKFAST.

MAKES OVER 40

INGREDIENTS

115g/4oz/generous ½ cup short grain
   pudding rice
900ml/1½ pints/3¾ cups mixed
   milk and water
30ml/2 tbsp caster (superfine) sugar
50g/2oz/½ cup plain (all purpose)
   flour
7.5ml/1½ tsp baking powder
5ml/1 tsp grated lemon rind
2.5ml/½ tsp ground cinnamon
1.5ml/¼ tsp ground ginger
generous pinch of grated nutmeg
2 eggs
sunflower oil, for deep frying
salt
icing sugar, for dusting
cherry or strawberry jam and thick
   cream, to serve

1 Put the rice in a pan and pour in the milk and water. Add a pinch of salt and bring to the boil. Stir, then cover and simmer over a very gentle heat for 15–20 minutes until the rice is tender.

2 Switch off the heat under the pan, then add the sugar. Stir well, cover and leave until completely cool, by which time the rice should have absorbed all the liquid and become very soft.

VARIATION
For a slightly spicy variation mix the icing sugar with some cinnamon and grated nutmeg before dusting.

3 Put the rice in a food processor or blender and add the flour, baking powder, lemon rind, spices and eggs. Process for about 20–30 seconds so that the mixture is like a thick batter.

4 Heat the oil in a wok to 160ºC/325ºF. Scoop up a generous teaspoon of batter and, using a second spoon, push into the hot oil. Add four or five more and fry for 3–4 minutes, turning them occasionally, until the calas are golden brown. Drain on kitchen paper and keep warm while cooking in batches.

5 Dust the calas generously with icing sugar and serve warm with fruit jam and thick cream.

Energy 50Kcal/206kJ; Protein 0.9g; Carbohydrate 3.5g, of which sugars 1.3g; Fat 3.6g, of which saturates 0.6g; Cholesterol 10mg; Calcium 16mg; Fibre 0g; Sodium 8mg.

RICH SPICED CARROT AND RAISIN HALWA

THIS IS ANOTHER UNUSUAL DESSERT THAT TASTES ABSOLUTELY DELICIOUS. HALWA IS A CLASSIC INDIAN SWEET, AND THERE ARE MANY VARIATIONS. HERE GRATED CARROTS ARE COOKED IN MILK WITH GHEE, SUGAR, SPICES AND RAISINS UNTIL MELTINGLY TENDER AND SWEET.

SERVES FOUR

INGREDIENTS
300g/11oz carrots
90g/3½oz ghee
250ml/8fl oz/1 cup milk
150g/5oz/¾ cup golden caster (superfine) sugar
5–6 lightly crushed cardamom pods
1 clove
1 cinnamon stick
50g/2oz/scant ½ cup raisins

COOK'S TIP
Ghee is clarified butter and is widely used in Indian cooking. It is an essential ingredient in halwa and is available in cans from Asian stores.

1 Peel and grate the carrots Place a non-stick wok over a low heat and add half the ghee. When the ghee has melted, add the grated carrot and stir-fry for 6–8 minutes, by which time the carrot will have softened and taken on more colour.

2 Pour the milk into the wok and bring to the boil, reduce the heat to low and simmer gently for 10–12 minutes.

3 Stir the remaining ghee into the carrot mixture, then stir in the sugar, crushed cardamom pods, clove, cinnamon stick and raisins.

4 Gently simmer the carrot mixture for 6–7 minutes, stirring occasionally, until thickened and glossy. Serve immediately in small serving bowls.

Energy 439Kcal/1838kJ; Protein 3g; Carbohydrate 56.7g, of which sugars 56.3g; Fat 23.8g, of which saturates 15.6g; Cholesterol 67mg; Calcium 120mg; Fibre 2.1g; Sodium 56mg.

COCONUT CRÈME CARAMEL

BASED ON THE CLASSIC FRENCH DESSERT, THIS VIETNAMESE VERSION IS MADE WITH COCONUT MILK.
POPULAR THROUGHOUT VIETNAM, IT IS SERVED BOTH AS A SNACK AND AS A DESSERT IN RESTAURANTS,
WHERE IT IS SOMETIMES GARNISHED WITH MINT LEAVES.

SERVES FOUR TO SIX

INGREDIENTS
   4 large (US extra large) eggs
   4 egg yolks
   50g/2oz/¼ cup caster (superfine)
     sugar
   600ml/1 pint/2½ cups coconut
     milk
   toasted slivers of coconut,
     to decorate
For the caramel
   150g/5oz/¾ cup caster (superfine)
     sugar

1 Preheat the oven to 160°C/325°F/
Gas 3. To make the caramel, heat the
sugar and 75ml/5 tbsp water in a heavy
pan, stirring constantly until the sugar
dissolves. Bring to the boil and, without
stirring, let the mixture bubble until it is
dark golden and almost like treacle.

2 Pour the caramel into an ovenproof
dish, tilting the dish to swirl it around
so that it covers the bottom and sides –
you will need to do this quickly.
Put the dish aside and leave the
caramel to set.

3 In a bowl, beat the eggs and egg
yolks with the caster sugar. Heat the
coconut milk in a small pan, but don't
allow it to boil. Then gradually pour it
on to the egg mixture, while beating
constantly. Pour the mixture through a
sieve (strainer) over the caramel in the
dish or individual ramekins.

4 Set the dish or ramekins in a bain-
marie. You can use a roasting pan or
wide oven dish half-filled with water.
Place it in the oven for about 50
minutes, or until the custard has just
set, but still feels soft when touched
with the fingertips. Leave the dish to
cool, then chill in the refrigerator for at
least 6 hours, or overnight.

COOK'S TIP
You can use this recipe to make six small
individual desserts using ramekin dishes
instead of a large dish.

VARIATION
If you are not keen on coconut, you can
use full-fat fresh milk instead of coconut
milk and infuse it with a vanilla pod,
orange peel or aniseed.

5 To serve, loosen the custard around
the sides using a thin, sharp knife.
Place a flat serving plate over the top
and invert the custard, holding on to the
dish and plate at the same time. Shake
it a little before removing the inverted
dish, then carefully lift it off as the
caramel drizzles down the sides and
forms a puddle around the pudding.

6 Decorate the custard with fresh grated
coconut and mint leaves, and serve.

VARIATION
For an alternative garnish, try toasted
coconut or make a small batch of sugar
syrup with finely shredded ginger or
orange peel.

Energy 256Kcal/1078kJ; Protein 9g; Carbohydrate 31g, of which sugars 31g; Fat 11g, of which saturates 4g; Cholesterol 338mg; Calcium 79mg; Fibre 0.4g; Sodium 200mg

CARAMELIZED PLUMS <u>WITH</u> COCONUT RICE

RED, JUICY PLUMS ARE QUICKLY SEARED IN A WOK WITH SUGAR TO MAKE A RICH CARAMEL COATING, THEN SERVED WITH STICKY COCONUT-FLAVOURED RICE FOR A SATISFYING DESSERT. THE GLUTINOUS RICE IS AVAILABLE FROM ASIAN STORES, BUT REMEMBER THAT YOU HAVE TO SOAK IT OVERNIGHT.

SERVES FOUR

INGREDIENTS
  6 or 8 firm, ripe plums
  90g/3½oz/½ cup caster
  (superfine) sugar
For the rice
  115g/4oz sticky glutinous rice
  150ml/¼ pint/⅔ cup coconut cream
  45ml/3 tbsp caster (superfine) sugar
  a pinch of salt

1 First prepare the rice. Rinse it in several changes of water, then leave to soak overnight in a bowl of cold water.

2 Line a large bamboo steamer that will fit in your wok with muslin (cheesecloth). Drain the rice and transfer it to the lined steamer.

3 Cover the rice and steam over simmering water for 25–30 minutes, until the rice is tender. (Check the water level and add more if necessary.)

4 Transfer the steamed rice to a wide bowl and set aside for a moment.

5 Combine the coconut cream with the sugar and salt and pour into a clean wok. Heat gently and bring to the boil, then remove from the heat and pour over the rice. Stir to mix well.

6 Using a sharp knife, cut the plums in half and remove their stones (pits). Sprinkle the sugar over the cut sides.

7 Heat a non-stick wok over a medium-high flame. Working in batches, place the plums in the wok, cut side down, and cook for 1–2 minutes, or until the sugar caramelizes. You may need to wipe out the wok with kitchen paper in between batches.

8 Mould the rice into rounds and place on warmed plates, then spoon over the caramelized plums. Alternatively, simply spoon the rice into four warmed bowls and top with the plums. Drizzle any syrup remaining in the wok over and around the fruit.

VARIATION
Try this with greengages. They look very pretty when piled on the discs of sticky rice. Red plums taste good if you add just a touch of balsamic vinegar to the syrup on serving.

Energy 298Kcal/1265kJ; Protein 3.6g; Carbohydrate 71.7g, of which sugars 50.2g; Fat 0.7g, of which saturates 0.1g; Cholesterol 0mg; Calcium 53mg; Fibre 2.4g; Sodium 47mg.

INDEX